Asian Christianities

ASIAN CHRISTIANITIES
History, Theology, Practice

The Edward Cadbury Lectures

Peter C. Phan

ORBIS BOOKS
Maryknoll, New York 10545

ORBIS BOOKS
Maryknoll, New York 10545

Fathers and Brothers
MARYKNOLL™

Founded in 1970, Orbis Books endeavors to publish works that enlighten the mind, nourish the spirit, and challenge the conscience. The publishing arm of the Maryknoll Fathers and Brothers, Orbis seeks to explore the global dimensions of the Christian faith and mission, to invite dialogue with diverse cultures and religious traditions, and to serve the cause of reconciliation and peace. The books published reflect the views of their authors and do not represent the official position of the Maryknoll Society. To learn more about Maryknoll and Orbis Books, please visit our website at www.maryknollsociety.org.

Library of Congress Cataloging-in-Publication Data

Names: Phan, Peter C., 1943– author.
Title: Asian Christianities : history, theology, practice / Peter C. Phan.
Description: Maryknoll : Orbis Books, 2018. | Series: The Edward Cadbury lectures | Includes bibliographical references and index.
Identifiers: LCCN 2018004224 (print) | LCCN 2018014602 (ebook) | ISBN 9781608335152 (e-book) | ISBN 9781626980938 (pbk.)
Subjects: LCSH: Catholic Church—Asia. | Christianity—Asia. | Theology—Asia.
Classification: LCC BX1615 (ebook) | LCC BX1615 .P48 2018 (print) | DDC 230/.25—dc23
LC record available at https://lccn.loc.gov/2018004224

In Memory of
Hundreds of Thousands of Asian Migrants
Who Died in Search of a Better Life

Contents

PART III: PRACTICE

Preface

This book originates from the Edward Cadbury Lectures that I delivered at the School of Philosophy, Theology, and Religion of the University of Birmingham, United Kingdom, April 12–16, 2010. The overall theme of these lectures is the Roman Catholic Church of Asia and its history and theology. In using "Asia" to designate the largest continent of Earth I am deeply aware of the multiple and diverse realities constituting "Asia" and the danger of essentializing what is called "Asia"—a kind of internalized "Orientalism." By restricting my considerations of the Catholic Church to a few countries of East Asia, both Northeastern and Southeastern, namely, China, Vietnam, Indonesia, Japan, Korea, and the Philippines, I hope that there are both enough commonality and specificity to justify the generic use of "Asia." Thus, in this book "Asia" refers mainly to East Asia, North and South.

Of course, Asian Christianity is not only Roman Catholic. In addition to the Catholic Church, there are in Asia other Christianities: Orthodox, Anglican, Baptist, Protestant, Evangelical, Pentecostal, and Independent/Indigenous/Marginal churches, each church possessing its own varieties within itself and its own distinctive history and theology. Given that I am a Vietnamese Roman Catholic and that Asian Catholic theology is what I know best, albeit regretfully not enough, I elected to focus the Cadbury Lectures on matters in which I would least likely commit blunders and howlers. Furthermore, even the Asian Catholic Church is far from homogeneous. Beneath its veneer of uniformity there are enormous differences in the Catholic Church of Asia—for example, between the Catholic Church of India and that of China, to cite the two largest countries of Asia. "Christianities" (in the plural) in the title of the book is intended to draw attention to this fact of ecclesial diversity and pluralism.

The subtitle of the book, *History, Theology, Practice* indicates the three areas that are under consideration. Again, my intention is not to offer a comprehensive history of Asian Catholic Christianities—there are already excellent works on this. Rather, my intention is to highlight their contemporary situation, especially in the aftermath of the Second Vatican Council. As for theology, I focus on some key issues in theological methodology, biblical hermeneutics, systematics, and interreligious dialogue. I am profoundly conscious of the diversity and multiplicity of Asian Catholic theology. Other

Asian Catholic theologians will no doubt choose to discuss other themes, and I welcome the opportunity to learn from their approaches and ideas.

Not all the chapters of this book were presented as the Cadbury Lectures as such; the limited number of lectures and the amount of time allotted to them did not permit this. Furthermore, several years have elapsed from when the lectures were delivered. In a way I do not regret the delay, because in the intervening time, having completed several book projects, I have learned a good deal more about Asian Christianities and have been able to incorporate the new knowledge into this book. In fact, all the chapters are new. However, all the *ideas* contained in them were discussed at one time or another during the six days on which the Cadbury Lectures were held. I hope that the original audience of the Cadbury Lectures will find here answers to the many questions they raised then.

There remains for me the most pleasant duty to thank publicly and in print the various people at the University of Birmingham who made it possible for me to deliver the Cadbury Lectures. Professor R. S. Sugirtharajah first suggested the possibility, and while I was in Birmingham, he and his wife, Professor Sharada Sugirtharajah, graciously invited me to their home and treated me to Sri Lankan cuisine. Professor Allan Anderson, then Head of the School of Philosophy, Theology, and Religion, officially extended the invitation. Professor Edmond Tang took care of all the practical business to make my stay as enjoyable as possible. Thanks to his generous hospitality and familiarity with the city, I was able to enjoy most of the best Chinese restaurants in Birmingham! The staff of the Woodbrooke Quaker Study Centre, where I stayed, were most gracious hosts and impressive by their deep prayerful spirit.

One of the many signs of divine providence during my stay at the University of Birmingham was that at the end of the Cadbury Lectures I could not fly back to the United States because of the ashes spewed forth by the Eyjafjallajoekull volcano in Iceland. I had to extend my stay for another week before there were flights available to go home—a free, lovely vacation, indeed! (A colleague of mine suggested that the British authorities did not allow me to leave because I failed to spell the name of the volcano correctly!) I am grateful to then-doctoral student Alex Chow, now a professor at the University of Edinburgh, and his wife, Betty, for taking time out of their busy lives to show me around Birmingham and the nearby cities during this extra week.

One precious lesson I learned from this travel debacle is that one cannot—and must not—always trust one's naked eyes. While the ashes of the volcanic eruptions swirling thirty thousand feet above us forced the cancellation of thousands of flights in Britain and elsewhere, the sky in Birmingham was unbelievably blue and cloudless, and the temperature balmy, which gave conspiracy aficionados a field day to concoct theories about collusion between governments and businesses for control and financial gain. Similarly, in matters religious and theological, one must not always trust what meets the eye. What you see is not always what you get. A dose of healthy skepticism and deconstructionism may be in order.

Part of the stipulations of the Cadbury Lectures is that they be published. I am deeply grateful to Robert Ellsberg, publisher of Orbis Books, for his gentle and constant encouragement to complete this book (and a few others), and his warm support throughout the years. Needless to say, I, more than he, am relieved that the manuscript is seeing the light of day after a considerable delay. In a sense, as mentioned earlier, the delay was a blessing in disguise in that it allows me to see the church—and the Catholic Church of Asia—with new eyes. During the composition of this book, a momentous change occurred with the resignation of Pope Benedict XVI and the election in 2013 of Jorge Mario Bergoglio, Archbishop of Buenos Aires, Argentina, as Bishop of Rome. The first Jesuit and the first person from the Global South to be elected pope, Francis has brought a new joy (his favorite word), a new simplicity of life, and a new vision of church that resonate deeply with the Asian people, as his visits to Asia have amply demonstrated.

Original Sources

The essays that make up this book have appeared in various books and journals. The author is grateful to the publishers of the journals and books in which they have appeared for permission to reprint them here, at times in extensively modified form.

Chapter 1, originally published as "Reception of and Prospects for Vatican II in Asia," *Theological Studies* 74, no. 2 (June 2013): 302–20.

Chapter 2, originally published as "An Asian Christian? Or a Christian Asian? Or an Asian-Christian? A Roman Catholic Experiment in Christian Identity," in *Asian and Oceanic Christianities in Conversation: Exploring Theological Identities at Home and in Diaspora*, ed. Heup Young Kim, Fumitaka Matsuota, and Anri Marimoto. Amsterdam: Rodopi, 2011, 57–74.

Chapter 3, originally published as "The Protestant Reformations in Asia: A Blessing or a Curse?," in *The Protestant Reformation and World Christianity: Global Perspectives*, ed. Dale T. Irvin. Grand Rapids, MI: Eerdmans, 2017, 120–53.

Chapter 4, originally published as "Christianity in Vietnam: 1975–2013," *International Journal for the Study of the Christian Church* 14, no. 1 (2014): 1–19.

Chapter 5, originally published as "Chinese Catholics in Ho Chi Minh City (Saigon), Vietnam, 1865–2012," in *Polycentric Structures in the History of World Christianity*, ed. Klaus Koschorke and Adrian Hermann. Wiesbaden: Harrassowitz, 2014, 141–52.

Chapter 6, originally published as "Doing Theology in World Christianity: Old Tasks, New Ways," in *Relocating World Christianity*, ed. Joel Cabrita, David Maxwell, and Emma Wild-Wood. Leiden: Brill, 2017, 115–42.

Chapter 7, originally published as "Can We Read Religious Texts Interreligiously? Possibilities, Challenges, and Experiments," in *Postcolonial Interruptions*, ed. Tat-siong Benny Liew. Sheffield: Sheffield Phoenix Press, 2009, 313–31.

Chapter 8, originally published as "An Interfaith Encounter at Jacob's Well: A Missiological Interpretation of John 4:4–42," *Mission Studies* 27, no. 2 (2010): 160–75.

Chapter 9, originally published as *"Sensus Fidelium, Dissensus Infidelium, Consensus Omnium*: An Interreligious Approach to Consensus in Doctrinal Theology," in *Learning from All the Faithful: A Contemporary Theology of the* Sensus Fidei, ed. Bradford E. Hinze and Peter C. Phan. Eugene, OR: Pickwick Publications, 2016, 213–25.

Chapter 10, previously unpublished.

Chapter 11, originally published as "L'Esprit Saint comme fondement du dialogue interreligieux," in *Le dialogue interreligieux*, ed. Fabrice Blée and Achiel Peelman. Montreal: Novalis, 2013, 21–41.

Chapter 12, originally published as "Catholicism and Confucianism: An Intercultural and Interreligious Dialogue," in *Catholicism and Interreligious Dialogue*, ed. James Heft. Oxford: Oxford University Press, 2012, 164–206.

Chapter 13, originally published as "Christian Social Spirituality: A Global Perspective," in *Catholic Social Justice: Theological and Practical Exploration*, ed. Philomena Cullen, Bernard Hoose, and Gerard Mannion. London: T&T Clark, 2007, 18–40.

Chapter 14, originally published as "Local Spiritualities, Popular Religions, and Christian Higher Education," in *Local Spiritualities and Everydayness: Promoting Religious Conversation in Christian Higher Education*, ed. Hadrianus Tedjoworo. Bandung, Indonesia: Unpar Press, 2017, 1–27.

Chapter 15, originally published as "'Always Remember Where You Came From': An Ethic of Migrant Memory," in *Living With(out) Borders: Catholic Theological Ethics on the Migration of Peoples*, ed. Agnes M. Brazal and María Teresa Dávila, Maryknoll, NY: Orbis Books, 2016, 173–86.

Chapter 16, originally published as "Care for Our Common Home: Ecology and the Catholic Church in Asia," *Bulletin of Ecumenical Theology* 28 (2016): 68–87.

INTRODUCTION

Asian Christianities
Why Another Book?

If you need proof that the history of Christianities in Asia and Asian theology are alive and well, I can point to the shelves of my personal library sagging under the weight of heavy tomes (and more often than not, when space runs out, stacked on the floor), in English and other tongues, recently published in the United States and abroad. Not only is their quantity notable but their scholarship is also outstanding. They are authored by Catholics, Protestants, and increasingly by Evangelicals and Pentecostals. This mention of the size of my personal collection of books on Asian Christianity and theology may sound like an unseemly boast, but it is also a liability. If there is already a large number of excellent books on these subjects on the market, why write another one?

In this case, there is the self-serving answer: my long-overdue obligation to the University of Birmingham to have the Edward Cadbury Lectures published in book form. But apart from this, I dare to hope that this book will make a contribution, albeit small, to the understanding of what is called "Asian Christianities" (please note the plural!). If you use Word software and type "Christianities," it will be underlined in red to warn you that there might be a spelling error. This prompt reflects the common assumption that Christianity, especially in its Roman Catholic tradition, is a monolithic organization. Such a perception is, of course, shattered in the face of the actual realities of Christianity in Asia, a fact I try to show in this book.

The first part of the book, "History," attempts to convey the multiplicity and diversity, at times dizzying, of Asian Christianity. Of course, it is impossible to describe Christianity in all the countries of Asia. I limit my narrative chiefly to East and South Asia. This ecclesial multiplicity and diversity are strongly promoted by the Second Vatican Council (1962–65) in the Catholic Church with its *ressourcement* and *aggiornamento* programs, as can easily be seen in the fifty-year aftermath of the council. A survey of how Vatican II has been "received" by the Catholic Church in Asia, both *ad intra* and *ad extra*, especially through the Federation of Asian Bishops' Conferences and the Asian Synod, highlights the complexity and challenges of a new "way of being church" in Asia. At the same time, this project of inculturation of Christianity into local cultures poses the highly vexed question of Christian identity: Are Asian Christians primarily Asian and secondarily Christian or vice versa? Or are they by necessity persons of hyphenated identity: Asian-Christian and Christian-Asian? An overview of the long history of Asian Catholicism shows that the answer to these questions is anything but simple.

Plurality and diversity are even more striking in the Protestant churches in Asia. As we commemorate the 500th anniversary of Luther's Reformation in 1517, a look at the enormous variety of Asian Protestant churches—mainline and marginal—is helpful to chart their future on the continent. Lacking a unifying central authority and with the astounding rise of Evangelicals and Marginals, for example, in China, the Protestant churches are facing numerous daunting challenges, both within and without. Whether they will have a bright future in Asia or not depends on their ability to remain faithful to Luther's and other Reformers' theological insights and church reform agenda and at the same time pull their common resources together in ecumenical endeavors to meet the socio-political, cultural, and religiously diverse challenges of Asia today. Here the work of the Christian Conference of Asia is highly promising.

I then turn to the Catholic Church in Vietnam, arguably one of the most fascinating cases, along with China, of church–state relations. Since the Communist takeover of the former South Vietnam in April 1975, the Catholic Church and the Communist government have been performing an intricate pas de deux, sometimes harmonious, at other times stepping on each other's toes, but hopefully achieving a beautiful ballet. This relationship between the Vietnamese Catholic Church and the Vietnamese Communist government will remain problematic as long as they perceive each other as competitors, which is well-nigh unavoidable, given their long history of mutual antagonism. However, in the last forty years since the Communist victory, the Vietnamese Catholic Church has proved itself a valuable, and even indispensable, partner in the reconstruction of postwar Vietnam for the country's common good. I end this historical part by paying homage to a little-known church in Vietnam, namely, the community of Chinese Catholics in Ho Chi Minh City (Saigon). This is a small and belated, but heartfelt and sincere token of thanks to the Chinese Catholics in Vietnam, an eloquent symbol of the resiliency and vitality of the Christian faith amidst suffering and adversity.

The second part, "Theology," explores various themes of systematic theology under three perspectives, namely, world Christianity, migration, and interreligious dialogue, realities that are prominent in Asia. How do we do theology in this new triple context? Are there new ways of carrying out the old task of "faith in search of understanding"? What are the specifically Asian "resources" for theology? In light of world Christianity, how do we interpret the basic Christian symbols such as God, Christ, Holy Spirit, and church?

In particular, given the fact that, as Vatican II puts it, scripture is the "soul" of theology, and that non-Christian religions have their own sacred scriptures and classics, how do we interpret our Bible in dialogue with these sacred scriptures and classics? Can they be regarded as containing divine "revelation"? Can they be used to enrich our Christian prayer and spirituality? Does this religious use make us "belongers" to these religions? Is multiple or double religious belonging theologically possible, and even desirable, in Asia? As an example, what new and surprising insights will a missiological and interreligious reading of the well-known narrative of Jesus' encounter with the Samaritan woman at Jacob's well (John 4:4–42) yield?

One of the most difficult problems for the church in the contemporary context of religious pluralism is forming consensus on doctrinal matters. The fifth-century monk Vincent of Lérins's triple criteria of *semper* (always), *ubique* (everywhere), and *ab omnibus* (by everyone) for ascertaining orthodoxy, as elaborated in his *Commonitorium*, were once obvious and incontrovertible when the world was predominantly Catholic, but now seem highly problematic in world Christianity. In the formation of doctrinal consensus in the past, a dominant, even exclusive, role was given to the hierarchical magisterium (pope and bishops) and, secondarily, to theologians. Little attention was given to the *sensus fidei* (faith instinct) of the laity, especially the poor and the marginalized among them, and of course no heed at all was paid to the beliefs and practices of non-Christians. Today, in world Christianity, what importance must be given to the beliefs and practices of the last three groups of people? How can we bring together the voices of all the five magisteria, namely, bishops, theologians, the laity, the poor, and believers of other religions to form a *consensus omnium* (consent of all) in matters of faith and morals? Furthermore, given the fact that we live in the "Age of Migration," how do we construct an ecclesiology in which migration functions as the perspective to understand the nature and mission of the church? Can there be church outside of migration (*extra migrationem nulla ecclesia*), and, more radically, can there be salvation outside migration (*extra migrationem nulla salus*)?

It is commonly agreed that dialogue among religions is a top priority for the church in Asia, as the continent is the birthplace of all world religions and where religious harmony in religious diversity can make a significant contribution to peace and justice. What is the common doctrinal basis for interreligious dialogue? What is its most productive starting point: church, or Christ, or God? What theological advantages would accrue to interreligious dialogue if we start not from any of these three doctrines (ecclesiology, Christology, and trinitarian theology) but from the Spirit instead? Can pneumatology provide a basis for both universality and particularity of a religious claim? Finally, so far interreligious dialogue has been carried out mostly between Christianity on the one hand and Buddhism, Hinduism, and—to a lesser extent—Islam on the other. Because Confucianism is considered more as an ethical and even political system and less as a religious tradition, it has not received the attention it deserves, except in mainland China, Hong Kong, Macau, and in the West, from a handful of scholars specializing in Chinese philosophy. To remedy this lacuna I devote some reflections on Catholic–Confucian dialogue.

The last part, "Practice," discusses four urgent issues demanding concrete action on the part of Asian Christians: social spirituality, the practice of popular devotions, an ethic of migration, and ecological responsibility. These issues, especially climate change brought about by human activity, are by no means mere theoretical problems nor hoaxes concocted by anticapitalistic and anti-American governments to harm American economic interests. Rather, they are literally life-and-death issues; unless drastic concerted measures and programs are taken by all countries, and now, millions of Asians will perish and huge migrations will take place across Asia, creating unimaginable and permanent havoc. Christian faith, especially as articulated by Pope Francis in his encyclical *Laudato Si'*, offers effective concrete steps to bring about a socially engaged, religiously harmonious, respectful of human rights, and ecologically healthy way of life.

History, theology, and practice are but three helpful approaches to understand Asian Christianities. They by no means guarantee results that one can make bombastic boasts about, à la Trump, that rightly cause derision. Asian Christianities will never be able, nor do they ever want, to claim to be the best, the hugest, the most stupendous, the most amazing thing that ever exists. Rather, they will remain in the foreseeable future a "small flock," a "tiny mustard seed"—to use evangelical images—and a sign and instrument of the reign of God on the immense continent of Asia. The reflections offered in the following pages are a humble invitation to scholars of Asian Christianities, much more learned and experienced than I, to correct and improve what I have written and to enlarge our understanding of and love for Asian Christians or Christian Asians.

Part I

HISTORY

1

Asian Catholicism
in the Post–Vatican II Era

The focus of this chapter is quite precise and narrow: the impact of the Second Vatican Council on Asian Catholicism, or to put the matter from the perspective of the positive role of the Asian Catholic churches, their "reception" of Vatican II since its convocation five decades ago. It is not a historical study of the contributions of the Asian churches to the council as such.[1] Nor does it treat of the theoretical issues such as the principles that should guide the interpretation of Vatican II as an "event" and of its sixteen documents,[2] the various "narratives" of the council,[3] and the "rupture/discontinuity" and/or "reform/continuity" between the council and the alleged "pre-Vatican II church.[4] The goal of this chapter is to paint a portrait of the Catholic Church

---

1. A comprehensive and critical-historical study of the contributions of the bishops of Asia to Vatican II during the antepreparatory, preparatory, and conciliar periods is still to be written. The celebrated five-volume *Storia del concilio Vaticano II*, ed. Giuseppe Alberigo (Bologna: Il Mulino, 1995–2001), ET, *History of Vatican II*, ed. Joseph Komonchak (Maryknoll, NY: Orbis Books, 1996–2006), provides only sketchy information on this subject. This study is now made easier by the publication of all the official documents of the council: *Acta et documenta Concilio Oecumenico Vatican II apparando: Series I—Antepraeparatoria* (Vatican City: Typis Polyglottis Vaticanis, 1960–1961); *Series II—Praeparatoria* (Vatican City: Typis Polyglottis Vaticanis, 1964–1994); *Acta Synodalia Sacrosancti Concilii Oecumenici Vatican II* (Vatican City: Typis Polyglottis Vaticanis, 1970–1999). For a brief survey of the presence and contributions of the bishops of Asia at Vatican II, see Peter C. Phan, "'Reception' or 'Subversion' of Vatican II by the Asian Churches? A New Way of Being Church in Asia," in *Vatican II Forty Years Later*, ed. William Madges (Maryknoll, NY: Orbis Books, 2005), 26–32.
2. On the hermeneutics of Vatican II, see the magnificent articles celebrating the fiftieth anniversary of the council in the pages of *Theological Studies*: John O'Malley, "'The Hermeneutic of Reform': A Historical Analysis," *Theological Studies* 73 (2012): 517–46; and Ormond Rush, "Toward a Comprehensive Interpretation of the Council and Its Documents," *Theological Studies* 73 (2012): 547–69.
3. On the three "narratives"—ultratraditionalist, ultraliberal, and neoconservative—of the council, see Massimo Faggioli, "Vatican II: The History and the Narratives," *Theological Studies* 73 (2012): 749–67.
4. On the debate on the "continuity" and "discontinuity" of Vatican II, see Gerald O'Collins, "Does Vatican II Represent Continuity or Discontinuity?" *Theological Studies* 73 (2012): 768–94).

in Asia by examining the ways in which it received Vatican II and met its various challenges both within itself and toward the world.

A few preliminary remarks are in order before undertaking the proposed assessment. First, by "Vatican II" is meant of course the council itself and its sixteen documents. However, since Vatican II could not implement its own reform programs and even called for the establishment of postconciliar commissions to carry out its reform policies, it is reasonable that in assessing the impact of Vatican II attention should be paid to the major postconciliar documents and institutions, indeed, to the pontificates of Paul VI, John Paul II, and Benedict XVI.[5]

Second, "reception" refers to the ongoing process by which the community of faith, with its *sensus fidei/fidelium*, makes a teaching or a practice of the faith its own, acknowledging thereby that it is a true and authentic expression of the church's faith. Reception is not to be understood as a juridical ratification by the community of such a teaching or practice whose truth and validity would derive from such ratification. Rather, it is an act whereby the community affirms and attests that such teaching or practice really contributes to the building up of the community's understanding and life of faith.[6] Such a process of reception, however, is not a simple act of obedience and passive absorption. It is not always and necessarily a full acceptance of what is enjoined by ecclesiastical authorities. It may at times involve a partial and even total rejection of what has been taught or commanded. Thus, reception is necessarily a remaking, an "inventing" of, a creative fidelity to the tradition in the light of the contemporary situation; and the reception of Vatican II is no exception.[7]

---

5. Note that the issue here is not a distinction between the "letter" and the "spirit" of Vatican II, which figures prominently in the recent debate on the hermeneutics of the council. Rather it is a recognition that the impact of Vatican II cannot fairly and fully be assessed apart from what has been officially promulgated as council-mandated reforms (e.g., new liturgical books and rites, the 1983 Code of Canon Law, the *Catechism of the Catholic Church*, the reform of the Roman Curia and so on) and is thus a measure of its impact itself.

6. On reception, see the classic by Yves Congar, *Tradition and Traditions: An Historical and a Theological Essay*, trans. Michael Naseby and Thomas Rainborough (New York: Macmillan, 1967). Other useful works include Robert Dionne, *The Papacy and the Church: A Study of Praxis and Reception in Ecumenical Perspective* (New York: Philosophical Library, 1987); Hans Robert Jauss, *Toward an Aesthetic of Reception* (Minneapolis: University of Minnesota Press, 1982); Edward J. Kilmartin, "Reception in History: An Ecclesiological Phenomenon and Its Significance," *Journal of Ecumenical Studies* 21 (1984): 34–54; and Dale T. Irwin, *Christian Histories, Christian Traditioning: Rendering Accounts* (Maryknoll, NY: Orbis Books, 1998).

7. On the reception of Vatican II, among the immense bibliography see Giuseppe Alberigo, Jean-Pierre Jossua, and Joseph Komonchak, eds., *The Reception of Vatican II*, trans. Matthew J. O'Connell (Washington, DC: Catholic University of America Press, 1987); René Latourelle, ed., *Vatican II: Assessment and Prospectives: Twenty-five Years After (1962–1987)*, 3 vols. (New York: Paulist Press, 1988–89); Pierre-Marie Gy, *The Reception of Vatican II: Liturgical Reforms in the Life of the Church* (Milwaukee: Marquette University Press, 2003); Austin Ivereigh,

Since the reception of Vatican II in Asia consisted in a conscious attempt at applying the council to the specific contexts of Asia and the Asian churches, I begin with a brief overview of these manifold contexts. Next, since Vatican II's achievements, as many commentators on the council have suggested, can be categorized *ad intra* and *ad extra*, I consider how they have impacted Asian Catholicism under both of these aspects. I end with reflections on the prospects of the Asian Catholic Church in the light of Vatican II.

THE CHURCH IN THE ASIAN CONTEXT

Many Asian theologians have argued that the church in Asia must be not simply *in* but *of* Asia, that is, a fully and wholly inculturated church.[8] The context is not merely the location in which the church exists; rather it determines the church's self-understanding and its mode of being. Consequently, to understand how Vatican II has shaped the church of Asia requires knowledge of the contexts in which the church exists and to whose challenges the church seeks to respond theologically and pastorally.

With regard to Asia, several features should be kept in mind, and it will be clear that its extreme diversities make it a near impossibility to refer to anything—Christianity included—as "Asian." First, immense geography and population. Conventionally divided into five regions, namely, Central Asia (mainly the Republics of Kyrgyzstan, Tajikistan, Turkmenistan, and Uzbekistan), East Asia (mainly China, Japan, Korea, and Taiwan), South Asia (mainly Bangladesh, India, Myanmar, Nepal, Pakistan, and Sri Lanka),

---

ed., *Unfinished Journey: The Church 40 Years after Vatican II* (New York: Continuum, 2003); Günther Wassilowsky, ed., *Zweites Vaticanum: Vergessene Anstösse, gegenwärtige Fortschreibungen* (Freiburg: Herder, 2004); Ladislas Orsy, *Receiving the Council: Theological and Canonical Insights and Debates* (Collegeville, MN: Liturgical Press, 2009); Christoph Theobald, *La réception du concile Vatican II, I: Accéder à la source* (Paris: Cerf, 2009); Christoph Theobald, *"Dans les traces . . ." de la constitution "Dei Verbum" du concile Vatican II: Bible, théologie et pratiques de la lecture* (Paris: Cerf, 2009); Gilles Routhier, *Vatican II: Herméneutique et réception* (Montreal: Fides, 2006); Gilles Routhier, ed., *Réceptions du Vatican II: Le concile au risque de l'histoire et des espaces humaines* (Louvain: Peeters, 2004); Gilles Routhier and Guy Robin, eds., *L'autorité et les autorités: L'herméneutique théologique du Vatican II* (Paris: Cerf, 2010); James L. Heft and John O'Malley, eds., *After Vatican II: Trajectories and Hermeneutics* (Grand Rapids, MI: Eerdmans, 2012); and Massimo Faggioli, *Vatican II: The Battle for Meaning* (Mahwah, NJ: Paulist Press, 2012).

8. The Jesuit Filipino bishop Francisco Claver (1929–2010) reports that during the Asian Synod in Rome (1998) a curial cardinal told the assembled Asian bishops that they must not use the expression "Church *of* Asia" but "Church *in* Asia." See Francisco Claver, *The Making of a Local Church* (Maryknoll, NY: Orbis Books, 2008), 2. Indeed, Pope John Paul II's Post-Synodal Exhortation" (1999) is entitled *Ecclesia in Asia*. Among Asian theologians who have strongly argued for a church *of* Asia is the Sri Lankan Jesuit Aloysius Pieris.

Southeast Asia (mainly Cambodia, Indonesia, Laos, the Philippines, Singapore, Thailand, and Vietnam), and South-West Asia (the countries of the Middle East, Near East, or West Asia), Asia is the largest and most populous continent, with nearly two-thirds of the world's seven billion population.

Second, overwhelming poverty. Despite the presence of some economically developed countries such as Japan and the so-called Four Asian Tigers (Hong Kong, Singapore, Republic of Korea/South Korea, and Taiwan) and despite the dramatic rise of China and India as global economic powers, Asia still remains mired in widespread poverty, with some of the poorest countries on Earth (e.g., North Korea, Cambodia, Laos, Myanmar/Burma, and Bangladesh).

Third, political heterogeneity. In addition to having the largest democratic country, namely, India, Asia also features the three remaining Communist countries of the world, namely, China, Vietnam, and Democratic People's Republic of Korea (North Korea), and several countries struggling to transition from military dictatorship or single-party state to democratic forms of government and from a socialist economy to a market economy.

Fourth, cultural diversity. Though East, South and Southeast Asia are dominated by the Indic and the Sinic cultures, and West and Central Asia by the Arabic-Islamic culture, Asia is a tapestry of extremely diverse cultures and civilizations, often within the same country. For instance, ethnically and culturally, India and China are teeming with staggering diversity, and more than 100 languages and more than 700 languages are spoken in the Philippines and Indonesia respectively.

Fifth, religious pluralism. Asia is the cradle of all world religions. Beside Christianity, other Asian religions include Bahá'í, Bön, Buddhism, Confucianism, Daoism, Hinduism, Islam, Jainism, Shinto, Sikhism, and Zoroastrianism, and innumerable tribal and primal religions.

It is within the context of these mind-boggling diversities—geographic, linguistic, ethnic, economic, political, cultural, and religious—that Christianity and, more narrowly, the Catholic Church in Asia should be broached, especially when assessing the impact of Vatican II. With regard to Asian Christianity, several features should be kept in mind.[9]

First, ancient historical roots. Christianity may be said to be an Asian religion since it was born in Palestine, part of West Asia or the Middle East. Furthermore, though West Asia is now dominated by Islam, it was until the Arab conquest in the seventh century the main home of Christianity. The

---

9. For an introduction to contemporary Asian Christianity, see Peter C. Phan, ed., *Christianities in Asia* (Oxford: Wiley-Blackwell, 2011). For a history of Asian Christianity, see Samuel H. Moffett, *A History of Christianity in Asia. Volume I: Beginnings to 1500* (Maryknoll, NY: Orbis Books, 1992) and *A History of Christianity in Asia. Volume II: 1500–1900* (Maryknoll, NY: Orbis Books, 2005).

conventional narrative of Christianity as a Western religion, that is, one that originated in Palestine but soon moved westward, with Rome as its final destination, and from Rome as its epicenter, spread worldwide, belies the fact that in the first four centuries of Christianity, the most active and successful centers of mission were not Europe but Asia and Africa, with Syria as the center of gravity. But even Asian Christians outside West Asia can rightly boast an ancient and glorious heritage, one that is likely as old as the apostolic age. For instance, Indian Christianity, with the Saint Thomas Christians, can claim apostolic origins, with St. Thomas and/or St. Bartholomew as its founder(s). Chinese Christianity was born in the seventh century with the arrival of the East Syrian (misnamed "Nestorian") monk Aloben during the T'ang dynasty. Christianity arrived in other countries such as the Philippines, Japan, Vietnam, Thailand, Cambodia, and Laos as early as the sixteenth century.

Second, colonial heritage. One of the bitter ironies of Asian Christianity is that though born in Asia, it returned to its birthplace and is still regarded by many Asians as a Western religion imported to Asia by Portuguese and Spanish colonialists in the sixteenth century, and later by other European countries such as Britain, France, Germany, Denmark, and the Netherlands, and lastly by the United States.

Third, numerical minority. In 2010, in Asia, Christians predominate in only two countries, namely, the Philippines and the Democratic Republic of Timor-Leste (East Timor)—over 85 percent of their populations are Christian (mainly Catholic)—but their total Christian population remains relatively small.[10] In South Korea and Vietnam, Christians constitute an important but by no means numerically overwhelming presence.[11] In other countries, especially China, India, and Japan, to name the most populous ones, and in countries with a Muslim majority such as Bangladesh, Indonesia, Malaysia, and Pakistan, and in those countries where Buddhism predominates such as Cambodia, Hong Kong, Laos, Mongolia, Myanmar, Nepal, Singapore, Sri Lanka, Taiwan, and Thailand, Christians form but a minuscule portion of the population.[12] Without counting the Middle

---

10. The total Christian population of these two countries is approximately 84 million (83 million in the Philippines and slightly over one million in Timor-Leste). These and the following statistics are taken from Todd M. Johnson and Kenneth R. Ross, eds., *Atlas of Global Christianity 1910–2010* (Edinburgh: Edinburgh University Press, 2009).

11. South Korea's Christianity (overwhelmingly Protestant) accounts for about 41.1 percent of the population of 50 million; Vietnamese Christianity (overwhelmingly Roman Catholic) represents 8.6 percent of the population of 85 million.

12. The following numbers represent the percentages of Christians vis-à-vis the population of each country in 2010 (though it must be remembered that the statistics are notoriously unreliable, especially in Communist countries): China (8.6), Taiwan (6.0), Japan (2.3), North Korea (2.0), Mongolia (1.7), Sri Lanka (8.8), India (4.8), Nepal (3.1), Pakistan (2.3), Bangladesh (0.59), Brunei (15.3), Singapore (16.1), Myanmar (8.0), Malaysia (9.1), Cambodia (2.0),

East, Christians constitute only slightly over 9 percent of the Asian population.[13]

Fourth, ecclesial diversity. Asia is the home of many different Christian ecclesiastical traditions, rites, and denominations so that it is more accurate to use "Christianities" in the plural to describe them. Thanks to its past extensive missions in Asia, Roman Catholicism is the largest church. Older than the Roman Catholic Church is the Malabar Church of India ("Saint Thomas Christians"). The Orthodox Church also has a notable presence in China, Korea, and Japan. The Anglican Church (including the Anglican Church of Canada) is well represented, especially in Hong Kong, India, Malaysia, and Pakistan. Various Protestant churches have also flourished in almost all Asian countries, e.g., the Baptists (especially in North India), the Lutherans, the Mennonites, the Methodists, the Presbyterians (especially in Korea), and the Seventh-Day Adventists.[14]

Fifth, extensive migration. One of the best-kept secrets about Asian Christianity is that migration, national and international in scope, forced and voluntary in nature, economic and political in intent, has changed the face of many Asian churches. Thanks to the ground-breaking research of scholars such as Kanan Kitani and Gemma Cruz, a fuller picture of contemporary Asian Christianity has emerged in which migration has played a key role in reshaping the membership and organization of the local churches and producing difficult pastoral and spiritual challenges for the churches.[15]

Indonesia (12.1), Thailand (0.6), Laos (3.1), Kazakhstan (13.4), Kyrgyzstan (5.9), Tajikistan (1.4), Turkmenistan (1.5), and Uzbekistan (1.3). Dyron Daughrity provides helpful statistics of Asian Christianity in his *Church History: Five Approaches to a Global Discipline* (New York: Peter Lang, 2012), 234–38.

13. There are currently 350 million Christians in Asia, out of the population of almost four billion. In absolute numbers Asia has more Christians than Western Europe, Eastern Europe, or North America. However, in relation to the total population of Asia, Christians constitute only a minority and will likely remain so in the foreseeable future. On the place of Asian Christianity in world Christianity, see Dale T. Irwin and Scott W. Sunquist, *History of the World Christian Movement. Volume 1: Earliest Christianity to 1493* (Maryknoll, NY: Orbis Books, 2001); Dale T. Irwin and Scott W. Sunquist, *History of the World Christian Movement. Volume II: Modern Christianity from 1454–1800* (Maryknoll, NY: Orbis Books, 2012); Dyron B. Daughrity, *The Changing World of Christianity: The Global History of a Borderless Religion* (New York: Peter Lang, 2010); Dyron B. Daughrity, *Church History: Five Approaches to a Global Discipline* (New York: Peter Lang, 2012); Douglas Jacobsen, *The World's Christians: Who They Are, Where They Are, and How They Got There* (Oxford: Wiley-Blackwell, 2011); Noel Davies and Martin Conway, *World Christianity in the 20th Century* (London: SCM Press, 2008); and Charles E. Farhadian, ed., *Introducing World Christianity* (Oxford: Wiley-Blackwell, 2012).

14. Helpful guides to Asian Christianity include Scott W. Sunquist, ed., *A Dictionary of Asian Christianity* (Grand Rapids: Eerdmans, 2001); and Felix Wilfred, ed., *The Oxford Handbook of Christianity in Asia* (Oxford: Oxford University Press, 2014).

15. K. Kitani has focused on the Pentecostals and Evangelicals, especially in Japan, and Cruz on Roman Catholics, especially in Hong Kong. See K. Kitani, "Invisible Christians: Brazilian

Sixth, the rapidly growing presence of Pentecostals and Evangelicals. These recent comers to Asia, often part of the waves of migration, have grown by leaps and bounds, particularly among ethnic minorities and disenfranchised social classes, and their brands of Christianity, with their emphasis on the literalist interpretation of the Bible, glossolalia, prophecy and healing, differ greatly from, and often are in severe conflict with those of mainline Christian churches. The popularity of Pentecostals is well illustrated by the Yoido Full Gospel Church, located in Seoul, Korea, which is the largest Pentecostal church in the world, with nearly one million members. Furthermore, Pentecostal Christianity with its system of house churches is believed to be spreading like wildfire in China (such as the True Jesus Church and the Jesus Family) and to pose a serious threat to the government because it is unregistered and, hence, beyond government control.[16]

Finally, indigenous and independent Christianity. Numerous indigenous and sectarian Christian churches and movements have been established, often inspired by nationalism, biblical fundamentalism, or charismatic leadership, and possessing few or no relationships among themselves or with mainline Christianity. Among the most famous are the Iglesia Filipina Independiente (founded by Gregorio Aglipay in 1902) and the Iglesia ni Cristo (founded by Felix Ysagun Manalo in 1914), both in the Philippines. In 1951 the Three-Self Patriotic Movement was formed to unite all Protestant churches in China and to promote a strategy of self-governance, self-support, and self-propagation. In 1957 the Chinese Catholic Patriotic Association was established to enable China's Religious Affairs Bureau to exercise control over Chinese Catholics. In 1980 the China Christian Council was founded as the umbrella organization for all Protestant churches in the People's Republic of China, allowing them to participate in the World Council of Churches.

This bird's-eye view of both Asia and Asian Christianity serves as the indispensable background and context for understanding the impact of Vatican II on the Asian Catholic Church. Indeed, it may be argued that the Asian Catholic Church's reception of Vatican II consisted mainly in appropriating the council's teachings and reform agenda to meet the challenges posed by this double context. Asian Catholic Christianity's reception of Vatican II, like the council itself, has an essentially "pastoral" character. It "received"

Migrants in Japan," in *Latin America between Conflict and Reconciliation*, ed. Susan Flämig and Martin Leiner (Göttingen: Vandenhoeck & Ruprecht, 2012), 195–214; and G. Cruz, *An Intercultural Theology of Migration* (Leiden: Brill, 2010).

16. On Pentecostalism in general, see the works of Walter J. Hollenweger and Allan H. Anderson. On Pentecostalism in Asia, the most authoritative and informative book is Allan Anderson and Edmond Tang, eds., *Asian and Pentecostal: The Charismatic Face of Christianity in Asia* (Oxford: Regnum Books International, 2005). From the Roman Catholic perspective, John Mansford Prior, *Jesus Christ the Way to the Father: The Challenge of the Pentecostals*, FABC Papers 119 (Hong Kong: FABC, 2006) is ground-breaking.

the council only to the extent that the teachings and the pastoral policies emanating from the council have proved helpful in meeting both the external challenges of Asia—geographical and demographic immensity, linguistic and ethnic diversity, economic poverty, Communist and military regimes, cultural richness, and religious pluralism—and the challenges internal to the church itself—ancient historical roots, colonial heritage, numerical minority, ecclesiastical diversity, widespread migration, Pentecostalism and Evangelicalism, and the emergence of independent and charismatic churches. These two distinct sets of challenges correspond to Vatican II's *ad intra* and *ad extra* foci, and it is under these two aspects that an assessment of the Asian Catholic Church's reception of the council will be offered. Of course, these two aspects cannot be fully separated from each other. Indeed, they mutually influence each other: the better the church understands itself, the better it can relate to the world, and vice versa, a better relation of the church with the world leads to the church's deeper self-understanding. Nevertheless, considering them separately serves as a useful heuristic device to put some order to what will otherwise prove a mass of unmanageable data about the Asian churches' recent past.

Before describing this process of reception it may be useful to take into account the helpful distinction suggested by the historian John O'Malley between "reception" and "trajectory." He writes: "Whereas 'reception' generally indicates a direct application (or nonapplication) of explicit norms or directives, such as the revised liturgical forms, 'trajectory' suggests something less obviously based on the council's norms and directives. It is related to reception, and perhaps can be considered a species of it. Introduction of it as a category of interpretation expands what we usually mean by reception."[17] In what follows I speak of "reception" in the expanded sense of "trajectory," as suggested by O'Malley.

AD INTRA RECEPTION OF VATICAN II

Vatican II is the first council to reflect at great length on its own nature (*Lumen Gentium*) and the various aspects of its internal life such as worship (*Sacrosanctum Concilium*), reception of divine revelation (*Dei Verbum*), the role of the laity (*Apostolicam Actuositatem*), episcopal and priestly ministry (*Christus Dominus* and *Presbyterorum Ordinis*), religious life (*Perfectae Caritatis*), and the Eastern Catholic Churches (*Orientalium Ecclesiarum*). In addition to these *ad intra* issues, the council has also considered the *ad extra* relations and tasks of the Catholic Church vis-à-vis the outside world: other Christian churches and communities (*Unitatis Redintegratio*), other believers (*Nostra Aetate*), evange-

---

17. Heft and O'Malley, eds., *After Vatican II*, xii.

lization and mission (*Ad Gentes*), education (*Gravissimum Educationis*), the mass media (*Inter Mirifica*), religious freedom (*Dignitas Humanae*), and the modern world in general (*Gaudium et Spes*).

Of course, Vatican II as a corpus of sixteen official documents has had a decisive impact on the Asian Catholic Church. Asian Catholicism has received all of these documents as authoritative guides for its *ad intra* and *ad extra* activities. However, as to be expected, it grants priority to some over others. From the frequency of citations, *Lumen Gentium*, *Sacrosanctum Concilium*, *Dei Verbum*, *Gaudium et Spes*, *Ad Gentes*, and *Nostra Aetate* have obtained pride of place. Important as Vatican II as a textual corpus has been for the Asian churches, it would be a mistake in assessing the council's impact on the Asian churches to limit our attention to its sixteen documents, even if interpreted as a coherent and intertextually integral theological corpus. One must also attend to Vatican II as "event," that is, a happening in, to, and by the church brought about under the impulse of the Holy Spirit in which the participants of the council as well as the church as a whole underwent a profound religious "conversion" that requires a new language and a new rhetoric to express itself adequately.[18] Among Asian theologians who have eloquently and insistently argued for a reception of Vatican II as an "event" is the Sri Lankan Jesuit Aloysius Pieris. Contrasting "reform" with "renewal," Pieris calls Vatican II a "crisigenic" council, a "council of renewal not a council of reform,"[19] the latter starting from the center, often forced upon the periphery and designed to proceed smoothly and gradually, the former beginning from the periphery and moving to the center, from the bottom to the top, and often with a stormy process.

With regard to Asian Catholicism's *ad intra* reception of Vatican II, one helpful way to chart this appropriation is by examining the teachings and activities of what is without the slightest doubt the most important organizational

---

18. John O'Malley has identified four issues with which Vatican II had to deal: "how to deal with change, how to deal with the implications of a truly world church, with the relationship between center and periphery, and with the style in which the church conducts its mission" (Heft and O'Malley, eds., *After Vatican II*, xiv).

19. See A. Pieris, *Give Vatican II a Chance: Yes to Incessant Renewal, No to Reforms of the Reforms* (Gonawala-Kelaniya: Tulana Research Centre, 2010). Pieris recounts the astonishing advice that Karl Rahner gave to his young audience during his *lectio brevis* at the Facoltà Teologica San Luigi in Naples: "Don't waste time on Vatican II." By this Rahner means that the task of expounding Vatican II should be left to him and the cohorts of his age (the younger theologians have other tasks to do) because in Rahner's view, "*his* own contemporaries (the older generation to which he belonged, including some of the bishops who signed the documents) would find it well-nigh impossible to grasp the totally *new perspective* within which the council was formulating its message. If this new orientation was not recognized, the teachings of Vatican II could be misinterpreted along the beaten track of a theology which it was trying to leave behind as inadequate" (ibid., 70). This "new perspective" is what O'Malley and others refer to as "event."

innovation of the Asian Catholic Church as a whole, namely, the Federation of Asian Bishops' Conferences (FABC).[20] The Asian bishops at the Asian Bishops' Meeting in Manila, Philippines, in 1970 decided to establish a permanent structure, not unlike the Latin American Episcopal Conference (CELAM), to help implement their resolutions. Approved by the Holy See in 1972, the FABC is a voluntary association of episcopal conferences in Asia. Its decisions have no juridically binding force on its members; acceptance of them is more an expression of collegial responsibility and ecclesial solidarity than canonical compliance. Its goals and objectives, to quote from its mission statement, include:

1. To study ways and means of promoting the apostolate, especially in the light of Vatican II and postconciliar official documents, and according to the needs of Asia.
2. To work for and to intensify the dynamic presence of the church in the total development of the peoples of Asia.
3. To help in the study of problems of common interest to the church in Asia, and to investigate possibilities of solutions and coordinated action.
4. To promote intercommunication and cooperation among local churches and bishops of Asia.
5. To render service to episcopal conferences of Asia in order to help them to meet the needs of the People of God.
6. To foster a more ordered development of organizations and movements in the church at the international level.
7. To foster ecumenical and interreligious communication and collaboration.[21]

It is clear from these goals and objectives, especially the first, with its explicit insistence on following Vatican II and the postconciliar documents, that the FABC intends to be an official organ for the reception of Vatican II in Asia, as it seeks to implement episcopal collegiality, ecclesial communion, and dialogue as the mode of being church, the three ecclesiological principles advocated by the council. On the other hand, it is equally clear that the FABC could not have come into being without the impetus of Vatican II. Thus, it is as much the most mature fruit of the process of reception of the council as the most effective instrument for the implementation of the council's teaching and reform agenda.

In constituting its membership, the FABC has also sought to meet most if not all the above-mentioned challenges facing Asian Christianity. Geographi-

---

20. For information on the FABC, see its website: http://www.fabc.org. For a history of the FABC's first three decades, see Edmund Chia, *Thirty Years of FABC: History, Foundation, Context and Theology*, FABC Papers 106 (Hong Kong: FABC, 2003).

21. See http://www.fabc.org under the section "About Us."

cally, the eighteen episcopal conferences that are the FABC's full members and the nine that are its associate members hail from all the five regions of Asia, including Central Asia.[22] Linguistically, ethnically, economically, politically, and culturally, the FABC is marked by the same kind of diversity and multiplicity prevalent in Asia. (English is by default the common language.) Also represented are churches of ancient origins, with their different rites and ecclesiastical disciplines, and their presence provides unique opportunities for the implementation of the council's decree on the Catholic Eastern Churches (*Orientalium Ecclesiarum*). In this way, more than any other continental episcopal conferences, the FABC embodies the ideals and reality of the "world church" that Vatican II ushered in.

The structure of the FABC also promotes and facilitates collaboration among the churches and among the laity and the clergy. Besides the General Assembly, which is its supreme body and meets in regular session every four years,[23] the FABC has the Central Committee (composed of the presidents

---

22. The episcopal conferences which are the FABC's full members come from Bangladesh, East Timor, India (comprising three episcopal conferences based on their distinctive "Rites," namely, the Conference of Catholic Bishops of India [the Latin Rite], the Syro-Malabar Bishops' Synod, and Syro-Malankara Bishops' Conference), Indonesia, Japan, Kazakhstan, Korea, Laos-Cambodia, Malaysia-Singapore-Brunei, Myanmar, Pakistan, Philippines, Sri Lanka, Taiwan, Thailand, and Vietnam. The FABC's associate members come from Hong Kong, Macau, Nepal, Novosibirsk (Russia), Kyrgyzstan, Tajikistan, Turkmenistan, and Uzbekistan. To be a full member, an episcopal conference must have a minimum of three dioceses. The absence of an official organization representing the bishops of mainland China is conspicuous.

23. The General Assembly is composed of (1) all the presidents of the episcopal conferences that are members of the FABC, or their official bishop-designates, (2) bishop-delegates elected by the episcopal conferences that are full or associate members, and (3) members of the Standing Committees.

Up to 2013 there have been ten General Assemblies, each with a distinct theme. The last assembly met in Vietnam, December 10–16, 2013, with 111 official participants. That the Communist government allowed the FABC's Tenth General Assembly to be held in Vietnam was in itself an extraordinary diplomatic success for the Vietnamese church leaders. At the conclusion of each assembly the FABC issues a "Final Statement."

For the Final Statements of the first seven General Assemblies, see FABC and its various institutes; see also Gaudencio Rosales and Catalino G. Arévalo, eds., *For All the Peoples of Asia: Federation of Asian Bishops' Conferences. Documents from 1970 to 1991*, Vol. 1 (New York/Quezon City: Orbis Books/Claretian Publications, 1992); Franz-Josef Eilers, ed., *For All the Peoples of Asia: Federation of Asian Bishops' Conferences. Documents from 1992 to1996*, Vol. 2 (Quezon City: Claretian Publications, 1997); Franz-Josef Eilers, ed., *For All the Peoples of Asia: Federation of Asian Bishops' Conferences. Documents from 1997 to 2002*, Vol. 3 (Quezon City: Claretian Publications, 2002); Franz-Josef Eilers, ed., *For All the Peoples of Asia: Federation of Asian Bishops' Conferences. Documents from 2002 to 2006*, Vol. 4 (Quezon City: Claretian Publications, 2007). These four volumes also contain the documents of the various "offices" of the FABC. Most of the documents related to the FABC are available online and at the FABC Documentation Centre located in Bangkok, Thailand, which is part of the General Secretariat of the FABC located in Hong Kong.

of the member episcopal conferences, or their officially designated bishop-alternates), the Standing Committee (composed of five bishops elected from the five regions of Asia), and the Central Secretariat. Though the members of the Central and Standing Committees are all bishops, the members of the General Secretariat, which is the principal service agency and an instrument of coordination of activities within and outside the FABC, is composed of nine "offices" whose members are mostly priests, religious, and lay and whose expertise and work are vital to the FABC.[24] These offices regularly organize workshops and seminars for all kinds and levels of church minsters, thus enabling an effective collaboration among the bishops, among the bishops and their collaborators, and among the local and national churches. The written statements and summaries of these meetings, readily accessible online, serve as a convenient and reliable means for church leaders and rank-and-file Asian Catholics to update themselves on the current issues and problems confronting the Asian churches and their possible solutions. From the names of these nine offices it is clear that no area of Christian life is left untouched by the FABC, and through it, the teachings and reforms of Vatican II itself.

In addition to the FABC, a, if not the, major landmark in the history of Asian Catholicism's reception of Vatican II is the Special Assembly of the Synod of Bishops. Convoked by Pope John Paul II to celebrate the second millennium of Christianity, the Asian Synod met in Rome, April 18–May 14, 1998. It has been rightly hailed as the coming of age of the Asian Catholic Church. A careful reading of the responses of the Asian episcopal conferences to the *Lineamenta*, the individual bishops' speeches during the synod, and John Paul II's postsynodal apostolic exhortation *Ecclesia in Asia* readily shows how far the Asian Catholic Church has moved forward, from its barely noticeable contributions to Vatican II to the Asian Synod, and all that thanks to its whole-hearted reception of Vatican II, or more precisely, the council's trajectories.[25]

RECEPTION OF VATICAN II FOR
THE CHURCH'S RELATIONS *AD EXTRA*

While the reception of Vatican II by the Asian Catholic Church *ad intra* has been extensive and enduring, especially through the agency of the FABC and as demonstrated by the Asian Synod, ironically, if one were to survey the rather extensive official documents of the FABC and the writings of Asian

---

24. The nine offices are Human Development, Social Communication, Laity, Theological Concerns, Education and Student Chaplaincy, Ecumenical and Interreligious Affairs, Evangelization, Clergy, and Consecrated Life.

25. On the Asian Synod, see Peter C. Phan, ed., *The Asian Synod: Texts and Commentaries* (Maryknoll, NY: Orbis Books, 2002).

theologians, one would be struck by the dearth of explicit treatments of what is commonly referred to as ecclesiology or the theology of the church. If anything, there is a conscious shying away from "churchy" themes such as papal primacy and infallibility, apostolic succession, magisterium, episcopal power, the hierarchical structure, canon law, the Roman Curia, women's ordination, and the like. Not that these issues are of no importance for the Asian churches. Of course, they are. But they do not occupy the central position on the theological radar of the Asian churches.

Instead of developing an ecclesiocentric or church-centered ecclesiology, Asian bishops and theologians have fostered what may be called a regnocentric or kingdom-of-God-centered way of being church. Their emphasis is not on establishing new church organizations or instituting structural reforms, much less elaborating a theoretical ecclesiology. Rather their main, if not exclusive, concern has been implementing, pastorally and spiritually, ways of being church that are appropriate to the socio-political, economic, cultural, and religious contexts of Asia, as these have been sketched out above. In other words, in appropriating Vatican II, the Asian Catholic Church has been more interested in those conciliar and postconciliar documents that deal with the church's *ad extra* relations. Among these *Gaudium et Spes*, *Ad Gentes*, and *Nostra Aetate* have been most frequently invoked.

A quick glance at the themes of the past ten General Assemblies as well as those of the innumerable seminars and workshops organized by the FABC's nine offices will confirm this assessment.[26] In addition to these official and semi-official documents, the FABC also publishes what it calls "FABC Papers." These booklet-size publications are theological writings, mainly by native Asian theologians, addressing particular issues affecting Asian churches.[27] By and large all these writings focus on what has been become a mantra among Asian Catholic Churches, namely, the "triple dialogue": dialogue with the poor (liberation), dialogue with cultures (inculturation), and dialogue with other Asian religions (interreligious dialogue). By dialogue is meant not theoretical discussions among religious experts but the fundamental mode-of-being-church toward the outsiders, be they other Christians (ecumenical dialogue), non-Christian believers (interreligious dialogue), or nonbelievers (humanistic dialogue). This dialogue takes a fourfold form:

---

26. The themes of the FABC's General Assemblies are evangelization (first, 1974), life of the church (second, 1978), church as community of faith (third, 1982), the laity (fourth, 1986), a new way of being church (fifth, 1990), discipleship (sixth 1995), church as love and service (seventh, 2000), family (eighth, 2004), the Eucharist (ninth, 2008), and new evangelization (tenth, 2012). The tenth General Assembly celebrated *inter alia* the fortieth anniversary of the approval of the statutes of the FABC by the Holy See and the fiftieth anniversary of the convocation of Vatican II. Underlying these diverse themes is the leitmotif of the new way of being church in Asia.

27. These booklets, numbering over 150, are available online on the FABC website.

common life, working together for the common good, theological discussion, and sharing of religious experiences.

Continuing further the assessment of the impact of Vatican II on Asian Catholic Christianity, I will examine how this triple dialogue has been understood by the FABC and some influential Asian Catholic theologians. Here, John O'Malley's distinction between "reception" and "trajectory" is highly relevant. In fact, this triple dialogue belongs more to extending the council's trajectories than to its reception. Needless to say, all three dialogues have been recommended by the council, as the three conciliar documents mentioned above, repeatedly invoked by the FABC, testify. It is true as well that liberation theology is the original contribution of the Latin American church (with an emphasis on liberation from economic poverty) and that inculturation has been a deep concern of African Christianity (with a stress on liberation from cultural and anthropological domination). Nevertheless, it is the Asian Catholic churches that have consistently, insistently, and officially adopted the three dialogues in all their reciprocal and intrinsic connections as the overall agenda for pastoral ministry, church life, and spirituality, so much so that "dialogue" has become synonymous with the new-way-of-being-church in Asia.[28]

Perhaps the most comprehensive summary of this new way of being church is found in the Final Statement of the FABC's Seventh General Assembly (2000), with its theme "A Renewed Church in Asia: A Mission of Love and Service." The General Assembly sees the thirty-year history of the FABC as woven by seven movements: toward a church of the poor and the church of the young, toward a truly local and inculturated church, toward an authentic community of faith, toward active integral evangelization and a new sense of mission, toward empowerment of lay men and women, toward active involvement in generating and serving life, and toward the triple dialogue with other faiths, with the poor, and with the cultures.[29] This new way of being church had been elaborated at length by the Fifth General Assembly (1990), with its theme "Journeying Together toward the Third Millennium." Its Final Statement envisions "alternative ways of being church in the Asia of the 1990s" and describes them as constituting the church in Asia as a "communion of communities," a "participatory church," a "church that faithfully and lovingly witnesses to the Risen Lord Jesus and reaches out to people of other faiths and

---

28. See Peter C. Phan, *Christianity with an Asian Face: Asian American Theology in the Making* (Maryknoll, NY: Orbis Books, 2003); Peter C. Phan, *In Our Own Tongues: Perspectives from Asia on Mission and Inculturation* (Maryknoll, NY: Orbis Books, 2003); and Peter C. Phan, *Being Religious Interreligiously: Asian Perspectives on Interfaith Dialogue* (Maryknoll, NY: Orbis Books, 2004).

29. See the full text of the Final Statement in Eilers, ed., *For All the Peoples of Asia*, vol. 3, 1–16. See also Peter C. Phan, "A New Way of Being Church in Asia: Lessons for the American Catholic Church," in T. Frank Kennedy, ed., *Inculturation and the Church in North America* (New York: Crossroad, 2006), 145–62.

persuasions in the dialogue of life towards the integral liberation of all," and as "a prophetic sign daring to point beyond this world to the ineffable Kingdom that is yet to come."[30]

This "new-way-of-being-church" is the consistent and pervasive perspective in which Vatican II has been received and its trajectories carried forward in Asian Catholic Christianity. This is supremely true not only of the FABC and its offices in general but also of most Asian Catholic theologians of the older and younger generations. Among the former group mention has already been made of Aloysius Pieris, who may rightly be regarded as one of the most innovative theologians of Asia. Together with him are to be named Cardinal Luis Antonio Tagle, Carlos H. Abesamis, Georg Evers, Felix Wilfred, Michael Amaladoss, Virginia Fabella, Kathleen Coyle, José M. De Mesa, Jacob Kavunkal, Jacob Parappally, Soosai Arokiasamy, Antoinette Gutzler, Mark Fang, James Kroeger, John Mansford Prior, Vu Kim Chinh, and many others.[31] Among the younger generation mention should be made of Jonathan Tan, Edmund Chia, Gemma Cruz, Vimal Tirimanna, and the theologians associated with the FABC's Office of Theological Concerns.[32] A growing number of doctoral dissertation and master's theses have been written on the FABC and Asian theology.[33]

TRAJECTORIES OF VATICAN II IN ASIA

As we celebrate the fiftieth anniversary of the convocation of the Second Vatican Council and as we take stock of the council and its reception throughout the world, it is clear that the Catholic Church as a whole is at a crossroads. There is a widespread sense of an urgent need for a renewal and even a moral and spiritual purification in the whole church *a capite ad calcem*. This realization is made more insistent by the discouraging perception that Vatican II's "reforms" have been "reformed" during the last few decades and by the

---

30. For the full text of the Final Statement, see Rosales and Arévalo, eds,. *For All the Peoples of Asia*, vol. 1, 273–89.

31. See M. Amaladoss and R. Gibellini, eds., *Teologia in Asia* (Brescia, Italy: Queriniana, 2006), which also contains essays by non-Catholic theologians. Deserving special mention is James H. Kroeger, an American Maryknoller and long-time professor of missiology at the Loyola School of Theology, Manila. With his prolific writings he is a tireless and ardent promoter of the FABC and Asian Catholic theology.

32. See Vimal Tirimanna, ed., *Harvesting from the Asian Soil: Towards an Asian Theology* (Bangalore, India: Asian Trading Corporation, 2011); and Kathleen Coyle, ed., *40 Years of Vatican II and the Churches of Asia and the Pacific: Looking Back and Moving Forward. East Asian Pastoral Review* 42, no. 1/2 (2005).

33. See James H. Kroeger, *Theology from the Heart of Asia: FABC Doctoral Dissertations I (1985–1998)* and *Theology from the Heart of Asia: FABC Doctoral Dissertations II (1998–2008)* (Quezon City, Philippines: Claretian Publications, 2008).

numerous scandals of various sorts (not only of a sexual nature!) that have wrought havoc to the credibility of the church as a sign of God's presence in history. By happenstance, as this essay was being composed, the cardinals were meeting in Rome to elect a new pope after the unexpected resignation of Pope Benedict XVI, who felt no longer up to the task of shepherding the church because of alleged advanced age and ill health.

The question naturally arises: Can the Asian Catholic Church, with its manifold attempts at receiving Vatican II *ad intra* and *ad extra*, provide some useful hints for the "renewal" (and not simply "reform," to reprise Pieris's expressions) of the church? In other words, are there "trajectories" or unfinished businesses at Vatican II that need to be carried forward to achieve a true renewal of the church at this critical juncture? Like any genuine church renewal, this renewal must be both *ressourcement* and *aggiornamento*, the two movements working in tandem and in support of each other.

Perhaps an answer may be derived from the Final Statement of the FABC's Tenth General Assembly, which has as its theme "Renewed Evangelization for New Evangelization in Asia." As the General Assembly sees it, the fundamental task of the church is to respond to the specific challenges of our time, and, like Vatican II, it sets out "to read the signs of the times." Its *instrumentum laboris*, entitled "FABC at Forty Years: Responding to the Challenges of Asia: A New Evangelization," analyzes fifteen megatrends currently affecting Asia and Asian Christianity: (1) globalization as an economic process and a cultural phenomenon; (2) a secular, materialist, consumerist, and relativist culture; (3) widespread and systemic poverty; (4) the phenomenon of migrant workers and refugees; (5) the oppression of the indigenous peoples; (6) rapid increase in population; (7) threat to religious freedom; (8) threats to life in general; (9) the increasing role of social communications; (10) endangerment of ecology; (11) the lack of empowerment of the laity; (12) discrimination against women; (13) the majority of youth in the population; (14) the presence of Pentecostalism; and (15) the rise of Asian missionary societies.

An essential part of the effort to meet these challenges, according to the FABC's Tenth General Assembly, is continuing the process of reception of Vatican II and expansion of its trajectories, as is clear from the introductory statement: "The same Spirit who animated Vatican II now summons us to become **renewed evangelizers for a new Evangelization**" (bold in the original). This reception and expansion require a new spirituality: "To be renewed as evangelizers we have to respond to the Spirit active in the world, in the depths of our being, in the signs of the times and in all that is authentically human. **We need to live a spirituality of New Evangelization**" (bold in the original).

To elaborate this spirituality of New Evangelization, the General Assembly lists ten recommendations: (1) personal encounter with Jesus Christ;

(2) passion for mission; (3) focus on the kingdom of God; (4) commitment to communion; (5) dialogue as a mode of life and mission; (6) humble presence; (7) prophetic evangelization; (8) solidarity with victims; (9) care for creation; and (10) boldness of faith and martyrdom.[34]

It is interesting to note that in accord with the FABC's mode of receiving Vatican II, the ten recommendations, deeply rooted in Christian spirituality, are all oriented *ad extra*, as ways-of-being-church toward the others in contemporary Asia. The FABC's dominant concern is centered on the kingdom of God (not the institutional church), mission (not inward self-absorption), communion (not splendid isolation), dialogue (not imperialistic monologue), solidarity with victims (not blaming victims and withdrawal into an otherwordly "spirituality"), care of creation (not exploitation of natural resources), and witness/martyrdom (and not cowardly compromise and self-promotion).

Perhaps it is not too far-fetched to see in this reception of Vatican II and the expansion of the council's trajectories by the Asian Catholic Church a possible way forward for the entire Catholic Church in these dark times? If so, we will come full circle: the gift that Rome gave to Asia fifty years ago is now brought back to back to Rome, enlarged, enhanced, enriched.

---

34. For the full text of the Final Statement of the Tenth General Assembly, see the FABC's website.

2

An Asian Christian? Or a Christian Asian? Or an Asian-Christian?

A Catholic Experiment in Christian Identity in Asia

The central issue of this chapter is the identity of Asian Christianity. What does "Asian Christianity" mean, beside its geographical location? Are there characteristics—historical, socio-political, economic, cultural, and religious—that distinguish Asian Christianity from other Christianities? Is "Asian Christianity" itself a monolith susceptible of a common description or a variegated and heterogeneous entity, so that it is more appropriate to speak of "Asian Christianities"? Is the search for a unified identity of Asian Christianity not condemned to be a Sisyphean labor from the start? I hope to contribute to the discussion of the identity of Asian Christianity by looking at how the Catholic Church has historically dealt with this issue.

Of all the Christian churches in Asia, the Catholic Church is the largest and, in spite of its tendency toward uniformity and centralization, also the most diverse. This diversity is a function of the geography of Asia, the world's largest and most varied land mass: its teeming people, who constitute two-thirds of the world population; its immense array of languages, ethnic groups, cultures, and religions; the extreme differences in its economic and social realities represented by some of the richest and the poorest countries on Earth; its opposite political systems, comprising the largest democratic and the largest Communist states in the world. Within the Catholic Church itself, there are ancient and at times competing "rites," or, more accurately, vastly different theological, liturgical, and canonical traditions.

Throughout the long history of Catholicism in Asia, the question of Christian identity has been broached differently, and various answers have been given. At the risk of oversimplification, these answers can be classified along a three-stage trajectory. In the first, the word *Christian* functions as a substantive, with *Asian* as an adjective qualifying it, and hence the emphasis is on promoting "Christianness." In the second stage, *Asian* functions as a substantive and *Christian* as an adjective, and the stress is on preserving "Asianness." In the third and current stage, *Asian* and *Christian* are hyphenated together, both functioning as substantives, mutually transforming each other to produce a *tertium quid*, a new identity, whose configurations are still blurred but in which neither "Christianness" nor "Asianness" is jeopardized, but rather each is brought to full flourishing. In what follows I will attempt to interpret the history of Asian Roman Catholicism with the lens of this three-stage trajectory.

AN ASIAN CHRISTIAN: IMPOSING THE WESTERN CHRISTIAN IDENTITY

Roman Catholics appeared in China for the first time during Kublai Khan's reign (1260–94) under the Mongol/Yuan dynasty (1279–1368). They were preceded by Syrian Christians of the Church of the East, often mislabeled as "Nestorian," who under the leadership of the monk Aluoben [A-lo-pen] had come to China in 635. These Roman Catholics included Italian merchants (the best known were the Polo brothers, Niccolò and Maffeo, and their more famous son and nephew, Marco), a small number of slaves deported after the Mongol invasion of Eastern Europe, Franciscan missionaries and papal legates (the best known were Giovanni da Montecorvino and Odoric da Pordenone), and Chinese and non-Chinese converts.[1] Niccolò and Maffeo first arrived in Khanbalik [Beijing] in 1265 and, on a second voyage, accompanied by Marco, in Shangdu, Kublai Khan's summer capital, in 1275. These Italian merchants and others helped establish Catholic missions in Khanbalik, Quanzhou, and Yangzhou.

In an attempt to establish reunion between the Church of Rome and Eastern Christians and to enlist the help of Mongolians to put an end to the Muslim occupation of the Holy Land, various popes sent legates, mostly Franciscans, to the Mongolian court. Two Franciscan missions arrived at Qaraqorum, the Mongolian pre-Yuan capital (in present-day Mongolia), between 1245 and 1253, headed by Giovanni dal Piano del Carpini and Willem van Rubroek. Another friar, Giovanni da Montecorvino, arrived in Quanzhou in 1293. In 1307, seven more Franciscans (six of whom were bishops) were sent to reinforce the Chinese mission. Of the six bishops only three arrived in Quanzhou. In 1313, Giovanni da Montecorvino was consecrated the first archbishop of Khanbalik and patriarch of the Roman Catholic Church in the East.

Little is known of these missionaries' work in China except from their letters and travelogues and sundry archeological finds.[2] From these we learn that

---

1. On these early Roman Catholics in Mongol China, see Nicolas Standaert, ed., *Handbook of Christianity in China. Volume 1: 635–1800* (Leiden: Brill, 2001), 68–78.

2. For a description of these written sources and archeological finds, see Standaert,

most conversions occurred among non-Chinese people, such as the Öngüt tribe, the Armenians, and the Byzantine Alans (who had no clergy of their own and who were not allowed to use the Nestorian churches), and other non-Chinese groups (Giovanni da Montecorvino reported to have baptized six thousand of these). Of the Mongolians and the Chinese themselves, no mention is made of their conversions.

One of the reasons for this slim success among the native population is no doubt the missionaries' inability to adapt to the local culture or, in current parlance, the lack of contextualization, or inculturation. When evangelizing the people whom they called "idolaters," that is, the native Chinese, missionaries preached by means of interpreters, often through a double interpretation, from a European language to a Turco-Mongolian language and then to Chinese. Furthermore, Catholic missions courted the good will and support of the Mongolian rulers, especially Kublai Khan, who were foreign occupiers, and when the Yuan dynasty dissolved in 1368, Catholic Christianity also disappeared with it. What S. Moffett writes, with poignant sadness, of Chinese Christianity under the Mongolian rule speaks volumes about the missionaries' unconcern for the Asian identity:

> It is no surprise that the church fell with the old dynasty. This was the pattern of past Chinese history. But the Christians of the Yuan dynasty compounded the errors of their forerunners under the T'ang who had disappeared with their imperial patrons four hundred years before. That earlier Christianity had at least been unitedly Nestorian. The China of the fourteenth century, however, could not fail to note the enmity between Nestorians and their newly arrived rivals, the Catholics, and both were considered foreign by the Chinese. Compounding the handicap this imposed on the church, the Mongol dynasty itself was foreign. So to the Chinese, Christianity appeared as a foreign religion protected and supported by a foreign government. Catholic missions gave the impression of being even more foreign than the Nestorians, who were almost entirely Mongol, for they received far more visible support from outside China than ever was true of the Nestorians either in the ninth or fourteenth century.[3]

While such unconcern for the Asian cultures among these early missionaries was most probably unintentional and even unavoidable, the hostile attitude of later missionaries who came to Asia in the wave of the European

---

Handbook, 46–49, 59–61. The sources include four letters and four books; the finds include tombstones, remnants of churches, a bible, a pyx, and a host-iron.

3. Samuel Moffett, *A History of Christianity in Asia, Volume I: Beginnings to 1500* (Maryknoll, NY: Orbis Books, 1998), 474.

conquest of Asia since the sixteenth century is hardly blameless. Of course, there were brilliant attempts at what is now termed "inculturation," and we will describe some of them in detail later. But there are undeniable evidences pointing to an attitude of cultural and religious chauvinism on the part of most missionaries who required converts to adopt European ways of life and to condemn Asian religions as superstition and the work of the devil.

In India, with the main exception of Roberto de Nobili and other Jesuits such as Gonçalo Fernandes, Diego Gonsalvez, and Jacobo Fenicio, the general policy was to force Indian Christians to behave and even to dress as Portuguese. Alexandre de Rhodes (1591–1660), a French Jesuit missionary to Vietnam in 1624–1645, noted during his sojourn in Goa how Indians who had become Christians were forced to abandon their ancient customs. For example, they were dressed in Portuguese clothes, so that in public places one could tell which Indian was a Christian and which was not. Needless to say, this practice and others (e.g., meat-eating instead of vegetarianism) created a separate identity for Indian Christians, making them more Christian than Indian. Later on, de Rhodes found that in China men who became Christian had to cut off their long hair, again making them more European/Christian than Chinese. He wryly remarked: "For my part, I well know that in China I vigorously opposed those who wanted to compel new Christians to cut their long hair, which the men all wear as long as the women's, and without which they would not be able to move around the country freely nor be part of the society. I used to tell them that the Gospel obliged them to lop off their spiritual errors but not their long hair."[4]

From the religious perspective, however, nothing betrays a rejection of Asian cultures and religious practices by the Catholic Church more clearly than the so-called Chinese Rites Controversy.[5] At issue was the cult of ancestors, which lies at the heart of the Confucian tradition. In spite of the support of it by some Jesuits, church authorities as a whole—Popes Clement XI and Benedict XIV in particular—and most of the missionaries, especially the Dominicans and the members of the Société des Missions Étrangères de Paris, condemned the cult as superstition and prescribed an oath against the Chinese rites on missionaries to the East. While the factors that contributed to the Catholic Church's condemnation of ancestor veneration and its eventual reversal in 1939 are multiple and complex, there is no doubt that it represents

---

4. See Peter C. Phan, *Mission and Catechesis: Alexandre de Rhodes & Inculturation in Seventeenth-Century Vietnam* (Maryknoll, NY: Orbis Books, 1998), 42.

5. For a brief history and theological evaluation of this controversy, see Peter C. Phan, *In Our Own Tongues: Perspectives from Asia on Mission and Inculturation* (Maryknoll, NY: Orbis Books, 2003), 109–29. See also George Minamiki, *The Chinese Rites Controversy from Its Beginnings to Modern Times* (Chicago: Loyola University Press, 1985); and David E. Mungello, ed., *The Chinese Rites Controversy: Its History and Meaning* (Nettetal: Steyler Verlag, 1994).

the most vigorous attempt at imposing orthodoxy and the Christian identity
not only on the Chinese but also on all Asians influenced by Confucianism,
even at the risk of eliminating what is most sacred and dear to them and of
jeopardizing the whole missionary enterprise.

As a result, Christianity was so identified with the West that in the seventeenth century, to become a Christian meant to become a Portuguese. One
indication of this Western identity is the Vietnamese interpreters' translation
of the question in the baptismal rite: "Do you want to become a Christian?" as
"Do you want to become a Portuguese?"[6] Of course, this was not how Christian missionaries themselves translated or would have translated the baptismal question. Francisco Buzomi, an Italian Jesuit missionary who arrived in
Vietnam in 1615, was horrified when he discovered the erroneous translation
and immediately devised a new translation of the question as "Do you want to
enter the Christian religion?"[7] But the fact that the Vietnamese interpreters
translated "Christian" as "Portuguese" speaks volumes about how Christianity was perceived by the natives.

Later Catholic missionaries took pains to clarify that Christianity is not
the religion of the West or of the Portuguese. Alexandre de Rhodes, in his
famous catechism, the first to be written in the alphabetical script, insists that
Christianity is not the religion of the Portuguese but that, like the sun, it
belongs to all peoples, even though it may shine on some countries first:

> Do not say that this law is the law of the Portuguese. The holy law of the
> Lord of heaven is a light greater and older than the light of the sun itself.
> For example, when the sun sends its rays on a kingdom, it illuminates it,
> though the other kingdoms on which it has not sent its rays still remain
> in darkness. Nevertheless, no one says that the sun belongs to that king-
> dom upon which it sends its rays first, because the sun is common to the
> whole world and exists before the kingdom it illuminates. Similarly, the
> holy law of God, though it has appeared to other kingdoms first, should
> not be seen as belonging to this or that kingdom, but as the holy law of
> God, the Lord of all things.[8]

A CHRISTIAN ASIAN:
CHRISTIANITY IN ASIAN GARB

It is partially the catholicity or universality of Christianity that allows
seventeenth-century missionaries, mostly Jesuits, to Asia, in particular in
India, Japan, and China, to adopt a more positive attitude toward Asian cul-

---

6. See Phan, *Mission and Catechesis*, xv.
7. Ibid.
8. Ibid., 223.

tures and religions. As is well known, Catholic missions from the sixteenth century were carried out under the patronage of either Spain or Portugal. As a result of the Treaty of Tordesillas in 1494, missions to Asia, and more specifically, to India, Japan, China, and the Philippines, were entrusted to the Portuguese *padroado* (in 1565, Spain took over the Philippines, in violation of the Treaty of Tordesillas).

With the capture of Goa by the Portuguese in 1510, Roman Catholicism was introduced to India. Twenty-four years later, Goa was made a diocese, with jurisdiction stretching from the Cape of Good Hope to China. As mentioned above, the common practice of the church was to make Indian Catholics more Christian than Indian, even in their costumes and behavior. There were exceptions, however. Among the Jesuits in India, Roberto de Nobili (1577–1656) proposed and practiced the method of adaptation or accommodation. In Madurai, where he arrived in 1606, de Nobili led the life of a *sannyāsin* (renouncer) and attempted to convert the Brahmins. To show that Indians need not abandon their cultural customs, de Nobili carefully distinguishes between cultural norms and practices on the one hand and religious beliefs and practices on the other, the former contained mostly in the *Laws of Manu* and the latter divided into three groups, namely, the "atheists," the "idolaters," and the "wise." The "atheists" are the Buddhists, who do not speak of God; the "idolaters" are those who indulge in all kinds of superstitions; and the "wise" are the Brahmins, a group of learned and highly regarded scholars, who should be the missionaries' preferred conversation partners and targets for conversion. To this last group de Nobili addressed his books, chief of which are *Report Concerning Certain Customs of the Indian Nation*; *The Dialogue on Eternal Life*; and *The Inquiry into the Meaning of "God."*[9]

As an appropriate missionary strategy de Nobili counsels the avoidance of two extremes, i.e., accepting everything and condemning everything Indian. Instead, he suggests that one "should weigh with all care and discernment which of these customs are purely social, and which are tainted by superstition."[10] De Nobili goes on to examine three categories of things, namely, certain insignia (e.g., the thread, the tuft of hair, the sandal paste, and the scholar's mark) used in idol worship, certain actions performed in the performance of rituals, and certain objects dedicated to idols. To evaluate these, he offers two guidelines:

> The first rule is that wherever in the customs of this country we find anything that has no relation to civil adornment, anything that does not serve as a sign of distinction, anything that is not adapted to common

---

9. For a translation of these three works, see Roberto de Nobili, S.J., *Preaching Wisdom to the Wise*, trans. and intro. Anand Amaladass and Francis X. Clooney (St. Louis: Institute of Jesuit Sources, 2000).

10. Ibid., 195.

usage, but is exclusively oriented towards the veneration and worship of an idol, such a thing can in no way be permitted to Christians. . . . The second rule is the following. If, in the aforesaid matters, i.e., in practices which of their own natural constitution or by popular convention have been established to meet either needs in the ordinary course of nature or the common needs of civilized life, the people here should adopt a line of conduct that is reprehensible, as for instance by overlaying some practice with incantations or rites of superstitious character, or by associating it with some frivolous ideas of merit and demerit—then in that case, these practices are not be condemned, as the theologians say, regarding their substance, but solely regarding the objectionable mode connected with it, and that offensive mode is surely to be discarded.[11]

With this distinction between culture and religion, and between the "substance" and the "mode" of customs and things, de Nobili opens up the possibility of an inculturated Christianity, or to put it in terms of the identity of Asian Christianity, of being a Christian Asian and not simply an Asian Christian.

De Nobili's distinction between culture and religion would be of great interest to missionaries in China. Roman Catholicism reentered China in 1583 with the coming of Michele Ruggieri and Matteo Ricci. For the following fifty years (1580–1631), all the missionaries were Jesuits, operating under the Portuguese *padroado*. In the next fifty years (1631–1684), they were joined by Spanish Dominicans and Franciscans, Capuchins, Augustinians, and Carmelites, all under the Spanish *patronato*. From 1684, other missionaries, in particular members of the Société des Missions Étrangères de Paris, arrived, not under the Portuguese or Spanish patronage but under the authority of the Congregation for the Propagation of the Faith (Propaganda Fide). This variety of religious orders, ecclesiastical jurisdictions, national interests, and missionary strategies makes for profound differences in how to deal with Chinese customs, in particular the veneration of Confucius and the ancestors.

Under the leadership of Alessandro Valignano (1539–1606), the Jesuits' policy was one of accommodation to the local culture.[12] This strategy includes the learning of the local languages; adaptation of the lifestyle and etiquette of the Confucian elite of *literati* and officials; evangelization "from the top down," beginning with the emperor and his court; indirect evangelization by means of science and technology; and openness to and tolerance of Chinese values.[13]

---

11. Ibid., 210–11.

12. On Alessandro Valignano, see Andrew C. Ross, *A Vision Betrayed: The Jesuits in Japan and China, 1542–1742* (Maryknoll, NY: Orbis Books, 1994), 32–46.

13. See Standaert, *Handbook of Christianity in China*, 310–11.

This policy, later dubbed the "Ricci Way," in honor of Matteo Ricci, the most famous practitioner of it, was by no means universally adopted by the Jesuits in China, but there is no doubt that it played a key role in the Jesuits' stance in the so-called Chinese Rites Controversy. As mentioned above, the position of the Friars, especially the Dominicans (in particular Juan Bautista Morales and Domingo Fernández Navarrete), and the members of the Société des Missions Étrangères de Paris (in particular Bishop Charles Maigrot), was negative toward the cult of Confucius and the ancestors, which they considered superstitious and therefore to be proscribed. By contrast, the Jesuits regarded it as a "civil and political act," without religious significance, and therefore permissible.[14] The Jesuit position, at first condemned by several papal interventions, won the day in 1939, when Propaganda Fide issued the instruction *Plane compertum est* permitting the Chinese cult of Confucius and the ancestors insofar as it is a civil and political, and not religious, act. Whether the judgment about the nature of the Chinese cult is correct, it is clear that de Nobili's distinction between culture and religion would have been directly apropos to the debate about the Chinese Rites and that the Jesuit position would favor the Asian identity of Christians.

Another important document of the Roman Catholic Church that also favors the Asian identity is the instruction that Propaganda Fide issued to the first vicars apostolic of Tonkin and Cochinchina (1659), François Pallu (1626–84) and Pierre Lambert de la Motte (1684–79), both members of the Société des Missions Étrangères de Paris. The bishops are instructed to observe four principles in their missions: first, to form an indigenous clergy from whom future priests and even bishops can be selected; second, to preserve a close union with Rome; third, to keep away from national politics; and fourth, to respect local cultures and customs and to adapt to them with prudence. Given the path-breaking character of its directives, the instruction, unfortunately little known, deserves a detailed and thorough study. Limited space, however, allows the citation of only passages relevant to the issue of Asian identity of Christians, i.e., those dealing with the first and fourth principles:

> The main reason which induced the Sacred Congregation to send you as bishops to these regions is that with every possible way and mean you so form the youth as to make them capable of receiving the priesthood. You will then ordain them and assign them in those vast territories, each to his own region, with the mission to serve Christianity there with utmost diligence and under your direction. You must therefore always keep in

14. For a collection of Roman Catholic documents on the Chinese Rites Controversy, see Ray R. Noll, ed., *100 Roman Documents Concerning the Chinese Rites Controversy (1645–1941)* (San Francisco: University of San Francisco, 1992).

mind this goal: to lead as many and as suitable candidates as possible to the priesthood, to educate them, and to promote them in due course.

If among those whom you have promoted there are some worthy of the episcopacy, you must not, under the strictest prohibition, elevate anyone of them to this high dignity, but first make known to the Sacred Congregation by letter their names, qualities, age, and whatever other useful information, such as where they could be consecrated, to which dioceses they could be appointed. . . .

Do not in any way attempt and do not on any pretext persuade these peoples to change their rites, customs and mores unless these are clearly contrary to religion and good morals. For what could be more absurd than to bring France, Spain, Italy, or any other European country over to China? It is not these countries but faith that you must bring, the faith that does not reject or jeopardize the rites and customs of any people as long as these are not depraved, but rather desires to preserve and promote them. It is, as it were, written in the nature of all peoples that the customs of their country and especially their country itself should be esteemed and loved above anything else. Nothing causes more hatred and alienation than changing the customs of a country, especially those by which the memory of their ancestors is preserved. This is particularly so if these customs are abrogated and then replaced with those imported from your country. Never make comparisons between the customs of these peoples and those of Europe. On the contrary, be anxious to adapt yourself to them. Admire and praise whatever deserves praise. As to things that are not praiseworthy, they should not be extolled, as is done by flatterers. On the contrary, exercise prudence in either not passing judgment on them or in not condemning them rashly and exaggeratedly. As for what is evil, it should be dismissed with a nod of the head or by silence rather than by words, though without missing the opportunity, when people have become disposed to receive the truth, to uproot it without ostentation.[15]

Besides the Jesuits, mostly Portuguese and Italian, working under the Portuguese *padroado*, there were also French Jesuits, sent by King Louis XIV as "Mathématiciens du Roy," who arrived in China in 1687 independently of the *padroado*. Their main mission was to work as scientific advisors to the court of the emperor Kangxi. With respect to the Asian identity of Chinese Christians, the theory known as "figurism," which was developed by some of these French Jesuits, most notably Joachim Bouvet, Jean-François Foucquet, and

---

15. For an English translation of excerpts of this instruction, see Jacques Dupuis, ed., *The Christian Faith in the Doctrinal Documents of the Catholic Church* (New York: Alba House, 2001), 468–70.

Joseph de Prémare, is of great relevance.[16] Using typological exegesis, "ancient theology" (*prisca theologia*), and the doctrine of Jewish kabala, these Figurists argue that the Chinese classics, in particular the *Yijing* [the Book of Changes] and the *Daode jing* [the Book of the Way and Its Power], contain "examples" (*figurae*) of Christian doctrines such as those concerning God the creator, the Trinity, Wisdom, and the awaited messiah. The point of figurism is to show that the ancient Chinese had already known about the Christian mysteries, and, therefore, being a Christian does not require abandoning Chinese culture and religion.

It may be argued that this accommodationist policy—of Roberto de Nobili, Alessandro Valignano, Matteo Ricci, Alexandre de Rhodes, Propaganda Fide, and the Figurists—admittedly innovative, and even revolutionary in comparison with previous practices—is only what it is: mere accommodation or adaptation. Though it enables a more respectful approach to Asian cultures and religions, and hence, promotes a stronger Asian identity in Christians, it still weighs more heavily on the Christian identity than on the Asian identity. Indeed, it has been pointed out, and correctly so, that for de Nobili and his Jesuit confreres there is ultimately only one valid mode of religious thinking and acting, namely, the Christian. The Indian and Chinese cultures and religions are not respected in themselves but only to the extent that they do not contradict the Christian truths and values or at best confirm them.[17] There is no genuine appreciation for and an attempt to learn from these cultures and religions, much less a recognition that they may contain truths and saving grace given by God. For this next step, one would have to wait for Vatican II (1962–1965) and its reception in Asia.

ASIAN-CHRISTIAN/CHRISTIAN-ASIAN: A NEW WAY OF BEING CHURCH

As is well known, for Roman Catholicism Vatican II represents both a returning to the ancient sources of the faith (*ressourcement*) and a radical renewal (*aggiornamento*) to meet the challenges of the times. Nowhere, arguably, is the discontinuity between Vatican II and the pre–Vatican II period of the Catholic Church more obvious than in matters regarding the possibility of salvation of non-Christians and the value of their religions. With regard to the salvation of non-Christians, Vatican II, reversing the church's centuries-old condemnation of non-Christians to hell,[18] affirms that "those who have not

---

16. On figurism, see Standaert, *Handbook of Christianity in China*, 668–74.

17. See the critique of Anand Amaladass and Francis Clooney in R. de Nobili, *Preaching*, 34–48.

18. See, for instance, the Council of Florence's decree to the Jacobites (1442): "(The Holy

yet received the Gospel are related to the People of God in various ways."[19] Among these people the council explicitly mentions five groups: Jews; Muslims; those seeking the unknown God in shadows and images through their religions; those who do not practice any specific religion but sincerely seek God; and those who, without any fault on their part, have not yet arrived at an explicit knowledge of God (e.g., atheists). All these people, the council says, "may achieve eternal salvation," though of course not without the grace of Christ.[20]

With regard to non-Christian religions themselves, Vatican II acknowledges that the "rites and customs of peoples," including therefore their religions, should be "saved from destruction" and "purified and raised up, and perfected for the glory of God."[21] In its Decree on the Church's Missionary Activity (*Ad Gentes*), the council affirms that these religious elements "may lead one to the true God and be a preparation for the gospel."[22] These "elements of truth and grace" are the "secret presence of God"[23] and "the seeds of the word."[24] In its Declaration on the Relation of the Church to Non-Christian Religions (*Nostra Aetate*), Vatican II mentions the primitive religions, Hinduism, Buddhism, Islam, and Judaism. Of these religions the council affirms: "The Catholic Church rejects nothing of what is true and holy in these religions. It has a high regard for the manner of life and conduct, the precepts and doctrines which, although differing in many ways from its own teaching, nevertheless often reflect a ray of that truth which enlightens all men and women."[25] The council goes on to urge Catholics to "prudently and lovingly,

---

Roman Church) . . . firmly believes, professes and preaches that 'no one remaining outside the Catholic Church, not only pagans, but also Jews, heretics and schismatics, can become partakers of eternal life; but they will go to the 'eternal fire prepared for the devil and his angels' (Matthew 25:41), unless before the end of their life they are joined to it.' English translation is taken from Joseph Neuner and Jacques Dupuis, eds., *The Christian Faith in the Doctrinal Documents of the Catholic Church* (New York: Alba House, 2001). For an excellent analysis of the Roman Catholic teaching on "outside the church there is no salvation," see Francis A. Sullivan, *Salvation outside the Church? Tracing the History of the Catholic Response* (New York: Paulist Press, 1992).

19. See Vatican II's Dogmatic Constitution on the Church (*Lumen Gentium*), no. 16. English translations of Vatican II's documents are taken from Austin Flannery, gen. ed., *Vatican II: Constitutions, Decrees, Declarations* (Northport, NY: Costello Publishing, 1996).

20. *Lumen Gentium*, no. 16. In its Pastoral Constitution on the Church in the Modern World, *Gaudium et Spes*, Vatican II explains how this possibility of salvation for non-Christians is realized: "For since Christ died for everyone, since all are in fact called to one and the same destiny, which is divine, we must hold that the holy Spirit offers to all the possibility of being made partners, in a way known to God, in the paschal mystery" (no. 22).

21. Ibid., no.17.

22. *Ad Gentes*, no. 3.

23. Ibid., no. 9.

24. Ibid., no. 11.

25. Ibid., no. 2.

through dialogue and collaboration with the followers of other religions, and in witness of Christian faith and life, acknowledge, preserve, and promote the spiritual and moral goods found among these people, as well as the values in their society and culture."[26] Needless to say, such teachings of Vatican II on the possibility of salvation of non-Christians and the "elements of truth and grace" of non-Christian religions have extensive and profound implications for how Asian Catholics understand their identity and relate to believers of other religions.[27]

Though the contributions of the Asian churches to Vatican II were not significant, they did not delay in "receiving" its doctrinal teachings and pastoral orientations. "Reception" refers to the ongoing process by which the community of faith acknowledges that a teaching or a practice enjoined by church authority is a genuine expression of the church's faith and therefore true and binding, and makes that teaching or practice its own. It is an act whereby the community affirms and attests that such teaching or practice really contributes to the building up of the community's life of faith.[28] Such a process of reception, however, is not a simple act of obedience, a mere application of a rule. It is not always an acceptance or at least a full acceptance of what is enjoined. It may at times involve rejection, total or partial. At any rate, it is *always* a remaking, an "inventing" of the tradition, and at times a subversion of it.[29]

It is in the light of this process of reception of Vatican II, in the sense of both acceptance of and going beyond the council, that the question of Christian identity for Catholic Asians can best be answered. A central role

---

26. *Nostra Aetate*, no. 2. For a comprehensive study of this document, see Charles L. Cohen, Paul F. Knitter, and Ulrich Rosenhagen, eds., *The Future of Interreligious Dialogue: A Multireligious Conversation on* Nostra Aetate (Maryknoll, NY: Orbis Books, 2017).

27. For a critical evaluation of *Nostra Aetate*, see Peter C. Phan, "Reading *Nostra Aetate* in Reverse: A Different Way of Looking at the Relations among Religions," *Studies in Christian-Jewish Relations*, 10, no. 2 (2015): 1–14.

28. On reception, see the classic by Yves Congar, *Tradition and Traditions: An Historical and a Theological Essay*, trans. Michael Naseby and Thomas Rainborough (New York: Macmillan, 1967). Other useful works include Robert Dionne, *The Papacy and the Church: A Study of Praxis and Reception in Ecumenical Perspective* (New York: Philosophical Library, 1987); Hans Robert Jauss, *Toward an Aesthetic of Reception* (Minneapolis: University of Minnesota Press, 1982); Edward J. Kilmartin, "Reception in History: An Ecclesiological Phenomenon and Its Significance," *Journal of Ecumenical Studies* 21 (1984): 34–54; Dale T. Irwin, *Christian Histories, Christian Traditioning: Rendering Accounts* (Maryknoll, NY: Orbis Books, 1998); and Terrence Tilley, *Inventing Catholic Tradition* (Maryknoll, NY: Orbis Books, 2001).

29. For an extensive bibliographical survey of post–Vatican II developments in Asia, see Peter C. Phan, "Reception of Vatican II in Asia: Historical and Theological Analysis," in Phan, *In Our Own Tongues*, 201–14. On the reception of Vatican II by the Asian Catholic Churches, see Peter C. Phan, "'Reception' or 'Subversion' of Vatican II by the Asian Churches? A New Way of Being Church in Asia," in William Madges, ed., *Vatican II: Forty Years Later* (Maryknoll, NY: Orbis Books, 2006), 26–54.

in this reception has been played by the Federation of Asian Bishops' Conferences (FABC), which was founded in 1970 during a meeting of 180 Asian bishops with Pope Paul VI. Since its foundation to 2006, the FABC has held ten plenary assemblies, at the end of which it issued a Final Statement. In addition to the plenary assembly, which is its supreme body, the FABC also has permanent offices that promote various activities and publish documents of their own.[30]

With regard to the question of Christian/Catholic identity in Asia, the FABC approaches it indirectly by speaking of "a new way of being church." This new way consists in shifting the mission of the church from "saving souls" and "planting the church" to promoting the reign of God among all peoples. Put more technically, to be a Christian in Asia is to be "regnocentric" (kingdom-of-God-centered) rather than "ecclesiocentric" (church-centered). To be "regnocentric" is to be focused ultimately on God, that is, to be "theocentric" (God-centered) rather than "Christocentric" (Christ-centered). In this new way of being church it is not a matter of choosing one and rejecting the other, to be either ecclesiocentric or regnocentric, either Christocentric or theocentric. Rather it is a question of theological *prioritizing* that orders the activities of the church's mission according to their importance and defines the Christians' relations to the cultures and the religions in which they live.[31] The goal of these activities is to make Christianity a religion not only *in* but *of* Asia.

How does being regnocentric and theocentric promote a real Asian identity of the Christians better than being ecclesiocentric and Christocentric? In a context as religiously and culturally pluralistic as that of Asia, anything that incites animosity and rivalry between Christianity and other religions should be avoided. Historians have shown that promoting the institutional interests of the church in Asia had often been done at the expense of other religions, and, sadly, at times with the sword. Eschewing ecclesiocentrism does not imply that work to expand the church geographically and numerically is not legitimate. Rather, it is legitimate only to the extent that it serves God's reign of peace, justice, reconciliation, and the integrity of creation, to which the followers of other religions are invited to contribute. Asian Catholics are urged to share life and collaborate with non-Christians for the integral human development and liberation of all people, especially the poor, the Dalits, the

---

30. For a history of the Federation of Asian Bishops' Conferences (henceforth, FABC), see Chapter 1.

31. See Peter C. Phan, "Kingdom of God: A Theological Symbol for Asians?," in Peter C. Phan, *Christianity with an Asian Face: Asian American Theology in the Making* (Maryknoll, NY: Orbis Books, 2003), 75–97; and Peter C. Phan, "Proclamation of the Reign of God as Mission of the Church: What for, to Whom, by Whom, with Whom, and How?," in Phan, *In Our Own Tongues*, 32–44.

tribals, the victims of patriarchy and sexual exploitation, women and children, refugees and migrants, and so on.

Again, historians have also shown that the proclamation of Jesus as the unique and universal savior had often been done in Asia with the belittling of the founders of other Asian religions and wisdom teachers such as the Buddha and Confucius. To avoid Christocentrism does not, however, mean that Christians should abandon their belief that God in Christ has reconciled the world to himself and has offered God's gift of salvation to all. Rather, in adopting theocentrism they should make utterly clear what the truth of Christ's universality and uniqueness is all about, namely, that *God* in Christ has made an offer of salvation to the whole humanity, with *Christ* as the decisive and constitutive mediator, and that Christ's role as savior does not exclude the fact that the *Spirit* of God also makes God's truth and grace available to all in other ways, particularly in non-Christian religions. A verbal proclamation of Christ as the unique and universal savior, and especially of the church as the superior religion, if unaccompanied by a life of selfless service and love, both at the personal and institutional levels, is nothing but sheer arrogance and of course convinces no one.

Clearly, then, regnocentrism does not exclude ecclesiocentrism but includes it and protects it from theological distortions. Similarly, theocentrism does not exclude Christocentrism but places it in a theologically fruitful framework in which the role of the Holy Spirit, in addition to that of Christ the Logos, in the history of salvation is given due recognition.

As far as the identity of Asian Christians is concerned, this new way of being church moves beyond both the first and second paradigms of understanding and shaping Christian identity as described above. The first paradigm is *colonization*, both cultural *and* religious, in which both Western cultures (e.g., Portuguese) and a form of Christianity (e.g., Latin) are presented as the universal norm to be imposed on Asians, and in which Asian cultures are regarded as barbaric and Asian religions are condemned as rank superstition. In this paradigm a Christian has nothing to learn from either Asian religions or Asian cultures. In becoming Christian one must renounce both of them and become Christian inside and outside, religiously and culturally.

The second paradigm is *fulfillment*, but only religious and not cultural. With a neat distinction and separation between culture and religion, proponents of this second paradigm are able to appreciate and even appropriate the cultural customs and philosophical ideas of the Asian people. However, as far as Asian religions are concerned, their beliefs and practices are good only to the extent that they correspond to Christian beliefs and practices. At best, they may be regarded as *preparatio evangelica* or "seeds of the Word," and their fullness can be fulfilled only when "converted" to Christianity. In this paradigm, Christians may learn something from Asian cultures but have nothing to learn from Asian religions; what needs to be done is clothing the Christian truths and practices in Asian garb. Asian Christians are Christian on the inside but Asian on the outside. Ultimately, this paradigm is an instrumentalization of Asian cultures and religions for the sake of mission and evangelization.[32]

The third paradigm is called an Asian new way of being church. It goes beyond the paradigms of both colonization and fulfillment. It is the paradigm of *mutuality* or *partnership*. Here the ideal Christian identity is Asian *and* Christian, both inside *and* outside, both culturally *and* religiously. It is imperfectly signified by the hyphenated Asian-Christian and Christian-Asian, with both "Asian" and "Christian" functioning equally as adjective and noun. Conversion or becoming a Christian does not require that one abandon, much less condemn, either one's culture or one's religion. Indeed, one affirms both and brings them to their full flowering. Conversion is not to be understood primarily as rejecting one religion and joining another but rather promoting the values of the reign of God in and through the impulses of one's culture, one's previous religion, and Christianity.[33] In this sense conversion does not prevent but rather encourages certain forms of "multiple religious belonging" by which a person, though not an official member of more than one religious organization, accepts the beliefs and practices of two or more religious systems.[34]

To achieve this new way of being church, the FABC proposes *dialogue* as the modality par excellence of living the Christian life in Asia. This dialogue is threefold: with the people of Asia, especially the poor and the marginalized (liberation and integral development), Asia's cultures (inculturation), and Asian religions (interreligious dialogue).[35] This dialogue is carried out at four levels. The first is the dialogue of *life*, where people of different faiths live together as friendly neighbors and share their joys and hopes together. The second is the dialogue of *action*, by which people collaborate with one another to achieve peace, justice, and reconciliation. The third is the dialogue of *theological exchange*, the purpose of which is to remove misunderstandings and to

---

32. This model seems to be that of John Paul II in his encyclical *Fides et Ratio*. See Peter C. Phan, "Inculturation of the Christian Faith in Asia through Philosophy," in Phan, *Christianity with an Asian Face*, 47–71.

33. On conversion understood as conversion to the reign of God, see Peter C. Phan, "Conversion and Discipleship as Goals of the Church's Mission," in Phan, *In Our Own Tongues*, 45–61.

34. On multiple religious belonging, see Peter C. Phan, "Multiple Religious Belonging: Opportunities and Challenges for Theology and Church," in Peter C. Phan, *Being Religious Interreligiously: Asian Perspectives on Interfaith Dialogue* (Maryknoll, NY: Orbis Books, 2004), 60–81

35. See among the FABC's many texts on these three dialogues: *For All the Peoples of Asia: Federation of Asian Bishops' Conferences (FAPA)*: FAPA (1992), 14–15, 22–23, 42–43, 100–101, 266–67; FAPA (1997), 167–71, 197–98, 203–5; FAPA (2002), 44–45, 120–25, 133–38, 139–45, 307–8.

deepen one's appreciation for one's religious traditions as well as those of others. Finally, the fourth is the dialogue of *religious experience*, in which people, while rooted in their own traditions, share their spiritual riches, especially with regard to prayer and contemplation, with people of other faiths.[36]

In conclusion, who is an Asian-Christian or a Christian-Asian in the Roman Catholic perspective? This question of the Christian identity in Asia is, as has been shown above, a complex one, and the answers to it are historically conditioned and varied. In the course of the history of Asian Catholicism, at first, the emphasis is on the Christian side of the binary identity; later, the emphasis is on its Asian side. More recently, thanks to the pioneering insights of Vatican II, the FABC, and the Asian Synod on the church's mission,[37] the identity of Asian Christianity is conceived of as the unity of "Christianness" and "Asianness," in which both elements gain full recognition and are enabled to achieve full flourishing. In short, an Asian-Christian or a Christian-Asian is one who is culturally and religiously Asian *and* culturally and religiously Christian, committed to a triple dialogue, that is, with the Asian poor and marginalized people, the Asian cultures, and the Asian religions, in the service of the kingdom of God. This is indeed a new way of being church *in* Asia and *of* Asia that Roman Catholicism sets out for itself. This new way of being church is no mere optional matter but one of life and death for Asian Catholicism, as the colloquium on ministries in the church held in Hong Kong in 1977 puts it starkly: "If the Asian Churches do not discover their own identity, they will have no future."[38]

---

36. See *FAPA* (1997), 169–71.

37. On the Asian Synod, see Peter C. Phan, ed., *The Asian Synod: Texts and Commentaries* (Maryknoll, NY: Orbis Books, 2002).

38. *FAPA* (1992), 70.

3

The Protestant Reformations in Asia.
A Blessing or a Curse?

Historical, Theological, and Missiological Perspectives

Recent historiography of the sixteenth-century Protestant Reformation has highlighted the staggering multiplicity of its actors, localities, theologies, and institutional forms as well as the manifold reforms undertaken by the Roman Catholic Church, which non-Catholic historians have dismissively labeled "Counter-Reformation," as if their whole scope and purpose were restricted to fighting the Protestant Reformation.[1] It is now generally recognized that sixteenth-century Europe underwent not *the* Reformation but *many* Reformations, including the Catholic Reformation prior to and concomitant with the Protestant Reformations as well as the reform promoted by the Council of Trent (1545–63).

With regard to the Protestant Reformation, in addition to its center-stage stars—Martin Luther, Ulrich Zwingli, and John Calvin—scholarly focus is also turned on the lesser-known Radical Reformers, such as the Anabaptists (Conrad Grebel, Menno Simons, Jacob Hutter, Melchior Hoffman, Hans Denck, and Adam Pastor), the Spiritual Reformers, whom Luther nicknamed the *Schwärmer* (Gaspar Schwenckfeld, Sebastian Franck, and Thomas Müntzer), and the Evangelical Rationalists. These Radical Reformers espoused dizzyingly divergent theologies and practices that are opposed not only to the magisterial (that is, led by academics [*magistri*] and magistrates) Protestant Reformation but also to each other, and which later found expres-

---

1. Currently two expressions are used to describe the reforms of the Roman Catholic Church in the sixteenth century: "Roman Catholic Reform/Reformation" to indicate significant movements of renewal within the Catholic Church before and during the Protestant Reformation, and "Counter-Reformation," first used in the seventeenth century to describe efforts by ruling authorities to restore their territories to the Roman obedience, and now used to refer mainly to the doctrinal and disciplinary measures adopted by the Catholic Church, especially at the Council of Trent, to combat the Protestant Reformation.

sion in various institutions classified under the umbrella term of "Pietism."[2]

Furthermore, in current scholarship the geography of the Reformation is seen to have extended beyond the countries of western and central Europe such as Germany, Switzerland, France, the Netherlands, England, and Scotland. It is expanded to include the Nordic countries (Denmark, Norway, Iceland, Sweden, and Finland), the Baltic countries (Lithuania, Latvia, and Estonia), and Eastern Europe (Prussia, Poland, Bohemia, Moravia, Silesia, Hungary, Slovenia, and Croatia). Attention is also shifted from the role played by the ordained and theologians to that of the laity, especially women, and the peasants.[3]

Acknowledgment of the multiplicity and diversity of the Protestant Reformations does not of course intend to deny the fact that the Reformers, though sharply different among themselves, shared a common goal, namely, restoring the church—deeply corrupted, in their view—to its original purity and authenticity by returning to the Word of God enshrined in the Bible as the sole norm for the Christian faith. Rather this recognition of diversity and multiplicity, in addition to being an imperative of historical scholarship, serves as an indispensable vantage point from which to evaluate the Reformation's five-century-old global impact and to shape its legacy for the future of Christianity. A serious challenge to this legacy is the fact that the Protestant Reformers' opposing theologies, methods, and means to achieve their reform agenda have unfortunately led to violence and war and to still-ongoing divisions among the Christian churches.

Keeping in mind the diversity and multiplicity of the Protestant Reformation and its differentiation from Roman Catholicism is especially important to understand its role and impact in Asia. For one thing, only in Asian countries, even in those that are not in principle hostile to Christianity, are Protestantism and Catholicism legally categorized as two different *religions*, alongside other religions such as Hinduism, Buddhism, Judaism, and Islam, and not just two branches of one single religion. Furthermore, in Asia, to the great detriment of Christian missions, historical divisions of Christianity continue to exist, not only between the Roman Catholic Church and the various Protestant churches but also among the different "denominations" within Protestantism, often as different "churches" competing with one another for membership and influence, and in the eyes of most Asian governments, as separate "religions."

---

2. On the Radical Reformers, see George Hunston Williams, *The Radical Reformation*, 3rd ed. (Kirksville, MO: Truman State University Press, 2000); Michael G. Baylor, ed., *The Radical Reformation* (Cambridge: Cambridge University Press, 1991); and Leonard Verdun, *The Reformers and Their Step Children: Dissent and Nonconformity* (Paris, AR: The Baptist Standard Bearer, 2001).

3. Among recent histories of the Reformations to be noted is Diarmaid MacCulloch, *The Reformation: A History* (New York: Viking, 2003).

In light of the foregoing observations the title of my essay on the impact of Protestant Reformations on Asia is intentionally phrased as a question: Are the Protestant Reformations a blessing or a curse for Asia?[4] The answer, of course, depends on how Protestant missions, past and present, in Asian countries are viewed. To gain a fair and balanced picture of these missions, it is necessary, in the first part, to describe, albeit summarily, the current situation of Protestant churches in countries of Asia.[5] In the second part I examine the most challenging theological issues facing the Protestant churches in Asia today. The last part indicates the way forward and ahead for the missions of Protestant churches in Asia.

THE PROTESTANT REFORMATIONS IN ASIA

As is well known, in contrast to the Orthodox Church and the Roman Catholic Church, which had undertaken extensive missionary work in Asia and Latin America, the latter since the fifteenth century with the support of the Spanish and Portuguese crowns under the *patronato/padroado real* system, the first Protestant Reformers were not concerned with mission outside Europe, partly because of their urgent need to consolidate their churches within their own countries and partly because of their belief that the apostles had completed the work of evangelization and that the end of the world was imminent. Of the three founders of the Reformation only Calvin saw a connection between the church as the *regnum Christi* and the duty of evangelizing non-Christians, and attempted a short-lived mission by sending a group of Genevans on a Huguenot colonial venture in Brazil in 1557.

---

4. For our present purposes, by Asia is meant primarily South Asia (in particular India, Pakistan, and Sri Lanka); Northeast Asia (especially China, Japan, and Korea), and Southeast Asia (particularly Myanmar, Laos, Thailand, Vietnam, Malaysia, Singapore, the Philippines, Brunei, Indonesia, and East Timor). I will leave out of consideration Western Asia (the Middle East) and Central Asia. Furthermore I will concentrate on countries where the churches issued from the Reformations maintain a significant presence, namely, India, Sri Lanka, China, Japan, (South) Korea, Myanmar, Singapore, the Philippines, and Indonesia. For comprehensive resources on Asian Christianity, see Scott W. Sunquist, ed., *A Dictionary of Asian Christianity* (Grand Rapids, MI: Eerdmans, 2001); and Peter C. Phan, ed., *Christianities in Asia* (Oxford: Wiley-Blackwell, 2011).

5. In this chapter the churches of the Reformations in Asia refer to (1) the mainline Protestant churches, including especially the Lutheran, the Reformed (Presbyterian), the Baptist, and the Methodist churches; (2) the Anglicans; (3) the Evangelicals; (4) the Pentecostals; and (5) the Independents. I will leave out of consideration the Roman Catholics, the Orthodox, and the so-called Marginal Christians (that is, those who claim to be Christians but do not hold the basic Christian doctrines, such as the Church of Jesus Christ of the Latter-Day Saints (Mormons), Jehovah's Witnesses, the Unification Church, Family International, and the Iglesia ni Cristo in the Philippines.

Early Protestant Missions in Asia: The Pietist Danish-Halle Mission and the Moravian Church

Historically speaking, the first Protestants to come to Asia in the seventeenth century were not missionaries but Dutch traders of the Dutch East India Company whose primary interest was trade and not evangelization. There were Calvinist chaplains accompanying these traders to Indonesia (1601), Formosa (Taiwan, 1642), and Ceylon (Sri Lanka, 1656), but their mission was not to Christianize the natives but to provide to the spiritual needs of their fellow coreligionists. Some of these chaplains— Justus Heurnius in Indonesia, Georgius Candidius and Robert Junius in Taiwan, and Philip Baldaeus in Sri Lanka—did try to evangelize the indigenous people, but their efforts were individual and sporadic.[6]

In terms of organized missions it was not the main Reformers who played the key role but the seventeenth-century followers of those who are referred to as the Radical Reformers and who were associated with the Pietist movement. "Pietism," originally a term of abuse and derision used in the 1670s to refer to the followers of Philipp Jakob Spener, describes a highly complex theological and spiritual movement of renewal that was deeply rooted in the traditions of medieval mysticism and the Radical Reformers and sought to overcome the crisis affecting seventeenth-century Protestantism caused by the church-state system, denominational conflicts, an overemphasis on institutions and orthodoxy, and failures to bring about a reform of Christian life in church and society.[7] The Pietist remedy lies in personal sanctification, interior experience and devotion, and Bible study and prayer, especially in small groups or conventicles (*ecclesiola in ecclesia*).

The Pietist movement had its first home in Germany. It was inspired by the devotional literature of the English Puritans and the writings of Johann Arndt (1555–1621), Philipp Jakob Spener (1635–1705), August Hermann Francke (1663–1727), and Count Nikolaus von Zinzendorf (1700–1760). The main center of Pietism was the University of Halle, founded by Frederick III, Elector of Brandenburg, in 1691, where Francke was appointed a professor in 1692. It was here that a plethora of Pietism-inspired activities were organized such as theological training, orphanages, educational work, Bible societies, and care of Christians outside their native countries (the "diaspora").

---

6. For an account of the early Protestant presence in Asia, see Samuel Hugh Moffett, *A History of Christianity in Asia. Volume II: 1500–1900* (Maryknoll, NY: Orbis Books, 2005), 213–35.

7. It is customary to distinguish between "Reformed Pietism" and "Radical Pietism"; the latter, headed by August Hermann Francke and the Petersens (Johann Wilhelm and his wife, Johanna Eleonora), promotes anti-establishment, nondenominationalist tendencies, and millenarian and apocalyptic views.

Another important activity of the Pietists, which is of interest here, is mission outside Europe, especially in Asia. It is in connection with the University of Halle that the first extensive "foreign" Protestant missions were undertaken, thanks to which the Pietist movement soon spread to Scandinavia, Russia, North America, and Asia. The occasion for the Protestant mission from Halle to India was the decision of King Frederick IV of Denmark in 1706 to establish a mission in the Danish colony of Tranquebar (Tharangambadi) in southeast India. Unable to find Danish missionaries, the king entrusted the mission to two Halle University Lutheran Pietist professors, Heinrich Plütschau (1676–1752) and Bartholomäus Ziegenbald (1683–1719), whose work marked the beginning of the Tamil Lutheran Christianity in India.

Besides the University of Halle, another center of Pietist missionary activity is Herrnhut, an estate of Count von Zinzendorf, who in 1722 welcomed there a group of Bohemian Brethren (the Unitas Fratrum), known in Europe as the "Herrnhutter," who constituted the Moravian Church or the United Brethren. These Pietist Christians believed that their particular task is to witness to Christ to non-Christians rather than establishing new churches in places that are already Christianized. Moravian missionaries constituted the first large-scale and officially organized Protestant missionary movement. Within three decades of its founding, the Moravian Church sent hundreds of missionaries worldwide, including the Caribbean, North and South America, Labrador, Greenland, South Africa, and (Central) Asia. In 1760, fourteen Moravians landed in Tranquebar.[8] Later, twenty-four Moravians were sent to another Danish colony, the Nicobar Islands, in the Bay of Bengal, where, however, their mission foundered because of the eventual deaths of all of them. They were more successful in the northern Danish trading colony Serampore, near Calcutta (Kolkata), where they went in 1777 but from which they departed in 1803 because of the denominational jealousy of the Lutherans.

"The Great Century" (1784–1860): Expansion of Protestant Missions in Asia

The nineteenth century has been dubbed by the church historian Kenneth Scott Latourette "The Great Century" of Protestant missions. Actually, the Great Century began before 1800, toward the latter half of the eighteenth century. The scene moved from Germany to Britain, with Anglican missionaries serving as "evangelical chaplains" to the British East India Company, notable among whom are David Brown (1763–1812), Claudius Buchanan (1766–1815), and Henry Martyn (1781–1812). Missionaries societies were

---

8. On the German Pietist Danish-Halle mission to Tranquebar (1706–1846), see Moffett, *A History of Christianity in Asia, Volume II*, 236–50.

founded, such as the Society for Promoting Christian Knowledge (SPCK, 1698), the Society for the Propagation of the Gospel in Foreign Parts (SPG, 1701), the London Missionary Society (LMS, 1785), and the Church Missionary Society (CMS, 1799), all of which carried out extensive missionary work in Asia during the "Great Century."

But the "father of the modern [Protestant] missionary movement" is no doubt the English Baptist William Carey (1761–1834), a cobbler and self-taught multilinguist. With his 1782 famous tract *An Inquiry into the Obligation of Christians, to Use Means for the Conversion of the Heathens*, Carey successfully led the leaders of the Northampton Baptist Association to establish in 1792 a "society for propagating the gospel among the heathen," the Baptist Missionary Society (BMS). In 1793 Carey and his family arrived in Kolkata, where after a stint as manager of an indigo plantation, he moved in 1799 to the Danish colony of Serampore, some thirteen miles north of Kolkata, where he was joined by Joshua Marshman (1768–1837) and William Ward (1769–1823). In a fruitful partnership governed by the famous "Serampore Covenant," Carey, Marshman, and Ward, dubbed the "Serampore Trio" (characterized by Carey as himself Erasmus, Marshman as the theologian, and Ward as Luther), engaged in activities such as Bible translation (in whole or part, into some twenty-four languages and dialects), education (Carey as professor of Sanskrit, Bengali, and Marathi at Fort William College for thirty years and establishing schools for girls), and social reform (promotion of the abolition of the practice of burning widows). The educational work in India was further promoted by Alexander Duff (1806–1882), on behalf especially of upper-class Brahmins.[9]

In the first half of the nineteenth century, Protestant missions were extended to China with the arrival of Robert Morrison (1782–1834), a missionary of the LMS, in 1807. Together with his colleague William C. Milne (1785–1822), also of the LMS, he translated the Bible into Chinese and established the Anglo-Chinese College in Malacca. Following the example of the LMS, the American Board of Commissioners for Foreign Missions (ABCFM), an independent and interdenominational mission society founded in 1811, sent American missionaries to China, especially to work in the medical field. The Netherlands Missionary Society joined the Chinese missions in 1827 by sending the talented Lutheran Karl Friedrich Augustus Gützlaff (1803–1851), who founded the Chinese Union with the goal to distribute Bibles in mainland China. Sadly, the Opium Wars (1839–1844; 1856–1860)

---

9. The most comprehensive resource on Christianity in India and South Asian Christianity in general is Roger E. Hedlund, chief editor, *The Oxford Encyclopedia of South Asian Christianity*, 2 vols. (Oxford: Oxford University Press, 2012). An informative one-volume history of Indian Christianity is Robert Eric Frykenberg, *Christianity in India: From Beginnings to the Present* (Oxford: Oxford University Press, 2008).

and the Taiping Revolution (1851–1864) compromised and destroyed much of the Protestant (and Catholic) missionary work in China.[10]

Meanwhile Protestant missionaries penetrated other Asian countries. The Congregationalist-turned-Baptist Adoniram Judson (1788–1850) and his wife were sent by the BCFM to Burma and founded the Burma Baptist Church among the Karens. Later, during British rule, especially after the third Anglo-Burmese War (1885–1886), missions were carried out to the Kachins, mostly by Karen Baptist converts. The Anglican Church came to Ceylon (Sri Lanka) in 1802, when the British took it from the Dutch who had wrestled it from the Portuguese in 1796 and ruled for the next 300 years. For its work the church was largely dependent on the colonial power for material support. Unfortunately, the missions were badly damaged by the controversy in the mid-1840s between the High Church, represented by the Society for the Propagation of the Gospel, and the Low Church, represented by the Church Missionary Society, which was not resolved until the disestablishment of the Anglican Church in 1881.

In 1828, the peripatetic Karl Gützlaff, who had left the Netherlands Missionary Society and turned independent, and Jacob Tomlin of the LMS were the first Protestants to enter Siam (Thailand). They were followed by the missionaries of the ABCFM, the Presbyterians (the Presbyterian Board of Foreign Missions), and the American Baptists. The focus of these missions was health care and education. Unfortunately, despite the work of able missionaries, mostly Presbyterians, such as Samuel G. McFarland (1830–1897) and Daniel McGilvary (1828–1911), Protestant missions in Thailand did not produce many conversions, except a few in the northeast (Chiang Mai). The main reason for this failure is that most Thais identify being Thai with being Buddhist.[11]

The Dutch Reformed Protestants came to Malacca (Malaysia, including Singapore), whose Christianity had been largely Catholic under the 130–year rule of Portugal, when it was colonized by the Netherlands, which ruled it for 154 years. Next came the Anglican Church when the country fell under British rule in 1819. Because of its close connection with British colonization and

---

10. Two very helpful overviews of Christianity in China are Jean-Pierre Charbonnier, *Christians in China: A.D. 600 to 2000*, trans. M. N. L. Couve de Murville (San Francisco: Ignatius Press, 2007); and Daniel H. Bays, *A New History of Christianity in China* (Oxford: Wiley-Blackwell, 2012). See also Daniel H. Bays, ed., *Christianity in China: From the Eighteenth Century to the Present* (Stanford, CA: Stanford University Press, 1996). The most authoritative and comprehensive treatment of Chinese Christianity is the following massive two-volume work: Nicolas Standaert, ed., *Handbook of Christianity in China. Volume One: 635–1800* (Leiden: Brill, 2000); and R. G. Tiedemann, ed., *Handbook of Christianity in China. Volume Two: 1800–Present* (Leiden: Brill, 2009).

11. For a survey of Protestant Christianity in Thailand, see Kenneth E. Wells, *History of Protestant Work in Thailand, 1828–1958* (Bangkok: Church of Christ in Thailand, 1984).

because it was perceived as an exclusively white concern, the Anglican Church did not make much progress. The most successful Protestants in Malaysia/ Singapore were the American Methodists, with the American James M. Thoburn (1836–1922) as the first bishop and the Indian-born Englishman William B. Oldham (1854–1935) as the founder of the Methodist mission in Singapore.[12]

As noted earlier, the first Protestants to arrive in Indonesia were not missionaries but Dutch traders associated with the Dutch East India Company. In 1833, the ABCFM sent two missionaries, Samuel Munson and Henry Lyman, to work among the Bataks in Sumatra. Tragically, they were killed by the natives, but their efforts brought about the largest single Protestant denomination in the islands, the Batak Christian Protestant Church. Protestant missions in Indonesia, particularly in the Moluccas, received a boost in the middle of the nineteenth century when there was a renewal of missionary enthusiasm in Holland. Between 1858 and 1861 three missionary societies were founded: the Netherlands Missionary Union, the Utrecht Missionary Society, and the Dutch Reformed Missionary Association. The LMS too entered the field, with Joseph Carel Kam (1769–1833), the "Apostle of the Moluccas."[13]

As the nineteenth century was drawing to a close, Protestant missions made rapid advance in India, thanks in part to the support of Queen Victoria, after the government of India was taken away from the British East India Company and turned into a crown colony. There were mass conversions to Protestant Christianity from the Dalits (the outcasts) and the tribals, as Western missionaries made the momentous decision to shift their targets from the rich, the powerful, and the educated to the poor and the outcasts. In the northeastern states of Meghalaya, Nagaland, and Mizoram the American Baptists and the Welsh Calvinistic Methodists (later changed to Welsh Presbyterians) had great success, mostly through the evangelizing work of the native converts themselves.

The closing decades of the nineteenth century also witnessed a rebirth of Protestant missions in China with the coming of the Englishman Hudson Taylor (1832–1905) in 1853 and 1866, who founded the China Inland Mission, an evangelical nondenominational organization aiming at the evangelization of all the provinces of China. Equally if not more famous is Timothy Richard (1845–1919), a Welsh Baptist of the BMS, who spent forty-five years in China and was widely praised as evangelist, relief worker (especially

---

12. For a history of Protestant Christianity in Malaysia/Singapore, see Robert Hunt, Lee Kam Hinh, and John Roxborough, eds., *Christianity in Malaysia: A Denominational History* (Petaling Jaya: Pelanduk Publications, 1992).

13. For a comprehensive resource on Christianity in Indonesia, see Jan Sihar Aritonang and Karel Steenbrink, eds., *A History of Christianity in Indonesia* (Leiden: Brill, 2008).

during the 1876–1879 famine), social reformer, and educator. Another excep-
tional China missionary is the Episcopal Jewish bishop Samuel Isaac Joseph
Schereschewsky (1831–1906), who went to China under the sponsorship of the
Domestic and Foreign Missionary Society of the Protestant Episcopal Church
of the United States. A linguistic genius, Schereschewsky spoke thirteen languages and could read twenty, and is best remembered for his translation of the
Bible into popular Chinese (a "Bible for the poor"), typed with one finger (the
"One-Finger Bible"). In addition to evangelism, Protestant missions in China
produced an extensive network of schools, from elementary and high school
to university, notably the Hangchow Christian University (Presbyterian), St.
John's College (American Episcopal), Nanjing University (Methodist), Shan-
tung Christian University (American Presbyterian and English Baptist), and
Yenching University (a union of smaller Presbyterian, Methodist, and Congre-
gational schools). Tragically, as it was during the Opium Wars and the Taiping
Revolution, Christian missions (both Catholic and Protestant) were heavily
damaged by the anti-foreign Boxer Rebellion (1900).

In Japan, where Christianity had been banned since the middle of the
seventeenth century and was not fully permitted until 1873, Protestant missions were not initiated until 1859, when Japan formally opened three treaty
ports of Kanagawa, Nagasaki, and Hakodake to nondiplomat foreigners.
The first denominations to arrive were Episcopal, Presbyterian, American
Dutch Reformed, and Free Baptist. After the Meiji Restoration in 1868, with
the removal of the last anti-Christian edicts in 1873, five major Protestant
denominations were actively working in Japan: Presbyterian/Reformed, Con-
gregationalist, Methodist, Episcopal, and Baptist. Part of the reasons for the
early success of Protestant missions in Japan lies not only in the active role of
Japanese student groups called "Bands" in evangelism and church leadership,
but also in the fact that Christianity was perceived as identical with Western
civilization, which would be useful for Japan's way to modernization.[14]

Protestant missions also came to Korea thanks to the country's openness
to the West. As with Roman Catholicism, Protestant Christianity was first
brought to Korea not by expatriate missionaries but by Koreans themselves,
the former by Peter Yi Sunghun in 1784 and the latter by Suh Sang-Yun (1848–
1926), who in 1883 carried a Korean translation of the Gospel of Luke back
to his village and organized a house church. Immediately after Korea signed
its first treaty with the United States in 1882, foreign missionaries, mostly
Americans, arrived, notably the Presbyterian medical doctor Horace N. Allen
(1858–1932), the Presbyterian Horace G. Underwood (1859–1916), the
Methodist Henry G. Appenzeller (1858–1902), and the Presbyterian Samuel A. Moffett (1864–1939). These early Methodist and Presbyterian mis-

---

14. A resource on Japanese Christianity is Mark R. Mullins, ed., *Handbook of Christianity in
Japan* (Leiden: Brill, 2003).

sionaries—the two main Protestant denominations in Korea—carried out evangelism mainly through medicine (Allen's Royal Hospital) and education (Yonsei University and Ewha Womans University). The two denominations eventually experienced a phenomenal growth, thanks partly to the adoption of the "Nevius Plan" or "Three-Self Plan" (self-government, self-support, and self-propagation) and thanks partly to Korean Christians' support for Korea's struggle for liberation from Japanese colonization (1910–1945).[15]

The predominantly Catholic Philippines was introduced to Protestantism after the United States took the country over from Spain in 1898. The first permanent Protestant presence began with the establishment of the YMCA in the following year. Next a variety of American mission agencies rushed in: Northern Presbyterian, Methodist, and American Baptist. To avoid counter-productive rivalries, these mission boards agreed to a cooperation comity arrangement by adopting the common name of *Iglesia Evangelica* and by dividing up the country for their missions. Manila and the rest of the island of Luzon were divided in half between the Presbyterians and the Methodists, and Panay Island was assigned to the Baptists. These denominations were later joined by the American Episcopalians, among whom Bishop Charles Henry Brent played a key role in missions to non-Catholic Filipinos.[16]

The World Missionary Conference (Edinburgh, 1910) to the Present

There is no doubt that the World Missionary Conference (Edinburgh, 1910) marked a momentous new beginning for Protestant missions worldwide at the beginning of the twentieth century. As is clear from its title, the explicit focus of the conference is Christian mission; its aim is, in W. H. Findlay's words, "to be a Grand Council for the Advancement of Missionary Science." Furthermore, its scope is intended to be global, even though in fact its participation was restricted to the representatives of Protestant and Anglican missionary societies. Nor was the conference geographically all-inclusive; Africa, Latin America, the Pacific Islands, and the Caribbean were absent. With regard to Asia, of 1,215 official delegates to the conference, only eighteen were Asian: eight Indians, four Japanese, three Chinese, one Korean, one Burmese, and one of Turkish origin.[17] Given these restrictions, it might be

---

15. On Korean Protestantism, see Lak-Geoon George Paik, *The History of Protestant Missions in Korea, 1832–1910*, 2nd ed. (Seoul: Yonsei University Press, 1971).

16. For a resource on Protestantism in the Philippines, see K. J. Clymer, *Protestant Missionaries in the Philippines, 1895–1916: An Inquiry into the American Colonial Mentality* (Urbana and Chicago: University of Illinois Press, 1986).

17. The best history of the World Missionary Conference is Brian Stanley, *The World Missionary Conference, Edinburgh 1910* (Grand Rapids, MI: Eerdmans, 2009). Helpful studies of the conference with the focus on mission are Kenneth R. Ross, *Edinburgh 2010: Springboard for Mission* (Pasadena, CA: William Carey International University Press, 2010); David A. Kerr

argued that the World Missionary Conference would not have the intended worldwide influence.

With regard to the impact of the conference on Protestant mission, John R. Mott's slogan "The evangelization of the world in this generation," which may be taken as expressing the ultimate goal of the conference, admirable though it is for its zeal, has been criticized as wildly naïve. No doubt the two world wars, which wrought terrible havoc on Christian missions worldwide, prevented the conference from implementing its "Missionary Science." Despite its potential limitations, however, the conference can serve as a useful benchmark to evaluate Protestant missions in Asia in the twentieth century and beyond.[18]

First of all, some numbers. In 1910, Protestants in Asia (including East, South, and West Asia) numbered 22,119,000 and Anglicans 778,000. In 2010, they numbered 87,379,000 and 864,000 respectively. The growth rate of Protestants in Asia (average annual growth, percent per year, between 1910 and 2010) was 2.68 and that of Anglicans 0.10.[19] From 1910 to 2010, Christianity as a whole (Anglican, Catholic, Independent, Marginal, Orthodox, and Protestant) grew at twice the population growth (2.68% vs. 1.41%); still, in 2010 Christianity represented only 8.5 percent of the Asian population (352,239,000 Christians out of the population of 4,166,308,000). (One significant fact, which is of great import for Christian mission and to which we will return, is that the number of atheists and agnostics grew the fastest, from 60,000 in 1910 to 600 million in 2010. Asia became the most nonreligious continent in 2010!). Another important fact is that in 1910 the majority of Christians in Asia were Roman Catholic and Orthodox; in 2010, it shifted to the Independent and Marginal churches, especially in China. The fastest current growth rates are found in East Asia, especially China, and in South Central Asia. In 2010, the Asian countries with the largest numbers of Christians are, in descending order, China, the Philippines, Indonesia,

---

and Kenneth R. Ross, eds., *Edinburgh 2010: Mission Then and Now* (Oxford: Regnum Books, 2009); and Daryl Balia and Kirsteen Kim, eds., *Edinburgh 2010: Witnessing to Christ Today* (Oxford: Regnum Books, 2010).

18. The two most informative sources for twentieth-century Christianity are Todd M. Johnson and Kenneth R. Ross, eds., *Atlas of Global Christianity 1910–2010* (Edinburgh: Edinburgh University Press, 2009); and Patrick Johnstone, *The Future of the Global Church: History, Trends and Possibilities* (Downers Grove, IL: InterVarsity Press, 2011). On world Christianity, consult the many works by Dyron B. Daughrity, especially *To Whom Does Christianity Belong? Critical Issues in World Christianity* (Minneapolis: Fortress Press, 2015); Douglas Jacobsen, *Global Gospel: An Introduction to Christianity in Five Continents* (Grand Rapids, MI: Baker Academic, 2015); and Sebastian Kim and Kirsteen Kim, *Christianity as a World Religion* (London: Bloomsbury, 2008).

19. All the statistics, here and below, are taken from Todd and Ross, eds., *Atlas of Global Christianity 1910–2010*, 134–49.

South Korea, Vietnam, Myanmar, and Japan. In terms of percentage of the population, the Philippines has the highest (86.2), followed by Timor (84.8), South Korea (41.4), Singapore (16.1), and Brunei (15.3). Urban areas that have the number of Christians exceeding one million in 2010 are, in descending order, Manila (11,068,000), Seoul (4,366,000), Jakarta (2,433,000), Shanghai (2,368,000), Mumbai (2,004,000), Pusan (1,835,000), Incheon (1,482,000), Tangu (1,142,000), Tokyo (1,064,000), and Hong Kong (1,001,000).

Statistics, albeit informative, do not tell the whole story, very complex and often underreported, of the presence of the Reformation in Asia. Clearly, the number of the spiritual descendants of the Reformation, especially the Protestants, has increased dramatically during the last hundred years, as the figures above show. There are many reasons for this explosive growth, chief among which is, as we will see, the staggering and unexpected rise of Christianity in China after the 1980s. Yet, the percentage of Christians in Asia's total population (over four billion) remains small in 2010 (8.5 percent, with 352,239,000 members) after centuries of mission. The discomforting question inevitably arises as to whether anything was wrong with Christian evangelization in Asia, and whether new missionizing methods, a new "Advancement of the Missionary Science" advocated by the Edinburgh Conference, will produce in Asia the kind of demographic growth we have witnessed in Africa and Latin America—the three continents forming the Global South. We will take up these questions in the second and third sections of this essay. Meanwhile we will take a closer look at the Protestant churches in Asia in the last century.

In *South Central Asia*, with the end of British colonization and many of the countries constituted along ethnic or religious lines and gaining national independence, Christian churches underwent tremendous political, economic, military, and religious turmoil. The countries with the largest number of Christians in 2010 are, in descending order, India (58,367,000), Pakistan (3,923,000), Sri Lanka (1,714,000), Nepal (935,000), and Bangladesh (859,000). Countries with the highest percentage of Christians (not only Protestants) are, in descending order, Sri Lanka (10.7), India (4.8), Nepal (3.3), and Pakistan (2.3). Among the descendants of the Reformation in South Asia, in 2010 there were 55,100 Anglicans (a huge decrease from 657,000 in 1910), 20,734,000 Independents (up from 101,000 in 1910), 167,000 Marginals (up from 200 in 1910), and 23,998,000 Protestants (up from 856,000 in 1910). Clearly, there has been a tremendous growth among Protestants, Independents, and Marginals.

In terms of church life and missionary activities, there have been five significant trends toward indigenizing Christianity to the South Asian context. First, ecumenically, there has been a movement toward church union for collaboration on national and international levels: the Church of South India (1947), the Church of North India (1970), the Church of Pakistan (1970), and the Church of Bangladesh (1971). In addition, collaboration in mission is also fostered by the formation of the National Council of Churches, which is affiliated with the World Council of Churches. Second, liturgical reforms and introduction of new worship styles (notably, the production of the *Book of Common Worship* in the Church of South India) provide the people with a rich source of spirituality. Third, a vibrant development of contextualized theology, especially in dialogue with other religions, in particular Buddhism, Hinduism, and Islam, and for the liberation of the oppressed (e.g., Dalit theology), has brought new insights to the understanding and practice of the Christian faith. Fourth, the churches have engaged extensively in the traditional fields of health care and education, especially for the outcasts and the tribals.[20] Fifth, Indian churches have organized missionary societies such as Discipling a Whole Nation (DAWN) and the India Mission Association (IMA), an independent evangelical mission-networking organization that links various conservative-evangelical missionary agencies, with more than 41,000 Indian missionaries in 2001. Given the influence of Christianity in South Asia, quite disproportionate to their numbers, it has recently met with opposition, often violent, from extremist Hindus in India (the Hindutva), Muslims in Pakistan, and Buddhists in Sri Lanka.

In *Southeast Asia*, during the twentieth century all the countries where Christianity had a significant presence, such as the Philippines, Vietnam, and Indonesia, underwent violent struggles for independence from colonial powers and engaged in the arduous task of nation building, and Christian churches were unavoidably implicated in these political and economic processes. Given the strong anticolonial sentiments, foreign missionaries, both Catholic and Protestant, were perceived as agents of Western domination; in Myanmar and Vietnam, they were expelled. Some native Christians called for a mission moratorium. The situation has changed substantially for the better in the last decades of the twentieth century. In 2010, there were 537,000 Anglicans (up from 47,300 in 1910), 28,498,000 Independents (up from 2,188,000 in 1910), 1,253,000 Marginals (up from 60 from 1910), and 27,184,000 Protestants (up from 705,000 in 1910). Clearly, the children of Protestant Reformations have been doing extremely well in Southeast Asia in the last century! Countries with the highest number of Christians (not only Protestants) in 2010 are, in descending order, the Philippines (83,151,000), Indonesia (23,992,000), Vietnam (7,796,000), Myanmar (4,002,000), Malaysia (2,530,000), Timor (1,077,000), Thailand (849,000), Singapore (740,000), Cambodia (305,000), and Laos (194,000). Countries with the highest percentage of Christians are, in descending order, the Philippines (89.4), Timor (84.8), Singapore (16.1),

---

20. Ibid., 142–43.

Brunei (15.3), Indonesia (12.1), Malaysia (9.1), Vietnam (8.6), Myanmar (8.0), Laos (3.1), and Cambodia (2.0).

Protestantism came to all East Asian countries, except Thailand, through Western colonization, Dutch, British, and American successively. (The Catholic Church came to Vietnam, Cambodia, and Laos through French colonization.) Like elsewhere, Protestant missions were carried out chiefly through health care and education, the two areas in which notable benefits would be enjoyed by converts. Two issues present significant challenges to Christian missions. First, the relation between church and state: Though all Southeast Asian countries now recognize religious freedom in their constitutions, religious practice is closely monitored by the government through the registration system and at times suppressed, especially when a particular church, particularly an unregistered Pentecostal church, is perceived as a threat to national security. Second, the process of indigenizing the Christian faith ("inculturation"): To what extent should the Christian faith be adapted to local cultural customs, such as marriage and funeral rituals, and especially indigenous religious practices ("popular religiosity"), such as the veneration of ancestors and sacrifices to spirits, without adulterating the Christian faith and Christian identity?

Lastly, in *Northeast Asia*, the situation of Christianity in the last century is anything if not extremely complex. Seismic political events such as the Boxer Uprising (1900), the establishment of the Communist government in China in 1949, the Japanese occupation of Korea (1910–1945), the defeat of Japan in 1945, the Korean War (1950–1953), and the Cultural Revolution (1966–1976)—just to cite a few—not only transformed the political landscape but also did untold damage to Christian missions. By 2010, however, an astonishing and explosive phenomenon had occurred in the Reformation in Asia: it would be a gross understatement to say that the situation of Protestantism in Northeast Asia had ameliorated. Anglicans numbered 176,000 (up from 43,500 in 1910), Independents 93,002,000 (up from 12,400 in 1910), Marginals 1,662,000 (up from 0 in 1910), and Protestants 35,974,000 (up from 475.000 in 1910). The countries with the highest number of Christians (not only Protestants) in 2010 are, in descending order, China (115,009,000), South Korea (20,150,000), Japan (2,903,000), Taiwan (1,420,000), North Korea (484,000), and Mongolia (47,100). Countries with the largest percentage of Christians are, in descending order, South Korea (41.4), China (8.6), Taiwan (6.0), Japan (2.3), North Korea (2.0), and Mongolia (1.2).[21]

This demographic explosion, especially of the Independents and the Marginals in China, does not mean that Christianity in Northeast Asia is problem free. On the contrary, there are no places on earth where Christianity is

---

21. Note that the number of Christians in China, as will be seen below, is much debated.

facing more political conflicts and apparently intractable internal problems than Northeast Asia and Western Asia (the Middle East). Of the Northeast Asian countries listed above, only South Korea is one in which the Reformation churches (as well as the Catholic Church) have enjoyed a vigorous expansion. Moreover, Korean churches, especially the Presbyterian Church, the largest denomination in Korea, have sent a large number of missionaries overseas, estimated at 16,000 in 2006, the second largest number of foreign missionaries after the United States. Part of the reasons for this flourishing is the fact that Korean Protestants, in spite of the apolitical stance of their foreign missionaries, have played a decisive role in the struggle against Japanese occupation, especially during the 1919 March First Independence Movement.

By contrast, in Japan, where in 1941, under government coercion, thirty-two Protestant denominations (except the Anglican Church and the Holiness Church) joined together to form the United Church of Christ in Japan (*Nippon Kirisuto Kyōdan*), church growth has been anemic, perhaps because of the fact that chastened by their acquiescence to the country's past military adventures, Christian churches have tended to abstain from political involvement and as a result have little impact on Japanese society.

China represents an extremely complex case of its own. After the Boxer Uprising (1900), xenophobic hostility to Christianity subsided and Protestant missions resumed with great vigor, especially in the five eastern coastal cities, with a new emphasis on social services, particularly through health care and education, so much so that 1902–1927 has been dubbed the "Golden Age" of Protestant missions in China. Between 1900 and 1925 the number of Protestant missionaries increased fourfold—from 2,000 to 8,000. At the same time, there began a movement toward building an indigenous church, through the "Three-Self" movement, that is, self-administration, self-financing, and self-evangelization, a plan eloquently advocated by the twenty-eight-year-old Chinese delegate Cheng Jingyi at the World Missionary Conference in a speech that was judged by the Boston *Missionary Herald* "without question the best speech" made at Edinburgh. Cheng further proposed that an interdenominational, or nondenominational, Protestant Church be established in China for the sake of mission.[22] The idea of a "Chinese Church" that is confessionally, ecclesiastically, and institutionally a single church was taken up at the National Christian Conference of the China Continuation Committee of the World Missionary Conference, of which Cheng Jingyi was chairman, in Shanghai in 1922. Out of this all-China conference two organizations were created: the National Christian Council and the Church of Christ in China

---

22. For a helpful presentation of the voices of the Asian delegates at the World Missionary Conference, see Stanley, *World Missionary Conference*, 91–131.

(*Zhonghua Jidujiaohui*), with a significant degree of Chinese leadership. The Church of Christ in China was not established until 1927; unfortunately, several members of the conservative Bible Union of China refused to join, objecting to its allegedly modernist theology, including the Christian and Missionary Alliance, the China Inland Mission, the U.S. Southern Presbyterians, the Anglican Communion, the Southern Baptists, the American Methodists, the Church of the Nazarene, and the Assemblies of God. Thus Cheng Jingyi's and the National Christian Council's dream of the one and unified Chinese Church was still-born.

It is also during the first decades of the twentieth century that an extremely significant phenomenon took place, namely, the rise of Independent Chinese Christianity, without any foreign leadership whatsoever, though their founders were influenced to varying degrees by foreign missionaries. These include, with the names of their founders in parentheses: The True Jesus Church (Wei Enbo, 1876–1916), the Jesus Family (Jing Dianying, 1890–1957), and the Christian Assembly, commonly known as the Little Flock (Ni Tuoshen Watchman Nee, 1903–1972). In addition to these Independent churches, there were indigenous Pentecostal-like and charismatic movements such as the Spiritual Gifts Society (*Ling'en hui*) in Feixian (Southern Shandong), the "Shandong Revival" (started by the freelance Norwegian missionary Marie Monsen), the Christian Tabernacle (*Jitudu Huitang*), initiated by the conservative Wang Mingdao (1900–1991), and the Bethel Worldwide Evangelistic Band, founded by the revivalist preacher John Sung (Song Shangjie, 1901–1944). These Independent churches, with emphasis on speaking in tongues, prophesying, miraculous healing, emotional worship, and apocalyptic expectation, also engaged in enthusiastic evangelism, especially of the western parts of China, with their "Chinese Back-to-Jerusalem Evangelistic Band," dedicated to evangelizing the vast reaches of Xinjang and the far west.[23]

The Golden Age of Protestant missions in China, with its enviable achievements in health care and education and its bright future, and of Chinese Christianity as a whole was dashed to pieces by the Communist Party's victory over the Nationalist Party (*Guomindang*) and the establishment of the People's Republic of China in 1949. Missionaries were expelled; church properties nationalized; and religious leaders forced to undergo reeducation, imprisoned, condemned to hard labor, or killed. Ironically, the dream of one unified and nondenominational (Protestant) Chinese Church, long pursued by the National Chinese Council and the Church of Christ in China, and fiercely

---

23. For an informative account of Independent and Marginal Protestants in China, see Lian Xi, *Redeemed by Fire: The Rise of Popular Christianity in Modern China* (New Haven: Yale University Press, 2010).

resisted by the more conservative groups, was realized by a stroke of the pen in 1954, when separate denominational organizations were abolished and all Chinese Protestants came under the oversight of the Three-Self Patriotic Movement (TSPM).[24] (Later, in 1957, the Catholic Church met the same fate, with the founding of the Catholic Patriotic Association.) In the new China, all religions came under the control of the government Religious Affairs Bureau, now called the State Administration for Religious Affairs (SARA).

Protestantism is known as "New Religion of Christianity" (*Jidujiao xinjiao*), whereas Catholicism is the "Religion of the Lord of Heaven" (*Tianzhu jiao*), and they are legally categorized as two different "religions." In 1980, in addition to the TSPM, the China Christian Council (*Zhonguo Jidujiao Xiehui*, CCC) was founded as the umbrella organization for all Protestant churches in China responsible for activities promoting their internal church life such as Bible translation, theological education, worship, and church order. (Together the TSPM and the CCC are called the "Two Associations" [*liang hui*], the former more political, the latter more ecclesiastical.) Through the CCC, registered Protestant churches join the World Council of Churches. The chief leaders of the TSPM are Wu Yaozong (Y. T. Wu, 1895–1971) and his successor, in 1980, the Anglican bishop Ding Guangxun (K. H. Ting, 1915–2012). Of course, not all Chinese Christian churches accepted incorporation into the TSPM, notably the Evangelical and Independent groups. (Needless to say, the majority of Chinese Catholics did not.)

In addition to the historical irony concerning the establishment of a nondenominational church mentioned above, there is another huge historical irony, this time to the chagrin of the Communist Party. The requirement for all churches to register with the TSPM brought about the rise, within both Protestantism and Catholicism, of the so-called underground churches (*dixia jiaohui*), which refuse to register and be controlled by the government. The number of Christians in underground churches, which is hard to count, is likely much larger than that of the official churches.[25] There have been tensions between the TSPM and the CCC on the one hand and unregistered Protestant churches on the other. (Within the Catholic Church such tensions have been much more pronounced, especially due to the ordination of bishops appointed by the government without the consent of the Vatican. In recent times, however, some progress has been made toward reconciling the regis-

---

24. On the TSPM, see Philip L. Wickeri, *Seeking the Common Ground: Protestant Christianity, the Three-Self Movement, and China's United Front* (Maryknoll, NY: Orbis Books, 1988).

25. In 2010, the State Administration for Religious Affairs (SARA) put the number of registered TSPM Protestants at 16 million. Other scholars believe that SARA intentionally underestimated that number and suggested that the likely number is near 90 million. The Pew Research Center (2011) estimates 50 million to 70 million Christians practice in nonregistered churches.

tered and unregistered Catholic groups. In general, the relation between the Vatican and the Chinese government is a pas de deux, with one step forward and two steps backward.)

Two more political events contributed to the devastation of Chinese Christianity: the "Great Leap Forward" (1958–1966), Mao Zedong's social and economic campaign to transform China's agrarian economy into a socialist society through rapid industrialization and collectivization. The program caused a great famine in which millions, estimated between 18 and 45, died of starvation. It also closed over 90 percent of the churches that were still open, especially in rural areas. The next maelstrom into which Chinese society and Christianity were plunged was the "Great Proletarian Cultural Revolution" (1966–1976), also promoted by Mao Zedong (1893–1976), during which Christianity as a whole seemed to be about to be wiped out in China.

In and through these extremely adverse conditions, however, there occurred the third historical irony, one of immense impact on the descendants of the Reformation. Unable or forbidden to worship in public, Chinese Protestants conduct religious services in the homes of believers without government approval. These informal gatherings, generally small in cities but large in rural areas, are called "spontaneous private meetings" by authorities but "house churches" (*jiating jiaohui*) by believers. These house churches in practice function as independent churches, though there are a few networks of house churches stretching over many provinces and even the entire country. These house churches are an enormous boon for Protestantism. In 2009, a one-year government-commissioned study on house churches puts the number of Protestants worshiping in house churches between 45 and 60 million, with another 18 to 30 million attending registered churches. House churches generally are either evangelical, emphasizing their historical and doctrinal connections with former Western missionaries and conservative Chinese pastors (for example, Wang Mingdao) and adopting a literalist interpretation of the Bible, or charismatic, with emphasis on personal religious experiences and the gifts of the Spirit, particularly miraculous healing and speaking in tongues.

In addition, there is a large group of new and bewilderingly varied religious movements that are inspired by or connected to Protestantism, especially of the Pentecostal type, and which are usually categorized as "Marginal Christians." These movements, with colorful and biblical-sounding names, can pop up anywhere with charismatic founders, quickly attract a large following, and are not officially registered. These include the Local Church (also known as the Shouters), the Established King Sect, the Lightning from the East, the Lord God Sect, the All Scope Church, the South China Church, the Disciples Sect (also known as the Narrow Gate in the Wilderness), the Three Ranks of Servants, the Cold Water Sect, the Commune Sect, the New Testament Church (also known as the Apostolic Faith Sect), the Resurrection

Sect, the Dami Evangelization Association, and the World Elijah Evangelism Association.[26] The Chinese government criminalizes these as "evil cults" and arrests, fines, and imprisons their leaders and followers, especially those of the Local Church and its offshoot, the Lightning from the East. Ostensible reasons for this suppression are their heterodox beliefs (end-time predictions and deification of leaders), superstitious practices (derived from folk religion and Pentecostal healing practices), and threat to public order (large-scale activities and meetings), but their large size, rapid growth, and avoidance of government control also play a key role. The above-mentioned house churches assiduously distinguish themselves from these groups, which they themselves condemn as heretical, partly because they do not want to be lumped with them as "evil cults," a deadly legal categorization, partly because these groups try to recruit members from them.

Finally, after Deng Xiaoping's economic opening in the late 1980s, there has been an increase of interest in the role of religion, and Christianity in particular, in the "public sphere" or "civil society." As the result of Deng's massive restructuring of the economy, the growth of Chinese Protestantism moved from rural areas to cities, especially those of the southeast coast in the Shandong, Zhejiang, and Fujian provinces. At the same time, there was a group made up of intellectuals, university professors, and upper-class elites who have a great sympathy for Christianity as a system of cultural, moral, and religious principles, which they consider helpful for China's cultural and moral reconstruction. These are dubbed "Cultural Christians" (*wenhua jidutu*), who occasionally attend church services but do not seek baptism. They promote the academic study of Christianity, and currently there are more than twenty university-based centers or institutes for the study of Christianity. Unfortunately, the impact of these "Cultural Christians" on Chinese Christianity and Chinese society still remains minimal.

With regard to the Chinese government's treatment of Protestants, in general it is quite varied. By and large, Protestants can freely worship at registered churches associated with the TSPM and the CCC. Of course, many—perhaps a larger number—do not, as we have seen above. Government authorities make periodic attempts at forcing them to join the registered churches, mostly with half-hearted measures, sometimes by more severe actions such as confiscation or destruction of church properties, imprisonment of church leaders, and dispersal of the church into smaller communities. As a whole, more tolerance is shown in cities than in rural areas, and the treatment of Christians varies from place to place, depending on the local authorities. The one exception is with the groups that the government calls "evil cults," whose leaders and members the government openly persecutes.

---

26. See Fenggeng Yang, *Religion in China: Survival and Revival under Communist Rule* (New York: Oxford University Press, 2012).

CHALLENGES AND OPPORTUNITIES

I have lingered over the presence of the Protestant Reformation in China partly because in many ways it epitomizes both the challenges and the opportunities facing the Protestant churches and their missions in Asia and partly because it helps in answering the question of whether the Protestant Reformations are a blessing or a curse for Asia as a whole. The challenges and opportunities can be divided into two types, those concerning the relations of Protestantism to the outside world (*ad extra*) and those that are internal to the life of the churches (*ad intra*). Limited space will allow me to mention only the most significant ones.

The Reformations Encountering the World of Asia: External Challenges

1. As mentioned above, Protestantism (as well Catholicism) entered Asia (except Thailand) on the back of Western colonialism. This colonialist legacy, and the subsequent complicity of some foreign missionaries as well as indigenous Christians either by collaborating with colonialist powers or by seeking to benefit from privileges attached to their Christian status such as extraterritoriality, judicial immunity, health care, education, and job opportunities, must ever be borne in mind with repentance and humility by both local Christians and foreign missionaries. Governments such as China, Vietnam, and North Korea may be forgiven for being suspicious of Christianity, especially those denominations that have financial and organizational ties with foreign institutions located in the West, especially the United States (and for Catholics, the Vatican). But even in countries that are not in principle hostile to Christianity, such as India, Sri Lanka, the Philippines, Malaysia, Singapore, and Indonesia, the history of Western colonialism and its lingering impact on Protestant missions must not be forgotten by Christians engaged in evangelization.

2. In several countries, harassment, intimidation, arrest, imprisonment, persecution, and even killing of Christians and destruction of church properties are a fact of life. These violent acts are motivated by religious hatred (in some Islamic countries such as Pakistan and Malaysia), political ideology (the Hindutva and anticonversion laws in India), or concern for state and party security (Vietnam and China). While pressure must be applied and measures taken to defend and protect the right to religious freedom, Christians must not return violence for violence, and, when absolutely necessary, must be ready to suffer and even to lose their lives to bear witness to Christ. Martyrdom, not deliberately sought but faithfully accepted, is no doubt the most efficacious form of evangelization.

3. In broader terms, Protestant churches must face the extremely complex issue of church-state relations. Although most if not all Asian countries

recognize the right to religious freedom in their constitutions, the actual practice is fraught with difficulties in many countries such as China, Vietnam, Laos, Myanmar (especially in the case of the Christian Karen), and India (especially in the northeastern majority-Christian states of Meghalaya, Mizoram, and Nagaland). At times, discrimination takes on subtle forms, as in Malaysia recently, where there is an attempt to ban the use of "Allah" to refer to the Christian God. In Islamist countries and in Hindu-majority India, there exist severe restrictions to evangelization, the presence of foreign missionaries, and conversion. This is particularly true with Evangelicals and Pentecostals, who generally practice a rather aggressive form of proselytization without due respect for local customs and religions, and whose churches are mostly unregistered. The challenge for Christians is to seek out ways to collaborate with the government to promote the common good, especially in health care, education, and social services, particularly for the benefit of the marginalized and the oppressed such as the Dalits and the tribals, ethnic and religious minorities, women, and workers, without surrendering to the unjust religious policies of the government and being co-opted by it.

4. One of the most difficult challenges for Protestant mission is to indigenize Christianity in all its beliefs and practices. By and large, Catholics have been more willing to take on this task of inculturation and more successful than Protestants, except in Bible translation. This is not of course always the case. In China, for instance, except for the efforts of the Jesuits in the seventeenth century, it was the Protestants who were seriously engaged in building a Chinese church on the basis of the three-self principles, and even if they were not successful on their own to bring about one unified Church of Christ in China, they finally achieved their goal by the Communist Party's fiat through the creation of the TSPM and the CCC. However these two associations are judged, there is no doubt that they have performed an indispensable role in keeping the Protestant churches alive during the harrowing decades following the Communist victory and continue to do so today. To the extent that is possible, the three-self principles should be the guide for creating indigenous churches elsewhere in Asia.

Another important aspect of inculturation is the adoption of cultural customs and popular religious practices. In contrast to Catholics, Protestants have tended to look upon them with suspicion, especially when local customs and practices such as marriage customs, sexual mores, the veneration of ancestors, and sacrifices to the spirits seem at first sight contrary to Christian faith and morality. The challenge is to discern with prudence and humility, in broad consultation with all the local churches, what may and should be adopted and what should be changed and rejected, and avoid imposing Western cultural norms and practices as an essential part of the Christian faith.

5. Lastly, one recent phenomenon that is presenting serious challenges to Christian missions in Asia is migration. According to one statistical report, in 2013, 232 million people—3.2 percent of the world's population—lived outside their countries of origin. It is predicted that the immigration rate will continue to increase over time. A 2012 Gallup survey determined that nearly 640 million adults would want to immigrate if they had the opportunity to.[27] Global population movements today are so global and immense that our time has been dubbed "The Age of Migration."[28] In 2010 Asia hosted some 27.5 million immigrants. India had 9 million emigrants, Bangladesh 7 million, and China 6 million. Pakistan, the Philippines, Afghanistan, Vietnam, Indonesia, South Korea, and Nepal were also important countries of emigration. Top Asian countries of destination include India (6 million), Pakistan (3 million), Hong Kong (2.5 million), Japan (2.1 million) Malaysia (2 million), South Korea (1 million), Iran (2 million), and Saudi Arabia (2 million).[29] Asian migration is fueled mainly by the search for jobs through labor contract (especially to the Middle East). The majority of migrants are women (the "feminization of migration"), whose typical jobs include domestic work, entertainment (a euphemism for the sex industry), restaurant and hotel service, and mail-order marriage. That migrants, and especially refugees, face a host of enormous problems of various kinds needs no elaboration. What has not been sufficiently studied is the religious life of migrants, especially of Christians in Christian-minority countries (the Middle East in particular). It is here that Christian missions are most urgently needed.[30]

Varieties of Reformations in Asia: Internal Challenges

Turning now to the internal life of Protestant churches in Asia, it is important to recall that the first sustained initiatives in Protestant missions were not taken by the early Reformers but by the eighteenth-century (Moravian) Pietists who stood within the tradition of the Radical Reformers. The Pietist emphasis on personal sanctification, interior experience and devotion, reception of the gifts of the Spirit, and Bible study and prayer, especially in small groups or conventicles (*ecclesiola in ecclesia*) was imported to Britain and the

---

27. See Boundless, "Dimensionalizing Immigration: Numbers of Immigrants around the World." Boundless Economics. Boundless, July 21, 2015. https://www.boundless.com. There are legions of websites dedicated to the study of migration.

28. This is the title of the best one-volume study of international migration; see Stephen Castles, Hein De Haas, and Mark J. Miller, *The Age of Migration: International Population Movements in the Modern World*, 5th ed. (New York: Guilford Press, 2014).

29. On migration in the Asia-Pacific region, see ibid., 147–71.

30. For a study of migration and theology, see the trilogy edited by Elaine Padilla and Peter C. Phan, *Contemporary Issues in Migration and Theology* (2013); *Theology of Migration in the Abrahamic Religions* (2014); *Christianities in Migration: The Global Perspective* (2016) (New York: Palgrave/Macmillan).

United States and bore fruit in the various Awakening and Revival move-ments. It is from these movements in Germany, Britain, and the United States that Protestant missions to Asia were undertaken.

In the second half of the twentieth century many elements of this Pietist tradition are alive and well in the various Evangelical, Charismatic, Pentecos-tal, and Pentecostal-like churches and movements in Asia which have enjoyed phenomenal growth.[31] Recall the demographic explosion of the Independents and the Marginals in Asia from 1910 to 2010: the former from 2,301,000 in 1910 to 142,737,000 in 2010 and the latter from 290 in 1910 to 3,139,000 in 2010. On the other hand, this demographic explosion has proved to be both a blessing and a curse for Protestant Christianity in Asia (as well as in Africa and Latin America). Again, space permits a listing of only some of the chal-lenges facing Protestant Christianity *ad intra*.

1. To most Asians the seemingly unlimited number of Protestant churches and denominations, often in the same city, is a mind-boggling mystery. Worse, as Cheng Jingyi put it succinctly at the World Missionary Conference in 1910, "Denominationalism has never interested the Chinese mind. He finds no delight in it, but sometimes he suffers for it."[32] Ironically, Cheng's dream of a nondenominational, interdenominational, or postdenominational church for China became a reality only thanks to the Communist government. In India and Pakistan denominationalism was overcome by creating church unions, and elsewhere by establishing national councils of churches which then join the World Council of Churches. In countries where such collaboration is absent, to the scandal of non-Christians, the evils of denominationalism are exacerbated by rivalries, "sheep-stealing," and mutual condemnation.

Denominationalism is the pivot of a much more complex issue confront-ing Christian churches in Asia, namely, ecumenism. The World Missionary Council at Edinburgh is generally regarded as the starting point of ecumeni-cal dialogue among Protestants. The Catholic Church gave a strong impe-tus to work for Christian unity at the Second Vatican Council (1962–1965). After bursts of enthusiasm and intense ecumenical activities in the immediate aftermaths of the council, fervor for ecumenism cooled down considerably toward the end of the last century. This state of affairs causes much damage to the cause of Christian missions in Asia. Unfortunately, it is largely ignored in Evangelical and Pentecostal missiology and missionizing practice, which give pride of place to church planting and thus perpetuate denominationalism.

2. A related, and much more complex, internal challenge for the Reforma-tion in Asia is the dramatic explosion of Independent and Marginal churches and groups, especially in China. Independent churches, as the name implies,

---

31. See Allan Anderson and Edmond Tang, eds., *Asian and Pentecostal: The Charismatic Face of Christianity in Asia* (Oxford: Regnum Books, 2005).

32. Quoted in Stanley, *World Missionary Conference*, 109.

represents a new paradigm of being church, which, ironically, represents a form of, to coin an oxymoronic phrase, "sectarian postdenominationalism." They are "postdenominational" insofar as they minimize traditional doctrines, forms of worship, and church structures, which they regard as too rigid, formal, and authoritarian. On the other hand, in spite of its post-, or pan-denominationalism, they are "sectarian" insofar as, with few exceptions, they tend to be organized as local units ("house churches") along experiential, ethnic, or generational rather than doctrinal lines. Indeed, one group often claims to be the sole true church and is not slow to condemn all the others as heretical. For them, the guidelines for ecumenical unity, or to use a less exacting term, "convergence," as proposed by the World Council of Churches in its Faith and Order Paper No. 214, *The Church: Towards a Common Vision* (2013), have little if any relevance.

The same thing is even more true of Marginal Christians (the preferred term to "sect" and "cult"), who, though self-describing as Christian and adopting certain Pentecostal-like practices, reject certain fundamental Christian beliefs such as the Trinity, the divinity of Jesus and his role as God's final revealer and savior, and key sacraments (for instance, the Eucharist and ordination). This is the case of all the movements classified as "evil cults" by the Chinese government and a host of new religious movements in Korea (for instance, the Unification Church), the Philippines (for instance, the Iglesia ni Cristo), and Japan.[33] The fact that these Marginal churches have historical and theological affinity with the Reformation and their phenomenal growth beyond church and government control makes the issue of their Christian identity all the more urgent for Protestantism in Asia.

3. Regarding evangelization itself, as reported, many Protestant churches, especially in India, Korea, China, and Japan, have undertaken missions not only nationally but also internationally, "from everywhere to everywhere," reversing the direction of missions from north to south to south to north and south to south. This is one of most significant contributions of the Reformation, especially in its Pietist heritage, in Asia. Nevertheless, there are problems. The first concerns the very concept of mission itself. By and large, mission is taken, particularly in Evangelical and Pentecostal circles, to mean primarily conversion (baptism) and church planting, and the success of missions is measured in terms of numerical growth. Second, there is the category of "sympathizers," who accept the teachings of Jesus but who do not seek baptism, such as the "Cultural Christians" in China and the *Khrist Panthis* ("Christ followers") in India, that is, Hindus who find a home for devotion and worship of Jesus within Hindu religious structures. They are not unlike the "God-fearers" (*yirei Hashem* and *theophobes/pheroumenoi tou theou*) in

---

33. On indigenous Christian movements in Japan, see Mark R. Mullins, *Christianity Made in Japan: A Study of Indigenous Movements* (Honolulu: University of Hawai'i Press, 1998).

antiquity. Third, as mentioned earlier, in the last century the number of atheists and agnostics grew the fastest, from 60,000 in 1910 to 600 million in 2010. As capitalism and consumerism spread to Asia through globalization, this last category is expected to grow exponentially. Fourth, again as mentioned above, massive numbers of the Asian population have shifted from rural areas to cities, making person-to-person evangelism for conversion extremely difficult if not impossible. All these factors call for a rethinking of the concept of and strategies for mission.

4. Finally, in encountering Asia, the Reformation cannot ignore the fact that Asia, despite the growing phenomenon of agnosticism, is a religiously plural world, with believers of different religions living everywhere cheek-by-jowl with one another. Indeed, religious pluralism is perhaps the greatest challenge facing Christian missions in Asia, especially in the encounter with Hinduism and Islam. Theologically, it calls for a radical reassessment of the exclusivist theology of religions that is implicit in the thought of the Protestant Reformers, operative in early Protestant missionaries, and vigorously maintained in many Protestant churches active in Asia today. A new theology of religions, one that is responsive to the reality of religious pluralism, will leave no Christian doctrine untouched, from the presence of the Spirit of God and salvation outside Christianity, the role of Christ as the unique and universal savior, the function of the church as community and symbol of God's grace, and the necessity and goal of mission.

THE WAY FORWARD AND AHEAD

The Reformation(s) in Asia: A blessing or a curse? The historical survey and theological reflections above do not lend themselves to a clear-cut, either/or answer. As a human enterprise sustained by God's grace, it is unavoidably both, a truth that Reformation theology of *simul justus et peccator* will have little difficulty in admitting. There was, of course, the ambiguous relation between evangelization and colonization, which was sometimes collaboration, and at other times resistance and subversion. On balance, however, the overall picture is more of light than darkness.

First, the Reformation has offered an *alternative* religious vision and an *alternative* way of life, one that brings hope and liberation to Asians who are oppressed and marginalized by their own political systems and religions. In particular, the Reformation, especially in its Pietistic tradition that emphasizes the personal and immediate relation to God, affirms the inalienable value and dignity of the individual over the interests of the group. Second, in addition to bringing the Word of God to Asia, the Reformation brought to the continent vast improvements in education at all levels and for all (girls included), mass printing, Western medicine and health care, nationalism, democracy, and human rights. In the process, a great number of Protestant missionaries have made innumerable and heroic sacrifices; some have lost their lives, all for the sake of the Gospel.

As has been argued by Scott H. Hendrix, the Reformers, who, despite their different agendas, ended up by confessionalizing their reform, were all united in one common goal, namely, re-Christianizing Europe, a process that had suffered serious deficiencies (according to the early Reformers), or had utterly failed (as the Radical Reformers thought) during the medieval process of Christianization.[34] It was the genius of the descendants of the Radical Reformers who first initiated the project of Christianization outside Europe, which was later joined by other mainline Protestants.

In Asia today this process of "Christianization" is encountering severe challenges without and within. It is even highly debatable whether "Christianization," as envisioned by the Reformers, is the right term and goal for Protestant missions in Asia. That Protestant missions should go *forward* and meet all these challenges is not an option but an act of obedience to the Lord and a way to consolidate the legacy of the Reformation in celebration of its five-hundredth jubilee. With regard to Asia, what Aiming Wang writes about the Reformation jubilee and Christianity in China indicates the way *ahead* for Asia as a whole as well. Asians' knowledge of Luther, Melanchthon, Zwingli, Calvin, and Knox, Wang notes, is still rudimentary, and the legacy of the Reformation cannot be established without a profound knowledge of its founders Wang listed above, and I must add, especially with reference to Protestant missions in Asia, the lesser-known but no less important Radical Reformers. As the Chinese character for "crisis" implies, it means both danger and opportunity. Some dangers have been described above; the opportunity is well expressed by Wang: "The Reformation Jubilee can become a historical opportunity for Chinese Christians to draw up a road map for a promising future; the legacy of the great reformers and their spirit could increasingly become a tradition of relevance to Chinese Christianity."[35]

---

34. Scott H. Hendrix, *Recultivating the Vineyard: The Reformation Agendas of Christianization* (Louisville and London: Westminster John Knox, 2004).

35. Aiming Wang, "The Reformation Jubilee and Christianity in China," in Petra Bosse-Huber, Serge Forneroad, Thies Gundlach, and Gottfried Locher, eds., *Reformation: Legacy and Future* (Geneva: World Council of Churches, 2015), 298.

4

Church and State Relations
in Vietnam, 1975–2015

From Enemies to
Collaborators for the Common Good

Two anniversaries prompt the reflections on church and state presented in this essay. The year 2013 marked the 1,700th anniversary of the Edict of Milan, in which Constantine and Licinius granted Christians as well as the followers of other religions the right to practice their religions freely and openly. As far as Christianity is concerned, this edict initiated what the Mennonite theologian John H. Yoder calls the "Constantinian shift," during which secular authority assumes the role of protector of the church, providing it with financial support, enforcing its doctrinal and disciplinary decisions with penalties, interfering in its internal affairs, turning it into a state church, and together with the church constituting what is known as Christendom. The year 2015 marked the fortieth anniversary of the victory of the (Communist) Democratic Republic of Vietnam (North Vietnam) over the (pro-Western) Republic of Vietnam (South Vietnam). After the country was reunified the following year under the name of the Socialist Republic of Vietnam, the state adopted a series of measures toward religion in general and the Christian churches, both Catholic and Protestant, in particular, that adversely affected the free exercise of religious freedom. Though the Edict of Milan and the religious policies of Vietnam represent polar opposites, they do share certain common features that invite serious examination, such as the constitutional affirmation of religious freedom, toleration of religious practices, and a marked propensity to regulate the church's internal affairs.

Against the background of the Constantinian shift, this essay surveys the situation of Christianity in Vietnam since the Communist victory in 1975. The predominant form of Vietnamese Christianity being Roman Catholic, the bulk of the essay is devoted to it. But attention will also be given to the Protestant and Evangelical/Pentecostal Churches. (There is no Orthodox

Church in Vietnam.) Of course, Christianity is not the only religion in Vietnam. It is the latest comer to the scene, after Buddhism, Daoism, Confucianism, and Islam. There are as well indigenous religions, principally Caodaism and Hoa Hao Buddhism. Of these non-Christian religious traditions only passing remarks will be made.[1]

ORIGINS OF THE VIETNAMESE CATHOLIC CHURCH

The history of Roman Catholicism in Vietnam dates back to the early sixteenth century, with sporadic visits by Spanish Franciscans and Dominicans from Malacca and the Philippines. Only at the beginning of the next century were missions to the country undertaken by Jesuit missionaries, with stable personnel and permanent residences, in what was known as Cochinchina in 1615, and in Tonkin in 1626.[2] It was the French Jesuit Alexandre de Rhodes (1591–1660) who, after twenty years of off-and-on missionary activities in both Tonkin and Cochinchina (1624–45), petitioned Rome to establish a hierarchy with the local clergy in Vietnam. As a result of his efforts, in 1659 two French missionaries, François Pallu and Pierre Lambert de la Motte, both members of the newly founded Société des Missions Étrangères de Paris (MEP), were appointed bishops and apostolic vicars of Tonkin and Cochinchina respectively.[3] These French missionaries and their successors came to Vietnam under the direct aegis of the Propaganda Fide in an attempt to bypass the restrictive and highly inefficient Portuguese *padroado* system which required that missionaries to Asia obtain the permission of the Portuguese crown (except to the Philippines, where the Spanish *padronado* applied).[4] The fact that these newcomers operated outside of the *padroado* system caused no small conflicts with the Jesuits working under such a system (largely Portuguese, Italian, and Spanish) and exacerbated their national and

---

1. For a helpful introduction to Vietnamese history, politics, and culture, see Keith W. Taylor, *A History of the Vietnamese* (Cambridge: Cambridge University Press, 2013); George E. Dutton, Jayne S. Werner, and John K. Whitmore, eds., *Sources of Vietnamese Tradition* (New York: Columbia University Press, 2012). For a collection of wide-ranging essays on various aspects of the history of Vietnam, see K. W. Taylor and John K. Whitmore, eds., *Essays into Vietnamese Pasts* (Ithaca, NY: Cornell University Press, 1995).

2. For a brief account of the earliest Christian missions in Vietnam, see Peter C. Phan, *Mission and Catechesis: Alexandre de Rhodes & Inculturation in Seventeenth-Century Vietnam* (Maryknoll, NY: Orbis Books, 1998), 8–13.

3. On the presence of the members of the MEP in Vietnam, see Claude Lange, *L'Église catholique et la société des Missions Étrangères au Vietnam: Vicariat apostolique de Cochinchine XVIIe et XVIIIe siècles* (Paris: L'Hamattan, 2004).

4. On the Portuguese *padroado* system in Asia, see Roland Jacques, *De Castro Marim à Faïfo: Naissance et développement du padroado portugais d'Orient des origines à 1659* (Lisbon: Fundação Calouste Gulbenkian, 1999).

religious rivalries. The suppression of the Society of Jesus (1773–1814) further lessened the influence of Jesuit missionaries on the Vietnamese church. Eventually, Catholic missions in Vietnam were taken over by other religious orders, principally the Franciscans, Dominicans, Augustinians, and Discalced Carmelites, but the majority of missionaries were members of the MEP.

The preponderant presence of French missionaries presented an enormous political and religious problem for the better part of the nineteenth century,[5] during the Tây Sơn uprising (1773–1802),[6] and especially under the two emperors of the Nguyen dynasty, Minh Mang (1791–1841) and Tu Duc (1829–1883), who carried out bloody persecutions against Vietnamese Catholics between 1820 and 1883.[7] Under the pretense of protecting its French citizens, France sought to extend its commercial ties with Asia by colonizing Vietnam, beginning in 1858 and later dividing it into three parts, Cochinchina (the south), which it made into a colony, and Annam (the center), and Tonkin (the north), which it ruled as protectorates.[8]

---

5. On the role of the French clergy, especially that of Bishop Pigneau de Béhaine, in helping Nguyen Anh, the founder of the Nguyen dynasty, in defeating the Tây Sơn revolutionary brothers, see George Dutton, *The Tây Sơn Uprising: Society and Rebellion in Eighteenth-Century Vietnam* (Honolulu: University of Hawai'i Press, 2006); and Wynn Cox, *Allegories of the Vietnamese Past: Unification and the Production of a Modern Historical Identity* (New Haven: Yale University Press, 2011), esp. 37–83.

6. The Tây Sơn rebellion was led by three brothers, Nguyen Nhac, Nguyen Lu, and Nguyen Hue, who came from the small village of Tây Sơn near Qui Nhơn against the rule of the Nguyen in the southern region (đàng trong), and later that of the Trinh in the northern region (đàng ngoài). Contrary to the Communist interpretation of the Tây Sơn uprising as a triumph of an oppressed peasantry by the royal courts and rich landowners, in the judgment of George Dutton, "the uprising was not an ideologically coherent movement seeking to articulate a uniform political agenda. Rather, it was an event whose course was guided by constantly changing circumstances, the whims of its leaders, and the reactions of a wide range of challenges" (*The Tây Sơn Uprising*, 17).

7. For a historical study of the Nguyen dynasty, see Li Tana, *Nguyen Cochinchina: Southern Vietnam in the Seventeenth and Eighteenth Centuries* (Ithaca, NY: Cornell University, 1998); and Choi Byung Wook, *Southern Vietnam under the Reign of Minh Mang (1820–1841): Central Policies and Local Response* (Ithaca, NY: Cornell University, 2004).

8. For a detailed study of the place of the Catholic Church in the relations between France and Vietnam, see the monumental studies by Étienne Vo Duc Hanh, *La place du catholicisme dans les relations entre la France et le Viet-Nam de 1851 à 1870*, 2 vols. (Lille: Service de reproduction des thèses, Université de Lille, 1975); *La place du catholicisme dans les relations entre la France et le Viet-Nam de 1870 à 1886*, 4 vols. (Berne: Peter Lang, 1992); *La place du catholicisme dans les relations entre la France et le Viet-Nam de 1887 à 1903*, 3 vols. (Berne: Peter Lang, 2002). For a more focused study of the Catholic Church from the Nguyen dynasty to the emergence of Vietnam as an independent nation, see Charles Keith, *Catholic Vietnam: A Church from Empire to Nation* (Berkeley: University of California Press, 2012); and Jacob Ramsey, *Mandarins and Martyrs: The Church and the Nguyen Dynasty in Early Nineteenth-Century Vietnam* (Stanford, CA: Stanford University Press, 2008). For a general history of French colonialism in Vietnam, see Pierre Brocheux and Daniel Hémery, *Indochina: An Ambiguous Colonization, 1858–1954*,

French colonization of Vietnam ended in 1954, and the Geneva Accords (July 21, 1954) temporarily partitioned Vietnam into two zones with the 17th parallel as the military demarcation line, with the north under the control of the Communists (with Ho Chi Minh as leader) and the south under a pro-Western government (with Catholic Ngo Dinh Diem as leader).[9] This political settlement stipulated that a plebiscite be held in 1956 to determine the type of political system for the eventually unified country. It also provided for the possibility for people of each zone to move north or south, according to their political preferences. This provision for internal migration proved to be a disaster for northern Vietnamese Catholic Christianity, as it was decimated by the departure of about half a million of its Catholic population (about two-thirds of the entire Catholic population of Vietnam at the time) to the south. This sudden influx also produced enormous challenges for Catholic Christianity in the south.[10]

The stipulated plebiscite was never held, and soon war erupted between North and South, as part of the Cold War, the North assisted by the People's Republic of China and the Soviet Union, the South by the United States. The internecine twenty-year war ended on April 30, 1975, with the victory of the Communist North, and the country was reunified the following year under the name of the Socialist Republic of Vietnam.

This event was both a bane and a boon for Vietnamese Christianity. On the one hand, it abruptly arrested the growth of the church in the south. Hundreds of thousands of Christians emigrated abroad, mostly to the United States of America, once again to escape Communism.[11] In addition, in the

---

trans. Ly Lan Dill-Klein et al. (Berkeley: University of California Press, 2009); and J. P. Daughton, *An Empire Divided: Religion, Republicanism, and the Making of French Colonialism, 1880–1914* (Oxford: Oxford University Press, 2006).

9. For a study of the Vietnamese Catholic Church during the war of independence from France, see Tran Thi Lien, "Les catholiques vietnamiens pendant la guerre d'indépendance (1945–1954) entre la reconquête coloniale et la résistance communiste" (Ph.D. diss., Institut d'Études Politiques de Paris, 1996).

10. On this migration of Catholics of northern Vietnam to the south and its impact on the church in the south, see Peter Hensen, "The Virgin Heads South: Northern Catholic Refugees in South Vietnam, 1954–1964" (Ph.D. diss., Melbourne College of Divinity, 2008). According to *Informations catholiques internationales* 158 (December 15, 1961), there were 860,026 refugees from the north to the south. Of these 80 percent (676,384) were Catholics, that is, almost half of the Catholic population of the church in the north. There were 5 bishops and 700 priests (two-thirds of the clergy of the north). In addition, almost all the male religious and a greater part of the female religious of the northern church also moved south. Remaining behind were 7 bishops, 374 priests, and a few religious serving 750,000 faithful in 10 dioceses.

11. Contrary to the 1954 exodus, this time the Vietnamese Episcopal Conference in South Vietnam was opposed to, though did not forbid, emigration. The bishops were committed to remaining with their fellow citizens and urged their clergy and religious to do so. Most Vietnamese refugees settled in the United States, though there are sizable Vietnamese communities in

immediate aftermath of its victory, the Communist government sought to destroy many structures of the church, Catholic as well as Protestant. On the other hand, with the unification of the country, it was possible for first time in twenty years for the Catholic Church to function as a single body and to establish regular contacts between the churches of the north and those of the south. In 1980 the Vietnamese Episcopal Conference was reestablished and since then has been able to hold its annual meetings regularly.

Currently the Catholic Church in Vietnam is organized into twenty-six dioceses grouped under three ecclesiastical provinces: Hanoi (ten dioceses), Hue (six dioceses), and Ho Chi Minh (ten dioceses). There are eight officially approved diocesan seminaries for the training of future priests. In addition to the secular clergy (c. 2,600 priests), there is large number of religious orders, both male and female, with c. 4,700 members. According to *Catholic Hierarchy Catalog* (2013), there are 5,658,000 Catholics in Vietnam, representing 6.87 percent of the total population, the fifth largest Catholic population in Asia, after the Philippines, China, India, and Indonesia.[12]

THE VIETNAMESE CATHOLIC CHURCH AND COMMUNISM, 1975–1990

Any account of contemporary Christianity in Vietnam must deal with its relationship to the Communist Party and government.[13] This relationship has had a long and fraught history. Following his declaration of independence of Vietnam from France on September 2, 1954, Ho Chi Minh wanted to found a state, or at least state-managed, "patriotic" Catholic Church in the mold of the Catholic Patriotic Association in China. His primary goal was to destroy the Vietnamese Catholic Church, which he perceived as a threat to national liberation. Soon, however, realizing that such a project could not be achieved, given the tightly knit organization of the Vietnamese Catholic Church, especially its loyalty to the Vatican, Ho convoked in Hanoi at the beginning of 1955 what was dubbed the "Assembly of Vietnamese Catholic Representatives" to gain control of the church. Attendees were appointed by the government and a "Liaison Committee of Catholics for Patriotism and Peace" was

France, Canada, and Australia. On the Vietnamese Catholics in the United States, see Peter C. Phan, *Vietnamese-American Catholics* (Mahwah, N.J.: Paulist Press, 2005).

12. As is well known, statistics of Christians in Asia, especially in Communist countries, are notoriously unreliable. Some put the current number of Vietnamese Catholics at 8 million out of the population of 86 million.

13. Some of the materials that follow can be found in my earlier essay "The Roman Catholic Church in the Socialist Republic of Vietnam, 1989–2005," in *Falling Walls: The Year 1989/90 as a Turning Point in the History of World Christianity*, ed. Klaus Koschorke (Wiesbaden: Harrassowitz, 2009), 243–57.

established, with two priests as president and vice-president and three other priests as members of its central board. The committee's main task was to rally Catholics behind governmental policies and projects. Despite financial support from the government, the committee failed to achieve anything of significance because it was boycotted by the faithful.

The Vietnamese Communist Party versus the Vietnamese Catholic Church before 1975

With total and absolute control over North Vietnam after the partition of the country in 1954, the Vietnamese Communist Party (VCP) adopted a Marxist-inspired attitude toward religion in general and toward Christianity in particular. Its ultimate goal was to destroy religion, especially Christianity. In its eyes, religion is the cause of self-alienation and an instrument of exploitation for capitalism, colonialism, and imperialism. The VCP's strategy to destroy the Vietnamese Catholic Church was threefold: eliminating its leadership, demolishing its structures, and impeding its activities.

Nevertheless, officially, the VCP recognized religious freedom. In the 234-SL Decree, which both Ho Chi Minh and Prime Minister Pham Van Dong signed on June 14, 1955, and which contained five chapters and sixteen articles, the freedom to preach and teach religion was granted, though only to be done within the confines of churches, pagodas, and temples (Article 1). Article 5 permitted the establishment of institutions for the formation of religious leaders, and Article 9 that of private schools. Article 10 allowed religions to keep a certain amount of land for the maintenance of religious personnel. Most significantly and surprisingly, Article 13 stipulated that the government not interfere in the internal affairs of religions.

Arguably the decree was a ploy to dispel the fears of North Vietnamese Catholics about repression under the Communist regime and to keep them from migrating to the south. If that were the intent of the decree, it failed miserably, because perhaps as many as 500,000 Catholics, as mentioned above, fled south. In spite of official assurances of religious freedom, the Catholic Church in North Vietnam after 1954 suffered continual harassment and persecution: expulsion of foreign missionaries, severance of diplomatic relations with the Vatican, restrictions on priestly and episcopal ordinations, prevention of appointments and movements of the clergy, isolation of the priests from their bishops and of bishops from their colleagues, arrests of prominent and influential religious leaders, and general intimidation of the faithful who were classified as second-class citizens and hence ineligible for benefits such as higher education and civil service. By 1975 the church in the north was decimated: Two-thirds of the Catholic population had emigrated to the south; of the 370 priests in 1955 only 277 survived, mostly old and feeble; a great number of churches were in dilapidated condition.

The Communist State and the Catholic Church
in Vietnam, 1975–1990

After the fall of South Vietnam in 1975, the religious policies that had been in force in North Vietnam were applied to the newly conquered territory.[14] With the 297-HDBT government decree dated November 11, 1977, the VCP added new restrictions on religious practices and organizations, while affirming the freedom of religious belief and nonbelief. Included among various new rules and regulations were segregation of believers from public and civic life, prohibition of preaching and religious education outside of religious buildings, governmental approval of candidates to the priesthood and especially to the episcopacy, and nationalization of church properties for the purposes of education, social services, and health care.

In general, from 1975 to 1989, the VCP was vigorously engaged in its triple strategy toward religion, i.e., elimination of the leadership, demolition of organizational structures, and restrictions of religious activities. With regard to the elimination of leadership, foreign missionaries were expelled, including the apostolic delegate Henri Lemaitre. Archbishop (later Cardinal) Nguyen Van Thuan was not permitted to take up his post as bishop of Saigon and was imprisoned for thirteen years. Later, Bishop Huynh Van Nghi was prevented from succeeding Archbishop Nguyen Van Binh as bishop of Saigon. About three hundred priests were sent to "re-education camps" for an extended number of years. Several dioceses were left vacant since episcopal candidates were blocked by the government.

To demolish the organizational structures of the church, in November 1983, the VCP promoted the formation of the *Uy Ban Doan Ket Cong Giao Yeu Nuoc* [Committee for the Unification of Patriotic Catholics], like the "Liaison Committee of Catholics for Patriotism and Peace" in 1955, with the help of a group of Catholics known as *Cong Giao va Dan Toc* [Catholicism and People]. The committee, which is part of the National Front and which publishes a journal named *Cong Giao va Dan Toc*, is the official organ for relations between the state and the Catholic Church. The VCP's implicit intent in founding such a committee was to nullify the authority of the Vietnamese Catholic hierarchy and to establish a national "patriotic" church with no ties to the Vatican and the universal church. Once again, this project failed utterly since the committee was boycotted by the faithful and has had no influence on the life of the church as a whole. The committee held a national meeting

---

14. For an informative overview in Vietnamese of the Catholic Church in Vietnam 1975–2005, see the collection of essays in *Ba Muoi Nam Cong Giao Viet Nam Duoi Che Do Cong San 1975–2005* [Thirty Years of the Vietnamese Catholic Church under the Communist Government 1975–2005] (No place of publication or publisher, 2005); and Bui Duc Sinh, *Giao Hoi Cong Giao o Viet Nam 1975–2000* [The Catholic Church in Vietnam 1975–2000] (Westminster, CA: Asian Printing, 2001).

in Saigon in August 1983, followed shortly afterward by another meeting in Hanoi.[15]

To impede church activities, the government confiscated many religious institutions, notably St. Pius X Pontifical University in Da Lat, and properties belonging to the Society of Jesus, the Franciscans, the Salesians, the Redemptorists, and the Congregation of Mary Co-Redemptrix (a local religious order). All Catholic schools as well as social and health care centers were shut down. Though worship activities within church buildings were still allowed, they were often impeded by conflicting schedules of work and civic duties. Permission was required for religious instruction, priests' retreats, bishops' conferences, and other extraordinary activities (e.g., processions and pilgrimages). The agenda of the bishop's meetings was required to be communicated to the government beforehand, and reports of the meetings subsequently submitted.

An incident before 1989 worth mentioning is Pope John Paul II's decision to canonize 117 martyrs of Vietnam (of whom 96 were Vietnamese, 10 French, and 11 Spaniards) on June 19, 1988. The pope's decision was strenuously and publicly opposed by the Vietnamese government. Its objection was threefold: beside the fact there had been no prior consultation with the Vietnamese government, the canonization would be honoring those killed by order of the Vietnamese kings and glorifying French and Spanish spies. The government organized petitions against the canonization, canvassed the collaboration of the Committee for the Unification of Patriotic Catholics, and sponsored several national conferences to propagate its point of view. It also pressured the Vietnamese Episcopal Conference to make a statement against the canonization. On March 2, 1988, the Conference, which had petitioned for the canonization in 1985, simply stated that the canonization was strictly a decision of the Vatican on which it had no say.

The Catholic Church under the Communist Government, 1975–1990

Like all other religious organizations in South Vietnam, the Catholic Church was caught completely unprepared for the victory of Communist North Vietnam on April 30, 1975. Its stance toward Communism had been one of rejection and condemnation, consistent with that of the universal church until the end of the Second Vatican Council (1962–65). The new challenge was how to

---

15. It is important to note, however, that the Vietnamese Communist Party did not intend to found a patriotic church like that of China with its own organization, with the power to nominate and ordain bishops independently of the Vatican. Perhaps its leadership realized that such a plan would not work with the Vietnamese Catholic Church. Furthermore, its control over the nomination of bishops is far more benign than that of the Chinese government, limited as it is to veto power. There is in Vietnam no schismatic church and no "underground church" opposed to the "official" or "patriotic" church.

exist as church and fulfill its mission under a Communist regime. Fortunately, the archbishops of Hue and Saigon were able to exercise much-needed leadership. On April 1, 1975, after the city of Hue had fallen to the Communists, Nguyen Kim Dien, archbishop of Hue, sent a personal letter to the Catholics of his diocese asking them to thank God for the end of the war and urged them to work with the new government to build a peaceful, just, and prosperous country. Eight days later, addressing the Liberation Front of Hue, the archbishop emphasized the church's readiness to collaborate with the Front to build an independent, free, and compassionate society; and, appealing for religious freedom, he pledged that Catholics would fulfill all their obligations toward the country and God.

Nguyen Van Binh, archbishop of Saigon, took the lead in guiding the church in this new phase of its existence. In the immediate aftermath of the Communist takeover, on May 5, 1975, the archbishop sent a personal letter to his Catholics urging them to share in the lives of their fellow citizens and to carry out the civic duties imposed by the Provisional Revolutionary Government. In a more elaborated circular of June 12, 1975, he reminded them of their duty to collaborate with the new Communist government and at the same time to remain in communion with the universal church, especially with the pope, so as to avoid at any cost creating an autonomous, "patriotic" church. On the other hand, he also asked the new government to respect religious freedom in accord with the above-mentioned 234-SL Decree signed by Ho Chi Minh and Pham Van Dong in 1955. Again, as the unification of the North and South was being planned by the VCP, the archbishop sent out another letter on November 22, 1975, in which he asserted that national unification could be God's "visitation," a providential opportunity, and urged his clergy and laity to discern the positive contributions of socialism in terms of social justice.

Twenty-one bishops of the Vietnamese Episcopal Conference of the South held their regular meeting on December 15–20, 1975, in Ho Chi Minh City, the first time since the Communist takeover, and at the end of their meeting were received by the representatives of the Provisional Revolutionary Government. Clearly, the most urgent task for the church was to formulate a pastoral approach appropriate for the new situation. It was a most challenging and difficult task as the bishops had to shift from a traditional rigidly anti-Communist stance to one of openness, dialogue, and collaboration, in the footsteps of Vatican II. On July 16, 1976, the bishops issued a statement in which they acknowledged fundamental differences between Marxist-Leninist ideology and the Christian faith, yet argued that such differences should not prevent Catholics from collaborating with the Communist government for the common good of the country. In this and several later statements, the bishops repeatedly urged Catholics to be good and faithful citizens. In particular, they emphasized that Vietnamese Catholics as a whole must not form a political party or bloc in opposition to the Communist government or the VCP.

The most important and widely disseminated document expounding the attitude of the church toward Communism and outlining its ministry under the Communist regime is no doubt the first pastoral letter of the now reconstituted Vietnamese Episcopal Conference, composed of the thirty-three bishops of both North and South. It was issued on January 5, 1980, and titled "Living the Gospel in the Midst of the People." Beginning with an emphatic affirmation that the church of Jesus Christ must live in the midst of the people, the letter asserts that Vietnam is the place where God calls Vietnamese Catholics to live as children of God and that the Vietnamese people are the community that God gives to Catholics to serve as both citizens and members of the People of God.

Unfortunately, subsequent events showed that the church's conciliatory stance and willingness to collaborate with the Communist government were not reciprocated. On the contrary, repressive measures against the Catholic Church were taken, as mentioned above, to eliminate its leadership, destroy its organizational structures, and impede its activities. Under the pretext of national security, in November 1980, the government confiscated the properties of the Jesuits in Ho Chi Minh City. In 1987–88, tensions between the government and the church reached a fevered pitch on the occasion of the canonization of 117 Vietnamese martyrs, as recounted above. Meanwhile, the VCP could not ignore world events, with the impending collapse of the U.S.S.R., and their possible impact upon the course of Vietnam's economy and politics.

RELIGIOUS POLICIES AND CHRISTIANITY IN VIETNAM, 1990–2015

As is often the case, politics and religion are trumped by economics. By the 1980s it was clear that Vietnam was facing an economic catastrophe, even with massive financial aid from the Soviet Union, China, and Eastern Europe amounting to U.S. $3 to $4 billion, plus roughly U.S. $1.5 billion of pledged aid from Western nations. This dire economic situation forced the VCP to introduce economic reforms at the Fifth National Party Congress in 1982, resulting in the Third Five-Year Plan (1981–85). The plan adopted a number of capitalist enterprises, especially in the south, to boost production. It also emphasized the development of agriculture by adopting the end-product contract system whereby farming peasants were allowed to keep the surplus production, sell it on the free market, or sell it to the state for a negotiated price.

In 1986, the Fourth Five-Year Plan (1986–90) was launched to facilitate a "socialist-oriented market economy." Agricultural collectives were abolished, price controls on agricultural goods removed, and private businesses and foreign investments, including foreign-owned enterprises, encouraged. In practice, the free-market system was sanctioned and promoted.

Along with economic innovation, some important changes in the political system were advanced under the rubric of *Doi Moi* [renovation]. Unlike *perestroika* in the Soviet Union where it was officially accompanied by political *glasnost*, *Doi Moi* was not undergirded by a new political ideology of openness. Nevertheless, no doubt it represented the most significant reforms not only economic but also political in post-1975 Vietnam.

The United States lifted the economic embargo on Vietnam in 1994 and reestablished diplomatic relations with it in 2000. Government control of the economy and a nonconvertible currency spared Vietnam from a severe economic downturn from the East Asian financial crisis in 1997. In July 2000, Vietnam signed the Bilateral Trade Agreement with the United States, providing for the normal trade relations status of Vietnamese goods in the U.S. market. In 2001 the VCP approved a Ten-Year Plan for economic development, enhancing the role of the private sector and at the same time reaffirming the primacy of the state. In November 2006, Vietnam became the 150th member of the World Trade Organization.

In spite of all these *Doi Moi* changes toward the free-market system, the VCP, like the Chinese Communist Party, did everything to retain its status as the only party with the power to govern Vietnam. Occasionally, laws and policies were enacted and ordinances and decrees issued to protect human rights, including religious freedom, especially if these measures could improve Vietnam's standing in the international community and attract economic foreign investments. Nothing, however, would be tolerated if it could challenge or jeopardize the party's exclusive grip on power. Nevertheless, it must be acknowledged that in the 1990s, there was some relaxation in the government's attitude toward religious freedom and practices in general. New laws and policies in religious matters were issued. With regard to the Catholic Church, diplomatic relations were established between the Vietnamese government and the Vatican.

Laws and Policies on Religious Freedom in Vietnam, 1990–2013

Mention has been made of the 234-SL Decree of 1955 and the 297-HDBT Decree of 1977 that severely limited the activities of religious institutions and curtailed the rights of Catholics. Widely and sharply criticized as a repressive policy, the 297-HDBT Decree was subsequently replaced by the Constitution and several government directives, decrees, ordinances, and resolutions.[16]

---

16. For a progovernment exposition of religious laws and policies in Vietnam, see Nguyen

The 1992 Constitution of the Socialist Republic of Vietnam, emended in 2001 and again in 2013, stipulates that "citizens have the right to freedom of belief and religion, and may practice or not practice any religion. All religions are equal before the law. Public places of religious worship are protected by law. No one has the right to infringe on the freedom of faith and religion or take advantage of the latter to violate State laws and policies" (Article 70).

Basic to the VCP's stance toward religious freedom is the distinction between religion as faith and belief (*tin nguong*) and religion as religious organization and activities (*ton giao*). For the former, there is a guarantee for complete freedom of believing and not believing; for the latter, there are restrictions, especially to protect "national security." Accordingly, the Directive No. 37–CT/TW of July 2, 1998, of the Central Committee of the VCP requires party committees and administration at all levels "to encourage religious followers to promote their traditional patriotism, to take an enthusiastic part in the renovation cause, to fulfill religious tasks and citizens' duties, to build and defend the Fatherland, and to continue to implement the policy of the Party and State on religion."[17]

The directive spells out the government's position toward religion in the following principles:

1. To respect and guarantee the freedom of religion and belief and the freedom of nonreligion and nonbelief of citizens. All citizens are equal before the law with regard to their obligations and rights, irrespective of adherence/nonadherence to religion and of difference between religions.
2. To unite and cohere all religious and nonreligious people in the great bloc of all-people unity.
3. All individuals and organizations engaged in religious activities must observe the Constitution and law, are duty-bound to protect the interest of the Socialist Fatherland of Viet Nam, to safeguard national independence and sovereignty.
4. Religious activities beneficial to the people and country and conforming to the legitimate aspirations and interests of religious followers are guaranteed. Cultural and ethical values of religions are respected and promoted.

Quang Minh, *Religious Issues and Government Policies in Viet Nam*, trans. Nguyen Huy Dung (Ha Noi: Gioi Publishers, 2005), which contains the English texts of these government documents. For a recent report of the U.S. Department of State on the current religious situation in Vietnam, see the "International Religious Freedom Report 2007." The report is available online at www.state.gov. On the religious situation in contemporary Vietnam, see Philip Taylor, ed., *Modernity and Re-enchantment: Religion in Post-Revolutionary Vietnam* (Singapore: Institute of Southeast Asian Studies, 2007).

17. Nguyen, *Religious Issues*, 155–56.

5. All acts of making use of religious activities to cause social disorder and insecurity, to harm national independence, to sabotage the policy on the unity of all people, to counter the State of the Socialist Republic of Viet Nam, to deteriorate the cultural and ethical values and lifestyle of the nation, to prevent religious followers and clerics from fulfilling their citizen's duties will be dealt with according to law. Superstitious practices must be criticized and eliminated.[18]

A much more detailed and specific list of stipulations regarding what is allowed and forbidden was given the following year in the Decree No. 26/1999/ND-CP (April 19, 1999), especially in articles 6–26. While this decree marks an advance over the 1998 directive inasmuch as it clarifies the kinds of religious activities that can "cause social disorder and insecurity" and are unlawful, it has been heavily criticized for its attempt to interfere in the normal internal affairs of religions. For example, it requires the approval of appropriate government authorities for extraordinary religious activities outside religious buildings (e.g., processions and pilgrimages), the appointment of religious officials (in particular bishops and their equivalents), the building of churches, the founding of seminaries and houses of formation, meetings and conferences of religious leaders at the national and local levels, and relations with foreign religious organizations. In addition, it is pointed out that the government is treading dangerous grounds when it pretends to define "superstitious practices" that must be eliminated.

On June 18, 2004, the government issued an "Ordinance on Belief and Religion" composed of forty-one articles. The ordinance gives precise definitions to terms such as "belief-related activity," "belief-related establishment," "religious organization," "grassroots religious organizations," "religious activity," "religious association," and "religious establishment." A key distinction is again made between "belief" (for which there is complete freedom as well as for nonbelief) and "religion" (for which there are restrictions). Again, this ordinance is an improvement over the 1998 decree and the 1999 directive. Of great interest is Article 6, which stipulates that

Relations between the Socialist Republic of Viet Nam and other States and/or international organizations in religion-related matters shall be based on the principle for each other's independence and sovereignty, non-interference in each other's internal affairs, equality, mutual benefit, and in conformity with each other's law and international law and practice.[19]

---

18. Ibid., 156–57.
19. Ibid., 180.

In spite of this stipulation, the ordinance continues the practice of government control and oversight of religious institutions and their activities. It requires "registration" and government approval for matters that are universally regarded as routine and internal to religious institutions such as the establishment of seminaries, enrollment of candidates to the priesthood, and activities outside of church buildings. In particular, for the appointment of bishops, since it involves "foreign elements" (read: the Vatican), the ordinance stipulates that "agreement with the central State management body for religious affairs shall . . . be required in advance" (Article 22, 1).[20]

The ordinance was shortly followed by a "Decree of the Government Guiding the Implementation of the Ordinance on Belief and Religion" (March 2005) containing thirty-eight articles. As implied by its title, this decree, which is so far the longest and most detailed legal document on religious institutions and practices, sets out procedures for registering "belief-related festivals" (Articles 3–5), "religious organizations" (Articles 6–19), "religious activities" (Articles 20–35). Again, the overriding concern of the government is control of religions and their activities, particularly by means of "registration." Without registration, no religion may legally function. As of 2007, the State, through the Committee for Religious Affairs, officially recognizes six religions: Buddhism, Catholicism, Protestantism, Islam, Caodaism, and Hoa Hao Buddhism.[21]

---

20. Ibid., 190–91.

21. With regard to Buddhism, the government requires that all Buddhist monks be approved and function under the officially recognized Buddhist organization, the Vietnam Buddhist Sangha. It continues to outlaw the United Buddhist Church of Vietnam. On Buddhism and Communism, see Shawn Frederick McHale, *Print and Power: Confucianism, Communism, and Buddhism in the Making of Modern Vietnam* (Honolulu: University of Hawai'i Press, 2004).

There are currently between 50,000 and 80,000 Vietnamese Muslims. According to the Song dynasty-era documents, Islam entered central coastal Vietnam—more precisely, the Champa Kingdom, now Ninh Thuan and Ninh Binh—in the late tenth and early eleventh centuries. After the collapse of the Champa Kingdom in 1471, the number of Muslims increased significantly with the arrival of Muslims from the Sultanate of Malacca. In the mid-nineteenth century, many Muslims emigrated from Cambodia into Vietnam and settled in the Mekong Delta region, especially in Chau Doc and An Giang. At the beginning of the twentieth century, Malaysian Islam began exerting influence on Vietnamese Muslims. After 1975 a large number of Vietnamese Muslims emigrated to Malaysia and Yemen. On the Champa Kingdom, see Tran Ky Phuong and Bruce M. Lockhart, eds., *The Cham of Vietnam: History, Society and Art* (Singapore: NUS Press, 2011). On Vietnamese Islam, see Seddik Taouti, "The Forgotten Muslims of Kampuchea and Vietnam," in Ibrahim Ahmad Datuk, Hussain Yasmin, and Sharon Siddique, eds., *Readings on Islam in Southeast Asia* (Singapore: Institute of Southeast Asian Studies, 1985), 193–202

Caodaism currently has about between 2.3 million members (according to the government) and 4 million (according to its adherents). Founded in 1926 by Ngo Minh Chieu (1878–1932) and his immediate followers, especially Pham Cong Tac (1890–1959), Caodai's most prominent organizer and writer, Caodaism—its full name is *Cao Dai Dao Tam Ky Pho Do* [Great Religion of the Third Period of Revelation and Salvation]—is a highly syncretistic religion combining

The most compelling criticism of this 2005 decree is that while it has relaxed many of the earlier restrictions on religious activities, in requiring "registration" for church organizations and intrachurch activities, it has created a system of "request-grant" (*xin-cho*) that is rife with abuse and corruption. While the government's concerns for national security are legitimate, the criteria for granting and denying requests for registration are arbitrary and undefined. Furthermore, because of the lack of due process in the legal system and inconsistent oversight, the implementation of the ordinance has been uneven and left to the discretion of the (often incompetent and corrupt) local authorities. The International Religious Freedom Report 2007 of the U.S. Department of State summarizes the current situation well:

> Despite progress during the reporting period, problems remained in the implementation of the country's legal framework on religion. These included slowness, and even in some cases inaction, in the registration of Protestant congregations in northern Vietnam and the Northwest Highlands; inconsistent application of procedures for congregation registration and other legal requirements; ongoing restrictions on religious recruitment; difficulties in the establishment of Catholic seminaries and Protestant training courses; and unresolved land expropriation claims involving a number of religious denominations.[22]

The report, however, recognizes that apart from isolated cases such as the government's crackdown on Catholic priest Nguyen Van Ly and Protestant pas-

---

elements of Daoism, Buddhism, and Christianity (especially Roman Catholicism, whose hierarchical structure and nomenclature it adopts). It has thirteen separate groups, the largest of which is headquartered in Tay Ninh, where it has its "Holy See." Politically, Caodaism was strongly opposed to both French colonialism and Communism and was submitted to harassment by both powers. It was only in 1997 that it was granted legal recognition by the Communist government. For a study of Caodaism, see Peter C. Phan, "Caodaism," in *A Dictionary of Asian Christianity*, ed. Scott W. Sunquist (Grand Rapids, MI: Eerdmans, 2001), 115–17; and Jayne Werner, *Peasant Politics and Religious Sectarianism: Peasant and Priest in the Cao Dai in Vietnam* (New Haven: Yale University Press, 1981).

Hoa Hao, another indigenous religion with deep roots in Buddhism founded in 1939 by Huynh Phu So (1920–1947), with most of its followers residing in the Mekong Delta, has between 1.2 million members (according to the government) and 3 million (according to its adherents). Hoa Hao claims to be a continuation of the nineteenth-century Buddhist tradition known as *Buu Son Ky Huong* [The Mysterious Perfume of the Precious Mountain]. Its emphasis is on agriculture and worship in the home rather than at an official pagoda. Politically it was anti-French colonialism and anti-Communist. After the Second World War, Hoa Hao organized its own army, which was later disbanded by President Ngo Dinh Diem. Though Hoa Hao was granted legal recognition by the Communist government in 1999, a number of its followers have resisted its incorporation by the State. On Hoa Hao, see Nguyen Long Thanh Nam, *Hoa Hao Buddhism in the Course of Vietnam's History* (New York: Nova Science Publishing, 2004).

22. See www.state.gov.

tor Nguyen Van Dai for alleged political activism, there have been significant improvements in the Vietnamese government's attitude and practices toward religious freedom. In 2004, then-Secretary of State Colin Powell designated Vietnam as a "country of particular concern" for severe violations of religious freedom. In 2006, however, Secretary of State Condoleezza Rice lifted this designation, recognizing that Vietnam was no longer a severe violator of religious freedom as defined by the International Religious Freedom Act.

The Vietnam Government and the Vatican, 1990–2015

As is clear from the above-mentioned directive and decrees, the Vietnamese Catholic Church, differently from other religious organizations, suffered special legal restrictions, especially in the appointment of bishops, because of its institutional connections with what the VCP calls "foreign elements," that is, the Vatican state. Mention has been made of the fact that the apostolic delegate was expelled from Saigon in 1975; Archbishop Nguyen Van Thuan was not allowed to function as the bishop of Saigon in 1976; Bishop Huynh Van Minh was not accepted as apostolic administrator of the same archdiocese after Archbishop Nguyen Van Binh's death; and the canonization of 117 martyrs in 1988 caused severe tensions between the Vatican and the Vietnamese government.

However, since 1989, after the collapse of the Soviet Union, there has been a remarkable rapprochement between the Vatican and the Vietnamese government. In March 1989, Archbishop Nguyen Van Thuan was permitted to go to Rome after his release in March 1988. In July 1989, Cardinal Roger Etchegaray visited Vietnam as a special envoy of Pope John Paul II and was able to travel from north to south to visit the main dioceses. From 1990 to 2004, there were thirteen official visits either by the Vatican delegation to Vietnam or by the Vietnamese delegation to Rome. Most significantly, in January 2007, the Vietnamese prime minister Nguyen Tan Dung visited the Vatican and met with Pope Benedict XVI, and in March of the same year, an official delegation of the Vatican reciprocated by visiting the country. Declarations were made that exchange of ambassadors between the Vatican and Vietnam would be a matter of time. In 2009, the president of Vietnam, Nguyen Minh Triet, visited Benedict XVI.

Matters under negotiation between the Vatican and the Vietnamese government since 1990 concerned mainly the appointment of bishops to the archdioceses of Ho Chi Minh City (with Archbishop Pham Minh Man, now cardinal, in 1998) and of Hue (with Archbishop Nguyen Nhu The in 1998), the appointment of bishops, the selection of candidates to the priesthood and religious life, the ordination and transfer of priests, and religious freedom in general.

A turning point in the relations between Vietnam and the Vatican occurred on January 13, 2011, when Archbishop Leopoldo Girelli was appointed apostolic nuncio to Singapore and apostolic delegate for Malaysia and for Brunei Darussalam, and nonresidential papal representative for Vietnam. He was the first papal representative of any kind to be appointed for Vietnam since the expulsion of the resident apostolic delegate in 1975. His appointment was approved by the Vietnamese government, even though apostolic delegates, being accredited not to the government but to the church in the country, are normally assigned without prior consultation of the government. Accordingly, the 2012 *Annuario* (the Vatican Yearbook) classified the papal representative office for Vietnam as an apostolic delegation, but referred to Archbishop Girelli not as an apostolic delegate but, generically, as papal representative for Vietnam. Since his appointment the papal representative has visited Vietnam ten times so far and was always given unimpeded access to the local churches throughout the country.

Another highly significant event is the government's permission to the Federation of Asian Bishops' Conferences (FABC) to hold its Tenth Plenary Assembly on December 10–16, 2012. Among seventy-one participants consisting of cardinals, archbishops, and bishops from more than twenty Asian countries was Pope Benedict XVI's special envoy, Cardinal Gaudencio Rosales, archbishop emeritus of Manila. Other participants included executive secretaries of various offices of FABC, fraternal delegates and guests from Oceania, Europe, and Latin America. Recently, on September 15–20, 2013, a seven-member delegation from the Vietnam Government Committee for Religious Affairs paid a working visit to the Vatican during which they met with Pope Francis to whom they presented a statue of Jesus as a gift. These official events signal a notable improvement in relations between the government of Vietnam on the one hand and the Vatican and the Vietnamese Catholic Church on the other.

THE PROTESTANT CHURCHES IN VIETNAM, 1975–2015

In most Asian countries, Protestantism (in Vietnamese, *Dao Tin Lanh* [The Good News Religion]) is officially and legally treated as a distinct "religion" from the Catholic Church. Introduced into Vietnam in 1911 by Robert A. Jaffray under the aegis of the Christian & Missionary Alliance (C&MA), Protestantism was organized in 1927 into a church known as the Evangelical Church of Indochina, later changed into the Evangelical Church of Vietnam (ECVN).[23] During the War of Independence (1945–54), the church adopted the policy of neutrality, restricting itself to the spiritual task of evangelizing. After the 1954 Geneva Accords, the ECVN was divided into two: ECVN

---

23. For a brief introduction to Vietnamese Protestantism, see Reg Reimer, *Vietnam's Christians: A Century of Growth in Adversity* (Pasadena, CA: William Carey Library, 2011).

North and ECVN South, and about one thousand members moved from the north to the south.

Soon, and especially during the Vietnam War, other Protestant denominations and groups joined the C&MA, notably, the Seventh Day Adventists (1929), the Mennonite Central Committee (1954), the Eastern Mennonite Board of Missions and Charities (1971), Southern Baptists (1959), and the Assemblies of God (1972).

Despite (or rather because) of persecutions by the government, since 1975 the number of Vietnamese Protestants grew from 160,000 to 1.4 million—nearly 900 percent. Originally the ECVN's missions were highly successful among the ethnic Vietnamese in the south, especially in My Tho and Can Tho, but less so in the north. Later the church focused its work on the ethnic minorities in the Highland Mountainous Region in the north (notably among the Hmong) and in the Central Highlands in the south (notably among the Koho, Ede, Jarai, Bahnar, Stieng, and Mnong). Even though the ethnic minorities make up only 13 percent of the Vietnamese population, they constitute over half of the Protestants in Vietnam.

A recent phenomenon deserving close attention is the emergence of the house church movement. In the late 1980s some ECVN young pastors (notably Dinh Thien Tu, Vo Van Lac, Tran Mai, and Tran Dinh Ai) were dissatisfied with the senior church leadership's accommodating attitude toward the government and advocated instead a confrontational approach. In addition, they favored Pentecostal doctrines of the Holy Spirit and worship style with emphasis on speaking in tongues and healing. They were subsequently expelled from the ECVN for insubordination. These pastors started the home church movement, which spread like wildfire. By 2009 there were an estimated 250,000 Christians in at least 2,500 home-based groups belonging to house church organizations. These organizations range from a single congregation to ones that have hundreds of congregations. Some of them have also tried to establish a connection with international denominations such as the Assemblies of God, the Nazarenes, the Methodists, the Mennonites, and the Presbyterians.[24]

The spread of Protestantism among the tribal people and the rise of the house church movement present great difficulties for the churches in relation to the government. Among the Central Highland tribes, there was in the 1960s a liberation movement called FULCRO. Most of its members were Protestants and were adamantly opposed to the Communists. In 2001 and 2004 there were extensive demonstrations among the Central Highlands tribes against confiscation of their lands and lack of religious freedom. These protesters, who called themselves "Dega" (the term is derived from the

---

24. See ibid., 71.

Ede-language phrase *anak ede gar,* meaning "children of the mountains"), were accused by the government to be working for the United States and were brutally crushed.

Another problem concerns "registration." In February 2005, as mentioned above, the government issued the "Decree of the Government Guiding the Implementation of the Ordinance on Belief and Religion," requiring that religious organizations "register" for "recognition" with the government to be allowed to function legally. The following month the prime minister issued "Special Directive No. 1 Concerning the Protestant Religion," directing commune- and city-level authorities to expedite the registration of Protestant house churches. Some of these have applied for registration and recognition. Two Protestant organizations, the ECVN North and the ECVN South, representing well over half of Vietnam's Protestants, have already had full legal recognition, the former in 1950 and the latter in 2001. Only 160 ethnic congregations associated with the ECVN North, out of over one thousand, have received provisional recognition. In 2009, church leaders reported that not more than one-tenth of the house churches' applications for recognition had been approved. Other house churches have refused to register on the grounds that such a process allows the government to control their religious activities. Obviously, the combination of the recent mushrooming of Protestant house churches without a central authority and the cumbersome process of registration conspire to make a harmonious relation between Vietnamese Protestantism and the Vietnamese government a well-nigh impossible reality.

In sum, the history of the relationship between Vietnamese Christianity and the Communist government is not a linear one. At times, it is an intricate pas de deux, with a step forward and two steps backward and with the partners occasionally stepping on each other's toes. This is the case with recent events that have attracted international notice. In early 2008 thousands of Catholics assembled to pray at the former residence of the apostolic nuncio and the Thai Ha property of the Redemptorists in Hanoi demanding the restoration of long-confiscated church properties. On September 19, 2008, the government ordered some of the buildings razed and the properties turned into a public park. Later, thugs and plainclothes police attacked the remaining chapel of the Redemptorists' property. In June 2010 the archbishop of Hanoi Nguyen Van Kiet, who had been vocal in his opposition to the government policies regarding religious freedom, mysteriously resigned for "health reason." Attacks were also carried out against the Hmong Protestants, who make up a full quarter of all Vietnamese Protestants. Because of their isolation and lack of organization, they are especially vulnerable to religious oppression.[25]

---

25. On the history of the Hmong Protestants, see ibid., 75–84.

THE FUTURE OF VIETNAMESE CHRISTIANITY: CHALLENGES AND OPPORTUNITIES

A fair assessment of the history of the relationship between the Vietnamese government and Vietnamese Christianity, both Catholic and Protestant, between 1975 and 2015, must recognize that there has been substantial progress in matters of religious freedom, a fact that justified the removal of Vietnam from the list of "countries of particular concern" for severe violations of religious freedom in 2006. In 2012 a process of revising the constitution was undertaken, and the National Assembly was scheduled to vote on constitutional amendments during the October 21–November 30, 2013, session. (The 1992 constitution had been amended in 2001.)

However, it may be argued that the changes in the VCP's religious policies and practices do not reflect a fundamental modification, much less a rejection, of the party's ideological stance toward religion in general and toward Christianity in particular. On January 2, 2013, the draft amendments were published and the public was invited to make suggestions. Thousands of Vietnamese (myself included) have submitted written suggestions to promote respect for human rights, including religious freedom. Unfortunately the Communist Party refused to accept any constitutional amendment that may jeopardize its total control over society. Most recently, on October 18, 2014, the prime minister of Vietnam Nguyen Tan Dung met with Pope Francis, as a result of which there were high hopes for an exchange of diplomatic relations between the Vatican State and Vietnam in the near future.

Two observations will be made with regard to this point. First, even if the Marxist-Leninist ideology and Ho Chi Minh's political thought still remain the VCP's official philosophy, and while the VCP still controls much of the nation's life, it is undeniable that Communism as a philosophy, though still officially spouted, is little more than an empty slogan that will cause a cynical smirk among the general population, especially the young. As globalization expands its reach in Vietnam, with the concomitant free-market economy and ubiquitous availability of communication media, it will be increasingly difficult if not impossible for the VCP to convince the Vietnamese people of the validity of Communism as a worldview and of socialism as an economic system.

Second, the Vietnamese government's policies toward religion and religious activities are governed by a concern for national security. Their goal is tight control and oversight of religious organizations. The older generations of Vietnamese Communist leaders were still operating under the notion that believers, especially Catholics, were a serious threat to Communism and national independence. In the case of Catholics, the fear was justified, partially at least, until the early 1960s, when the anti-Communist, at times vitriolic, rhetoric was rampant in the Catholic Church as a whole and in Vietnam in particular. The dramatic exodus of over half a million northern Catholics to the south in 1954 was eloquent proof of this. Death rather than coexistence with Communism was the oft-repeated slogan of Vietnamese Catholicism at the time. Such rhetoric was theologically undergirded, to be sure, but it was also motivated by the fear that Communist North Vietnam would take over democratic South Vietnam. This fear was confirmed and exacerbated by the oppressive measures and persecutions that the victorious Communist regime undertook against the Catholic Church, especially between 1975 and 1985.

Four decades of coexistence between Vietnamese Christianity and the Communist regime since 1975 have more than proved that the Christian churches have not been a threat to national security as the older political leaders had feared. A generation of new Communist leaders has come to realize that the Christian churches have been and can certainly be a powerful and irreplaceable ally in the promotion of economic well-being and social justice for all. It is surprising to read the following statement of the Seventh Plenum of the Ninth Party Central Committee on Religion-Oriented Work (March 2003): "Beliefs and religions are the spiritual demand of part of the population, which has been and will be present with the nation in the course of building socialism in our country. Religious believers are part of the national unity block."[26]

It is also encouraging that the same plenum recognizes that religions have a positive role to play in the life of the nation. According to it, one of the tasks of religion-related activities is "to step up a patriotic movement to build a lifestyle of 'good worldly and religious life' among followers, clergies, and religious practitioners from the grass-roots level and to build nationwide solidarity to successfully carry out the cause of renovation, national construction and defense."[27]

Those adamantly opposed to the Vietnamese Communist government do not put much stock in these official declarations of the VCP. "Do not believe what they say, watch what they do," they would probably say. Perhaps a similar retort should be addressed to the Vietnamese Communist leaders: "Do not believe what your predecessors say about Christianity, watch what it does." What Vietnamese Christianity has done in the last four decades has shown beyond doubt that far from being an enemy of the Vietnamese people, Christianity has been an effective contributor to the development of the country in all aspects of life. It has, to quote from the title of the Vietnamese Catholic bishops' famous 1980 pastoral letter, "lived the Gospel in the midst of the people." If the VCP realizes this, it will see that all the cumbersome and practically unenforceable rules and regulations about the "registration" of religious

---

26. Nguyen, *Religious Issues*, 244.
27. Ibid., 140 and 247.

institutions and their purely internal activities for the purpose of state control of religion are totally unnecessary and counterproductive to a vibrant national life. If and when this occurs, religion, and in particular Vietnamese Christianity, will have a bright future and a challenging task ahead.

In the meantime, as long as Vietnam maintains only a one-party political system, Christianity in Vietnam, both Catholic and Protestant, is challenged to find a peaceful *modus vivendi* with which to carry out its mission under a Communist-socialist government.[28] The first challenge concerns the relationship between Christianity and the state. Christianity was and to a certain extent still is perceived as a Western religion that has colluded with Western colonialism and is associated with foreign powers. The Catholic Church is seen as identical with the Vatican city-state (whose nature as a sovereign state distinct from the Holy See is recognized under international law), whereas the Protestant churches are perceived as in collusion with the United States. No doubt the colonialist legacy remains a heavy and scandalous baggage for Vietnamese Christians, which they must honestly acknowledge, even if historically Christian missions have made and continue to make significant contributions to their countries, especially in the fields of education, health care, and social welfare.

The second challenge to being Christian under Communist regimes concerns religious freedom. Christians must continue to press their governments for it since it is an inalienable human right and not a special favor to be secured through under-the-table deals or through diplomatic negotiations between their governments and the Holy See in the case of Roman Catholics. Furthermore, this struggle for religious freedom must be carried out on behalf of all believers and not just for Christians. It should also be pursued in concert with the followers of other religions, in particular Buddhists, as well as with non-believers, since they too suffer from a lack of religious freedom

The third challenge is internal, albeit originally caused by the Communist governments' religious policies, and that is the reconciliation of various groups and divisions in the church itself. These may take the form of patriotism (e.g., the so-called *quoc doanh* [national enterprise] church) vs. allegiance to a foreign power, or competition among different Christian denominations (e.g., Catholics vs. Protestants), or theological differences (e.g., mainline Christianity vs. Pentecostals/Charismatics). That these intra-ecclesial disputes have been exploited by the Communist governments against Christianity is plain and incontrovertible. Fortunately, in recent times, these divisions have been partially bridged through mutual recognition and collaboration, but much work remains to be done. Authentic and full Christian identity depends largely on the success of this ecumenical enterprise.

---

28. Ibid., 140 and 247.

Within this context it would be helpful to ask whether the traditional mis-sionary method of propagating Christianity along denominational lines is still appropriate. Once again we may wonder whether the Communist policy of uniting all Protestant denominations under one umbrella organization has not been a blessing in disguise for Christianity inasmuch as it forced different Christian denominations and communities to work together, a "unity" now being torn apart by the rivalry between the "registered" and "unregistered" churches, surely a *skandalon* to the credibility of the Christian message itself. Raising this question is of course not tantamount to committing oneself to pan- or postdenominationalism, but rather highlights, over against the gen-eral indifference if not skepticism toward church unity in the West in recent years, the urgency of ecumenical unity for Christian identity in Asia. Chris-tian unity, it is to be noted, has become a burning issue with the spectacular rise of Evangelicals and innumerable house churches. These "unregistered" churches, whose membership likely will outstrip that of the "registered" churches, will remain as one of the greatest challenges to Christian identity in Vietnam in the foreseeable future.

The fourth issue concerns the role of the Catholic, mainline Protestant, and Evangelical/Pentecostal churches of the Vietnamese diaspora, especially in the United States, Canada, and Australia. These Vietnamese Christian communities have greater material, academic, and personnel resources at their disposal. What is being advocated here is not old-style financial support and control by mission boards (for Protestants) or the Congregation for the Propagation of the Faith, now known as the Congregation for the Evange-lization of Peoples (for Catholics). The Three-Self Movement, whatever the Communist Party's exploitation of it, must remain the norm for Vietnamese Christianity. Rather, what is being suggested is that the Christian churches that enjoy political freedom and economic prosperity have a particular respon-sibility toward and solidarity with their counterparts in Vietnam, especially in matters of human rights.

The fifth challenge is the encounter with other religions. Though there has been a remarkable change in the position of the Roman Catholic Church toward non-Christian religions, at least since the Second Vatican Coun-cil, interreligious dialogue, even among Vietnamese Catholics, is still in its infancy. Moreover, the attitude of Vietnamese Protestants toward other reli-gions remains by and large condemnatory. An adequate theology of religions remains to be developed that acknowledges the positive role of non-Christian religions for the spiritual well-being of their adherents and Christians them-selves, beyond the so-called exclusivist, inclusivist, and pluralist categories made popular in recent decades. More than anywhere else, in Vietnam being religious is being interreligious, and Christian identity cannot be formed apart from a sincere and humble dialogue with the believers of other faiths and from the reality of multiple religious belonging. This dialogue is not only theological but must involve sharing of life, collaboration for the common good, and sharing of religious experiences.

The sixth, and perhaps the hardest, challenge to being Christian in Communist countries today, Vietnam included, is, ironically, the rapid encroaching of the market economy and rampant materialism and consumerism, especially among the young. Communism as an ideology, though still spouted and propped up by the Communist Party, is fast becoming an empty shell, and party leaders are quite cognizant of this state of affairs and are busy preserving their interests in an eventual postsocialist state. Today the greatest threat to Christianity in the Asian socialist countries is not (or no longer) the oppressive religious policies of the Communist Party or the cultural "dictatorship of relativism" for that matter. Rather it is complete indifference to Christianity as well as to any other religious way of life as the result of a relentless pursuit of wealth and all the pleasures it promises. Religious oppression produces faithful resistance, martyrdom sows seeds of conversion, and relativism at least still takes religion into account by declaring that all religions are equally effective. The threat to Christianity now comes from the new-found faith in the unbounded and unparalleled power of capitalism, whose sole creed is "Greed is good," as the panacea for all ills, the faith that swallows up all other faiths.

Seventeen centuries separate the signing of the Edict of Milan and the promulgation of an amended constitution for Vietnam. Despite their polar contrasts, the two documents share a common policy toward the church, namely, the ability of political authorities to intervene in the internal affairs of the church for the sake of "national security." Constantine was referred to by the church historian Eusebius of Caesarea as "a sort of bishop," and his son and successor Constantius II was styled as *episcopus episcoporum*." Both of them intervened frequently in favor of the church and in its internal affairs, not rarely because they believed that their actions would preserve and strengthen the Roman Empire. In the history of Christian missions in Vietnam in the late eighteenth and nineteenth centuries, there was no lack of high-ranking French missionaries such as Bishop Pierre Pigneau de Béhaine (1741–1799), Bishop François-Marie Pellerin (1813–1862), and Bishop Jean-François Puginier (1835–1892), who dreamed of establishing a Christendom in Vietnam in which the church would exercise a powerful influence on politics and society. In light of these events, it is not difficult to understand, though of course not justify, the Vietnamese Communist Party's efforts to maintain the right to veto all religious activities and organizations it deems detrimental to "national security," which is often a euphemism for party members' privileges and interests.

After half a century of coexistence with Communism, Vietnamese Christians have devised effective strategies for survival and, when persecuted, know how to resist and preserve the faith and have even found in Communism a kindred quest for social justice. Now faced with the near-universal dominance of capitalism, they are at a loss what to do to help their members, especially the young, resist the call of their sirens. It comes as no surprise that the so-called Prosperity Gospel has proved as attractive in Asian Communist countries as in the United States. Consequently, the most difficult challenge to being Christian in Asian Communist countries and in Asia as a whole may no longer be suppression of religious freedom but what to do with religious freedom when most people do not bother about it at all.

5

Chinese Catholics in Vietnam, 1865–2015

A Forgotten History

Seldom in modern times is a church the last refuge for chiefs of state seeking safety from coups d'état. This dubious honor belongs to Saint Francis Xavier church, popularly known as *Nha Tho Cha Tam* [Father Tam Church], in Cholon, Saigon (now Ho Chi Minh City). A brass plaque screwed onto a pew in the back of the church records the fact in English, French, and Chinese: "This is the pew on which the President Ngo Dinh Diem and his brother Ngo Dinh Nhu had sat before they were taken on the tank and were killed on the way to Saigon, on November 2, 1963."

Why Diem and his brother Nhu decided to take refuge in this Chinese parish remained shrouded in mystery. That the parish was under the direction of French priests, of the Société des Missions Étrangères de Paris (MEP), and could presumably offer the two politicians possibilities of negotiation through the French embassy with the generals involved in the coup, was a likely motivation.[1] Another possible reason is that the parish, composed predominantly of ethnic Chinese, was more favorable to the Diem government; indeed, a wealthy Chinese there was a close friend of theirs.[2] A more probable motive is that sensing their imminent ends, the two men, devout Catholics as they were, wanted to prepare themselves spiritually with the last sacraments.

Be that as it may, the name of Saint Francis Xavier church and parish was forever linked with the fate of the first president of the Republic of Vietnam and his brother. As the two walked out of the church, they were arrested by a contingent of soldiers who bound their hands behind their backs and forced

---

1. The pastor of the parish at the time was Fr. Eléazard Joseph Guimet (1919–1995, pastor 1953–1969); and the associate pastors were Fr. Gabriel Marie Joseph Lajeune (1926–, associate pastor 1953–1969) and Fr. Aimé Jean-Baptiste Pinsel (1920–, associate pastor 1953–1974). On E. J. Guimet, G. M. J. Lajeune, and A. J.-B. Pinsel, see http://archives.mepasie.org.

2. The Chinese are believed to have controlled up to 80 percent of the economy of South Vietnam before 1975.

them into an armored personnel carrier. On the way to the army headquarters in Saigon, they were repeatedly stabbed with bayonets and sprayed with bullets. The final moments and the murder of the two Ngo brothers catapulted the hitherto obscure Chinese Catholic parish in Cholon into the limelight of national and international news. It was but a fleeting and unwanted moment of notoriety on the political scene.

In the Vietnamese Catholic world, however, Saint Francis Xavier parish and its church have played a significant and lasting role in the lives of Chinese Catholics in Vietnam in the latter half of the nineteenth century and throughout the twentieth century. This chapter offers a sketch of this Chinese Catholic parish, the only ethnically Chinese parish of its kind in Vietnam, by outlining its origin, development, and current condition as a contribution to the history of world Christianity in the twentieth century that is constituted by transnational and intercontinental migrations.

"HERE THERE IS A VERITABLE BABEL
OF THE LANGUAGES OF CHINA"

In his letter written in Saigon dated September 20, 1865, to the Hong Kong-based procurator [financial officer] of the MEP Napoléon-François Libois (1805–72), Pierre-Marie Philippe (1831–71) spoke of the plan of Bishop Jean-Claude Miche (1805–73), vicar apostolic of the diocese of Western Cochin (Cochinchine occidentale) since 1864, to purchase a piece of land in Cholon, Saigon's Chinatown, located on the city's western bank.[3] Miche had been vicar apostolic to Cambodia and Laos (1850–64), and now as apostolic vicar to Cochinchina, he was anxious to evangelize the locals of his diocese, among whom there were the Chinese inhabitants in Cholon, and had asked Philippe to come to Saigon to undertake the work of evangelizing the Chinese in the Chinatown.[4]

The migration of the Chinese (known in contemporary Vietnamese as *Nguoi Hoa*) dates back to the second century BC; in fact the earliest Vietnamese kings were Chinese descendants. During the turbulent transition from the Western to Eastern Jin dynasty, from the third to the fifth centuries CE, many Chinese were encouraged to migrate from the Shaanxi and Shanxi provinces to the Tonkin area to implement the policy of assimilation of the Vietnamese into the Chinese culture, a process that lasted nearly a thousand years until

---

3. P.-M. Philippe's letter to N.-F. Dubois is found in the MEP Archives in Paris, Section Cochinchine occidentale, 02, 1861–1866, No. 492. On P.-M. Philippe and N.-F. Libois, see http://archives.mepasie.org.

4. On J. C. Miche, see http://archives.mepasie.org.

the Vietnamese established their independence from China in 938 under the leadership of Ngo Quyen. There were sporadic migrations of Chinese to Vietnam between the tenth and fifteenth centuries, but they were required to renounce their Chinese nationality and adapt to Vietnamese customs as conditions for their stay.

A large number of Chinese escaped to Vietnam when the Ming dynasty fell to the Manchu in 1644, and the majority of them chose to settle in Hue, Hoi An, and especially in Cochinchina, where they were not required to follow the Vietnamese way of life and were able to function as independent fiefdoms. In the early part of the eighteenth century, more Chinese sought economic trade with Vietnam, and two groups of Chinese migrants emerged: the early comers, mostly refugees of the Ming dynasty, known as the *Ming Huong* Chinese, and the migrants of the Qing dynasty, known as the *Thanh Nhan* Chinese.

These two groups settled mostly in Hoi An, Cholon, and the Mekong Delta, where they monopolized the export of rice to Southeast Asian countries. This economic hegemony greatly irked the Nguyen dynasty, who enacted several measures to control Chinese trade and to assimilate them culturally. During the French colonization of Vietnam from 1860 onward, Chinese immigration to Vietnam increased exponentially. Thanks to the Convention of Peking, part of the so-called Unequal Treaty, the Chinese were allowed to seek employment overseas, and the French government greatly favored the coming of the Chinese to Vietnam as laborers and merchants to stimulate trade and industry. Between the 1870s and the 1890s, some 20,000 Chinese settled in Cochinchina, mostly in Cholon; another 600,000 arrived in the 1920s and the 1930s. It is in the latter part of the nineteenth century that the story of the Chinese Catholics in Vietnam began.[5]

In his 1865 letter to Libois mentioned above, Philippe reported that he went to see the property four days after his arrival in Saigon and met with the (subsequently infamous adventurer) François Garnier (1839–73), the interim prefect of Cholon, who told him of the colonial government's plan to build in Cholon, in addition to the living quarters for missionaries, the city hall, a hospital for the Chinese, a school for boys and another for girls, and a chapel for the hospital, which would also serve as a church for the missionaries. Since this building project would take a long time, Garnier provided the missionaries with two Vietnamese-style thatch-roof houses, one serving as the chapel and the other as the home for the missionaries.

---

5. For accounts of the migration and commercial activities of the Chinese in Vietnam, see *Water Frontiers: Commerce and the Chinese in the Lower Mekong Region, 1750–1880*, ed. Nola Cooke and Tana Li (Lanham, MD: Rowman & Littlefield, 2004); and Tran Khanh, *Ethnic Chinese and Economic Development in Vietnam* (New York: Palgrave, 1993).

Philippe's first impression of Cholon was one of extreme linguistic confu-
sion. Cholon, he said, is "a veritable Babel of the languages of China."[6] He
told Libois, however, that if he had another missionary who could speak the
language of Hunan, the two of them could manage the work since he was
told that the language of Hunan is very close to the languages of Fujian and
Chaozhou.[7] While this missionary could work with the Chinese who spoke
these three languages, he (Philippe) could take care of the Chinese who spoke
Mandarin, Cantonese, and Hakka.[8] Fortunately, Philippe added, their work
would be facilitated by the fact that the Chinese population in Cholon was
concentrated in a narrow area of about three square kilometers. There were,
he estimated, 30,000 Chinese in Cholon, 6,000 in Saigon, and 300 in Cho
Quan. Of these Chinese there were only 180 to 200 Christians speaking different languages.

In another letter dated the same day to the associate procurator Pierre
Osouf (1829–1906, since 1877 bishop of Northern Japan),[9] Philippe reiter-
ated almost verbatim the same information about the colonial government's
building projects, the Chinese population in Saigon and Cholon, the number of Chinese Catholics, and their linguistic diversity.[10] To this he appended
a long list of things he requested to be sent to him, among which were the
twenty-ninth volume of Kangxi Chinese dictionary and a Chinese almanac so
that he could prepare the Christian calendar for the Chinese.

Thus began, in 1865, the Catholic mission to the Chinese in Vietnam.
Philippe continued to work among the Chinese in Cholon until 1869 when
his ill health forced him to return to France where he died in 1871 at the
age of 39. During his four-year work in Cholon, Philippe regularly reported
the progress of the establishment of the Chinese Catholic community and his
activities in his letters to Libois and Osouf.[11] On the economic condition of

---

6. "Ici c'est une vraie Babel des langues de la Chine."

7. About 57 percent of the Chinese in Vietnam speak the Fujian and Chaozhou languages.

8. "S'il y avait avec moi un missionaire parlant la langue de Haïnan, nous pourrions nous
tirer d'affaires, car on dit que cette langue a beaucoup de rapport avec celle de Fokien et de
Tchaotscheou. Alors ce missionnaire s'occuperait des gens parlant ces 3 patois et moi j'aurais les
gens parlant mandarin, cantonais et hakka."

9. On Pierre Osouf, see http://archives.mepasie.org.

10. P.-M. Philippe's letter to P. Osouf is found in MEP Archives in Paris, Section
Cochinchine occidentale, 02, 1861–1866, No. 493.

11. In addition to the letter to Osouf mentioned above, Philippe wrote twelve more letters to
his superior, which are found in the MEP Archives in Paris, Section Cochinchine occidentale, 02,
1861–1866, numbered 494, 501, 506, 513, 525, 536, 544, 547, 556/1, 562, 569, 590. Philippe
also wrote six more letters to Libois, found in the same archives, numbered 510, 517, 526, 532,
556/2, 591. Finally, he also wrote a letter, numbered 571, to the administrative council of the
seminary of the MEP in Paris defending himself against the rumor that he did not intend to stay
in Vietnam until his death.

the Chinese in Cholon he noted that two vices were keeping them in poverty, namely, gambling and smoking opium.[12]

In the letter dated October 22, 1865, he reported that his latest census showed that there were 109 Catholics and that many of them had not been able to go to confession for seven or eight years for lack of priests who could speak their languages. He also added that he had about twenty to twenty-five catechumens, without counting the sick at the hospital in Cho Quan. In a letter dated January 31, 1866, he reported that he had confessed some sixty Chinese Catholics and had about forty catechumens. He noted that conversions were rare among the Cantonese Chinese, because of their moral "disorders," spiritual "hardening," and "pride," and also among the Fujian Chinese, because of their "apathy," whereas the Hakka Chinese were more disposed to conversion.[13] In a later letter to Osouf, dated February 24, 1866, he asks the now-procurator to send him a Hakka-speaking catechist. Philippe also mentioned the work of the Sisters of Saint Paul de Chartres, especially in the hospital in Cho Quan, among them a young Cantonese sister who was "a real apostle among her compatriots."[14] Several times he mentioned the mother superior of the Sisters of Saint Paul de Chartres by the name of Benjamin, who, as we shall see, would play an important, albeit indirect, role in the life of the Chinese Catholic community in Cholon.[15]

FRANCIS XAVIER TAM ASSOU AND *NHA THO CHA TAM*

The building projects for the Chinese Catholics which Garnier, for whom Philippe had the greatest admiration, promised did not come to fruition

---

12. In Letter no. 513, Philippe mentions that Mr. Garnier was vehemently opposed to the use of opium and gambling among the Chinese: "deux choses qui amènent à la pauvreté dans les familles en ruinant les fortunes et empêchent la prospérité de la colonie, tout étant des obstacles à l'entrée de ces gens adonnés au jeu et à l'opium dans la religion chrétienne."

13. Letter no. 532: "Il n'y a guères que les Cantonais proprement dit qui, ici comme dans leur province, se font remarquer par leurs désordres et leur endurcissement à ne pas ouvrir les yeux à la vérité." A little later, Philippe writes, "D'ailleurs les Cantonais ne se convertissent pas, dit-on, à cause de leur orgueil, les Fokinois à cause de leur apathie."

14. Letter no. 532: "Et à Choquan il y a une petite soeur chinoise des environs de Canton qui est une véritable apôtre pour ses compatriotes."

15. Philippe notes that the Sisters of Saint Paul de Chartres would be working at the hospital where there were many Chinese patients and hopes that there would be many conversions. He notes with pleasure that the sisters were better appreciated in Vietnam than in Canton. Letter no. 526: "Un peu plus tard des Soeurs de Saint Paul de Chartres (*qu'on estime un peu mieux ici qu'à Canton* [emphasis in the original]) viendront prendre soin des malades d'un hopital chinois que l'on y construit aux frais de la ville."

until October 1866. In his letter to Osouf dated October 20, 1866, Philippe mentioned that the governor of the colony had given him twelve thousand franks to build a church in Cholon. Earlier in the year, a small house was bought on the then-Rue des Marins for use as a church. In 1866, the governor general of Cochinchina Pierre de Lagrandière (1807–76) paid a visit to the church during his tour of Cholon. Distressed by its dilapidated condition, the governor decided to use public funds to build a new church. Philippe joked that with this sum he could not pretend to build a basilica to rival that of Canton, but it would be, he admitted, "quite lovely nevertheless when it is finished."[16] Philippe hoped that the church would be ready for Easter the following year. This is the second church built for the Chinese Catholics in Vietnam on Paris Street, today located at 203 Hung Vuong Street, District 14, County 5, Saigon, were one to count the old house on the Rue des Marins as the first.

In a letter to his superior Libois dated October 20, 1866, Philippe mentioned the governor's financial gift for the building of the church but also noted with regret that he had not baptized as many as he had projected eight months earlier. He had baptized only eighteen adults, not counting forty at the hospital in Cho Quan *in articulo mortis*. Furthermore, the May–July French military campaigns forced many of his recent converts to go to Singapore and Thailand or to return to China to look for work. He lamented that he was the only missionary working for the Chinese since he was able to speak four of their six languages. (He excused himself for not being able to learn Vietnamese.)

After the departure of Pierre-Marie Philippe, the Chinese Catholic community experienced a decline, not least due to the frequent turnover of pastors and linguistic difficulties.[17] In 1898, noting the alarming decline in the number of Chinese Catholics—in 1891 there were 365 but only 40 in 1898—Bishop Jean-Marie Dépierre (1855–99) sent a Chinese priest, Francis Xavier Tam Assou, to revive the community. His thirty-six-year ministry (1898–1934) in the parish surely earns him the title of the Second Founder of the Chinese Catholic parish in Cholon, alongside that of Pierre-Marie Philippe; it was not

---

16. Letter no. 590: "Il est vrai qu'avec cette somme je ne prétends pas élever une basilique capable de rivaliser avec celle de Canton, mais elle sera tout de même bien jolie quand elle sera terminée."

17. After Philippe (1865–69), the following MEP priests were pastors or associate pastors of the Chinese Catholic community until the appointment of Francis Xavier Tam Assou in 1898: Jean-Joseph-Rémi Delpech (1869–73); Édouard Le Vincent (1873–75); François-Constant Derval and Félix Humbert (1875–76); Charles-Jean Baptiste Jacquemin (1876–79); Henri-Martin Brillet (1879–84); Jacques-Alexis Hirbec (1884–85); Louis-Marie Joseph Martin (1885–90); Lucien Mossard (1890–91, later vicar apostolic to Saigon); Charles Boutier (1891–95); Émile-François-Marie Moreau (1895–98).

for nothing that its church was popularly known as *Nha Tho Cha Tam* (Father Tam church).[18]

Francis Xavier Tam Assou (his Vietnamese name is Tam) was born in Macau in 1855. His parents sent him and his brother to the Sisters of Saint Paul de Chartres in Hong Kong. He was baptized by Bishop François-Marie Pellerin, vicar apostolic to Hanoi. After his brother's death, Francis Xavier, then eight years old, was taken by Mother Benjamin, mentioned above, to Saigon, where she entrusted him to the care of Pierre-Marie Philippe, then pastor of the Chinese Catholic parish in Cholon, where he learned the Fujian and Hakka languages. When he was thirteen, Philippine sent him to Penang for minor seminary studies, where he stayed for six years. At nineteen, he returned to Saigon, where he entered the major seminary. After his ordination to the priesthood in 1882 by Bishop Émile Genest Auguste Colombet (1849–1933), Father Tam was appointed associate pastor at the Saigon cathedral and teacher at the Taberd high school, where he served for sixteen years.

As mentioned above, in 1898 Fr. Tam was sent to the Chinese Catholic parish. He began planning to build a church to replace the church built in 1866 and found a piece of land of three hectares in the heart of Cholon. Unfortunately, the land was owned by nine different persons and could be sold only with the consent of all the owners. After an arduous but successful search for the owners who had moved to different parts of the country, Fr. Tam began constructing a church in Gothic style on what is today Tran Hung Dao Street, District 5. On December 3, 1900, the feast of Saint Francis Xavier, Bishop Lucien Mossard laid the cornerstone for the new church, and on January 10, 1902, he solemnly consecrated it. After the construction of the church, Fr. Tam built a school, a kindergarten, a boarding house, and several rental properties on the parish property. The number of Chinese Catholics then was four hundred.

Fr. Tam died in 1934 and was buried in the church. He was succeeded by Fr. John Baptist Huynh Tinh Huong (1934–49), who as a seminarian had played an extensive role in the construction of the church. Unfortunately, Saint Francis Xavier parish went through another period of decline and did not experience a renaissance until the return of the MEP priests in 1952 as pastors and with the help of a host of Vietnamese associate pastors.[19] In 1952 Fr. Robert Lebas opened a chapel in District 1 (today Our Lady of Peace par-

---

18. For a brief history of the parish, the building of the churches, and Fr. Tam Assou in Vietnamese, see http://titocovn.com.

19. The pastors who followed Fr. Huynh Tinh Huong until the fall of South Vietnam in 1975 were Maurice Bach Van Le (1949–52); Robert Lebas (1952–53); Joseph Guimet (1953–69, with several associate pastors); and Gabriel Lajeune (1969–76, with several associate pastors).

ish). In 1953 Fr. Joseph Guimet built a chapel in Binh Tay (today Binh Phuoc parish). In 1960 a minor seminary was founded at Our Lady of Peace parish to recruit Chinese boys for the priesthood.

In 1962 Fr. Guimet built another chapel for the Chinese in Phu Lam (today the Glorious Manifestation of Jesus parish). In 1963 another minor seminary named after Saint Charles was opened in Phu Lam. In 1968 Fr. Guimet built a church in honor of Saint Joseph on An Binh Street (today Saint Joseph parish). In the same year Fr. Gabriel Lajeune bought two more buildings to be used as a chapel (today Binh Thoi parish). In 1972, a pastoral council was established for Saint Francis Xavier parish, and its constitution and regulations were approved by Archbishop Nguyen Van Binh on December 30, 1972.

In 1974 the archdiocese of Saigon decreed that the pastors of Saint Francis Xavier parish were charged with the pastoral care of Vietnamese Catholics of Chinese descent all over Vietnam as well as with advising all the bishops in matters regarding the evangelization of Vietnamese Catholics of Chinese descent.

The missionaries' labors with the Chinese Catholics in Vietnam over a century, from 1865 to 1975, were abundantly blessed. In 1975 the number of parishioners at Saint Francis Xavier alone was 8,000, among whom there were 17 major seminarians and 32 minor seminarians. In addition, there were two religious societies for men and women, Saint John the Baptist and Saint Teresa, one minor seminary, one social center for Chinese Catholics, three chapels, three middle schools, four elementary schools, 118 rental apartments, one catechism school, one monthly newspaper, and one group of catechists who worked in all the provinces. In March 1975 Archbishop Nguyen Van Binh entrusted to the pastors of Saint Francis parish the direct administration of all the churches and institutions of the Chinese Catholics in the entire country.

AFTER 1975: THE PHOENIX RISING FROM THE ASHES

In December 2012 I visited Saint Francis Xavier parish and its church for the first time. The day was unbearably hot, humid, and overcast. I was received by the current pastor, Fr. Stephen Huynh Tru. Through a friend of mine I had tried to contact him, though he did not respond to me directly. A Vietnamese of Chinese descent, Fr. Tru spoke fluent Chinese and Vietnamese. He was in his late fifties, somewhat short, and thin. He was dressed in a white short-sleeved shirt, black pants, and sandals. He knew me only by reputation and had been told that I was coming to see him. He welcomed me into the rectory located on the right side of the church. At first his demeanor, though warm, was cautious and diffident, and later I understood why.

For the Vietnamese Catholic Church as a whole, the victory of Communist North Vietnam over the Republic of Vietnam was a disaster. This was also true of the Chinese Catholic parish in Cholon. In 1976 the last MEP pastor of Saint Francis Xavier parish, Fr. Gabriel Lajeune, was expelled. In his place Fr. Tru was appointed pastor. He had been an associate pastor at the parish from 1974 to 1976. However, after two years at his post (1976–78), for security reasons he had to go on leave. Fr. Dominic Nguyen Xuan Hy was appointed pastor (1979–80). Only in 1980 could he come back to the parish and was appointed pastor again and has been functioning in this capacity until today. Having suffered interrogations by the Communist agents for two years, Fr. Tru was understandably suspicious of anyone inquiring about the parish and its past, especially someone who comes from abroad. Indeed, during our conversation he repeatedly cautioned me not to trust strangers and supporters of Communism.

Eventually, however, he opened up and became deeply grateful that I wanted to write a history of his parish. I asked him about the historical records of the parish, and he told me that, sadly, during the first years of the Communist rule, the associate pastor of the parish, fearing possible incrimination, had all of them burned. He told me how after 1975 most of the parish's properties, except the church, were confiscated by the Communist government and a large number of Chinese Catholics emigrated. He pointed to a multistory building under construction on the former land of the parish overshadowing the church, presumably to be used as a hotel.

He then gave me a tour of the church and the two-story building on the left side of the church where various souvenirs of the church were stored. The church, inside and outside, is in excellent condition, having undergone recent repairs, with a new roof in 2011. In 2010 a high and imposing throne covered by a red and blue roof in Chinese-Vietnamese style was built in front of the church to house a large statue of Our Lady of Lourdes. The juxtaposition of Asian artistic style and Gothic architecture is jarring, and one cannot escape the feeling that the present complex is but a pale and pinched reflection of its former glory.

Fr. Tru's memories of Saint Francis Xavier parish in the pre-Communist era were suffused with nostalgia and sadness. So much has been achieved by and for the Chinese Catholics in Vietnam, and so much has been lost. But he was far from despondent. He spoke with pride of the recent renovations in the church. But more than material achievements he was proud of the vibrant spiritual life of the parish. There are two Masses a day, one in Vietnamese and the other in Chinese. On Sundays there are seven Masses, four for the Vietnamese and three for the Chinese. Attendance is always overflowing. There are four catechism classes for adult catechumens and fifteen for youth.

There are also marriage-preparation classes. Parish activities are coordinated by two pastoral councils, one Chinese and the other Vietnamese, and there are twenty-two associations and societies of various types, both religious and secular.

One cannot but notice that the predominantly Chinese character of Saint Francis Xavier parish, the only parish for the ethnic Chinese in Vietnam, has shifted to the Vietnamese population, which is now the majority of its members. In a sense, the two communities, the Chinese and the Vietnamese, are like two dragons twisted around each other, but this time not in order to dominate the other but to support the other. It is in this mutual Christian love that the phoenix of Saint Francis Xavier parish will rise again from its ashes.[20]

20. Fr. Tru has been assisted by the following associate pastors since 1980: Dominic Nguyen Xuan Hy (1980–2006); Joseph Doan van Thinh (1980–85); Martin Do Van Diep (1980–89); Louis To Minh Quang (1980–91); John Baptist Nguyen Van Hieu (1992–99); Peter Nguyen Van Tam (1998–2002); Joseph Dinh Duc Thinh (2002–9); and Francis Tran Duc Huan (2009–). I am deeply grateful to Mr. Tran Van Canh who generously provided me photocopies of the archival materials at the MEP Archives in Paris relevant to the Chinese Catholics in Vietnam and the Saint Francis Xavier parish. I am also deeply grateful to Fr. Huynh Van Tru for his gracious hospitality and assistance.

Part II

THEOLOGY

6

Doing Theology in World Christianities

Old Tasks, New Ways

It is intriguing that the last two volumes of the monumental nine-volume *The Cambridge History of Christianity* bear the subtitle *World Christianities*. Volume 8, edited by Sheridan Gilley and Brian Stanley, covers the history of Christianity of the nineteenth century (c. 1815–c. 1914),[1] and volume 9, edited by Hugh McLeod, that of the twentieth century (c. 1914–c. 2000).[2] What happened, one wonders, to Christianity in these two centuries that justifies describing it with the new sobriquet of "World Christianities," qualifying this Christianity as "world" and using "Christianity" in the plural? By giving this unusual title only to the last two volumes of the series, does *The Cambridge History of Christianity* imply that the Christianity that is narrated in volumes 1 through 7 was neither "world" nor "Christianities"?

The answer to the above question depends, of course, on what is connoted by both "world" and "Christianities." If by "world" is meant that Christianity is universal and open to all peoples and to all regions of the world—another expression for this is "catholic"—and if by "Christianities" is meant that Christianity is variegated in self-definition, cultural and confessional ethos, doctrinal formulation, liturgical worship, and organizational structure, then Christianity has undoubtedly been so since its very beginnings. Indeed, the goal of the first volume of *The Cambridge History of Christianity*, entitled *Origins to Constantine*, as stated by its editors Margaret M. Mitchell and Frances M. Young, is to emancipate past historiography from a schematized view of early Christianity as a uniform and invariant institution.[3] Indeed, as the

---

1. Sheridan Gilley and Brian Stanley, eds., *The Cambridge History of Christianity: World Christianities c.1815–c.1914* (Cambridge: Cambridge University Press, 2006).

2. Hugh McLeod, ed., *The Cambridge History of Christianity: World Christianities c.1914–c.2000* (Cambridge: Cambridge University Press, 2006).

3. Margaret M. Mitchell and Frances M. Young, eds., *The Cambridge History of Christianity: Origins to Constantine* (Cambridge: Cambridge University Press, 2006).

editors put it tersely, "the recognition of diversity within Christianity from the very beginning has transformed [the] study of its origins."[4]

While catholicity ("world") and diversity ("Christianities") are arguably constant features of Christianity as a whole, a persuasive case can be made that Christianity of the nineteenth and twentieth centuries is so different from that of the previous eighteen centuries in geographical expansion and internal diversity that it alone deserves to be dubbed "world Christianities." Curiously, neither Sheridan Gilley in his introduction to volume 8 nor its other contributors themselves use the expression "world Christianities." But the fact that, as Gilley notes, contrary to most other histories of eighteenth-century Christianity, this volume dedicates nearly a third of its six hundred pages to the new Christian churches outside Europe is an eloquent testimony to the transformation of eighteenth-century Christianity into a truly "world," or global, and highly diversified religion.

While still implicit in volume 8, the concept of world Christianities is elaborated at length in the next volume. Noting "the development of Christianity from a mainly European and American religion to a worldwide religion," its editor, Hugh McLeod, points out that one of its five major themes is that "Christianity becomes a worldwide religion."[5] Indeed, the entire volume can be viewed as offering a documentation of this global expansion of Christianity (Part II: Narratives of Change) and of the resulting variations and multiplicities within Christianity as it sought to respond to the many and diverse challenges of the modern and postmodern age (Part III: Social and Cultural Impact).

Of course, *The Cambridge History of Christianity* is not the only work, nor the first, that highlights the global and multiple character of contemporary Christianity. There has recently been a plethora of scholarly and popular studies in church history as well as—perhaps especially—in missiology, new journals and periodicals, courses and programs, and centers and institutes at both universities and seminaries that make world Christianities or Christianity in the non-Western world the object of research and teaching.

The immediate impact of the concept of world Christianities is, of course, on the discipline of church history, or, more accurately, history of Christianity, as evidenced by *The Cambridge History of Christianity*.[6] Another academic dis-

---

4. Ibid., xiii.

5. McLeod, ed., *World Christianities c.1914–c.2000*, 6.

6. On the distinction between "church history" and "history of Christianity," see Peter C. Phan, "World Christianity: Its Implications for History, Religious Studies, and Theology," *Horizons* 39, no. 2 (2012): 171–88. On how the concept of "world Christianities" demands new ways of doing church history, see the insightful and challenging works by Justo L. González, *The Changing Shape of Church History* (St. Louis: Chalice Press, 2002); and Paul V. Kollman, "After Church History? Writing the History of Christianity from a Global Perspective," *Horizons* 31, no. 2 (2004): 322–42.

cipline that has been significantly impacted by this view of world Christianity is missiology. Works by renowned missiologists such as David Bosch, Andrew Walls, Lamin Sanneh, Robert Schreiter, and Stephen Bevans, to cite only a few, have shifted the focus of mission from evangelization by foreign missionaries to the building of the local churches by native Christians, thereby contributing to the indigeneity and variety of Christianities.

In their comprehensive survey of world Christianity Sebastian Kim and Kirsteen Kim spell out six aspects in which Christianity as a "world religion" can be studied. Topographically, the mapping of Christianity will take into account its local varieties and types throughout the globe. Theologically, Christianity's claim to be both universally applicable and locally inclusive will need to be taken seriously. Geographically, its presence and impact in all parts of the globe must be recognized. Socio-politically, its diversities and multiplicities will be seen mainly as the result of attempts by indigenous and grassroots communities and not by expatriate missionaries to contextualize the Christian faith. Historically, Christianity's global expansion was never carried out by and from a single geographical and ecclesiastical center, exporting and imposing a homogeneous and identical form; rather Christianity was polycentric from its very beginnings, expanded in different directions and in diffuse fashion, and adapted itself to each locale and context. Lastly, structurally, Christianity is shown to be a transnational and transcontinental movement constituted by complex networks of diverse kinds.[7]

A parallel focus on the impact of world Christianities on systematic theology is also emerging, especially on the way theology should be done (methodology) and on how the various *loci theologici* are to be reformulated (systematics). Regrettably, theology has not yet dealt with the concept of world Christianities with the same vigor and intensity as the history of Christianity and missiology. One reason for this relative paucity of interest is that systematic theologians, whose field is doctrine, generally tend to be more concerned with permanence and less sensitive to historical changes than their colleagues in history and missiology. Furthermore, it comes as no surprise that most of the theological effort to respond to the challenges of world Christianities has so far taken place in the so-called Third World (or Two-Thirds or Majority World), that is, Africa, Asia, and Latin America, where new types and forms of Christianity are proliferating. However, Third-World theologians generally do not enjoy the same academic status as their Western colleagues, and their writings are for the most part unknown, unless they come under scrutiny and censure by ecclesiastical authorities, especially in the Catholic Church.

In what follows I will focus on the challenges of world Christianities to the theological enterprise, and more specifically, to dogmatic/systematic/

---

7. See Sebastian Kim and Kirsteen Kim, *Christianity as a World Religion* (London: Bloomsbury, 2013).

constructive theology, leaving to others the task of reflecting on its implications for other subdisciplines such as biblical, historical, moral, and practical theologies. I will first examine, under the rubric of "Theology in World Christianities: Old Tasks, New Ways," the new methods in which theology is being performed in world Christianities. Next, to flesh out this methodological section, I illustrate these new ways of doing theology with concrete examples on some key *loci theologici* taken from different parts of the Christian world ("Theologies *in* World Christianities"). Finally, I indicate how "world Christianities" entails a new understanding of Christianity itself ("Theology *of* Christianities").[8]

Critics of the notion of world Christianities point out that Christianity has always been diverse and indigenized, and therefore one must not overstate its alleged novelty. This might well be the case, since nothing is utterly new under the sun, and the caution against overstatement is well taken. However, it is beyond doubt that the change from Christianity as Christendom during the so-called Constantinian era to Christianity as world Christianities in the sense indicated above is so radical that it is perfectly legitimate to use the over-wrought, but in this case exquisitely accurate, expression "paradigm shift" to characterize it. Nowhere is this paradigm shift more evident, I contend, than in systematic theology.

THEOLOGY IN WORLD CHRISTIANITIES:
OLD TASKS, NEW WAYS

Theology as faith seeking understanding—*fides quaerens intellectum*, to use Anselm's celebrated definition—is as ancient as Christianity, but this old task is carried out in ever new ways throughout the course of Christian history, searching for understandings and practices of the faith that would be appropriate to different socio-political, economic, cultural, and religious contexts, as any historical survey of Christian theology readily shows. All theologies, without exception, just as rationality itself, are therefore unavoidably context-dependent, and any theology's pretensions to universal applicability and permanent validity can easily be unmasked as symptoms of either intellectual naiveté or hegemonic ambition. The question then is not whether world Christianities can or should shape theological method but rather *how* they actually do so. To see the impact of world Christianities on theology in recent decades one convenient way is to examine how they have affected the deployment of the six "sources," or to use John Macquarrie's expression "formative factors," of theology. Let us briefly consider each.

---

8. For a more extensive explanation of the concept of "world Christianities," see Phan, "World Christianity," 171–88.

1. *Experience.* Since theology is, to use Gustavo Gutiérrez's celebrated phrase, "critical reflection on praxis" that "rises only at sundown,"[9] its matrix must be the various concrete contexts in which world Christianities are located. In the West, at least since the eighteenth century, the primary experience for theology consists of such cultural shibboleths as secularism, atheism, agnosticism, and relativism, against which Christian thinkers have devised a whole array of philosophical arguments in defense of theism and objective truth. No doubt these Enlightenment-inspired ideologies are also present outside the West, but in these non-Western countries the pervasive reality from which theology arises is not centered on these epistemological and metaphysical issues but upon massive and dehumanizing material poverty and oppression bolstered by economic and political structures. Elsewhere, in Africa and Asia, the destructive legacy of Western colonialism has been enormous, and now, insidious and manifold forms of neocolonialist capitalism, with its Western models of economic development through monetization and technological modernization, are reducing millions of people who used to live on a subsistence economy to abject poverty because they have no role and are of no use in a global market economy. These new forms of economic domination challenge world Christianities to find new ways to speak about God and things pertaining to God.

Besides poverty, other forms of oppression such as racism, classism, and patriarchalism confront theology in as well as outside the West. Ecological degradation is another pressing worldwide issue. Other problems of global character include stateless terrorism, violence, and national and international migrations. By contrast, some problems are peculiar to certain countries such as the caste system, tribalism, and communalism. In light of these very diverse contemporary experiences many theologians in non-Western Christianities have abandoned an introspective, spiritualistic, and individualistic conceptions of experience as the context for theology. Instead they expand the nature of theology as *sapientia* (wisdom) and *sacra scientia* (rational knowledge) by doing theology as critical reflection on praxis that is animated by the "option for the poor" (*orthopraxis*). The basic questions for theology in world Christianities are therefore about *which* and *whose* experiences should be both its source and its hermeneutical lens.

2. *Revelation.* God's self-communication in the history of Israel and supremely in Jesus of Nazareth remains of course the definitive norm (*norma normans*) for Christian theology. However, more than ever, world Christianities are encountering other religions that also claim to be recipients of divine revelation, such as Hinduism with its *sruti* (that which is heard), Islam with its Qur'an, and the Church of the Latter Day Saints with its *Book of Mormon*,

---

9. Gustavo Gutiérrez, *A Theology of Liberation*, trans. Sister Caridad Inda and John Eagleson (Maryknoll, NY: Orbis Books, 1991), 9.

not to mention a host of other recent religious movements and sects with their respective founders' religious experiences and recorded utterances (e.g., the Unification Church, or the Moonies, with its "Divine Principle"). Whereas Christian theology has until recently limited itself to considering divine revelation exclusively in Israel and in Christianity, especially in the context of Jewish-Christian dialogue, theologians in world Christianities are today challenged to consider the possibility of divine revelation as the in-breaking and disclosure of Holy Mystery in religions other than Judaism and Christianity and relate it to God's self-gift in Jesus Christ. This in turn leads to a systematic reconceptualization of God, Christ, the Holy Spirit, church, and other *loci theologici.*

3. *Scripture.* Intimately connected with the possibility of divine revelation outside Judaism and Christianity is scripture. As alluded to above, many religions other than Judaism and Christianity possess scriptures whose origins are also attributed to divine communication and which are venerated as the inspired Word of God. Furthermore, even religions that do not claim divine origin have sacred texts, such as Buddhism (the Tripitaka), Jainism (the *Agamas*), Sikhism (the *Guru Granth Sahib*), Zoroastrianism (the *Avesta*), Confucianism (the Four Books and Five Classics), and Daoism (the *Daodejing*). In world Christianities, particularly in Asia, where Christians regularly encounter the followers of other religious traditions, it is imperative to reexamine the Christian doctrine of biblical inspiration and canonicity in light of the existence of non-Christian scriptures and sacred texts, especially in interreligious dialogue and shared religious rituals and prayer services.

In this connection the issue of biblical hermeneutics often comes up for discussion. Whereas in the West biblical scholars for the most part have adopted the historical-critical method and interpret the Bible as a self-standing text, and in some cases, only intratextually, theologians in other world Christianities are urged to practice an intertextual and even interreligious reading of sacred texts. This is the project of the emerging disciplines of cross-cultural and interreligious hermeneutics and "comparative theology." On the other hand, an almost opposite hermeneutical approach is widespread in several world Christianities, particularly those associated with Pentecostalism, the fastest-growing Christian church in Africa, Latin America, and in some Asian countries such as China. It privileges biblical elements that are largely dismissed in mainline churches such as prophecy, exorcism, glossolalia, and miraculous healing.[10] Thus theologians in world Christianities can no longer assume the historical-critical method that is regnant in Western academy as the standard, nor limit themselves to practicing an exclusively intratextual hermeneutics.

---

10. This point is strongly made by Philip Jenkins, *The New Faces of Christianity: Believing the Bible in the Global South* (Oxford: Oxford University Press, 2006).

4. *Tradition.* Also under intense debate in world Christianities is the nature of tradition and above all what should count as tradition. Rejection of tradition does take the form of *sola scriptura*, especially in Pentecostal churches of world Christianities. By and large however the necessity of tradition is readily acknowledged, particularly in cultures, such as those of Asian societies, where tradition is generally given a normative role. Rather, the debate centers on what should count as normative tradition. Ironically, Vincent of Lérins's triple canon formulated in his celebrated dictum, "That which has been believed everywhere (*ubique*), always (*semper*), and by all (*ab omnibus*)," which is commonly appealed to in conservative circles in defense of tradition, is given a new and surprising twist in light of world Christianities.[11] Geographical ubiquity, temporal antiquity, and numerical universality, which are often attributed to Western tradition as proof of its universality and normativity, are now turned on their heads. For the first time, it is argued, these three Vincentian criteria of Christian orthodoxy have been met—albeit never perfectly and unambiguously: Only in world Christianities is "everywhere" found, "always" instantiated, and "by all" realized. In world Christianities, the Western tradition of the past as well as the present is not given a privileged, much less normative, status. Western Christianity is not related to world Christianities as center to periphery with all the privileges attendant to the center; rather it is only one Christianity among other Christianities, no more, no less, and its traditions, often maintained through power and imposed by force, legal and otherwise, must be seen for what they really are: local, context dependent, and culture-bound historical particularities.

Needless to say, it is in local traditions that world Christianities embody their specific differences and peculiarities. These traditions embrace each and every aspect of church life: Bible translation, liturgical language, sacramental celebration, worship, prayer, sacred object, art and architecture, music, canon law, organizational structure, theology, spirituality, and so on. In world Christianities, variety in tradition is not simply the result of adapting previously existing—mainly Western—traditions to different local contexts through the process of translation, linguistic and cultural, though admittedly this did happen extensively thanks to the work of expatriate missionaries. Rather, in world Christianities new traditions are constantly "manufactured," especially in Pentecostal and Independent churches, with staggering variety and dazzling ingenuity, in a process of "globalization from below." This independent and unrestrained proliferation of traditions, often the work of charismatic leaders

---

11. The best critical edition of Vincent of Lérins's *Commonitorium* is by Roland Demeulenaere in Corpus Christianorum Series Latina 64 (1985), 127–95. An older edition, with a very informative introduction, is Reginald Stewart Moxon, *The Commonitorium of Vincent of Lérins* (Cambridge: Cambridge University Press, 1915). On the implications of Vincent of Lérins's teaching for the question of truth, see Chapter 9.

and without local, national, and international consultation and agreement, poses a serious threat to faithfulness to the Christian faith and church unity. How to achieve this faithfulness and unity without falling into uniformity and fostering "the tradition of the dead" is one of the most difficult tasks for theology in world Christianities.[12]

5. *Culture*. Nothing is more conspicuous in world Christianities than the fact that the gospel is expressed in a mind-boggling variety of languages and cultures, at times even within the same country, such as Indonesia with its more than seven hundred spoken languages.[13] Beneath the language lies a worldview or a common pattern of thought and behavior into which the Christian faith is contextualized, indigenized, or inculturated. Culture, in contrast to nature, is a human construction, and in the process of cultural creation, the powerful often arrogate for themselves the right to determine what belongs to culture and what does not, what is true and normal and what is false and deviant, and thus only what serves their interest is acceptable as culture. Furthermore, even where there is no conscious attempt at domination, certain cultural achievements by the elite are elevated to the status of "classical" or "high" culture, which alone deserves propagation and preservation. As a result, "popular" culture and the cultures of minority and tribal groups are neglected and even marginalized.

In inculturation, that is, the encounter between Christianity and local cultures, the same dynamics are at work. In the past, cultural indigenization was conducted between official Christianity and "world religions" with their canonical classics, hierarchical leaders, and approved theologians (for the most part, expatriate missionaries). This was the case, for instance, with Matteo Ricci and the Confucian literati in China and Roberto de Nobili and the Hindu Brahmins in India. In contemporary world Christianities, however, the dialogue between Christianity and cultures (note the plural) has eschewed this elitist bias, and much attention is now being paid to the local, regional, ethnic, and tribal "small traditions." For instance, in India, local Christianities are made up largely of Dalits and tribals, and in China, Catholic, Protestant, and Pentecostal churches gain the largest following in rural areas where Chinese folk religion is widely practiced. In Africa, African Independent/Initiated Christianity, whose membership increased from 50,000 in 1900 to 99 million in 2010, has incorporated many beliefs and practices of African Traditional Religion.[14] In general, it is the adoption

---

12. See Charles Farhadian, ed., *Christian Worship Worldwide: Expanding Horizons, Deepening Practices* (Grand Rapids, MI: Eerdmans, 2007).

13. For Christianity in Indonesia, see the over one-thousand-page work edited by Jan Sihar Aritonang and Karel E. Steenbrink, *A History of Christianity in Indonesia* (Leiden: Brill, 2008).

14. On African Christianity in general, see Adrian Hastings, *The Church in Africa 1450–1950* (Oxford: Clarendon Press, 1994). Hastings's book should be brought up to date with his

of these "small traditions" that is the distinguishing mark of Christianities in the Third World.[15]

In this context, an issue that is being hotly debated is popular religiosity, or popular devotions. In the past, a good number of these popular devotions were condemned as superstition, idolatry, and magic, and conversion to Christianity required a total renunciation of these practices. Witness the repeated proscription of ancestor worship by Roman authorities in the Catholic Church until 1939 (the so-called Chinese Rites Controversy). In world Christianities, especially in the Catholic Church, there has been a vibrant renaissance of popular piety, especially devotion to Mary and the saints, veneration of ancestors, and pious practices such as novenas, processions, and pilgrimages, particularly in Christianities influenced by Iberian spirituality such as those in Latin America, the Philippines, and Vietnam. Furthermore, "popular Catholicism" has become an important source for Catholic theology. In general, the relation between Christianity and local cultures has been widely discussed in contemporary theology, especially in missiology, and an abundant literature has been produced on the issue

---

own *A History of African Christianity 1950–1975* (Cambridge: Cambridge University Press, 1979); Elizabeth Isichei, *A History of Christianity in Africa: From Antiquity to the Present* (Grand Rapids, MI: Eerdmans, 1995); and Kwame Bediako, *Christianity in Africa: The Renewal of a Non-Western Religion* (Maryknoll, NY: Orbis Books, 1995). On African Independent/Initiated Churches and their bewildering varieties and multiplicities, the literature is growing rapidly. See David Barrett, *Schism and Renewal in Africa: An Analysis of Six Thousand Contemporary Religious Movements* (Nairobi: Oxford University Press, 1968); Bengt Sundkler, *Bantu Prophets in South Africa* (London: International African Institute, 1961); Allan Anderson, *Zion and Pentecost: The Spirituality and Experience of Pentecostal and Apostolic/Zionist Churches in South Africa* (Pretoria: University of South Africa Press, 2000); Allan Anderson, *African Reformation: African Initiated Christianity in the 20th Century* (Trenton, NJ: Africa World Press, 2000); Martin L. Daneel, *Quest for Belonging: Introduction to a Study of African Independent Churches* (Gweru: Mambo, 1987); John S. Pobee and Gabriel Ositelu II, *African Initiatives in Christianity* (Geneva: WCC Publications, 1988). It is extremely difficult to obtain the exact number of the members of the AICs, According to a report of the WCC, in 1981 AICs constituted 15 percent of the total Christian population in sub-Saharan Africa. Assuming a growth estimated at more than two million per year, their adherents probably numbered close to 100 million in 2010, thus constituting a significant section of African Christian demography.

15. With this statement I am only making a historical and phenomenological observation on the way Third-World churches have dealt with local cultures, and not a value judgment on their ecclesial character, that is, whether they are more, or less, authentic than mainline churches. Such a doctrinal judgment is of course predicated on a set of mutually agreed criteria for orthodoxy, which may not be available. With regard to AICs in particular, they no doubt had strong connections with Pentecostal missionary movements from the West, but they have consciously severed these connections by their attitude—generally by no means uniformly positive—toward African Traditional Religion and culture. Motivations for ecclesial independence are varied and include considerations that are political (freedom from Western imperialism), denominational (the Protestant tendency to divide and separate in situations of conflict), and cultural (adoption of the African worldview).

known under various names such as contextualization, indigenization, localization, or inculturation of the Christian faith.

6. *Reason.* The last formative factor in theology in Macquarrie's list is reason. Though originated from divine revelation and thus not rational in the sense of being derived from pure philosophy or autonomous reason, Christianity claims to be reasonable, not merely in the sense that it is not absurd and contrary to reason (*pace* Tertullian) but also in the sense that at a minimum it must give a justification for its hope. This is done not by appeal to divine authority and authorized tradition but by means of reasoned arguments with publicly available criteria of truth (apologetics and fundamental theology). Moreover, beyond this apologetical task, Christian theology has engaged in conversation, at times in friendly alliance, at other times in hostile confrontation with various philosophies, other human sciences such as history, anthropology, psychology, and sociology, and natural sciences. This, of course, has been the main way in which Western Christianity has interacted with reason.

In other Christianities, however, the dialogue between Christian faith and reason takes on unfamiliar forms. In many countries such as India, China, Japan, Korea, Tibet, and others, just to cite a few Asian countries, there are centuries-old and well-developed philosophies. Here, Hindu, Buddhist, Confucian, Daoist, and Islamic philosophical systems are in full vigor, expressed in sophisticated conceptual frameworks and in a huge number of multilingual writings, such that no one scholar can claim mastery of even one philosophical tradition.[16] Interestingly, many Asian philosophers are well versed in Western philosophy, which may facilitate the dialogue between Asian philosophy and Christianity, but the same cannot be said of Western theologians, for the majority of whom Asian philosophy still remains a closed book.

Furthermore, for the majority of people in world Christianities outside the West, where orality is predominant, philosophical worldviews are expressed not in philosophical texts but in myths, stories, proverbs, koans, songs, dance, rituals, festivals, and dramas. Here the dialogue between Christianity and these forms of rationality is no less theologically complicated and pastorally even more urgent.

Thus far I have shown through a cursory examination of the six formative factors in theology how in world Christianities doing theology has been vastly complexified, much more so than in Western theology. Both the resources of theology and their deployment have changed and multiplied as Christianity becomes global, requiring widely divergent approaches and methodologies and entailing new and different articulations of the basic Christian beliefs. In

---

16. A helpful one-volume guide to Asian philosophies is Brian Carr and Indira Mahalingam, eds., *Companion Encyclopedia of Asian Philosophies* (London: Routledge, 1997).

the following section I will highlight some of the ways in which the main *loci theologici* have been reconceptualized in world Christianities.

THEOLOGY *IN* WORLD CHRISTIANITIES

New contexts, new experiences, new resources, new methodologies, and a new generation of theologians inevitably bring forth new theological insights, and this is especially true of Christianities in the non-Western world. A rapid survey of theological developments since the second half of the twentieth century will show that apart from some significant trends in Germany and France, and to a lesser extent, Britain and the United States, the most challenging, and even revolutionary innovations in theology have taken place in Latin America, Africa, and Asia. In the Catholic Church, this general assessment is confirmed by the fact that under the leadership of then-cardinal Joseph Ratzinger as prefect of the Congregation for the Doctrine of the Faith, and later as Pope Benedict XVI, the two theologies that were attacked, and their key proponents censured, are liberation theology and theology of religious pluralism, both of which originated in the Third World, the former in Latin America and the latter in Asia.

This does not at all mean that these two and other theological trends developed by themselves, in isolation and without an extensive dialogue with and learning from Western theologies. On the contrary, in recent decades there has been an extensive and constant contact and exchange among various world Christianities. Both the Catholic Church with the Second Vatican Council (1962–65), the World Council of Churches with its numerous general assemblies and committees, and the World Evangelical Fellowship have greatly fostered the communication and collaboration among theologians in all parts of the world. In addition, the Ecumenical Association of Third World Theologians (EATWOT), founded at Dar es Salaam, Tanzania, in 1976, has been a fertile venue for worldwide theological exchange. Furthermore, thanks to innumerable academic conferences, church gatherings, international networks, and online communications, theological ideas and movements circulate the globe with a speed unimaginable only a couple of decades ago.

The theologies in world Christianities have been given different names in which the relation between Christianity and culture is described by various prefixes. If culture is deemed positive, these theologies are said to be *transcul-tural*, *multi*cultural, *cross*cultural, and *inter*cultural, each denoting a particular aspect of the dynamics of the encounter between faith and culture.[17] The

---

17. See Volker Küster, *Einführung in die interkulturelle Theologie* (Göttingen: Vandenhoeck

theologian's task is to mediate between faith and culture, and the goal is to express the contents of the faith in categories understandable to the people of a particular time and place and, if necessary, to jettison the traditional, even ecclesiastically sanctioned, formulations of Christian beliefs and practices to meet the needs of the age. On the other hand, theologies are dubbed *counter*-cultural and *anti*cultural if a particular culture is judged godless and hostile to the gospel ("culture" standing in for "world" in the Johannine sense of being opposed to God). In the latter case, the main task of theology is to critique, and, when necessary, resist and reject cultural trends that are judged to be inimical to the Christian faith, rather than seek ways to accommodate it to culture.

By and large, however, the terms "intercultural" and "contextual" as well as the underlying positive perceptions of culture are more common in world Christianities. "Intercultural" highlights the fact that contemporary theology is inevitably a culture-dependent and culture-bound intellectual production arising out of and at the same time shaping the encounter between the gospel and a particular culture. "Intercultural" makes it clear that this encounter is not between a culture-free, "pure" gospel and another culture (which the words "inculturation" or "incarnation," commonly used in Catholic circles, might misleadingly suggest), but always between an already culture-laden gospel (Jewish and Hellenistic) and a particular culture, or more likely, cultures in a given place that usually contain both values and disvalues. "Contextual," on the other hand, accentuates the fact that the cultural context is not a neutral geographical venue in which world Christianities are implanted but rather that which conditions and influences the very way theology is constructed.[18] Let us now review the main rearticulations of the Christian beliefs in world Christianities.

1. *God.* Whereas most Third-World theologians emphasize the need to start from an accurate social analysis of concrete socio-political, economic, cultural, and religious contexts in which theology is done—the first moment of the three-stage process of "see-judge-act"—the primary object of their theologies is not human experience as such but God and all things insofar as they pertain to God. This should be said in response to the criticism, often voiced by conservative theologians, especially those under the sway of Karl Barth, that Third-World theologies, allegedly heirs of modernity and liberal theology, are anthropocentric and immanentist in orientation and have lost sight of the real object or rather subject of theology, namely, God as the Absolute

---

& Ruprecht, 2011), 16–17. See also Mark J. Cartledge and David Cheetham, eds., *Intercultural Theology: Approaches and Themes* (London: SCM Press, 2011).

18. This connotation of "context" is implied in the subtitle of Timothy C. Tennent, *Theology in the Context of World Christianity: How the Global Church Is Influencing the Way We Think about and Discuss Theology* (Grand Rapids: Zondervan, 2007).

Transcendent and the Totally Other.[19] On the contrary, it must be acknowledged that God remains the central focus of many currents of theology in world Christianities, and therefore it is appropriate to begin the discussion of theology in world Christianities with God. However, what is new and distinctive of these theologies is that they take the vastly different experiences in world Christianities, as outlined above, and not the Bible and church teachings, as the starting point, perspective, and hermeneutical lens for a reconstruction of the traditional understanding of God. Broadly speaking, their method is more inductive than deductive.

Interestingly, this critique of the doctrine of God was undertaken first in Western Christianity where it took the form of a wholesale rejection of what is termed "classical theism." By this is meant a philosophy and theology of God in which under the legacy of Hellenism God's perfection is understood to imply aseity, self-sufficiency, immutability, impassibility, and total detachment from the change, pain, and suffering of the world. Leading this charge are Process philosophers and theologians such as Alfred North Whitehead, Charles Hartshorne, John Cobb Jr., Joseph Bracken, and a host of others. Akin to Process theology, in evangelical theology, proponents of Open Theism such as Clark Pinnock argue for a view of God that presents God as freely and intimately involved in a dynamic relationship of love with human beings, which makes God vulnerable to temporality, change, and suffering and in which God affects creatures and creatures affect God.[20]

Third-World theologies of God would resonate sympathetically with the basic understanding of God proposed by Process theology, especially its concept of a suffering God, However, their starting point, resources, and methodology, and hence their resulting theology of God, are substantially different. As mentioned above, their immediate context is not dissatisfaction with "classical theism," and their goal is not an elaboration of a speculative metaphysics in which God as, to use Process thought's expression, "responsive love" (God's "consequent nature") is subject to change and as a "fellow-sufferer who understands," acts in the world by persuasion and lure, and not by coercive power. By contrast, the context of Third-World Christianities is, as has been alluded to above, massive systemic impoverishment and exploitation. Seen

---

19. This criticism is often voiced by the proponents, especially John Milbank, of the so-called Radical Orthodoxy.

20. See Charles Pinnock et al., *The Openness of God: A Biblical Challenge to the Traditional Understanding of God* (Downers Grove, IL: InterVarsity Press, 1994); and John Sanders, *The God Who Risks*, rev. ed. (Downers Grove, IL: InterVarsity Press, 2007). In its early phase, from the 1930s to the 1960s, Process theology focused on God. After 1970s it turned its attention to other topics such as liberation (Schubert Ogden), feminism (Marjorie Suchocki), science (Ian Barbour, Philip Clayton, Ann Pederson), interreligious dialogue (John Cobb Jr., David Ray Griffin, Clark Williamson, Joseph Bracken), evil (Griffin, Suchocki, Bracken), and ecology (Jay McDaniel).

in this context, and from the Bible read in this hermeneutical lens, God is understood primarily as liberator of the oppressed who has made an option for the poor, and because of this option, "has shown strength with his arm; has scattered the proud in the thoughts of their hearts; has brought down the powerful from their thrones and lifted the lowly; has filled the hungry with good things, and sent the rich away empty" (Luke 1:51–53).

For liberation theologies, it is these acts of God in "lifting the lowly" and "filling the hungry with good things" that define the nature of God. What and who God is, is known in and through what God does, not in generic actions in the world such as creation, providence, and consummation (the customary categories in Western theology to describe God's activities in the world) but in specific, highly partial, and politically charged interventions to liberate those who are treated as nonpersons by the rich and the powerful, and in this way overturning the social order. Thus there has been in Third-World theologies of God a shift not merely from the immanent Trinity to the economic Trinity, as the two paragons of First-World theology, Karl Barth and Karl Rahner, have done, but from a generic understanding of the economic Trinity as the immanent Trinity self-actualizing in human history to an economic Trinity self-actualizing precisely in God's identification and solidarity with a specific group of people designated with the umbrella term "the poor."

Needless to say, these poor in turn reconceptualize God from their particular form of oppression, not because, as a black woman in Sue Monk Kidd's novel *The Secret Life of Bees* tells a white girl who wonders why there is a black Madonna: "Everybody needs a God who looks like them,"[21] but because it is precisely in these people with their specific forms of oppression that God has revealed what and who God is and for whom God "has shown strength with his arm." Thus, there is black theology (against racism), African theology (against cultural colonialism), Latin American theology (against economic oppression), feminist theology in its various forms (against patriarchy and androcentrism), Dalit theology (against the caste system), tribal theology (against marginalization and exploitation of minorities), *minjung* theology (against dictatorship and capitalism), theology of struggle (against state security ideology), ecological theology (against environmental degradation), and so forth. Because of their focus on particular forms of human oppression, these theologies run the risk of being perceived as anthropocentric and being accused of reducing salvation to the socio-political and economic dimensions. Furthermore, because these theologies are critical reflection on praxis, they may be liable to the charge that they foment class struggle and even violent revolution. In light of these misunderstandings, it is necessary to point out that when these theologians articulate their theologies of God, they are not

---

21. Sue Monk Kidd, *The Secret Life of Bees* (New York: Penguin Books, 2002), 141.

indulging their "need to have a God who looks like them" (Feuerbachian and Marxian theories of projection) but are seeking to reveal the real face of God as God has truly appeared in the world (the economic Trinity) and the specific ways in which God saves humanity and the cosmos (grace as freedom, salvation as liberation). In sum, in world Christianities God is one who is world-relational, all-inclusive, co-suffering, and saving-by-liberating.[22]

2. *Christ.* Because Jesus is the human face of God, it is in Christology that the distinctiveness of Third-World theologies is most evident. Indeed it is in Christology that the effort by world Christianities to contextualize the Christian faith has produced the largest amount of literature. Again, as in the theology of God, though the Bible still functions as the *norma normans*, it is the context that serves as the starting point, the perspective, and the hermeneutical lens for christological construction. As K. K. Yeo puts it concisely,

> Global Christologies seek creative dialogues toward: (1) a *catholic* faith based on biblical Christologies that honor multiple and interacting worldviews; (2) a global theology that respects cross-cultural and shifting contexts in which faithful communities embody real-life issues; (3) a translatability of the Scripture that upholds various dynamic vernaculars and hermeneutics; and (4) a round-table symposium of proclaiming and worshiping a biblical Christ portrayed in varied Christologies.[23]

Add to Yeo's list of missiological ("proclaiming") and doxological ("worshiping") goals the praxiological dimension (overturning and transformation of oppressive societal structures) of Third-World theology, and we can have a glimpse of the dazzling variety of non-Western Christologies. Within this framework it is possible to classify Christology in world Christianities according to the various concerns relating to race (black), ethnicity (Chinese, Indian, Latino/a, etc.), gender (white, womanist, mujerista, etc.), class (Dalit), tribe (American Indian, tribals in northeast India), geography (continents and countries), culture, and religion.

My point here is not to offer a bibliographical survey of these Christologies; any competent overview of contemporary Christologies will present their significant trends, their guiding concepts, and the writings of their promi-

---

22. An example of this theology of God can be found in the works of the Taiwanese Presbyterian theologian Choan-Seng Song. Among his many writings, see his *The Compassionate God: An Exercise in the Theology of Transposition* (Maryknoll, NY: Orbis Books, 1982). Of course this theology of God is not exclusive to Third-World theologians. Among First-World theologians Jürgen Moltmann must be counted as the foremost proponent of it.

23. K. K. Yeo, "Biblical Christologies of the Global Church: Beyond Chalcedon? Toward a Fully Christian and Fully Cultural Theology," in Gene L. Green, Stephen T. Pardue, and K. K. Yeo, eds., *Jesus without Borders: Christology in the Majority World* (Grand Rapids, MI: Eerdmans, 2014), 168.

nent proponents. Rather, I would like to examine the basic ideas that provoke, challenge, and shape the bewildering variety of christological reflections in world Christianities. One helpful way to understand their basic orientations is to group them under the three major concerns of world Christianities, namely, liberation, inculturation, and interreligious dialogue. It is, however, most important to remember that these three tasks are not distinct and unrelated; rather they are deeply intertwined and overlap with each other so that one task cannot be fully achieved without the other two, though each can be given a particular emphasis depending on the local context.

Under the first category, that is, liberation, which was developed first and foremost in Latin America, the focus is on the historical Jesus as the liberator with his message about the reign of God as reported primarily in the Synoptic Gospels. Jesus' words and deeds during his ministry, death, and resurrection are mined to highlight Jesus' preferential option for the poor and the liberative force of his actions against all kinds of oppression in all aspects of life, including the Earth. Here lie the major contributions of Latin American, black, feminist, and ecological Christologies.

The second category includes inculturation Christologies, which find a congenial home in Africa, where colonialism has wrought extensive cultural pauperization, and center on the retrieval and adoption of certain elements of indigenous cultures to present Christ as a universal person, "without borders" and crosscultural, and precisely for that reason, capable of being "African." Here the images that emphasize kinship and community obtain pride of place and are used to present Jesus as mother, elder brother, ancestor, chief, and healer. Again, the Synoptic Gospels as well as the other writings of the New Testament, especially the Pauline letters, provide ample materials for inculturated Christologies.

3. *Religious Pluralism and Interreligious Christology.* The third category of Christology, which falls within the ambit of interreligious dialogue, is so complex, vast, and controversial that it merits discussion under a separate heading. Of all the Christologies developed in world Christianities, interreligious Christology has the potential to be the most revolutionary trend, shaking Christianity to its foundations. In a real sense interreligious encounter is, of course, not new, as Western theologians from the earliest times had to present Christ in relation to—more precisely, *over against*—Judaism, pagan religions, and Islam.

What is novel and is causing deep reverberations in Christology in World Christianities is that first, interreligious dialogue is now taking place in all world Christianities, but for obvious reasons, particularly in Asia, the cradle of all world religions. Thanks to globalization and migration, religious pluralism is now a global phenomenon, with large and complex socio-political, economic, cultural, and religious implications, calling for interreligious dialogue, not least for the sake of world peace and harmony. Second, the encounter between Christianity and other religions is now conceived, at least by the majority of Christians, no longer as confrontation but *dialogue*, requiring a set of virtues, intellectual and moral, that make mutual understanding and cooperation among believers of different faiths possible.[24] Third, this interreligious dialogue now involves new partners, not only Judaism and Islam, with which Christianity has family resemblances and a common heritage, but with religions with which Christianity has little or no connections, such as Hinduism (nonpersonal theism), Buddhism (nontheism), Confucianism and Daoism (immanentism and humanism), and a host of other no less global religious traditions such as Jainism, Sikhism, and primal religions. Fourth, this dialogue has led to a radical and thorough reexamination of all the major Christian *loci theologici*; indeed, none of the reputed nonnegotiables of the Christian faith has been left undisturbed. These include not only Christology but also the doctrine of God and the Trinity, pneumatology, revelation, inspiration, biblical hermeneutics, church, worship, spirituality, and ethics, and, of course, as mentioned above, the six formative factors in theology.

Again, it is not my intention to provide here an overview of how Christian theology has been challenged by religious pluralism; informative surveys of interreligious dialogue are plentiful on the market.[25] What I would like to do is to outline the various challenges that religious pluralism poses to Christology and to outline the two main types of interreligious Christology in world Christianities.

First, regarding theological challenges, as alluded to above, the very foundation of traditional Christology has been shaken. With regard to Judaism, one major issue concerns supersessionism, that is, the doctrine that Christ, and hence Christianity, have "fulfilled" Judaism, and therefore the covenant or testament that God has made with the Jews has become obsolete or "old" and replaced by the "new," Christian covenant. It is now asked, with deep moral anguish, especially in light of the Holocaust, whether this anti-Jewish and anti-Judaic "teaching of contempt," albeit widespread in Christian tradition and claimed to be based on a number of statements of the New Testa-

---

24. This is not to say that dialogue occurs everywhere in world Christianities. Conflicts with, violence against, and persecutions of Christians in countries such as China, India, Sudan, Nigeria, and many Middle Eastern countries have been widely reported. What I intend to say is that even in these conflictive situations the only means to achieve peace, justice, and reconciliation is dialogue, especially in its fourfold mode, namely, common life, practical collaboration, interreligious conversation, and sharing of spiritual experiences.

25. See, for instance, Catherine Cornille, ed., *The Wiley-Blackwell Companion to Interreligious Dialogue* (Oxford: Wiley-Blackwell, 2013); David Cheetham, Douglas Pratt, and David Thomas, eds., *Understanding Interreligious Relations* (Oxford: Oxford University Press, 2013); and Karl Becker and Ilaria Morali, eds., *Catholic Engagement with World Religions: A Comprehensive Study* (Maryknoll, NY: Orbis Books, 2010).

ment, especially the Gospels of Matthew and John and Hebrews, is biblically grounded in view of God's eternal faithfulness to his word and of what Paul says about the Jewish covenant (see Romans 9–11). If this supersessionism is rejected, and in my judgment it must be, disturbing questions are raised about the number of covenants and "peoples of God" (note the plural!) outside the historical Jesus and Christianity and their mutual relation, and about the appropriateness of Christian mission to "convert" the Jews.

Furthermore, traditional claims regarding Jesus as the unique, universal, and eschatological revealer and savior have been challenged. Troubling questions are raised regarding the salvific function of non-Christian religions: Are they, as missionaries of generations past and in our time Karl Barth have held, merely human, mostly superstitious, idolatrous, and vain attempts to reach God, or, on the contrary, are they God-intended and God-initiated "ways of salvation" in themselves? And if the latter, how to relate them to Christ and Christianity? Are they parallel and independent ways, or mutually complementary? Contemporary theologies of religions, commonly categorized as exclusivism, inclusivism, pluralism, and a variety of combinations thereof, are too well known to require exposition here.[26]

Connected with this christological issue is biblical hermeneutics and the role of sacred books of non-Christian religions. It is not merely a question of how to interpret (critics would say: interpret away) exclusive-sounding texts that categorically affirm the uniqueness of Christ such as Acts 4:12, 1 Timothy 2:5; and John 14:6. It has been suggested that their seeming exclusiveness can be overcome by contextualizing them within an all-inclusive and universalistic orientation of the whole biblical tradition, expressed powerfully, for example, in John 1:9. However, the more challenging task is how to interpret the Bible in light of non-Christian sacred scriptures. It is here that Third-World biblical scholars and theologians such as Samuel Rayan, George Soares-Prabhu, R. S. Sugirtharajah, Archie C. C. Lee, and Kwok Pui-lan, just to mention a few, have made innovative contributions to interreligious hermeneutics. Furthermore, in some places, for example in India, experiments have been made to include selected texts from these non-Christian scriptures into worship and prayer. Implicit in this hermeneutical practice and liturgical usage is a theology of revelation and inspiration that acknowledges the activity of the Holy Spirit ("in-*spiration*") in the origination and composition of these sacred texts.

Second, concerning its basic approaches, contemporary interreligious Christology has pursued two lines of research. The first explores how Christ and Christianity have historically been viewed in non-Christian sacred texts and by non-Christian thinkers themselves. This task is somewhat straightforward in the case of Judaism and Islam, given the fact that they and Chris-

---

26. A very helpful introduction to these issues is Paul Knitter, *Introducing Theologies of Religion* (Maryknoll, NY: Orbis Books, 2002).

tianity are "religions of the Book," and given the long history of encounter among theologians of the three faiths. It is a commonplace, for example, that the Qur'an contains narratives about Abraham, the prophets, the Jews, Jesus, and Mary; that the Christian Bible includes the Tanak; and that there has been a lively conversation among Jews, Christians, and Muslims concerning their common theological heritage. Of course, the challenge is how to remove mutual misunderstandings, suspicions, and hostility embodied in these texts and to bring to full flowering the common heritage and shared convictions among these three Abrahamic religions.

The second line of research in interreligious Christology is much more arduous and controversial than the first, seeking to relate the figure of Jesus to other religious founders and moral teachers such as the Buddha and Confucius, and to read the Bible in the light of the sacred texts that have little historical and literary commonality with it, such as the Vedas, the Upanishads, the Tripitaka, the *Guru Granth Sahib*, and the Chinese classics. Fortunately, Christian theologians are neither the first nor the only ones to embark upon this task. Not a few Hindu, Buddhist, and Confucianist thinkers have attempted this comparative work, often out of a sincere admiration of Jesus, his life and his teaching, but without converting to Christianity. Thus, in this type of Christology, similarities as well as differences between Jesus and the other religious figures are highlighted, allowing Jesus to be spoken of as the Sage, the Way, the Guru, the Avatara, the Bodhisattva, the Satyagrahi, the Servant, the Compassionate, the Dancer, and the Pilgrim.[27] Obviously these new christological titles, notwithstanding their linguistic strangeness, resonate with those ascribed to Jesus in the New Testament, but clearly they also expand and enrich our traditional understanding of Jesus and speak meaningfully to Third-World Christians. At the same time, this interreligious Christology causes much anxiety among guardians of orthodoxy for its alleged downplaying of the uniqueness of Jesus and its syncretistic tendency.[28]

4. *The Holy Spirit.* Another momentous development in contemporary theology in world Christianities is the emergence of a vigorous and vibrant pneumatology, thanks in part to theological attempts to account for the activity of God outside of Jesus and Christianity. Appealing to Irenaeus's arresting metaphor of God the Father's "two hands" working in the world, namely, the

---

27. See Martien E. Brinkman, *The Non-Western Jesus: Jesus as Bodhisattva, Avatara, Guru, Prophet, Ancestor or Healer?* (London: Equinox, 2007); Gregory A. Barker, ed., *Jesus in the World's Faiths: Leading Thinkers from Five Religions Reflect on His Meaning* (Maryknoll, NY: Orbis Books, 2005); Michael Amaladoss, *The Asian Jesus* (Maryknoll, NY: Orbis Books, 2006).

28. Within the Roman Catholic Church, this anxiety is well known, especially in the Congregation for the Doctrine of the Faith; and the latter's attempts to censure writings by theologians such as Jacques Dupuis, Jon Sobrino, Roger Haight, Michael Amaladoss, and a host of others have been well chronicled.

Word of God and the Holy Spirit, a number of theologies of religion invoke the activities of the Holy Spirit before, during, and after the Incarnation of the Word of God in Jesus of Nazareth. The Holy Spirit, it is argued, functions not independently from (much less in opposition to) but in collaboration and harmony first with the Logos-not-yet-made-flesh (*Logos asarkikos*) and then the Logos-made-flesh (*Logos sarkikos*). But this collaboration between the Spirit and the Word of God should not be understood as the dependence of the former on the latter, which the traditional Western theology of the Trinity, with its conception of the linear procession of the Spirit from the Father and the Son (*Filioque*), might misleadingly suggest. On the contrary, as the "two-hands" metaphor implies, the Son and the Spirit work "autonomously," "single-handedly," albeit in mutual collaboration, in different places and times, in diverse modalities, and with varying degrees of impact.

The venue in which the Spirit is actively present outside the historical Jesus and Christianity is preeminently non-Christian religions, with their beliefs and practices. In interreligious dialogue there have been attempts at finding analogues for the Spirit in the teachings of non-Christian religions, similar to those made in Christology mentioned above. Again, this task is relatively straightforward in the case of Judaism and Islam, though the challenge to express the "personality" of the Spirit remains considerable. The task is much more complex in the case of Asian religions, given the great differences in conceptual frameworks. Contemporary research has singled out the concepts of *prana* (Hinduism) and *Qi/Chi* (Chinese thought), the energy or life force circulating in all things, as particularly illuminating analogues for the Spirit as immanent grace and life-giving power.[29]

However, the main catalyst for the current resurgence of pneumatology in world Christianities is not interreligious dialogue but the phenomenal growth of Evangelicalism/Pentecostalism—a new Pentecost—in Third-World Christianity, especially in Africa, Asia (especially South Korea, India, and China), and Latin America (especially Brazil and Guatemala). As a result, a different type of Christianity, quite different from the mainline churches of the First World, is spreading like wild fire, with a more literal understanding of the Bible and an exuberant panoply of the gifts of the Spirit.[30]

---

29. See, for instance, Kirsteen Kim, *The Holy Spirit in the World: A Global Conversation* (Maryknoll, NY: Orbis Books, 2007); Grace Ji-Sun Kim, *The Holy Spirit, Chi, and the Other: A Model of Global and Intercultural Pneumatology* (New York: Palgrave Macmillan, 2011); and Hyo-Dong Lee, *Spirit, Qi, and the Multitude: A Comparative Theology for the Democracy of Creation* (New York: Fordham University Press, 2014).

30. See Donald E. Miller, Kimon H. Sargeant, and Richard Flory, eds., *Spirit and Power: The Growth and Global Impact of Pentecostalism* (Oxford: Oxford University Press, 2013). Philip Jenkins has drawn the contrasts between the Christianity of the Global North and that of the Global South in his *The Next Christendom: The Coming of Global Christianity*, 3rd ed. (Oxford:

THEOLOGY *OF* CHRISTIANITIES:
DIFFERENT ECCLESIOLOGIES

This mention of the astounding global expansion of Pentecostal churches is the natural transition point to the last part of my essay. With all the developments in world Christianities hinted at above, what is aborning is not a new "Christendom" but a new Christianity, better, the birth of Christianities that explode the categories of traditional ecclesiology. Earlier I mentioned how the three Vincentian canons for orthodoxy, namely, antiquity (*semper*), ubiquity (*ubique*), and unanimity (*ab omnibus*), have been given a surprisingly new and ironic twist. Not that these criteria are no longer valid or helpful. Rather, it would seem that only in contemporary world Christianities do they obtain, albeit not fully, for the first time.

At the same time these criteria are stood on their heads. Whereas Vincent of Lérins deployed them not only as marks of orthodoxy but also as a means to foster ecclesiastical uniformity, or at least conformity, in today's world Christianities the precisely opposite effect occurs if they are applied consistently. When the "always," "everywhere," and "by all" are given their full scope in global Christianity, what comes into view is not similarity, much less uniformity, but mind-boggling multiplicity and even profound discordance. Of course, in churches where there is a powerful central control mechanism such as the Catholic Church, doctrinal and structural uniformity can be enforced, as was done under the pontificates of John Paul II and Benedict XVI. But even here appearances are deceiving. Perhaps one of the reasons for the latter's abdication is his inability to deal with not only scandals of various kinds that were buffeting the church but also the manifold and serious discrepancies between the grassroots and the hierarchical leaders that were cracking up the foundation of the ecclesiastical edifice, and this in spite of restorationist policies he had installed to slow down the reforms initiated by Vatican II and to quash ideas and practices he judged to be misinterpretations of the council. In world Christianities, however, attempts to revert to central control to ensure uniformity are doomed to failure.

Of course, variety, multiplicity, and polycentricity in global Christianity raise the question of Christian identity, ecumenical unity, and, more basically, the nature of being "church," since the Christian faith is essentially a social reality. In a nutshell, there is no Christian faith without Christianity and church. But what makes Christianity and church "Christian"? The urgency of this question in world Christianities can be gauged by noting how the breaking-up of Christianity today, should it occur, is far more devastating in

---

Oxford University Press, 2011). Jenkins has at times overdrawn these contrasts, but his general point about the difference between these two types of Christianity is well taken.

scope and depth than the eleventh-century division between the Greek and Latin churches and the sixteenth-century separation between Roman Catholics and Protestants within the Latin church combined.

For one thing, the eventual disunity is truly global for the first time, "ecumenical" in the etymological sense of the term. This time, instead of the Middle East and Europe only, Africa, Asia, Latin America, and Oceania, the so-called Global South, will be active partners in the dispute, where, according to some demographic projections, four out of five Christians will live by 2050.[31] Second, there will be no center that holds, at least in the way it did when divisions occurred in the past, since the dividing lines now run not merely among churches but in the midst of each church and denomination, especially where there is no central authority or recognized authoritative interchurch body. Third, there will not be a checklist of universally agreed-upon doctrinal nonnegotiables that can serve as a litmus test for Christian identity, such as a commonly formulated creed. Fourth, relations with other religions will enter into discussions on intrachurch matters, especially where Christians are but a minority, such as Asia and North Africa, since it is impossible to be religious without being interreligious in these parts of the world. Finally, political factors such as government intervention will play a more invasive role, especially where religious freedom is severely curtailed.

Lest it be thought that the above rumination is an alarmist doomsday scenario, let's consider the case of Pentecostal Christianity, especially in China. In his informative study of Chinese Christianity, *Redeemed by Fire*,[32] Lian Xi, professor of world Christianity at Duke University, focuses on what he terms Chinese "popular Christianity," that is, the Christian movements that developed in China outside of mainline Protestant Christianity and the Catholic Church since the Taiping Uprising (1850–64) and continue today in the explosive and bewildering mushrooming of unregistered "house churches." Popular Christianity is an attempt by Chinese Protestants to indigenize Christianity by drawing inspiration from antiforeign nationalism, Pentecostal revivalism, Chinese rural and grassroots utopian millenarianism,

---

31. Whereas in 1900 over 80 percent of all Christians lived in Europe and North America, by 2005 this proportion had fallen to under 40 percent, and will likely fall below 30 percent before 2050. In his *New Faces of Christianity*, Philip Jenkins, on the basis of various statistical projections, notes that in 2015 60 percent of the estimated two billion Christians in the world live in Africa, Asia, or Latin America. By 2050, there will be an estimated three billion Christians, 75 percent of whom will live in what is the "Global South." The two most helpful statistical studies of global Christianity are Todd M. Johnson and Kenneth R. Ross, eds., *Atlas of Global Christianity 1910–2019* (Edinburgh: Edinburgh University Press, 2009); and Patrick Johnstone, *The Future of the Global Church: History, Trends and Possibilities* (Downers Grove, IL: IVP Books, 2011).

32. Lian Xi, *Redeemed by Fire: The Rise of Popular Christianity in Modern China* (New Haven: Yale University Press, 2010).

and beliefs and practices of Chinese popular religion to form an indigenous Christianity.[33]

Lian Xi traces the roots of popular Christianity back to the Christian-inspired millenarian and utopian Taiping Heavenly Kingdom with its founder Hong Xiuquan (1814–64). Other charismatic leaders of attempts at autonomous, "self-supporting" churches in late-Qing coastal China include Xi Zichi, known as Xi the Overcomer of Demons, founder of the opium-refuge churches; Xie Honglai, organizer of the Chinese Christian Union; Yu Guozhen, founder of the China Christian Independent Church; Cheng Jingyi, who eloquently urged nondenominational Christianity at the 1910 Edinburgh World Missionary Conference; Ding Limei, founder of the Chinese Student Volunteer Movement for the Ministry; Yu Cidu, a Methodist revivalist itinerant preacher. In the post–Boxer Uprising, these Chinese Christians felt that the survival and growth of Christian communities in China now appeared to hinge on their ability to separate themselves from Western missions. However, due to the lack of personnel and financial resources, these movements toward autonomy succeeded only in fulfilling the missionary vision of a native church safely within the limits of mainline Western Protestantism.

What was still required for successful and lasting independent Protestant churches to arise is a millenarian vision of an impending end of the world and of the imminence of the Second Coming of Christ. Lian Xi traces the origins and chronicles the development of six such "churches" with their founders: the True Jesus Church (Wei Enbo, 1876?–1919); the Jesus Family (Jing Dianying, 1890–1957); the Shandong Revival and the Spiritual Gifts Society (Ma Zhaorui, Yang Rulin, and Sun Zhanyao); the Christian Tabernacle (Wang Mingdao, 1900–91); the Bethel Worldwide Evangelical Band (John Sung/Song Shangjie, 1901–44); and the Little Flock (Watchman Nee/Ni Tuosheng, 1903–72). In the two decades 1930–50 these churches experienced unprecedented growth. However, as the Communist government orchestrated the Three-Self movement to unify the Protestant churches in China, their phenomenal growth came to an abrupt end. However, their apocalyptic, premillenarian fire was smoldering and waited for the right time to burst into new Pentecostal flames.

Lian Xi ends his study with a survey of the stupendous explosion of unregistered, independent house churches after the Cultural Revolution (1966–76). It is, in his assessment, "in the unofficial churches where one would find the heartbeat of the Christianity of China's masses and glimpse the future of Chinese Protestantism, which, at the turn of the twenty-first century, was already poised to rival the CCP [Chinese Communist Party] in total membership."[34] These house churches grew mostly out of the six pre-1949 churches mentioned

---

33. For more detail on what follows, see Chapter 3.
34. Xi, *Redeemed by Fire*, 206.

above and have taken on lives of their own, spinning off into dizzying numbers of idiosyncratic and uncontrollable sects under charismatic leaders. True
to their Pentecostal origins, these churches prize glossolalia, visions, trances,
miracles, and exorcisms.

There is no doubt that Christianity in its apocalyptic, premillenarian form
is experiencing an explosive revival in China, so much so that some Western observers, such as David Aikman, have breathlessly predicted a "Christianized China" that will, together with Christian America, promote global
evangelism and contribute to world peace. Lian Xi is rightly skeptical of the
likelihood of such a scenario: "Persecuted by the state, fractured by its own
sectarianism, and diminished by its contempt for formal education (theological or otherwise), it [Chinese contemporary popular Christianity] will
probably also remain, as sectarian religious groups in the past, in the state of
'intellectual decapitation.'"[35] Lian Xi also astutely notes that as long as Chinese politics, Chinese society, and Chinese life in general evolve toward the
rule of law, stability, greater equality, and harmony, Chinese Christianity is
unlikely to foment popular uprising, and that even if it does, it is unlikely
to succeed, "given the historical tendency of messianic movements in China
toward utopian radicalism, internal strife, a plebeian estrangement of the
elite, and, ultimately, political incompetence."[36]

Of course, contemporary Chinese Christianity is sui generis, and many
of its features, especially those related to its cultural and political contexts,
are not found outside China. But its basic ecclesial characteristics are derived
from the evangelical/Pentecostal movement and are common to innumerable
communities throughout the globe, including Africa, Latin America, and the
United States. Together they form the fastest-growing Christian group today,
with an estimated membership of more than half a billion.

There is no doubt that most of these "Independent churches," though they
have some common networks among themselves, do not have a central authority and lack many of the essential attributes that traditional ecclesiology considers constitutive of "church."[37] Consider, for instance, The Faith and Order
Paper no. 214 of the World Council of Churches entitled *The Church: Towards
a Common Vision*, the final fruit of nearly twenty years of intense ecumenical
discussions, consultations, and conferences on the nature and mission of the

---

35. Ibid., 242.

36. Ibid., 247.

37. Though AICs have formed ecumenical organizations among themselves and some are
members of National Councils of Churches and of the WCC, most lack some of the features,
such as apostolic succession and the Eucharist, that are considered essential to authentic
"ecclesiality" by historic mainline churches.

church.[38] It has been presented "to the churches as a common point of reference in order to test or discern their own ecclesiological convergences with one another and so to serve their further pilgrimage toward the manifestation of that unity for which Christ prayed."[39] Thus, the ultimate validation and success of the document is measured by its ability to promote in the churches "a mutual recognition of each other as churches, as true expressions of what the Creed calls the 'one, holy, catholic and apostolic Church.'"[40]

In light of the criteria for genuine "ecclesiality" proposed by the document, especially historical episcopacy and valid Eucharist, clearly the Independent churches are not "church in the proper sense," to use the terse expression of the declaration *Dominus Iesus* of the Congregation for the Doctrine of the Faith of the Catholic Church.[41] Add to the Independent churches the churches that issued from the Reformation, including the Anglican Church, which according to *Dominus Iesus*, are also not "church in the proper sense," world Christianities without them would be neither "world" nor "Christianities."

There would be something wrong then with either our current ecclesiology or with world Christianities. But if there is no denying the abundant presence of the fruits of the Spirit among Independent and Pentecostal churches, a different ecclesiology is needed to honor their ecclesial character. Such ecclesiology should be formulated from grassroots experiences of church—from below—and not deductively, from above, on the basis of a priori conceptions of the four marks of the true church. Connected with this issue of ecclesial identity is how ecumenical unity is to be envisaged in world Christianities. It may be asked whether a certain conception of apostolic succession, and with it historic episcopacy and the validity of the Eucharist, and the very understanding of church unity itself are too restrictive to do justice to the reality of world Christianities.

In sum, from what has been said above about the formative factors of theology, the rearticulations of fundamental *loci theologici*, such as the theology of God, Christology, pneumatology, and the need for a different ecclesiology, the reality of world Christianities today presents an enormous challenge as well as rich opportunities for systematic theology. We are just beginning to espy the complex contours of such a theology, but try we must to discern their forward movement to respond to what God is saying to the churches.

---

38. *The Church: Towards a Common Vision* (Geneva: WCC Publications, 2013). For a history of this document, see pp. 41–46.

39. Ibid., 46.

40. Ibid., vii.

41. *Dominus Iesus* (August 2, 2000). Note that according to *Dominus Iesus*, only the Catholic Church and the Orthodox Churches are "church in the proper sense," excluding all the churches originating from the Reformation and the Anglican Church!

7

Can We Read Religious Texts Interreligiously?

Possibilities, Challenges, and Experiments

The fact that the title of this chapter is phrased as a question indicates the tentative and, in some quarters, controversial nature of my reflections. It is important to understand the reason for their tentativeness. In a certain respect, reading and studying religious texts other than those of one's own religious tradition is nothing new or startling. Scholars of comparative religion and even Western theologians have been doing this for centuries, of course, for various purposes and with different methods. Today, college students in departments of religious studies routinely study the scriptures of various religions. What is novel and may raise ecclesiastical eyebrows is that there are Christians—and they are some of the folks that fill the pews on Sunday mornings and their number seems to be increasing—who read the scriptures of other religions as *sacred scripture*, and not merely as literary, historical, philosophical, and theological documents.

Today rare indeed is a Christian congregation or parish in which there are not a few members who have not participated in some kind of interfaith worship during which the scriptures of non-Christian religions are read, various meditation techniques practiced, and prayers of different religious traditions recited. Church leaders are often at a loss about what to say to Christians who claim that their spiritual life has been challenged, corrected, and enriched by, let's say, the Hindu *Bhagavad Gītā*, the Buddhist *Dhammapada* or *Lotus Sutra*, the Confucian *Analects*, the Daoist *Daodejing*, the Sikh *Adi Granth*, the Qur'an, or the Church of the Latter-Day Saints' *Book of Mormon*. They may issue a stern warning against syncretism and a possible loss of faith in the interreligious reading of the sacred texts of other religions or, on the contrary, they may commend this practice as a source of intellectual and spiritual enrichment. That a straightforward and ecclesiastically approved answer to this question is not readily available intimates the

124

complexity of the issue, and hence, the tentative and provisional nature of any answer—including mine—to it.

While reading religious texts interreligiously—that is, reading the religious scriptures of other religions as *sacred texts* for oneself—is today not an unknown or even rare phenomenon among Christians, it is nevertheless not a theologically unproblematic or ecclesiastically approved activity. A host of complex and varied issues are implicated by it. For instance, *theologically*, what doctrines are presupposed in accepting non-Christian writings as sacred scripture? *Ecclesially*, how does one account for what seems to be a case of multiple religious belonging and syncretism? *Spiritually*, how can one use non-Christian texts for meditation, prayer, and guidance, especially if they reflect a nontheistic or polytheistic belief system? *Hermeneutically*, what is involved in the act of reading a sacred text of religions other than one's own? In what follows I will take up for consideration some of the issues contained in each of the four questions raised above regarding the theology, ecclesiology, spirituality, and hermeneutics of reading religious texts interreligiously. What are the possibilities, challenges, and methods of reading religious texts interreligiously? My perspective in tackling these questions is, of course, that of a Christian and, more specifically, a Roman Catholic. Non-Catholic Christians and non-Christians may or may not find reading sacred writings of other religions as scripture for themselves problematic, and if they do, they will no doubt approach the issue quite differently and arrive at conclusions diverging from mine.

NON-CHRISTIAN SCRIPTURES AS DIVINE REVELATION?

Among the many theological questions raised by the practice of reading religious texts interreligiously, from the Christian point of view, that of the scriptural status of these writings as depositories of a possible divine revelation is perhaps the most salient and also the most complex.[1] For Christians, at

---

1. Here by "scripture" is meant the *written* text of the sacred words (the "Holy Writ"), though in several religious traditions (e.g., Hinduism and Islam) their oral form still remains primary, and hence hearing them takes precedence over reading them. Moreover, even the written text acquires revelatory and transformative power only when it is recited orally and listened to, in public rituals or in private devotion. Supernatural power is attributed even to the sound of the sacred word. It is proper to note here the ambiguous and polyvalent meanings of the term *scripture* (*graphē* in Greek, *ketav* in Hebrew) and its various Indo-European semantic cognates. Other terms are used to refer to sacred writings: *gramma* (Greek, plural *grammata*), *littera* (Latin, plural *litterae*), or to books: *biblos* (Greek, plural *bibloi*) or the diminutive *biblion* (Greek, plural *biblia*), *biblia* (Latin, originally neuter plural, then later, feminine singular). In his magisterial work *What Is Scripture?: A Comparative Approach* (Minneapolis: Fortress, 1993), Wilfred Cantwell Smith points out that the use of the term *scripture(s)* to refer to sacred book(s) is highly complex and ambiguous. When Christianity was the dominant religion in the Mediterranean

least for those for whom the Bible is, in the words of the Evangelical theologian Tim Perry, "divinely inspired and is therefore the necessary, sufficient, clear and authoritative guide for theological construction,"[2] and I might add, Christian living, the scriptures of other religions, except the Hebrew Tanak, which makes up parts of the Old Testament of the Christian Bible, are at best irrelevant and unnecessary. If the Bible already contains all the "necessary, sufficient, clear and authoritative" teaching, why should Christians bother reading let's say the *Dhammapada* or the Qur'an as something to learn *from*, much less as the Word of God?

Worse than redundant and irrelevant, non-Christian scriptures were also regarded by not a few Christians as the work of the devil himself, full of lies and errors, immoral tales of the gods' sexual adventures, and other perversities, and therefore should be burnt rather than perused. The Qur'an, to cite the title of Frederick Quinn's recent book about the image of Islam in the West, was regarded as *The Sum of Heresies*.[3] Should one ever read these "pagan" literatures, one must do so for apologetical purposes, as past missionaries, with very few exceptions, were wont to do, in order to refute their errors and to demonstrate the absolute superiority and truth of the Bible.

Today, happily, condemnation of non-Christian scriptures is no longer common. As shelves of these texts in Western-language translations in even secular bookstores readily attest, there has been a noticeable appreciation of them as a fountain of wisdom and source of spirituality. But even with this increasing esteem of non-Christian texts, there still remains a fundamental question, so far not adequately considered, that conditions the very possibil-

---

region, *scripture(s)* was used as a proper-noun designation to refer specifically to the Christian Bible. Later, the term was extended to refer to the scriptures of other religions, as when Peter the Venerable (d. 1156) speaks of the Qur'an as *nefaria scriptura* in his *Summa totius haeresis saracenorum*. The Qur'an itself uses the term *scripture* (*kitāb*) in a generic sense when it calls Jews and Christians "people of scripture" (*ahl al-kitāb*). In 1879, when the translation of the sacred texts of Asian religions was undertaken, the series was called *The Sacred Books of the East*, thereby explicitly recognizing that there are holy and authoritative books or scriptures in religions other than the Bible and that they function "scripturally," in an analogous way to the Hebrew and Christian Bible. See also William A. Graham, "Scripture," *Encyclopedia of Religion*, 2nd ed., vol. 12 (Farmington, IN: Thomson Gale, 2005), 8194–8205. I will come back to the theological significance of this shift from *scripture* designating something specific (i.e., the Christian Bible) to designating something generic (i.e., the sacred texts of all religions).

2. Tim Berry, *Mary for Evangelicals: Toward an Understanding of the Mother of Our Lord* (Downers Grove, IL: InterVarsity Press, 2006), 17. Of course, any Evangelical theologian could have been cited, but Tim Perry's words seem to be especially apposite since he is one of the few Evangelicals who are open to the other two sources of theology, namely, reason and tradition, and who do not adhere to the principle of *sola scriptura*.

3. Frederick Quinn, *The Sum of Heresies: The Image of Islam in the West* (Oxford: Oxford University in the West, 2007). Recall Peter the Venerable's designation of the Qur'an as *nefaria scriptura*.

ity of reading religious texts interreligiously. That is, what scriptural, or more generally, theological status, from the Christian point of view, can be attributed to non-Christian texts? The qualification "from the Christian point of view" is deliberate, to highlight the precise import of the question, namely, how *Christians* should evaluate the nature of these non-Christian texts. That these scriptures—be they the *Vedas*, the *Bhagavad Gītā*, the Tripitaka, the *Avesta*, the *Adi Granth*, or the Qur'an, etc.—are for their adherents sacred, inspired, and revelatory and therefore contain a divine (or in nontheistic religions, transcendent) teaching that has been heard (*sruti*) or remembered (*smirti*) is beyond doubt. The question here is whether in reading these religious texts interreligiously Christians may regard them as divine revelation for themselves, analogous to the Bible.

It may be objected at once that applying the Christian concept of "divine revelation" or "Bible" to the scriptures of other religions is a category mistake. The point is well taken, partly because not all the texts that have many cultural, social, and often even religious functions are regarded as having a divine origin by the very people for whom they function as normative classics. For example, the Confucian five "classics" (*jing*) and four "books" (*shu*), though of immense importance in traditional Chinese culture, are not attributed to divine authorship, in the way the Tanak, the Bible, and the Qur'an are. More important, as W. C. Smith has argued, *"scripture is a human activity."*[4] By this he means that "no text is scripture in itself and as such. People—a given community—make a text into scripture, or keep it scripture: by treating it in a certain way."[5] As William Graham has correctly pointed out, "neither form nor content can serve to identify or to distinguish scripture as a general phenomenon. . . . A text, written, oral, or both, is only 'scripture' insofar as a group of persons perceives it to be sacred or holy, powerful or meaningful, possessed of an exalted authority, and in some fashion transcendent of, and hence distinct from, other speech and writing."[6]

From the fact that there are a variety of ways in which texts are considered scripture even though not believed to be of divine origin and that their scriptural status is created by the particular communities in which they function as sacred scripture an important theological corollary follows. That is, it is not logically possible for Christians to judge whether the texts that other religions accept as sacred scripture are objectively of divine origin and hence to convey divine revelation or not. Because the holiness or sacredness of a book is not an a priori, ontological attribute nor the characteristic of a particular literary genre but is a contextual and relational quality that the book acquires vis-à-vis a particular religious community, the only thing Christian officials are

---

4. Smith, *What Is Scripture?*, 18.
5. Ibid.
6. Graham, "Scripture," 8195.

entitled to do is to declare that though non-Christian scriptures function as sacred texts to non-Christians, they cannot be called "inspired texts," much less be allowed to function as such for Christians.

This is in fact what the declaration *Dominus Iesus* of the Congregation for the Doctrine of the Faith attempts to do. On the basis of the Christian belief that divine revelation attains "fullness" and "definitiveness" in Jesus Christ, the declaration draws a distinction between the "theological faith" of Christians and the "belief" in other religions.[7] The latter is, according to the declaration, only a "religious experience still in search of the absolute truth and still lacking assent to God who reveals himself."[8] With regard to the scriptural status of non-Christian scriptures, the declaration says:

> The hypothesis of the inspired value of the sacred writings of other religions is also put forward. Certainly, it must be recognized that there are some elements in these texts which may be *de facto* instruments by which countless people throughout the centuries have been and still are able today to nourish and maintain their life-relationship with God. . . . The Church's tradition, however, reserves the designation of *inspired texts* to the canonical books of the Old and New Testaments, since these are inspired the Holy Spirit.[9]

The declaration goes on to affirm that whatever "elements of goodness and grace" these non-Christian sacred writings may possess, "which in actual fact direct and nourish the existence of their followers," they "receive from the mystery of Christ."[10]

---

7. The declaration's distinction between the "faith" of Christians and the "belief" of non-Christians is theologically problematic if one admits, as most contemporary Catholic theologians do, that there is a general supernatural revelation—not "natural revelation"—(e.g., Karl Rahner's "supernatural existential") outside the special historical revelation of Jesus.

8. The English text of *Dominus Iesus* (*DI*) is available in Stephen Pope and Charles Hefling, eds., *Sic et Non: Encountering* Dominus Iesus (Maryknoll, NY: Orbis Books, 2002). The reference is to the number of the paragraph of the document. Here, 7. It is to be noted that Vatican II's decree *Nostra Aetate*, speaking of the faith of the Muslims, uses the word "faith" (*fides islamica*) and not belief (no. 3).

9. *DI*, 8. The hypothesis of the inspired value of non-Christian sacred writings the declaration refers to has been put forward by some Indian theologians who suggest that these writings can be regarded as analogous to the Old Testament.

10. Ibid. The declaration's assertion that the "elements of goodness and grace" found in non-Christian religions are received by them "from the mystery of Christ" is an essentially dogmatic affirmation. It still needs to provide a plausible explanation of how such reception of these "elements of goodness and grace" is historically and sociologically possible, especially if these religions preexist the revelation by Jesus and have no historical connection whatsoever with him. Would it not be more plausible to hold that, from the historical point of view, non-Christian religions acquire these elements of goodness and grace "on their own," through the teaching of their founders who have arrived at them by themselves, apart from the historical revelation of

Dominus Iesus is making several theological assertions in the above statement. First, it recognizes that non-Christian texts do contain "some elements" of truth and grace that have been of help in nourishing non-Christians' relationship to God, even though, the declaration hastens to add, non-Christian religions contain "gaps, insufficiencies and errors."[11] But, and this is its second important point, it refuses them the appellation of "inspired texts" since this term is reserved by the church's tradition to the Christian Bible insofar as it is "inspired by the Holy Spirit."[12] Third, the declaration implicitly denies that these texts function as scripture in non-Christian religions. Sure, they may contain some elements of truth and goodness, which they are said to derive from Christ, but they are not viewed as functioning as scripture for non-Christians as the Bible does for Christians. The theological reason for the declaration's refusal to see these texts as scripture either for Christians or for non-Christians is that in its view, divine revelation has been exclusively given in Christ and the church, and therefore only the books that transmit this revelation—the Christian Bible—deserve to be called "inspired texts" or sacred scripture. Clearly, then, for *Dominus Iesus*, there is no possibility of reading religious texts interreligiously, simply because there are no non-Christian inspired or scriptural texts to begin with.

I have dwelt at some length on *Dominus Iesus*'s position toward non-Christian religious texts, which may not be exclusive of Roman Catholic official teaching, because in principle it undercuts the possibility of the practice of reading religious texts interreligiously. The critical question, of course, is whether *Dominus Iesus* is on solid ground in denying the scriptural quality to non-Christian religious texts. Of course, church officials are within their right to say that the Bible is scripture for Christians since this is how the Christian community has created this function for those books that it eventually included into the canon of the Bible.[13] As W. C. Smith has correctly observed,

---

Jesus? On the other hand, if one wants to maintain some connection between these elements of goodness and grace in non-Christian religions and Jesus, there is the option of holding that these religions derive their elements of goodness and grace, which are by nature supernatural, from the Unincarnate Word (*logos asarkos*), who is active before the birth of Jesus and operates historically apart from him and/or from the Holy Spirit (*pneuma*), who is also active before the birth of Jesus and operates historically apart from him. There is, however, a connection between non-Christian religions and the Jesus of history to the extent that the Word has become incarnated in Jesus and that the Spirit is the gift of the risen Jesus.

11. The declaration quotes from John Paul II's encyclical *Redemptoris Missio* (1991), 55. The question here is whether Christianity, and not just individual Christians, throughout its history has not contained "gaps, insufficiencies and error," both in its teachings and in its moral practices. The answer to this question can, of course, be answered only empirically, and not dogmatically.

12. *DI*, 8.

13. It is to be noted that I am not asserting that revelation is created by the religious community. On the contrary, it is always a divine activity. Rather I am saying that a text does not become and function as scripture (and consequently considered "inspired" and "canonical")

"scripture is a human activity." But it is on shaky ground, I submit, when it denies the scriptural quality of non-Christian sacred texts in non-Christian religions since historically these communities have endowed them with such scriptural quality and since these texts have *de facto* played and continue to play the role of scripture for these communities.

Furthermore, *Dominus Iesus* is also on shaky ground when it implies that non-Christian scriptures cannot in principle function as scripture for Christians because they are allegedly not inspired by the Holy Spirit. The reason for this is that Christians are given to know where the Holy Spirit is active and exercises his inspiring function, that is, in Christianity and in the Bible, but not where the Holy Spirit is not active and does not exercise his inspiring function, except where there are errors and sins. And it is, of course, absurd to say that non-Christian religions and their scriptures contain nothing but errors and sins. Thus Christians can say that their Bible is inspired by the Holy Spirit but cannot affirm a priori and with absolute certainty that non-Christian scriptures are not inspired by the same Holy Spirit.

On the other hand, if a Christian has experienced that certain non-Christian scriptures are carriers of divine revelation and function as a source of wisdom and spiritual edification, and hence are scripture for him or her, it is incumbent on that Christian to develop a theology of revelation that can explain how there is or at least can be divine revelation outside the Bible.[14] Here it is not the place to show how such a theology of revelation and inspiration could be elaborated and how therefore an interreligious reading of religious texts is theologically justified.

This theology of revelation is, of course, part of a theology of religion that is neither exclusivistic nor inclusivistic nor pluralistic, to name the three strands of contemporary theology of religion.[15] Rather this Christian theology of revelation should grow out of concrete interreligious experiences and patient and careful experiments of reading non-Christian sacred texts by a community of Christian believers and scholars, in study, meditation, private prayer, and even public worship. These texts will, of course, be selective and will have diverse

---

unless the community accepts it as such and allows it to function as such. "Scripture" is essentially a relational concept and is the result of the community's tendency to "scripturalize," to use W. C. Smith's term.

14. For an example of an inclusive theology of revelation and inspiration that admits the existence of divine revelation outside Christianity and the Bible, see Karl Rahner, *Foundations of Christian Faith*, trans. William Dyck (New York: Herder & Herder, 1976), 153–75. Rahner himself has not drawn out the implications of his theology of revelation and inspiration for an interreligious reading of non-Christian religious texts.

15. For an excellent exposition of contemporary theologies of religion, see Paul Knitter, *Introducing Theologies of Religions* (Maryknoll, NY: Orbis Books, 2002). Knitter expands the three types of theology of religion into four models, which he terms "replacement," "fulfillment," "mutuality," and "acceptance."

significance for and impact on the Christian community, some more inspiring, others less.[16] The point here is that scripture is a human activity; a text is scripture only to the community that reads it as scripture. It is only from this communal reading of non-Christian scriptures that a theology of revelation and inspiration will eventually emerge that is both appropriate to the Christian traditional teaching on the Bible as the Word of God and adequate to the new experiences of non-Christian scriptures as the wellspring of wisdom and spirituality for Christians.

ECCLESIAL IDENTITY AND MULTIPLE RELIGIOUS BELONGING?

One of the many objections against reading religious texts interreligiously is the fear that such a reading will weaken ecclesial identity and foster syncretistic forms of multiple religious belonging. If one reads and especially prays with non-Christian texts interreligiously, is there not the possibility that one abandons Christianity and converts to one of the non-Christian religions or at least develops a hyphenated or hybrid religious identity? In any case, one's loyalty and fidelity to Christianity as the only true religion would be jeopardized.

Such a fear seems to lurk behind *Dominus Iesus*. The declaration emphatically asserts what it terms the "unicity," "unity," and "universality" of the church. It declares that "the Church of Christ, despite the divisions which exist among Christians, continues to exist fully only in the Catholic Church,"[17] and that other "churches" or more precisely, "ecclesial communities which have not preserved the valid Episcopate and the genuine and integral substance of the Eucharistic mystery are not Churches in the proper sense."[18] With regard to non-Christian religions, the declaration affirms that "if it is true that the followers of other religions can receive grace, it is also certain that *objectively speaking* they are in a gravely deficient situation in comparison with those who, in the Church, have the fullness of the means of salvation."[19]

---

16. Raimon Panikkar has produced a massive selection of Hindu sacred texts for non-Hindu believers: *The Vedic Experience: Mantramañjarī: An Anthology of the Vedas for Modern Man and Contemporary Celebration* (London: Darton, Longman & Todd, 1977).

17. *DI*, 16.

18. *DI*, 17.

19. *DI*, 22. It is to be noted that the declaration refers to the "objective" condition of non-Christians when it speaks of their "gravely deficient situation" in comparison with Christians. It must be pointed out, however, that non-Christians can be, subjectively speaking, in a salvifically more advantaged position if they practice the true teachings of their religions in comparison with Christians who do not practice their faith and are therefore "in a gravely deficient situation" with regard to salvation. Ultimately, orthopraxis is of greater import than orthodoxy, though, of course, they should not be regarded as mutually exclusive.

Such an insistence on the Roman Catholic Church as the only true church of Christ and on the objective "gravely deficient situation" of non-Christians is no doubt intended to draw firm and clear boundaries between the Roman Catholic Church and other Christian denominations on the one hand and between Christianity and non-Christian religions on the other. This has the effect of bolstering the ecclesial and social identity of Roman Catholics over against both non-Catholic Christians and non-Christian believers. Needless to say, reading non-Christian religious texts as scripture tends, in the eyes of the authors of *Dominus Iesus*, to fuzz those institutional boundaries.

There is no doubt that interreligious reading of religious texts may lead to a syncretistic mixing of incompatible religious ideas, scriptures, and spiritual practices. This has happened particularly in new religious movements where either new interpretations of the Bible are made that contradict the basic Christian beliefs, or altogether new scriptures based on the founders' new visions and divine encounters are composed and declared authoritative (e.g., Joseph Smith's *Book of Mormon*, Mary Baker Eddy's *Science and Health with Key to the Scriptures*, L. Ron Hubbard's *Dianetics: The Modern Science of Mental Health*, Anton LaVey's *The Satanic Bible*, Mark and Elizabeth Prophet's *The Lost Teachings of Jesus*, Sun Myung Moon's *Divine Principle*, and innumerable books of the amorphous New Age movement). In all of these cases, the new books are intended to replace the Bible as sacred scripture.

The interreligious reading of sacred texts of various religions I am proposing does not aim at fusing two or more religions with their various constitutive elements, including their scriptures, into a new religion or a new religious movement with its own new scriptures. It claims no new religious visions, new prophecies, new miraculous events, new charisms, or new encounters with God as the source for new interpretations, new scriptures, and new religious institutions. Rather, its goal is to understand the Bible itself better through a comparative reading of other religious texts.

To achieve this richer understanding of the Bible and, consequently, to live a more authentically Christian life, a Christian may decide not only to read and learn from the scriptures of non-Christians, but also to share life with them; to work with them for justice, peace, and the integrity of creation; to undertake a theological dialogue with them; and, above all, to share religious experiences with them, especially in prayer, meditation, and worship. This fourfold sharing of life, work, theological dialogue, and religious experiences with non-Christians is not extraneous to the effort to understand non-Christian scriptures but forms an intrinsic part of the hermeneutics of religious texts. In these activities, especially in the sharing of religious experiences, what is being practiced has been referred to as multiple religious belonging. To cite a celebrated confession of Raimon Panikkar, one of the most prolific and influential practitioners of interreligious hermeneutics and dialogue: "I 'left' as a Christian, 'found myself' a Hindu, and I 'return' a Buddhist, without having ceased to be a Christian."[20]

Recently there have been several prominent Christians who practiced this double belonging and through it have given us a fresh, rich, and challenging understanding of the Bible and of the Christian faith and life as a whole. To be mentioned, among many, are Henri Le Saux, also known as Swami Abhishiktananda, Hugo M. Enomiya-Lassalle, Charles de Foucauld, Thomas Merton, Bede Griffith, Raimon Panikkar, Aloysius Pieris, Lawrence Freeman, and the Episcopal priest Ann Holmes Redding, who through their reading of Hindu, Buddhist, Zen, and Muslim texts have vastly enriched our understanding of the Bible.[21]

As for their Christian, and more specifically, ecclesial identity, there has never been the slightest doubt in their minds that they are Christian through and through, even though church officials might question their orthodoxy and Christian identity. Indeed, their religious quest was deeply rooted in their Christian faith, and it is precisely their conviction that revelation and salvation, which is brought about by Jesus, are somehow present in other religious traditions that set them on their journey of multiple religious belonging.

That does not mean of course that such multiple religious belonging does not cause severe theological difficulties and personal anguish. To take the case of Swami Abhishiktananda as an example, this Catholic-Hindu Benedictine monk experienced acutely the antinomy between the Christian and Hindu conceptions of reality and the painful push-and-pull of his double identity as a Hindu-Christian monk. The *advaita* or nondualistic experience of the divine that he had as a Hindu seemed to run counter to his Christian faith in God as triune, in God's creative act *ex nihilo*, and in prayer as an I–Thou relationship to God. Abhishiktananda lived this anguish for nearly twenty-five years, never fully able to reconcile the two apparently opposing theologies on the theoretical level. Rather he counseled acceptance of this unresolvable tension without attempting to harmonize them.

Clearly, double religious belonging, and, within it, reading religious texts interreligiously, is by no means a facile compromise or a painless feat of intellectual balancing between two opposing worldviews and two sets of scriptures. Rather, it is a lived drama of intellectual and religious tension, never fully resolved on the theoretical level but affirmed at the existential plane in a quest for an ever-deeper understanding of reality and an ever-growing harmonious living with the divine, the self, and the cosmos, a goal that is ever elusive, provisional, and unfinished until one reaches "the other shore."

---

20. Raimon Panikkar, *The Intra-religious Dialogue* (New York: Paulist Press, 1978), 2.

21. On multiple religious belonging, see Peter C. Phan, *Being Religious Interreligiously: Asian Perspectives on Interfaith Dialogue* (Maryknoll, NY: Orbis Books, 2004), 60–83.

USING NON-CHRISTIAN SCRIPTURES
IN PRAYER AND SPIRITUALITY?

Other sites where interreligious reading of non-Christian texts presents the greatest threat of syncretism are prayer, spirituality, and worship, which usually are the most common areas where ordinary Christians read non-Christian scriptures. As is well known, scripture is primarily oral-aural; it is meant to be recited and proclaimed aloud, especially in public worship. It is only after the reading of the scripture is concluded with the announcement "This is the Word of the Lord" and the congregation answers "Thanks be to God," thereby acknowledging that God has spoken to them in that particular text, that the text becomes scripture. It is precisely here that syncretism is perceived as a "clear and present danger."

This danger was most vividly perceived by some senior Vatican officials when Pope John Paul announced on January 25, 1986, his plan to invite non-Christian leaders (in addition to non-Catholic Christians) to come to Assisi to pray for peace. The meeting was criticized as skirting dangerous syncretism. It was left to Bishop Jorge Mejía, then secretary of the Pontifical Council for Justice and Peace, to explain that the purpose of the Assisi meeting was not to have religious leaders "pray together"—that would be syncretism—but "to be together to pray." Subsequently, the concise formula "not to pray together, but to come together to pray" became the official mantra to justify interreligious prayer. In fact, in the actual event, after John Paul's welcome of religious leaders at the Portiuncula, religious leaders went to separate places in Assisi to pray with their coreligionists for ninety minutes and afterward gathered in the piazza in front of the basilica. There, each religious representative offered a prayer for peace according to his or her own religious tradition.

In his address to the religious representatives in Assisi, John Paul clarified the purpose of the meeting:

> The fact that we have come here does not imply any intention of seeking a religious consensus among ourselves or negotiating our faith convictions. Neither does it mean that religions can be reconciled at the level of a common commitment in an earthly project which would surpass them all. Nor is it a concession to relativism in religious beliefs, because every human being must sincerely follow his or her upright conscience with the intention of seeking and obeying the truth.
>
> Our meeting attests only—and this is its real significance for the people of our time—that in the great battle for peace, humanity, in its very diversity, must draw from its deepest and most vivifying sources where

its conscience is formed and upon which is founded the moral action of all people.[22]

Clearly, then, interreligious reading of non-Christian scriptures meets its real test—its rubber meeting the road as it were—when it is read in the context of prayer and public worship. The question is not only whether believers of different religions can use their scriptures to pray together even if they believe in the same God but also—and here it is a much more difficult question—whether Christians can pray together with members of religions that do not mention God or do not profess faith in a personal God.[23]

With regard to the first question, the answer is clear in the case of Judaism. Christians have since the very beginning read and prayed with the Hebrew scriptures, especially the psalms, in their liturgy and in their private devotion, even though Jews may object to the Christians' christological interpretation of their Tanak.

In the case of Islam, as Pope John Paul II has repeatedly asserted, Christians and Muslims worship the same God. In all his addresses to Muslims, John Paul II always highlights the fact that Christians and Muslims believe in the one God who is creator and expresses his admiration for the high ethical and religious demands Islam makes on its followers, especially in terms of prayer, fasting, and almsgiving. Nevertheless, even John Paul, despite his great respect and admiration for Islam, did not pray together with Muslims, as he did with Jews in their synagogues.[24] Pope Benedict XVI, during his visit to the Blue Mosque in Istanbul in November 2006, elected to pray in silence rather than uttering any prayer.

The reason for the difference in the attitude of Christians toward Islam lies in the fact that Islam claims to have superseded Christianity and to be a post-Christian (at times perceived as anti-Christian) religion, making it impossible for Christians to read and pray the Qur'an christologically. But even so, I suggest that common praying between Christians and Muslims on the basis of the Qur'an is not impossible. In this respect I refer to an extraordinary document entitled *Christians and Muslims: Praying Together? Reflections and Texts*, issued by the "Islam in Europe Committee" of the Council of European Bishops'

---

22. Francesco Gioia, ed., *Interreligious Dialogue: The Official Teaching of the Catholic Church from the Second Vatican Council to John Paul II (1963–2005)* (Boston: Pauline Books & Media, 2006), no. 535.

23. For a helpful discussion of interreligious prayer, see Jacques Dupuis, *Christianity and the Religions: From Confrontation to Dialogue* (Maryknoll, NY: Orbis Books, 2002), 236–52.

24. To be mentioned is John Paul's visit to the Roman Synagogue on April 13, 1986, the first pope ever to do so. He conceives the visit not just as a social or political gesture but as an explicitly religious act, the purpose of which is to pray together with Jews.

Conferences and of the Conference of European Churches.[25] The document acknowledges that Christians and Muslims "praying together is a reality, often spontaneously performed by individual members of different churches as well as by informal gatherings of Christians and Muslims together." It points out that on political, civic, social, and personal occasions such as the taking office of a Muslim politician, the beginning and ending of the school year, marriage between a Christian and a Muslim, etc., Muslims and Christians already have prayed together. It notes, with commendable frankness and humility, that "it is not churches that have taken the initiatives, but Christians, singly or in groups." It also makes a helpful distinction between "multireligious prayer," that is, a gathering at which different religious groups pray in their own distinctive ways in a serial manner (as at the Assisi meeting), and "interreligious prayer," where different religions subsume their distinctive idioms in common expressions and combine their perceptions of God in addressing prayers to God. Finally, it offers a sample of interreligious prayers for Christians and Muslims composed by both Christians and Muslims and a selection of psalms (e.g., 23, 90, and 104:24–35) and texts from the Qur'an such as the *Fatiha*, and suras 2:255; 49:13, and the litany of the ninety-nine names of God.

With regard to Christians praying with believers not of the Abrahamic family, in particular Hinduism, Buddhism, Confucianism, and Daoism, the situation is much more complex, especially with regard to nontheistic Buddhism. The theological question must be raised of whether Brahman of Hinduism, or Nirvana of Buddhism, or Heaven of Confucianism, or Dao of Daoism can be identified with the God of Abraham, Jacob, and Isaac who has revealed himself as the Father of Jesus of Nazareth. There is no doubt that the conceptual categories and frameworks of these Asian religious traditions are markedly different from those of Christianity, and that these fundamental differences must be acknowledged in interreligious prayer. Nevertheless, it is not impossible that Christians may make use of, e.g., the well-known passage of the *Brhadaranyaka Upanishad* (I, 3, 28), which Pope Paul VI cites in his address to the representatives of the various religions during his 1964 visit to Mumbai:

> From the unreal lead me to the real!
> From darkness lead me to the light!
> From death lead me to immortality![26]

Another text, from *Kena Upanishad* (I, 3–8), can also be used to address and praise God in God's ineffable transcendence (*neti neti*). And above all, the long

25. The text is available at www.cec-kek.org.

26. R. C. Zaehner, ed., *Hindu Scriptures* (London: Dent, 1966), 34; cited in Dupuis, *Christianity and the Religions*, 250.

and passionate prayer of praise and adoration that Arjuna sings to Krishna in *Bhagavad Gītā* can certainly be recited with devotion by any Christian.[27]

Jacques Dupuis summarizes well the value of interreligious prayer based on the scriptures of non-Christian religions:

> The practice of common prayer is based on a communion in the Spirit of God shared in anticipation between Christians and "others," which in turns grows and is deepened through such practice. Through common prayer, Christians and the "others" grow together in the Spirit. Common prayer seems then to be the soul of interreligious dialogue, the deepest expression of dialogue and at the same time the guarantee of a deeper common conversion of the partners to God and to the others.[28]

HOW TO READ NON-CHRISTIAN SCRIPTURES INTERRELIGIOUSLY

The last issue for our consideration is the hermeneutical question: How to read non-Christian religious texts interreligiously? The answer to this question cannot but be multiple and nuanced, depending on the type of reader, the goals sought, and the venues in which non-Christian scriptures are read. From what has been said so far, it is clear that non-Christian texts are read by various kinds of people—scholars of religion, theologians, church officials, people in the pews, and nonacademics; for different purposes—for intellectual enrichment, apologetical and missionary purposes, and spiritual nourishment; and in diverse venues—in the academy, liturgical settings, social festivities, meditation and contemplation centers, and private devotion.

Needless to say, the method of reading non-Christian texts varies widely, depending on the kinds of reader, purpose, venue, and a lot of other things. One hermeneutical method that may be appropriate to one type of reader, purpose, venue, and circumstance may not be so for another. This should come as no surprise since the Bible itself is read differently by Christians, with a multiplicity of methods, none of which should be allowed to assume a monopoly.

One possible way is to read the sacred texts of other religions as windows through which one sees oneself through the eyes of another. The metaphor of "window" for sacred texts and the goal of looking through—not at—this window is to understand oneself through the self-understanding of another. Of course, not everyone who reads non-Christian texts approaches them as

---

27. See Zaehner, *Hindu Scriptures*, 298.
28. Dupuis, *Christianity and the Religions*, 252.

"window." Other metaphors may be preferred such as lens, perspective, light, mirror, voice, symphony, food, wellspring, treasure, world, or worldview. These other metaphors, especially nonocular ones, though not excluding the "window" metaphor, may suggest a different set of hermeneutical strategies.

Furthermore, some Christians reading non-Christian texts may not seek as their primary goal a theoretical understanding of their self, though this goal is certainly valid and worthwhile. Rather, their primary purpose may be a richer knowledge of and a deeper love for God or Jesus or church or non-Christian neighbors, and the practice of a more inclusive spirituality that they do not find in Christianity alone or at least in an adequate measure.

The foregoing observations are by no means intended to invalidate the practice of using non-Christian scriptures as a window through which one understands oneself through the self-understanding of another. On the contrary, "seeing one's self through the eyes of another" is arguably an indispensable epistemological act for an understanding of God and world. The understandings of God, self, and world are intimately intertwined and strictly condition one another. The way we understand any one component of this triad necessarily impacts our understanding of the other two.

It may even be argued that the metaphor of "window" for non-Christian scriptures enjoys certain hermeneutical advantages over others. Windows are normally not things to be looked at in themselves, unless you happen to be a window cleaner or a window maker. Generally, one does not look *at* but *through* windows, just as one normally does not gaze on the finger pointing at the moon but rather on the moon itself. Windows act as openings into a hidden world that would not be accessible to us otherwise. Without them we would be in a bunker or in a box bereft of any means to know what is going on outside. Windows let in light by which we see and fresh air by which we breathe and live. Epistemologically, windows serve as heuristic devices by which we are enabled to understand reality, even though our understanding of that reality is framed and therefore limited by them. Consequently, as windows, non-Christian scriptures should not be studied for their own sake, merely as antique artifacts, of interest only to historians and antiquarians, or as linguistic or grammatical documents, of concern only to philologists and litterateurs. Rather as scripture, they must be approached as icons or sacraments of the Divine or the Real and as the Word of God made flesh in human words.

Furthermore, as metaphor for texts, "windows" suggests their objectivity, autonomy, and primacy over us as readers. Texts are not things readers create at their whim and pleasure. They exist before we discover them, they norm our reading, we submit ourselves to them, they make demands on us, even though it is readers that make them scripture. We must approach sacred texts reverently, with pure hands and humble minds and devout hearts, the way Jews venerate the scroll, Muslims kiss the Qur'an, and Christians incense and carry the Bible in liturgical procession. We must be willing and ready to accept the intellectual, moral, and spiritual demands they may make upon us. We do not read them only to confirm what we already know or justify what we already do. There is always the possibility and risk that these non-Christian scriptures will provoke in us Christians an intellectual, emotional, moral, and religious conversion, to use Bernard Lonergan's categories.

Hermeneutical theorists such as Hans-Georg Gadamer, Paul Ricoeur, and David Tracy speak of hermeneutics as ways of understanding the world *behind*, *in*, and *in front of* the text. The world *behind* the text stands for the historical contexts in which the text was written, which is discovered through the historical-critical method of textual, form, and redaction criticisms. The world *in* the text represents the literary world of the text functioning as the mirror in which we see ourselves, which is unfolded by means of the literary methods of narrative, rhetorical, and reader-response criticisms. The world *in front of* the text stands for the existential possibilities presented by the text as lure and invitation, beckoning and challenging us to appropriate them as new, transforming, and liberating ways of being in the world. Though the metaphor of "window" hints more readily to the world *behind* the text and emphasizes the iconic function of the sacred text, the other metaphors of text as mirror and as lure must not be excluded from our understanding of the nature and functions of sacred texts so as not to miss the worlds *in* and *in front of* them.

Lastly, it is suggested that in reading non-Christian scriptures we should try to see ourselves through the eyes of another. This is perhaps the most difficult and by the same token the most transformative aspect of reading religious texts interreligiously. It is difficult because it demands that we read non-Christian scriptures not simply in order to see and understand what they can teach us Christians. This, of course, is by no means an easy task; in itself it already requires intellectual humility and a willingness to acknowledge and reverence the presence of the divine Spirit and the existence of divine revelation outside of Christianity. By contrast, seeing oneself through the eyes of another is a deeply disturbing and threatening act of decentering oneself and one's religious institution. It demands that we Christians jettison our pervasive sense of moral and religious superiority and make ourselves vulnerable to transformation and even conversion to another religious tradition or at least to forms of multiple religious belonging.

However praiseworthy and fruitful this act of reading non-Christian scriptures in order to learn from them is, it is still seeing the other through one's own eye. In so doing the danger abounds that we only see what we are conditioned to seeing by our own scripture and religious traditions or want to see only what interests us. We are still looking through our own "windows" and see only similarities or equivalences between Christianity and other religions. The religious "other" serves only as a reflection of ourselves, as the mirror in which we see ourselves, albeit somewhat differently, but the alterity of the other does not yet function as the lens through which we see ourselves.

In religious matters, this alterity, or the eye of the other, is revealed by two distinct questions: How the religious others see themselves, which often is very different from how Christians see them; and how they see us, which often is very different from how we see ourselves and may be quite hostile to us. Taking into account this alterity of the other as other and these two questions as hermeneutical lenses seriously vastly complicates the interreligious reading of religious texts. For instance, some Christians reading the Qur'an may want to expand thereby their specifically Christian understanding of God, Abraham, Moses, Jesus, and Mary, or to enrich their practices of profession of faith, prayer, almsgiving, fasting, and pilgrimage. This is no doubt a laudable goal, but the glass of their "window" is basically a Christian-tinted one, and as a result the risk of missing what the Qur'an says about itself as God's revealed Word and what it says about the Bible and Christians is very high. Because they read the Qur'an through the Bible these Christians may not be open to taking seriously those statements of the Qur'an that contradict Christian faith and practice. Only by seeing oneself through the eyes of another—both through what the others say about themselves and what they say about us—is reading religious scriptures interreligiously truly interreligious. Such an approach to the religious other as other is all the more important when we expand interreligious reading to include interreligious dialogue where the historical relations between Christians and Muslims and between Islam and the West are fraught with mutual hatred, violence, and war.

As to reading strategies that will be helpful in interreligious reading of non-Christian texts, Francis X. Clooney, a Christian theologian and Hindologist and a professor at Harvard Divinity School, has offered valuable suggestions, and I mention them in concluding this essay. Clooney, along with a handful of other Catholic theologians, has been engaged in elaborating what is called "comparative theology." This new theological enterprise is highly relevant for the practice of interreligious reading of sacred texts since the latter may be regarded as an integral part of the former.

By *comparative* theology Clooney means not simply another specialization within theology such as the theology of religions or the theology of Christian mission but a project that "intends a rethinking of every theological issue and rereading of every theological text"[29] *after* a careful and detailed comparison of the Christian theological texts with those of other religious traditions. As a *theological* discipline, comparative theology, while akin to the comparative

---

29. F. Clooney, *Theology after Vedanta: An Experiment in Comparative Theology* (Albany: State University of New York University Press, 1993), 6.

study of religion, differs from it in "its resistance to generalizations about religion, its commitment to the demands of one or another tradition, and its goal of a reflective retrieval, after comparison, of the comparativist's (acknowledged) community's beliefs in order to restate them more effectively."[30]

As Clooney practices comparative theology, his main if not exclusive emphasis is on reading texts, and in his case, Hindu texts. Of course, the purpose of comparative reading is to discover both differences and similarities between two or more texts. To accomplish this task, Clooney suggests five reading strategies or models. The first two are derived from *Advaita* hermeneutics; the third from Hans-Georg Gadamer and David Tracy; the fourth from Philip Wheelwright; and the fifth from Jacques Derrida.

The first two Advaitic hermeneutical practices are called "coordination" (*upasamhāra*) and "superimposition" (*adhyāsa*). By "coordination" two texts are used together because of their common terms, themes, and parallel structures and conclusions in order to mutually illumine each other. By "superimposition" or juxtaposition, our own religious text is placed on top of or side by side another, thereby defamiliarizing our religious text by the proximity of another religious text so that an enhanced understanding of our own text may result. In the "conversation" model, one reads back and forth between the two texts as if in dialogue with them, listens to each text attentively and carefully, takes their questions and answers seriously, and remains open to possibilities of challenges and corrections and of new understandings. By "metaphor" or, more precisely, by the "semantic motion" implicit in the metaphor, the texts are imaginatively and creatively stretched out beyond their original meanings and are combined into new meanings and applications. By "collage," parts of the texts are excised, decomposed, and recomposed and recombined so that the collaged texts are made to meet, resist, and intrude on each other, destabilize each other's meanings, and unsettle the reader into constructing new meanings.

In sum, by coordination, superimposition, conversation, metaphor, and collage are meant:

> i. strategies by which one makes the reading together of compared texts a manageable but not reductive reflection; ii. the temporal arrangements by which one text is allowed to enhance the other; iii. the arrangement in multiple texts as the initiation of an ongoing and necessarily unpredictable conversation; iv. the construction of tensions by which the texts taken together are allowed to communicate more than either of them alone; v. the visualization of proximities by which the texts marginalize and destabilize one another.[31]

---

30. Ibid., 6–7.
31. Ibid., 174–75.

Finally, from the new understandings of one's own Christian texts obtained as the result of and *after* reading non-Christian texts, one will attempt to rearticulate one's understanding of the Christian beliefs. This is comparative theology proper. Here, of course, the question of truth unavoidably emerges. After crossing over to non-Christian scriptures one returns to one's Christian faith to rethink and reformulate its whole panoply of diverse and variegated forms of creed, cult, code, and community. One may ask whether these creedal, liturgical, moral, and ecclesial forms and formulations of the Christian faith are still valid or at least valid to the extent we think they are before our encounter with non-Christian texts.

Of course, one need not reject a priori these forms and formulations as false as a result of our reading religious texts interreligiously. Very often, the issue is not one of a stark either–or choice between the Christian creed, cult, code, and community and those of another religious tradition whose sacred scriptures one has read and absorbed. It is not a matter of choosing light vs. darkness, truth vs. error, goodness vs. evil, beauty vs. ugliness. Rather, it is more a matter of including and integrating the new insights one has gathered from an interreligious reading of non-Christian scriptures into a new formulation of Christian faith and practice.

Very often questions are asked, especially by the guardians of orthodoxy, whether the comparativist theologian's reformulations of the Christian faith and practice are correct and true, and punitive measures are taken against theologians whose views are judged ambiguous, misleading, and confusing. Of course, theologians must exercise their task of *fides quaerens intellectum* responsibly and humbly, avoiding sensationalism and celebrity. On the other hand, church officials and the community itself must understand and accept the fact that a reformulation of the Christian faith *after* and *in light of* an encounter with non-Christian texts and practices is an extremely difficult task that should not be foreclosed by a premature condemnation or by a mindless repetition of ancient formulas.

Given the increasingly multireligious and global character of our world, even in the United States, and given the necessary roles of religions in building justice and peace, especially in the post–September 11 context, reading religious texts interreligiously is no longer a narrow and obscure specialization of ivory-tower theologians or a rare and rarified practice of the spiritual elite. Rather, it is becoming a daily necessity for all, believers and nonbelievers alike. The task is extremely difficult, challenging, even threatening. Fortunately, it has been started, and it must be continued, with deep humility, generosity of spirit, and welcoming hospitality.

8

An Interfaith Encounter at Jacob's Well

A Missiological and Interreligious Interpretation of John 4:4–42

The encounter between Jesus and the Samaritan woman at Jacob's well, reported only by the Fourth Gospel (4:4–42), is, as typical of many Johannine texts, susceptible of several interpretations—quite different among themselves and yet equally plausible. The hermeneutical principle that texts are inherently polyvalent and hence admit of many possible readings, if ever valid, is no doubt supremely so of this text, precisely because it can be shown to contain several layers of meanings.[1]

---

1. There is a preliminary issue of the historicity of the incident. At first sight, the incident seems to be a theological construction of John, who is the only evangelist to mention a ministry of Jesus in Samaria. Jesus' missionary discourse in Matt 10:5 forbids his disciples to enter a Samaritan town. Of the Synoptics Luke seems to be the most sympathetic to the Samaritans: a Samaritan is held up as an example of the love of neighbor (10:29–37) and the only leper to thank him among the ten cured by Jesus is a Samaritan (17:11–19). But even Luke mentions that Jesus refuses to go to Samaria on his way to Jerusalem (9:52–53). The first explicit account of the Christian presence in Samaria is found in Acts 8:1–25 where it is reported that the Hellenist Christians took refuge in Samaria after Stephen's murder and that Philip, one of seven Hellenist deacons, proclaimed the Good News there and met with Simon Magus. Philip's preaching brought many Samaritans to accept baptism, which, however, did not impart to them the Holy Spirit. Consequently, Peter and John had to come from Jerusalem to lay hands on the new converts so that the Holy Spirit could descend upon them. The historical plausibility of the text is no doubt lessened by the fact that the text, especially the solemn discourse of Jesus, bears all the characteristics of Johannine theology and style. For example, misunderstandings and ironies abound in both the Samaritan woman and the disciples, and distinctive Johannine theological themes and expressions (e.g. *egō eimi*) underlie Jesus' discourse. However, given the fact that the text also contains a wealth of concrete and specific historical details about the location (the well at the foot of Mount Gerizim), the time (about noon), the Samaritans' legal impurity, their theology of true worship (on Mount Gerizim), and their expectation of a prophet-like-Moses seems to argue in favor of at least a basic substratum of a historical event on which John constructs his theology.

POSSIBLE INTERPRETATIONS

Of the many interpretations of John 4:4–42 the *christological* interpretation, which focuses on the question of Jesus' real identity, is perhaps the most common and obtains pride of place.[2] It is argued that the point of the dialogue between Jesus and the Samaritan woman is to correct the misunderstandings of the messiah by Jesus' contemporaries and to reveal that Jesus is the real messiah. The Samaritan woman first acknowledges that Jesus is a "prophet" (19). She then professes her belief in the coming of the messiah, as affirmed by the fifth article of the Samaritan creed ("I know that messiah is coming"), whose role is to "proclaim all things" to the Samaritans (25). Later she wonders aloud to her townsfolk whether Jesus is the messiah because he has told her everything she had ever done (29).[3]

However, at this stage of the dialogue, she doubts whether Jesus could be a "prophet like Moses" since he is a Jew, worshiping God in Jerusalem and not on her ancestors' sacred mountain, that is, Mount Gerizim. Though the familiar term "messiah" [the anointed one] is placed on the Samaritan woman's lips, its usage is inappropriate since the Samaritans did not expect a messiah in the sense of an anointed king of the Davidic lineage, a belief not contained in the Pentateuch, the Samaritans' only sacred scripture. Rather, they expected a *Taheb* (one who returns) in the tradition of Moses, a prophet like Moses. In response to his interlocutor's doubt, Jesus declares *"egō eimi"* (I am he). This celebrated Johannine phrase reveals Jesus' identity as the true messiah, that is, as divine[4] and as the true teacher and lawgiver, or, in Samaritan terms, as the true *Taheb*, and not as a royal nationalistic leader.[5]

A *pneumatological* reading highlights a major theme of the text, that is, how the Spirit, symbolized by the gift of water that Jesus gives, establishes a special relation between true worshipers and God the Father. The presence of

---

2. Commentaries on the Fourth Gospel are legion. Among those consulted are Raymond Brown, *The Gospel According to John (I–XII)* (Garden City, NY: Doubleday, 1966); Raymond Brown, *The Gospel According to John (XIII–XXI)* (Garden City, NY: Doubleday, 1970); Stanley B. Marrow, *The Gospel of John: A Reading* (New York: Paulist Press, 1995); Francis Moloney, *The Gospel of John* (Collegeville, MN: Liturgical Press, 1998); Herman N. Ridderbos, *The Gospel According to John: A Theological Commentary*, trans. John Vriend (Grand Rapids, MI: Eerdmans, 1997); Leon Morris, *The Gospel According to John* (Grand Rapids, MI: Eerdmans, 1995); Colin G. Kruse, *The Gospel According to John: An Introduction and Commentary* (Grand Rapids, MI: Eerdmans, 2004).

3. The question begins with *mēti*, thus implying a doubt on the Samaritan woman's part about Jesus' identity as the awaited messiah/prophet-like-Moses and perhaps a hope that he be one.

4. On the meaning of *egō eimi* as indicating divinity, see Brown, *Gospel According to John (I–XII)*, 533–38.

5. On the theology of the Samaritans, see J. Macdonald, *The Theology of the Samaritans* (London: SCM, 1964).

the Spirit produces and guarantees the authenticity of worship, which is not based on any discriminatory particularity such as geography, race, ethnicity, gender, and religion (23–24).

A *sacramental* interpretation will unearth a baptismal motif in the text by attending to its symbols of "living water" (10),[6] "living water" (11),[7] and "spring of water gushing up unto eternal life"[8] (14) and to their connection with "God's gift" and the Spirit (10).[9] Arguably, this baptismal motif is a continuation of the same theme already present in Jesus' earlier discourse to Nicodemus (3:2–6) and in the narrative of the baptism incident (3:22–30).[10] Perhaps even a Eucharistic motif, albeit much weaker, may be detected in Jesus' enigmatic answer to his disciples' urging that he eat something: "I have food (*brōsis*) to eat that you know nothing about" (32).[11]

Related to the pneumatological and sacramental interpretations is the *liturgical* one, which focuses on the nature and conditions of true worship. Jesus maintains that the Jews understand what they worship while the Samaritans do not; in this sense "salvation is from the Jews" (22).[12] Nevertheless, in the

---

6. "Living water" refers not to Jesus himself but to his spiritual gift. It is not eternal life itself but something "leaping up unto eternal life." In one interpretation, "God's gift" or Jesus' gift of living water is his teaching. In the Old Testament water often symbolizes God's life-giving wisdom (Prov 13:14; 18:4; Isa 55:1; and Sir 24:23–29). The rabbis as well as the Qumran community frequently refer to the Torah as "living water." In John "living water" is a parallel of "light" and "bread of life," all symbols of Jesus' revelation. That Jesus is divine wisdom replacing the Torah is a common Johannine theme, which the Samaritan woman inchoatively intuits when she proclaims Jesus "a prophet" (19) and "the Messiah" (29). In another, quite plausible, interpretation, "living water" refers to the Spirit given by Jesus. The connection between water and spirit is common both in the Old Testament and in the Qumran literature (e.g., 1QS 4:21). See Brown, *Gospel According to John (I–XII)*, 180–81.

7. "Living water" that Jesus gives is contrasted with and is presented as superior to, that is, more life giving than the still water of Jacob's well. The Greek term for "well" in 11–12 is *phrear*, literally "cistern," whereas that for "spring" (14) is *pēgē*. Though in LXX usage both terms are practically synonymous, here a contrast seems to be drawn between the still, inert water of Jacob's well (cistern, though previously designated with *pēgē* in 6) and the fresh, life-giving water of Jesus' spring.

8. The term for "gushing up" is *hallesthai*, which LXX uses for the "spirit of God" that falls on Samson, Saul, and David. The connection between the living water and the Spirit is thus made clear.

9. That the "gift of God" is the Spirit is affirmed in Acts 2:38; 8:20; 10:45; 11:17. Moreover, the Spirit is the gift of the risen Christ (John 15) and hence, the mark of the eschatological era.

10. The baptismal motif is hinted at in early catacomb art in which baptism is represented by the Samaritan woman at the well. An objection against the baptismal interpretation may be that in baptism the person is immersed in water and does not *drink* it. In reply, 1 Cor 12:13 may be cited: "For by one Spirit we were baptized into one body . . . and all were made to drink of one Spirit."

11. In a later verse (34) Jesus clarifies that his food (*brōma*) is "doing the will of him who sent me and bringing his work to completion."

12. Note that here the "Jews" refers not to the group of Jews hostile to Jesus, in particular the

eschatological time, which is already here (21, 23), true worship is one that worships the Father neither in Gerizim nor in Jerusalem (21) but "in spirit and truth" (23) since "God is spirit" (24).[13] Note that the contrast between the true worship "in spirit and truth" and the false worship is not one between the interior worship in the depths of one's heart or spirit (private devotion and piety) and the external and official worship (public liturgy). Rather, the contrast is between the public worship carried out on Mount Gerizim and in the Jerusalem temple and the equally public worship of the Father in the spirit who is Jesus' eschatological gift. This contrast is part of the Johannine comprehensive dualism between flesh and spirit, from below and from above, earth and heaven. Worship in spirit and truth (possibly a hendiadys) means worship in the Spirit of truth, that is, the Spirit of Jesus, who guides us to all truth (14:17; 15:26), or, simply, worship in Jesus, who is the truth (14:6) and who replaces the worship both in the Jerusalem temple and on Mount Gerizim.

More recently, inspired by *feminist* theology, another interpretation is put forth in which the role of women as courageous and forthright vindicators of their religious traditions and subsequently as effective apostles and evange-lizers is foregrounded. The Samaritan woman is portrayed as self-confident enough to challenge and even reprimand Jesus for speaking to her ("How is it that you, a Jew, ask a drink of me, a woman of Samaria?" [9]), question his ability to give water (11), and to assert her community's belief over against the Jewish—and by implication, Jesus'—belief ("Our ancestors worshiped on this mountain, but you say that the place where people must worship is in Jerusa-lem" [19]), and to state with clarity her own belief in the messiah ("I know that messiah is coming. When he comes, he will proclaim all things to us" [27]). Jesus himself deems the woman a worthy dialogue partner in acknowledging that she is speaking the truth when she affirms that she has no husband (18) and in addressing her as "Woman" (21), the Johannine Jesus' title of respect.[14] Above all, the Samaritan woman is presented as the first apostle to her towns-people, who came to believe in Jesus on the strength of her words (39).[15]

Jewish leaders, as it does in many other places in the Johannine Gospel, but to the Jewish people as a whole, in distinction from the other peoples, such as the Samaritans.

13. John offers three statements that are not definitions of God's inner essence but descriptions of God's external relations to humanity: "God is spirit" (4:24); "God is light" (1 John 1:5); and "God is love" (1 John 4:8).

14. Jesus uses the same title of respect in addressing his mother (2:1; 19:26–27) and Mary Magdalene (20:15). Jesus' addressing the Samaritan woman (as well as Mary Magdalene) with this title implicitly raises her to the dignity of his mother, and even to the status of the "universal woman."

15. For a feminist interpretation of John 4:4–42, see Sandra Schneiders, *The Revelatory Text: Interpreting the New Testament as Sacred Scripture* (Collegeville, MN: Liturgical Press, 1999), 180–99.

A MISSIOLOGICAL AND INTERRELIGIOUS READING

The five above-mentioned interpretations are, of course, not mutually exclusive. Each illumines the others and in turn is enriched by them. For example, the christological and pneumatological interpretations, when taken together, will throw a stronger light on the identity of both Jesus and the Holy Spirit. The feminist interpretation complements the christological one by revealing the kind of prophet and messiah Jesus is. And, of course, the pneumatological, sacramental, and liturgical interpretations are intimately related to each other. Moreover, each of them in its own way supports a missiological reading of the text by highlighting a particular dimension of Christian mission. The christological interpretation explains the content of Christian mission; the pneumatological its dynamism; the sacramental its immediate goal; the liturgical its ultimate purpose; and the feminist its agency. In addition, the encounter between Jesus and the Samaritan woman and their conversation as well as their interaction provide a model for interreligious dialogue. Finally, Jesus' discourse to the disciples explicates the very nature and dynamics of Christian mission. On its part, the missiological reading of John 4:4–42 lends thematic unity and practical relevance to the five foregoing interpretations.

Before attempting this missiological reading of John 4:4–42,[16] a brief word about its literary structure is in order.[17] The text is composed of two parts, the first narrating the dialogue between Jesus and the Samaritan woman (7–26), the second the dialogue between Jesus and his disciples (27–38). Part I is divided into two sections, the first about the living water (6–15) and the second about true worship of the Father in Spirit and truth. Each section contains two short dialogues, and each dialogue is composed of three exchanges. The first dialogue of each section is initiated by Jesus, responded to by the Samaritan woman, and concluded by Jesus. The second dialogue reverses the order, with the woman initiating, Jesus responding, and the woman concluding. Part II consists of Jesus' commentaries on two proverbs, the first concerning the interval between sowing and harvesting (35–36), the second about the difference between the sower and the reaper (37–38). The whole text begins with an introduction detailing the location and time of the encounter (4–6) and concludes with the narration of its result (39–42). Clearly, the text is a literary jewel sparkling with structural symmetry, literary symbols, and theological subtlety.

---

16. By "missiological reading" is meant a reading from the perspective of the church's mission of evangelization understood here as the task of witnessing to and proclaiming Jesus to those who have not yet accepted him as their savior and Lord.

17. Here I am following Brown, *Gospel According to John (I–XII)*, 176–77.

Whose Mission? Church's Mission as Missio Dei

That a missiological reading of John 4:4–42 is not arbitrary is confirmed by the use of the verb "send" in two key instances (the Latin *mittere* is the etymological root of the English "mission"). The first refers to the Father sending Jesus (34) and the second to Jesus sending the disciples (38). Note the strict temporal and theological chronological order of the two missions, with the second following and depending on the first, and this order is theologically significant for a correct understanding of the nature of Christian mission.

First of all, we are not missionaries by our own initiatives. We are not missionary entrepreneurs, determining for ourselves and on our own authority the goal, method, location, and time of our mission. John notes that Jesus "had to go through Samaria" (4). This is not a geographical necessity, since there is an alternative route from the Jordan valley, where he is (3:22), up to Galilee through the Bethshan gap, without having to pass through Samaria. Rather, the necessity of the trip, as everything else connected with Jesus' mission, is theological. It falls within God's will and plan for Jesus.

More than geography and time, the very origin and efficacy of Jesus' mission are rooted in his being sent by God. In the Johannine Gospel, Jesus repeatedly emphasizes that he has been sent by his Father and that everything he says or does he has learned from or seen done by his Father. Indeed, he *cannot* say or do anything unless enabled and authorized to do so by his Father (5:19–20, 30; 8:28; 12:49–50; 14:10). Challenged by his opponents to justify his ministry Jesus appeals to his being sent by his Father. In turn Jesus promises that the Spirit the Paraclete will be sent, either from the Father (14:15, 25) or from himself (15:7), and fulfills this promise during his apparition to the disciples after his resurrection. Christian mission then is essentially trinitarian, that is, from the Father to the Son, and from the Son to the Spirit, and from/in the Spirit to us. Ultimately their Christian mission/being sent originates from and prolongs the mission/being sent of the Son and of the Spirit by the Father.

Contemporary theology of mission has retrieved this trinitarian dimension and speaks of the church's mission as part of the *missio Dei*. This is to emphasize that the church's mission is not its own but rather comes from the Spirit, the Son, and the Father, in other words, from the triune God. As a consequence, the church cannot claim mission as its own possession nor can it control and implement it as it sees fit. Rather, acknowledging the root of its mission in the *missio Dei*, the church must obey the divine command and follow God's modus operandi in the world through God's Son and Spirit. By implication, as Christian missionaries, we are not sent by the church or by the mission board, though, of course, we are responsible to these bodies. Rather, we are sent by the Spirit, by the Son, and ultimately by the Father—again, note this theological taxis—as John asserts in 4:34 and 38 and in numerous other places of his gospel.

With regard to Jesus sending us, v. 38 poses a difficulty in that in it Jesus said: "I sent (aorist) you to reap that for which you did not labor." Up to this point in the Johannine Gospel no report has been made by John about whether or when Jesus did this. The difficulty may be resolved in two ways. First, it is assumed that there was a sending of the disciples on mission by Jesus, of which John has said nothing, but which is mentioned in the Synoptic Gospels (Luke 9:2; 10:1). Second, v. 38 is taken to be a retrojection into Jesus' earthly ministry of the postresurrectional sending of the disciples reported in 20:21, which makes the disciples apostles, that is, persons sent. In either case, it is clear that the church's mission is given by Jesus who in turn receives his mission from his Father: "As you have sent me into the world, so I have sent them into the world" (17:18).

Mission: To What End?

When Jesus is urged by the disciples to eat some of the foods they have brought back from the village, he says that he has food that they know nothing about. In his typical use of irony and misunderstandings John has the disciples wonder whether someone, probably the Samaritan woman, has brought food to their master during their absence.[18] Jesus replies, "My food is doing the will of him who sent me and to complete his work" (34).

In past theologies of mission popular in both Catholic and Protestant circles, the goal of mission is said to be saving souls and planting the churches. In his monumental study of mission David Bosch shows that Christian mission from 600 to 1500 is understood to have two basic goals: saving souls and church extension.[19] The first goal of mission is dependent on Augustine's view of humanity as radically corrupted by sin, both original and personal, which he develops in opposition to Pelagius. This anthropology entails that the goal of mission is saving the lost souls who in the mission fields are identified with non-Christians. In this perspective, mission is narrowed down to ensuring the individual's eternal salvation.

Another Augustinian doctrine also determines the second goal of mission. In his dispute with the Donatists, who insist that only those who are totally unblemished and perfect may be church members, Augustine argues that what is essential is not the personal moral and spiritual condition of the Christians but the church and its official institutions that are the necessary means of salvation. This ecclesiology entails that mission concentrates on bringing as many pagans as possible into the church, the only ark of salvation,

---

18. The disciples' misunderstanding about food parallels that of the Samaritan woman about water.

19. See David Bosch, *Transforming Mission: Paradigm Shifts in Theology of Mission* (Maryknoll, NY: Orbis Books, 1991), 214–19.

by blandishments and by forced conquest if necessary. Baptism is changed from a process of the individual's gradual incorporation into the church after a long and arduous moral and spiritual training (i.e., the ancient catechumenate) into a rite of entrance of the mass, sometimes of the whole tribe, into the church with a minimum of catechesis and often without real conversion. Hence, it is necessary to set up church structures as soon as possible in the missionary fields, a process known as "planting the church" (*plantatio ecclesiae*), which now becomes the second, and even the overriding goal of mission, on which most of the resources and energies of the missionary labor is spent. Consequently, the success of mission, not unlike the body count in war, is measured by the number of the sacraments administered, dioceses established, churches built, and money collected.

In contrast, John 4:34 states that Jesus' mission is to do the will of the Father who sent him and to bring his work to completion. If the church's mission is essentially a prolongation of Jesus' mission, then its goal must be identical with that of Jesus' mission. It is vitally important to discover what the Johannine Gospel means by doing God's will and bringing God's work to completion. God's will for Jesus, we are told, is to bear witness to his Father's teaching and work (5:30), to manifest the Father's glory (12:27–28).[20] In a later chapter John specifies God's will more explicitly: "And this is the will of him who has sent me: that I should lose nothing of all that he has given me, but raise it up on the last day. This is indeed the will of my Father, that all who see the Son and believe in him have eternal life; and I will raise them up on the last day" (6:39–40; see also 10:28–29). Elsewhere, this will, which Jesus' mission is to carry out, is that we have life, and life in abundance (10:10). This eternal life is said to consist in "knowing" two things: that the Father is the only true God and that Jesus is the one sent by him (17:3).

Jesus brought his Father's work to fulfillment not only by accepting his plan of the death on the cross but also by creating his new community, not of his servants but his friends (15:15). Such community must observe Jesus' new commandment, that they love one another as Jesus has loved them (13:34), and serve one another by washing each other's feet (13:14). The last chapter of the Johannine Gospel, which recounts the miraculous catch of fish (21:1–14) and Peter's threefold profession of love for Jesus (21:15–23), may be regarded as the *magna carta* of the Christian community. The miraculous catch describes the fruitfulness of the new community when it continues the mission of Jesus, and Peter's confession of love describes the condition for true discipleship.

In light of what John says about Jesus' mission as doing the will of the Father, the traditional understanding of the goal of mission as soul saving and church planting needs correction. While the concern for salvation remains,

---

20. Conversely, it is the Father who bears witness to his Son, Jesus (8:16).

eternal life is much less a matter of securing the individual's life after death with God as a reward for an upright life ("going to heaven," as the popular saying goes) than bearing witness before the world to God the Father's glory through word and, indeed, so that it may confess God the Father as the only true God and that Jesus is the only Son sent by him. Furthermore, with regard to church planting, the goal of mission is not so much extending the number of churches and their membership throughout the world (what is euphemistically referred to as "church growth") in order to increase the church's external influence and to bolster the power of the church's hierarchy as the deepening of the love and service that church members must render to one another. Baptism is still a desideratum, but not because without it the "pagans" would go to hell, but because through it a person can bear explicit witness to the love that God has for us in Jesus. Similarly, church planting is still an activity to be carried out, but not as a sign of God's favor, much less as a proof of one's denomination's superiority and success, but as a tangible way of extending God's love and caring for God's children, whether baptized or not, so that they may have life in abundance.

What Should the Church Proclaim in Mission?

In his conversation with the Samaritan woman Jesus presents her with two challenges, namely, to recognize God's gift and to discern Jesus' identity. As to the first, with Jesus' prompting, she recognizes that the water Jesus gives is not one from Jacob's well but the Spirit, who is the "living water" or a "spring of water gushing up unto eternal life" (14). As to the second, again Jesus leads the Samaritan woman to discern his identity by referring to her personal life and by praising her truthfulness. As a result, she acknowledges that he is a "prophet" (19). Furthermore, after Jesus affirms that true worship must be offered to God neither in Jerusalem nor on Mount Gerizim but "in spirit and truth," she professes her faith in a coming messiah. At that moment Jesus fully reveals himself as "I am he" (26).

The object of the church's proclamation then is twofold: first, Jesus as the prophet, the messiah, and "I am he/he who is"; and second, the Spirit as the living water giving eternal life. This is not the place to explicate the underlying Christology and pneumatology contained in the Johannine Gospel. Suffice it to say that, even if christological and pneumatological affirmations in John are invested with metaphysical weight, it is clear that they are functionally oriented.[21] That is, the point of Jesus' revelation about himself and the Spirit,

---

21. Put in terms of systematic theology, the main focus is on the "Economic Trinity"—the Trinity as present and active in history and the three divine persons' relations to humanity—and not on the "Immanent Trinity"—the inner, eternal relations among the Father, the Son, and the Holy Spirit. Of course, the Immanent Trinity and the Economic Trinity are not opposed to each other. Rather, what can be said about the former is derived from our knowledge of the latter, and

and ultimately about the triune God, is to lead the Samaritan woman not only to orthodoxy but also to "orthopraxis," which consists in worshiping God in spirit and truth: "God is spirit, and those who worship him must worship in spirit and truth" (24).

Fruits of Mission?

In his dialogue with the disciples, Jesus quotes two familiar and yet enigmatic proverbs. The first says: "Four months more, then comes the harvest" (35). The proverb seems to affirm a necessary interval between sowing and reaping. Yet, in commenting on this proverb, Jesus denies such an interval, since the fields are already "ripe for harvesting" (35), and notes that "the reaper is already receiving wages and is gathering fruit for eternal life" (36). The reason for this abolition of the interval between sowing and reaping is the presence of the eschaton, as Jesus informs the Samaritan woman: "The hour is coming, and is now here, when the true worshipers will worship the Father in spirit and truth, for the Father seeks such as these to worship him" (23). Clearly, then, the mission fields are not empty or "pagan" places to which missionaries bring the Good News for the first time, nor is the harvest the result of their sowing, which will come only after some necessary delay and which the missionaries have to wait for with anxiety. The Spirit of God is already working there, sowing and planting, so that missionaries should not claim whatever good things present there as the result of their labor. As a consequence, "sower and reaper may rejoice together" (36). Jesus' assurance of the immediate result of evangelization is, of course, no invitation to sloth or arrogance. Rather, it is a source of confidence and consolation for missionaries for whom discouragement and frustration are a constant temptation, especially when visible results (e.g., the number of "conversions") are long in coming.

Sowing and Reaping

The second proverb says: "One sows and another reaps" (37). At first blush the saying, which affirms the difference between the sower and the reaper, sounds pessimistic, suggesting that the sower may not able to enjoy the fruits of his or her labor.[22] But Jesus turns the proverb into a cause for rejoicing for the disciples, assuring them that they will reap what others and not they have sown: "I sent you to reap that for which you did not labor. Others have labored, and

---

because divine revelation is a self-communication of God (and not just something of God or information about God), we are guaranteed that what we say about the Economic Trinity is true of the Immanent Trinity. Indeed, we must say that the Immanent Trinity is identical with the Economic Trinity and vice versa. On this, see Karl Rahner, *The Trinity*, trans. Joseph Donceel (New York: Crossroad, 1997; orig., 1967).

22. Such pessimism is implied in Mic 6:15: "You shall sow, but not reap." See also Deut 20:6; 28:30; Job 31:8.

you have entered into their labor" (38). Whatever interpretation is given to "I sent," whether it refers to an earlier mission not reported by John or a retrojection of a postresurrectional event into Jesus' earthly ministry (as explained above), clearly the disciples—and by extension, missionaries—are allowed to reap the fruits of others' labor!

Who are the "others" the fruits of whose hard work missionaries are now allowed to reap? In the context of the Samaritans' conversions, Jesus is the one whose work produces the fruits that his disciples are allowed to reap. But because of the plural in "others," it has been suggested that Jesus includes the Father whose will and plan he accomplishes. Another suggestion is that "others" refers not to Jesus but John the Baptist and his disciples who had preached in Samaria, or to Jesus and John the Baptist. Another likely hypothesis is that "others" includes the Spirit in whom true worshipers worship. Indeed, recent mission theology has emphasized that the real agent of mission is the Holy Spirit who is already active in the hearts, cultures, and religions of peoples to whom the Good News is announced and whose presence alone makes the missionaries' labor fruitful.[23]

Whatever interpretation of "others" is preferred, it is clear that this second proverb, like the first, in Jesus' interpretation, gives joy and comfort to missionaries because their success in mission work is not due to their own efforts but to the work of those who precede them, to whom they must be grateful for the privilege of enjoying the fruits of their labor, and above all to the Spirit, whose grace already transforms all humans to listen to and welcome the Word into their hearts.

Interfaith Dialogue as Part of Mission? The Example of Jesus

In spite of the fact, according to the Synoptic Gospels, that Jesus did not send his disciples on mission to non-Jews but rather restricts his and their mission to the lost sheep of Israel,[24] during his ministry he did encounter people of non-Jewish faiths, marveled at and praised their faith, and performed miracles on their behalf.[25] In the Johannine Gospel, two encounters of Jesus with non-Jews are reported. Besides that with the Samaritan woman,

---

23. See John Paul II, *Redemptoris Missio* (Vatican City, 1990), nos. 21–30.

24. See Matthew 15:24.

25. With regard to Jesus' encounters with non-Jews, Bob Robinson notes: "However, the accounts of Christ's meeting with people of faiths other than Judaism are both few and brief, and in them it is the Gentiles who take the initiatives and not Jesus—although he is seen as open to their approaches and commends their faith. But his example offers nothing to justify dialogue as a common search for religious truth or in any of the other senses now usually attached to the enterprise of dialogue." See his *Christians Meeting Hindus: An Analysis and Theological Critique of the Hindu-Christian Encounter in India* (Carlisle, Cumbria: Regnum International Books, 2004), 210.

there is a presumed meeting between Jesus and some Greeks during his last trip to Jerusalem. These Greeks were non-Jews, either proselytes or simple sympathizers with Judaism. They approached Philip and told him that they would like to see Jesus. Philip told Andrew and with him went to tell Jesus of the Greeks' request. We are not told whether Jesus met with the Greeks in person or not, though it is very likely that he did, since he declared to the two apostles: "The hour has come for the glory of the Son of Man to be manifested" (12:23).

Jesus' encounter with the Samaritan woman and his interaction with her are unique. Here it is Jesus who initiates the encounter, the only time in all the four Gospels. This encounter is all the more surprising and even scandalous because she is a Samaritan and a woman. As is well known, Samaritans are despised by Jews as heterodox, of impure blood (as a result of mixed marriages between the remnant of the native Israelites and the foreigners brought in by the Assyrians), and of syncretistic religion. Calling someone Samaritan is one of the worst insults (8:48). The fact that Samaritans tried to prevent the Jewish restoration and in the second century BC helped the Syrian monarchs in their wars against the Jews and the high priest's destruction of the Samaritan temple on Mount Gerizim in 128 BC deepen the mutual hostilities. In addition, the Samaritans' refusal to worship in Jerusalem makes matters worse. As for Samaritan women, a Jewish regulation of 65–66 CE warns that Samaritan women are ritually impure from birth since they menstruate from the cradle, a legal decision that may reflect an earlier view of Samaritan women.[26] No wonder the Samaritan woman is deeply shocked by Jesus' attempt to strike up a conversation with her: "How is it that you, a Jew, ask a drink of me, a woman of Samaria?" (9). We are told that the disciples themselves are scandalized by Jesus' talking with a woman (27); and we can only surmise the depth of their shock when they find out that she is a Samaritan woman!

However, touched by Jesus' willingness to talk to her, his respect for her despite her personal immoral life, and his promise to give her the living water, the Samaritan woman confesses that Jesus is the prophet like Moses. Then she goes back to her townsfolk with the invitation: "Come and see a man who told me everything I have ever done!" (29).

There are several lessons here for our work in mission and in interreligious dialogue. First, start where your conversation partner is. Jesus begins with a request for a drink because the woman is going to draw water from the well. Our mission and interreligious dialogue can have any starting point. Here it is a daily need, but it could be anything close to life, whether it is happy or a sad event, a passing fad or a deep longing of the heart.

---

26. See Brown, *Gospel According to John (I–XII)*, 170.

Second, we must not be afraid to take the first step to initiate the encounter. At times we may hold back because history seems to suggest that the dialogue is doomed to failure on account of ill-will, prejudice, or outright refusal to meet. Perhaps there is between us and our dialogue partners a mutual hatred and contempt as deep and as old as that between the Jews and the Samaritans. But by taking the first step and making ourselves vulnerable to possible rejection but trusting unreservedly in the transformative power of the "living water" which is the Spirit, we work to bring about mutual trust, friendship, and reconciliation.

Third, we must not be afraid to challenge and let ourselves be challenged by our partners in dialogue. Here Jesus challenges the Samaritan woman to recognize God's gift and to discern Jesus' identity. She in turn challenges Jesus with her people's belief about the validity of their worship on Mount Gerizim. Furthermore, like her, perhaps we will be challenged by people of other faiths about the shortcomings in our own lives and our churches. In our conversation with them we will discover where we need to correct our theologies, our ways of worship, our church policies.

Fourth, like her, what we can and must do is to say to our non-Christian believers, "Come and see." It is not a debate, much less a condemnation, or an arrogant posture of religious superiority. Rather, it is an open invitation. And what they are humbly and gently invited to see is not a doctrine, a book (inspired or not), an institution, but a person, the person of Jesus, or as the Samaritan woman puts it, "Come and see a man who told me everything I have ever done!" What we show them is not our cultures and civilizations, our church buildings and our organizations, our universities and hospitals, our megacongregations and media centers, but the person who has forgiven our sins and failures, our own and those of our churches, and who has given us a new life and a new hope, because he has gone from death to life and because he is God-in-the-flesh, the "I am he."

Fifth, like the Samaritan woman, we must willingly accept the fact that soon we will no longer be necessary for the faith life of the community to which we have brought the Good News. As her townsfolk tell her, "It is no longer because of what you said that we believe, for we have heard for ourselves, and we know that this is truly the Savior of the world" (42).

To be taught all this by a woman, a Samaritan woman, a sinful Samaritan woman, and a nameless sinful Samaritan woman—is this not the very enrichment of mission and interreligious dialogue, of course only if one is willing to model oneself after Jesus—"he who is"—and be refreshed by the Spirit—the "living water."

9

Sensus Fidelium, Dissensus Infidelium, Consensus Omnium

An Interreligious Approach to Consensus in Doctrinal Theology

Ever since Vincent of Lérins (died ca. 445) formulated in his *Commonitorium*, written in 434 under the pseudonym "Peregrinus," his three criteria for orthodoxy, namely, geographical ubiquity, temporal antiquity, and numerical unanimity (*quod ubique, quod semper, quod ab omnibus creditum est*), have played a determinative role in the Catholic understanding of Tradition, and within it, of the *sensus fidei/fidelium*.[1] This role is briefly mentioned by the International Theological Commission (ITC) in its 2014 document entitled *Sensus Fidei in the Life of the Church*, which refers to Vincent of Lérins's triple criteria for discerning the *sensus fidei*: "Vincent of Lérins (died c. 445) proposed as a norm the faith that was held everywhere, always, and by everyone (*quod ubique, quod semper, quod ab omnibus creditum est*)" (no. 24).[2]

The purpose of this chapter is neither to expound the Lérinian's teaching on the three criteria for discerning Christian truth in his *Commonitorium*[3] and the various theses of the ITC's document *Sensus Fidei*, nor to evaluate and compare them as a whole and in detail. Obviously, such a task is impossible within the allotted space, as the issue of the *sensus fidei/fidelium*, as the ITC

---

1. The best critical edition of Vincent of Lérins's *Commonitorium* is by Roland Demeulenaere in Corpus Christianorum Series Latina 64 (1985), 127–95. An older edition, with a very informative introduction, is Reginald Stewart Moxon, *The Commonitorium of Vincent of Lérins* (Cambridge: Cambridge University Press, 1915). The English translation of the *Commonitorium* is by C. A. Heurtley in *Nicene and Post-Nicene Fathers, Second Series*, vol. 11, ed. Philip Schaff and Henry Wace (Buffalo, NY: Christian Literature Publishing Co., 1894). It is revised and edited by Kevin Knight and is available at http://www.newadvent.org.

2. The English text of the document is available at the website of the International Theological Commission.

3. A helpful recent commentary on the *Commonitorium* is Thomas G. Guarino, *Vincent of Lérins and the Development of Christian Doctrine* (Grand Rapids. MI: Baker Academic, 2013).

rightly notes, is intimately connected with a host of complex Christian doctrines such as biblical revelation; the prophetic function of Christ, the church, and in particular the laity; doctrinal development; the distinctive roles of the magisteria of bishops and theologians; hermeneutics; ecumenical unity; theological and spiritual qualifications of the subjects of the *sensus fidei*; popular religiosity; public opinion; and so on. Rather I focus on the narrow question of whether Vincent's three criteria of orthodoxy are to be modified and extended to be serviceable at all in the contemporary contexts of Christianity.

While Vincent's three criteria for orthodoxy appear unassailable in the abstract, there have been vigorous debates about their concrete applicability and usefulness. Doubts have been expressed as to whether any Christian doctrine can meet these three criteria fully, and whether it is possible to verify with historical accuracy the extent to which it satisfies them. More to the point of my inquiry, questions may be raised about the geographical extent of the *ubique*, the temporal length of the *semper*, and the people to be counted (and more disturbingly, *not* counted) among the *omnibus*. Obviously Vincent's "everywhere" (*ubique*) did not extend beyond the Mediterranean world and Africa; his "always" (*semper*) extended back only to the beginning of Christianity fewer than five hundred years earlier; and his "all" (*omnibus*) were exclusively Christians, and indeed mainly bishops, and these within a severely circumscribed area. It is highly unlikely that Vincent could envision, from his cell in a secluded monastery on an island in southern Gaul, the world of exuberant, often-conflicting, socio-political, cultural, and religious diversity and multiplicity that is ours today.

Given the globalized, and most importantly, multicultural and multireligious character of our contemporary world, and given the emergence of what is referred to as world Christianity, my reflections will explore the necessity of going beyond the theological ambit of the Vincentian canon. Even though Vincent never uses the expression *sensus fidei/fidelium* in his *Commonitorium*, it is beyond doubt that this concept, as will be shown below, is operative throughout the work. In light of world Christianity and in our current multireligious context my question may be rephrased as follows: What is the context in which the *sensus fidei* is formed today and should the *sensus fidelium* [the sense of faith of the Christians] be corrected, complemented, and enriched by the *dissensus infidelium* [the different sense of faith of non-Christians] to build up the *consensus omnium* [the shared sense of faith of all], that is, an interreligious understanding and reformulation of Christian doctrines among believers of diverse religious traditions?

I begin with a brief commentary on the import of the Vincentian canon in the *Commonitorium*. Next, I argue that today Vincent's three criteria for orthodoxy—ubiquity, antiquity, and universality—must be expanded to reflect the contemporary context of world Christianity and religious pluralism. Furthermore, I propose that Christian theologians take into account the *dissensus infidelium*, taking *dissensus* to mean not only doctrinal diversity but also doctrinal differences, and *infidelium* to refer to the adherents of other faiths (the so-called non-Christians). In my view, it is no longer possible to do Christian theology by drawing only on the *sensus fidelium*, with *fidelium* restricted to Christians. Rather, Christian theology must be an interreligious discipline; learning from the *dissensus infidelium* must be a constitutive part of the theological method. By radically expanding and redefining the three elements of the Vincentian canon I hope to show that the *consensus omnium*, inclusive of *sensus fidelium* and *dissensus infidelium*, is a historically conditioned and dynamic reality that finds its root and fulfillment in God's plan of salvation.

THE VINCENTIAN DOUBLE "RULE" IN THE *COMMONITORIUM*

The objective of Vincent of Lérins's work is well stated in its title: "For the Antiquity and Universality of the Catholic Faith Against the Profane Novelties of All Heretics."[4] The Lérinian's *aide-memoire* (*commonitorium*) is intended as a defense of what he takes to be the two essential characteristics of the true Catholic faith, namely, *antiquitas* and *universalitas*, in contrast to which all heresies are *"profanae novitates."* Little is known about the life of the author of the *Commonitorium* except that he was a monk of Lérins, a monastery in southern Gaul, who styled himself *peregrinus* (pilgrim). However, nothing is more certain and obvious about him than his all-consuming love for the truth of the Catholic faith, the obverse of which is his deep-seated concern—"obsession" is not too strong a word—with heresies and heretics. Hence, his dogged determination to discover "how and by what sure and so to speak universal rule" we can "distinguish the truth of Catholic faith from the falsehood of heretical depravity" (2, 4). Vincent finds this rule first and foremost (*primum*) in the scripture or "Divine Law," which is "complete, and

---

4. *Pro catholicae fidei antiquitate et universalitate adversus profanas omnium haereticorum novitates.* Vincent's own title might simply be *Commonitorium Peregrini adversus haereticos* (*haereses*). The work is currently made up of 33 chapters. At the end of chapter 28, however, the editor of the manuscript notes: "The Second Book of the Commonitory is lost. Nothing of it remains but the conclusion: in other words, the recapitulation which follows." Clearly then chapters 29–33, which deal with the Council of Ephesus—which took place three years prior to the composition of *Commonitorium*—are part of the Second Book. Vincent argues that the Council of Ephesus defends the doctrine of the *Theotokos* against Nestorius precisely on the ground of its ubiquity, antiquity, and universality. Quotations of the text are followed by the number of the chapter and the paragraph given in the English translation, e.g., 2, 4.

sufficient of itself for everything, and more than sufficient" (2, 5) and next (*deinde*) in the "Tradition of the Catholic Church" (2, 4).

However, as Vincent notes, because scripture is "capable of as many interpretations as there are interpreters" (2, 5) and because heretics themselves are fond of quoting scripture in defense of their novel teachings, he deems it necessary to formulate a "rule for the right understanding of the prophets and apostles . . . in accordance with the standard of ecclesiastical and Catholic interpretation" (2, 5). His formulation of this rule (which we will call "First Rule") deserves full quotation:

> In the Catholic Church itself, all possible care must be taken that we hold that faith which has been believed everywhere (*quod ubique*), always (*quod semper*), and by all (*quod ab omnibus*). For that is truly and in the strictest sense "Catholic," which, as the name itself and the reason of the thing declare, comprehends all universally. This rule we shall observe if we follow universality (*universitatem*), antiquity (*antiquitatem*), consent (*consensionem*). We shall follow universality if we confess that one faith to be true which the whole Church throughout the world (*tota per orbem terrarium ecclesia*) confesses; antiquity, if we in no wise depart from those interpretations which it is manifest were notoriously held by our holy ancestors and fathers (*sanctos maiores ac patres*); consent, in like manner, if in antiquity we adhere to the consentient definitions (*definitiones*) and determinations (*sententias*) of all, or at the least of almost (*paene*) all priests (*sacertodum*) and doctors (*magistrorum*) (6).

Later, in chapter 27, Vincent spells out in greater detail the process of distinguishing truth from falsehood in interpreting scripture. The basic method is to interpret the scripture "according to the traditions of the Universal Church and in keeping with the Catholic doctrine" and adhere to universality, antiquity, consent: "And if at any time a part opposes itself to the whole, novelty to antiquity, and the dissent of one or a few who are in error to the consent of all or at all events of the great majority of Catholics," then they must prefer "the soundness of the whole to the part," "the religion of antiquity to the profanes of novelty," and with regard to consent, "to the temerity of one or of a very few they must prefer, first of all, the general decrees, if such there be, of a Universal Council, or if there be no such, then, what is next best, they must follow the consentient belief of many and great masters" (27, 70). Among the other *loci theologici* of the Catholic faith, the Lérinian mentions the bishop of Rome, the *apostolica sedes* (6, 15), who acts within the whole college of overseers/bishops (*totum corpus praepositorum*, 22, 27), and all the faithful (*universa ecclesia*, 22, 27).

In insisting on ubiquity, antiquity, and universality as criteria of orthodoxy,

Vincent is by no means insensitive to doctrinal development. On the contrary, to the question of whether there has been progress (*profectus*) in the church, he enthusiastically replies: "Certainly; all possible progress" (23, 54). He hastens, however, to draw a sharp distinction between "*profectus*" (progress) and "*permutatio*" (alteration): "Yet on condition that it be real progress (*profectus*), not alteration (*permutatio*) of the faith. For progress requires that the subject be enlarged in itself (*res amplificetur*), alteration, that it be transformed into something else (*in aliud transvertatur*)." The Lérinian goes on to formulate what might be called his "Second Rule," which deserves to be quoted in full:

> The intelligence, then, the knowledge, the wisdom as well of individuals as of all, as well of one person as of the whole Church, ought, in the course of ages and centuries, to increase and make much and vigorous progress, but yet in its own kind (*in suo genere*), that is to say, in the same doctrine, in the same sense, and in the same meaning (*in eodem dogmate, eodem sensu, eadem sententia*) (23, 54).[5]

To explain this kind of organic development, Vincent uses two analogies: that of a child growing into an adult and of a seed becoming a fully formed plant. Just as in the child who has become an adult, in spite of all the changes, "his nature is one and the same, his person is one and the same," and just as in the seed that has grown into a plant, in spite of all the changes in shape, form, clarity (*species, forma, distinctione*), "the nature of each kind must remain the same," so Christian doctrines can "follow the same laws of progress, so as to be consolidated by years, enlarged by time, refined by age, and yet, withal, to continue uncorrupt and unadulterated, complete and perfect in all the measurement of its parts, and, so to speak, in all its proper members and senses, admitting no change, no waste of its distinctive property, no variation in its limits" (23, 56).

For the Lérinian, in a genuine development of doctrine, there must remain *idem sensus* (the same meaning). To describe this *profectus* he uses words such as: *crescere* (to grow), *proficere* (to advance), *evolvere* (to develop), *florere* (to flower), and *maturescere* (to mature). He never tires of repeating 1 Tim 6:20: "O Timothy, guard the deposit that has been entrusted to you." In this development, what is only permitted is the effort to express the universal and ancient doctrinal consensus (the *ubique, semper, et ab omnibus*) in a new way (*noviter*) and not new things (*nova*). Hence, the slogan: *noviter, non nova*. Therefore there can never be substantive novelty, let alone reversal. That would be *permutatio fidei*, a clear and unmistakable sign of heresy. Vincent's

---

5. This text is quoted by Vatican I in its *Dogmatic Constitution on Catholic Faith*, chapter 4. John Henry Newman adopts Vincent's rule in developing his own theory of development of doctrine. See Guarino, *Vincent of Lérins*, 43–80.

array of terms to characterize this *permutatio* includes "pervert," "adulterate," "corrupt," "maim," "mutilate," and "innovate." He abhors the "madness of novelty" (8, 13), the "profane novelties," which he calls the "garbage of heretical novelty" (8, 21). Contrary to heretics who itch for and peddle novelties,

> the true Church of Christ, the careful and watchful guardian of the doctrine deposited in her charge, never changes anything in them, never diminishes, never adds, does not cut off what is necessary, does not add what is superfluous, does not lose her own, does not appropriate what is another's, but while dealing faithfully and judiciously with ancient doctrine, keeps this one object carefully in view—if there be anything which antiquity has left shapeless and rudimentary, to fashion (*accuret*) and polish (*poliat*) it, if anything already reduced to shape and developed, to consolidate (*consolidet*) and strengthen (*firmet*), if anything already ratified and defined, to guard (*custodiat*) it (23, 59).

SENSUS FIDELIUM AND WORLD CHRISTIANITIES

From the Vincentian double rule of "*ubique, semper et ab omnibus*" and "*in eodem dogmate, eodem sensu, eadem sententia*" it is abundantly clear that for the Lérinian the principal and primary task of the church is to preserve what he calls the "*depositum*"—the faith "once delivered to the saints" (Jude 3) and to guard the "*regula fidei*" (and the plural "*regulae fidei*") and the "*regula credenda*." As he puts it pithily, the deposit is "a matter brought to you, not put forth by you, wherein you are bound to be not an author but a keeper, not a teacher but a disciple, not a leader but a follower" (22, 53). What Vincent means by *depositum* and *regula fidei* is referred to today as *sensus fidei* or *sensus fidelium*, the former referring to the instinct of faith possessed by "all" and "the whole church," and the latter that possessed by "individuals" and "one person" (23, 54).[6]

From Vincent's historical context, though we know next to nothing about his personal life, we may safely assume that by *ubique*, even though he does use the expression *orbis terrarum* (the whole world, 2, 6),[7] he has in mind (southern) Gaul, the countries where the councils of Nicea, Ephesus, and Ariminum

---

6. On the distinction between *sensus fidei* and *sensus fidelium*, see the ITC, *Sensus Fidelium*, no. 4. The "subject" of the former is the church as a whole, whereas that of the latter is the individual believer. Needless to say, the two realities are intrinsically linked with each other to form the *consensus fidelium*.

7. As Vincent says, "so many islands, provinces, kings, tribes, kingdoms, nations, in a word, almost the whole earth, have been incorporated in Christ the Head, through the Catholic faith" (24, 61). Still this enumeration of places is more for rhetorical effect and does not evince Vincent's real knowledge of them.

were held (Asia Minor, Greece, and Italy respectively), and the cities where the various people he mentions lived, chiefly Rome (Popes Celestine, Felix, Julius, Sixtus, and Stephen), Milan (Ambrose), Alexandria (Origen, Arius, and Cyril), Carthage (Cyprian and Donatus), and Constantinople (Nestorius). For a fifth-century monk who confesses to be dwelling "in the seclusion of a monastery, situated in a remote grange" (1, 2), this geographical list is admittedly impressive. Nevertheless, it is quite negligible when compared to the world in which Christianity existed in his day, especially beyond the Roman Empire, and, of course, as it exists today. The *semper*, that is, the ancient world in which the New Testament (leaving aside the Hebrew Bible) was composed, and the centuries in which the two chief doctrines that Vincent expounds, namely, Trinity and Christology, amounts to no more than five hundred years. Finally, the *omnes/omnibus* comprises chiefly ecumenical councils (Nicea and Ephesus), the bishops of Rome, other bishops, theological doctors, and, to a much lesser degree, "all the faithful of all ages, all the saints, the chaste, the continent, the virgins, all the clergy, deacons and priests" (24, 61).

However generous an interpretation is given to the Lérinian's double rule, taking his *ubique* to mean the inhabited world (the *oikoumene*), his *semper* to extend into the foreseeable future after his death, his *omnibus* to include all the Christians of the first five Christian centuries, and his *idem sensus* to connote the essential continuity between the original meaning of a Christian doctrine and all its virtual and enfolding meanings (John Henry Newman's "preservation of type"),[8] it is highly doubtful that Vincent's triple criteria for orthodoxy and his theory of doctrinal development are adequate for the peculiar contexts of Christianity of today. Of these I will mention only two, namely, the emergence of world Christianity and religious pluralism.

In the last two decades a sizable body of literature, especially in church history and missiology, has highlighted the emergence of what is called "world Christianity" or, better still, "world Christianities." To cite just an example: The last two volumes of the massive nine-volume *Cambridge History of Christianity* bear the subtitle *World Christianities*. Briefly, by "world Christianity" is meant Christianity as it currently exists globally, with a polycentric structure, that is, as a "world religion," and not a religious institution with centers of ecclesiastical power located in the West during the past several centuries, including Europe and North America, which was exported to other parts of the world through the missionary enterprise and colonial conquest. Since the twentieth century there has been a massive shift of the Christian population from the Global North to the Global South. As the church historian Justo L. González summarizes it crisply:

---

8. This is the tack taken by Guarino, whose magnanimous and spirited defense of Vincent's double rule as relevant for ecumenical unity is unpersuasive.

At the beginning of the twentieth century, half of all Christians in the world lived in Europe. Now that figure is less than a quarter. At the beginning of that century, approximately four out of five Christians were white. At the end of the century, less than two out of five. At the beginning of the century, the great missionary centers of Christianity were New York and London. Today more missionaries are sent from Korea than from London, and Puerto Rico is sending missionaries to New York by the dozens. A hundred years ago, there were less than 10 million Christians in Africa, less than 22 million in Asia, and some 5 million in Oceania; now those numbers have risen to 360 million, 312 million, and 22 million respectively. Meanwhile, growth in the North Atlantic has been much less spectacular (from 460 to 821 million), and in most cases has not kept up with population growth.[9]

This demographic shift requires a radical redrawing of the map of Christianity. A new cartography is needed to reflect this shift of the center of gravity of Christianity, a shift that Vincent of Lérins of the fifth century and, truth to tell, even many of us of the twenty-first century could not even remotely imagine when we hold on to the *ubique* and the *ab omnibus* as criteria of orthodoxy. There have been, of course, shifts of the centers of Christianity in the past— from Jerusalem to Antioch, to Constantinople, to Western Europe, and to the North Atlantic—each time the map of Christianity got bigger. The Lérinian was familiar with the first three shifts, and his triple criteria of orthodoxy might well be serviceable then. But this time the shift is radically different. In the previous shifts, one center was largely replaced politically, economically, and ecclesiastically by the next; by contrast, today, world Christianity is *polycentric*, that is, it has many concurrent centers, so that there are Christianit*ies*, each being a local/regional/national Christianity, with none capable of claiming superiority over and normative for the others. In other words, it is not simply a geographically larger Christianity but a qualitatively *different* Christianity.

Another extremely significant factor in world Christianity is the improbable and massive explosion of Evangelicalism/Pentecostalism across the globe in the last fifty years, currently with over 500 million members worldwide. Again, it is not so much a matter of numbers—though of course it is—as a theologically *different* type of Christianity, which emphasizes elements that are suspect to, if not despised by, mainline Christians such as belief in biblical inerrancy and apocalypticism, free-ranging styles of worship, unregulated ministries, and practices such as literalist interpretation of the Bible, prophecy, glossolalia, exorcism, miraculous healing, and conservative ethics, especially

---

9. Justo L. González, *The Changing Shape of Church History* (Saint Louis: Chalice Press, 2002), 9.

in sexual matters. The ITC's *Sensus Fidei* is to be applauded for its affirmation that separated Christians do participate in and contribute to the *sensus fidelium* (no. 86). The document states that "the Catholic Church therefore needs to be attentive to what the Spirit may be saying to her by means of believers in the churches and ecclesial communities not fully in communion with her" (no. 56). This is highly commendable, but it may be wondered whether the ITC is fully aware of the extreme complexity if not sheer impossibility in discerning the *sensus fidei* underlying these types of Christianities.

In addition to a new cartography, as Justo González suggests, world Christianity requires a new topography. Maps are flat and do not represent the terrain accurately. Hence, the saying: "The map is not the territory." However, what is badly needed is not the familiar church topography but a new topography, one that represents the systemic changes brought about by world Christianity. The old topography of church history is basically orography; it focuses on mountains and mountain chains. To shift the metaphor, the old topography of church history gives prominence almost exclusively to ecclesiastical leaders such as popes, bishops, and ecumenical councils. It is the ecclesiastical counterpart of the ancient secular historical genre *De viris illustribus* [note *viris*—males], as practiced by the father of church history Eusebius of Caesarea in his *Church History*. In this genre, church history is the narrative of the achievements of ecclesiastical elites and intellectual virtuosi; it is the equivalent of the contemporary idol and celebrity talk and television shows. It is from these church elites and virtuosi—popes, bishops, councils, the Roman Curia, academic theologians—that the *sensus fidei* is derived from and proclaimed in dogmatic formulas accompanied by anathemas, or encyclicals, or "notifications." While such a narrative can be informative and useful, it tends to lead to distortions and misrepresentations, as if these people were the only ones that constitute the church and the magisterium. No doubt Vincent of Lérins operates with an orographic topography, which focuses on the mountains and mountain ranges of the church. His *Commonitorium* contains a long list of heroes and villains—the former including popes, bishops, ecumenical councils, and theological doctors among the *omnes* guarding the ancient *depositum fidei*, and the latter being heretics with their "profane novelties," all of them equally elites and virtuosi. As noted above, Vincent does mention "all the faithful of all ages" (24, 61) and highlights the powerful witness to the truth by martyrs "adhering to religious antiquity" (5, 13), but their role in discerning and *producing* the *sensus fidei* remains woefully undervalued.

By contrast, what is needed today in world Christianities is a new topography that highlights the valleys out of which mountains arise, a *koiladology* —to coin a new word—which shows the beliefs and practices of ordinary Christians. Without them, church leaders could not have achieved the feats celebrated in past church history textbooks. Without their contributions, the *sensus fidei* could not have been produced and transmitted. Without them, in Newman's memorable phrase, the church would look foolish. Consequently, the new *koiladology* will privilege the voices of the poor and the marginalized, including women, the colonized, the Dalits, the people of color, the migrants and refugees, the young, and the people of the so-called Third World, where nearly four out of five Christians will live in 2050. The ITC's document deserves high praise for noting that "in the history of the people of God, it has often been not the majority but rather a minority which has truly lived and witnessed to the faith" (no. 118, ii) and that "sometimes the truth of the faith has been conserved not by the efforts of theologians or the teaching of the majority of bishops but in the hearts of believers" (no. 119). The million-dollar question is, of course, where these believers are to be found in world Christianity and how to listen to their "hearts."

Among the practices of the common faithful that merit highlighting is popular religion/religiosity. The ITC pays great tribute to popular religiosity since "both as a principle or instinct and as a rich abundance of Christian practice . . . popular religiosity springs from and makes manifest the *sensus fidei*, and is to be respected and fostered" (no. 110). Again, the question is how to discern the *sensus fidei* in popular religion when theologically we continue to speak of the liturgy as *fons and culmen* of Christian life and relegate popular religion to the rank of *"pia exercitia"* and "private devotions."

DISSENSUS INFIDELIUM OF OTHER RELIGIONS: CONSENSUS OMNIUM

Another striking feature of world Christianity, which is, of course, totally foreign to the monk of Lérins, and which is not even mentioned in the ITC's document, is its constant encounter with other religions. Thanks to globalization and migration, our world is becoming increasingly not only multicultural but also multireligious. Religious pluralism is now the air we breathe, so that being religious today is being interreligious. Given this fact of enormous theological significance, how is the *sensus fidelium* formed and preserved in the context of religious pluralism? For the Lérinian, who deals with trinitarian and christological doctrines and heresies in an exclusively Christian context, to ignore other religions is understandable. However, for us, members of world Christianities, who live our Christian faith amidst the followers of other religions, as a tiny minority in many parts of the world, framing the issue of the *sensus fidei* apart from the different, and at times conflicting, perspectives of the other faiths—the *dissensus infidelium*—would be a serious lacuna.

By *dissensus* is meant here simply beliefs and practices that are *different* from those of Christianity. It is to be remembered that these have not been formulated *over against*, in contradiction to, and in dissent from the Christian ones. Except for Islam, most world religions—Hinduism, Jainism, Buddhism, Confucianism, and Daoism—predated Christianity by several centuries, with their distinct beliefs and practices, some of which are similar to (albeit never identical with) and others different from those of Christianity. By *infidelium* is meant not infidels or unbelievers, as these terms are used pejoratively in older apologetical and missiological literature, but simply non-Christian believers or faithful. The *infideles* are simply the counterparts of Christian *fideles*. Contrary to *Dominus Iesus*, I hold that the adherents of religions other than Christianity (*infidels*) do not have mere "belief" but faith. I call them *infideles* not because they have no faith but because they have a faith different from that of Christians, the *in* of *infideles* not meaning *non* but *within*.

The question then is: Can the *dissensus infidelium*, that is, the *sensus fidei* of non-Christians, contribute to the shaping of the *sensus fidei* of Christians? Were he asked this question, Vincent would definitely answer with a resounding Barthian *Nein*! So, I suspect, would many Christians answer, especially if they accept the position of *Dominus Iesus*.

The ITC's document, as mentioned earlier, acknowledges the possibility of a positive contribution to the *sensus fidei* from the "separated Christians," that is, Christians of other churches and ecclesial communities, and its argument for its affirmative position is well taken. It does not, however, raise the question that I am raising here.

In the light of teaching of the hierarchical magisterium, especially that of Saint John Paul II as well as that of the Asian Bishops' Conferences, and adopting the insights of many theologians of interreligious dialogue and comparative theology, and drawing on the experiences of countless Christians of world Christianity who live among the faithful of other religions, I propose an affirmative answer to this question.

Perhaps one helpful way to support this thesis is to take a cue from the ITC's document *Sensus Fidei*. To the question whether non-Catholic Christians can contribute to the *sensus fidei*, the ITC gives an affirmative answer and explains the reason for it: "The Catholic Church acknowledges that 'many elements of sanctification and truth' are to be found outside her own visible boundaries, that 'certain features of the Christian mystery have at times been more effectively emphasized' in other communities and that the ecumenical dialogue helps her to deepen and clarify her own understanding of the Gospel" (no. 86, ii).

Since the faithful of other religions have faith, we may say that the *dissensus infidelium* can "deepen and clarify" the *sensus fidelium*, since, to quote *Nostra Aetate*, no 2: "The Catholic Church rejects nothing of what is true and holy in these religions. It has a high regard for the manner of life and conduct, the precepts and doctrines which, although differing in many ways from its own teaching, nevertheless reflect a ray of that truth which enlightens all men and women. . . . Let Christians, while witnessing to their own faith and way of life, acknowledge, preserve and encourage the spiritual and moral truths found among non-Christians, together with their social life and culture." There is an obvious parallel between what Vatican II affirms about non-Catholic Christianities and what it affirms about non-Christian religions. In both cases there are "elements of truth and grace"; in both cases, there are non-Catholic Christians and non-Christians who live lives of holiness that, to quote John Paul II, put Catholics to shame; in both cases, ecumenical and interreligious dialogues, respectively, help the Catholic Church "deepen and clarify her own understanding of the Gospel." In a word, the *dissensus infidelium* is necessary for the *sensus fidelium*, and vice versa.

The question then is not whether the *dissensus infidelium* can "deepen and clarify" the *sensus fidelium* (and vice versa) but how to bring about this process of mutual enrichment. This is a highly complex question, and a host of literature has been produced in recent years on interreligious dialogue and comparative theology to suggest ways in which Christian Scripture and Tradition can be corrected, complemented, and enriched by non-Christian religions and vice versa. There have been helpful works on what I call "interreligious" trinitarian theology, Christology, pneumatology, ecclesiology, ethics, and spirituality, just to name a few *loci theologici*.

In sum, Vincent of Lérins's triple canon formulated in his celebrated dictum, "That which has been believed everywhere (*ubique*), always (*semper*), and by all (*ab omnibus*)," which is commonly invoked in conservative circles to define orthodoxy, is thus given a new and surprising twist in light of world Christianities. Geographical ubiquity, temporal antiquity, and numerical unanimity, which are often attributed to Western tradition as proof of its universality and normativity, are now turned on their heads. For the first time, it may be argued, these three Vincentian criteria of Christian orthodoxy have been met—albeit never perfectly and unambiguously: Only in world Christianities is "everywhere" found, "always" instantiated, and "by all" realized. In world Christianities, Western tradition of the past as well as the present is not given a privileged, much less normative, status. Western Christianity is not related to world Christianities as center to periphery, with all the privileges attendant to the center; rather it is only one Christianity among other Christianities, no more, no less, and its traditions, often maintained through power and imposed by force, legal and otherwise, must be seen for what they really are: local, context-dependent, and culture-bound historical particularities. In world Christianity, the *sensus fidelium* and the *dissensus infidelium* work hand in hand, in mutual learning and teaching, with the hope that there may emerge one day the *consensus omnium*.

10

Doing Ecclesiology in World Christianity

A Church of Migrants and a Migrant Church

There are four terms in the title of this chapter that require preliminary clari-fication to determine its scope and methodology. First, by "ecclesiology" is meant a treatise in dogmatic/systematic theology that investigates, from the faith perspective, the church as, in the words of Vatican II's *Lumen Gentium*, "a sacrament—a sign and instrument, that is, of communion with God and of the unity of the entire human race."[1] "Ecclesiology" is, of course, not the church itself; the church is a living reality that is, again according to Vatican II, "already prefigured at the beginning of the world . . . prepared in marvel-ous fashion in the history of the people of Israel and in the ancient alliance . . . established in this last age of the world, and made manifest in the outpouring of the Spirit . . . [and] will be brought to glorious completion at the end of time."[2]

Second, in contrast to the church as a cosmic mystery in which God— Father, Son, and Spirit—is present in history from creation to the end of time as a gracious communion, "doing ecclesiology" is a human and ever-inadequate attempt at understanding this saving mystery, that is, an act of *fides quaerens intellectum*, in St. Anselm of Canterbury's celebrated expression. Indeed, as a theological exercise, apart from anticipations in the writings of Giacomo of Viterbo at the beginning of the fourteenth century and of Juan de Ragusa and Juan de Torquemada in the fifteenth century, serious "doing ecclesiol-ogy" was not undertaken until the Protestant Reformation in the sixteenth century, when the issues of the true religion (*De Vera Religione*) and the true church (*De Vera Ecclesia*) were hotly contested among Catholics and Protes-tants. Ecclesiological reflections at Vatican I (1869–70) were interrupted by

---

1. Vatican II, *Dogmatic Constitution on the Church* (*Lumen Gentium*), no. 1, ET, Austin Flannery, general editor, *Vatican II: Constitutions, Decrees, Declarations* (Northport, NY: Costello Publishing, 2007), 1.

2. *Lumen Gentium*, no. 2.

the Franco-Prussian war and resulted in a badly lopsided ecclesiology that was limited to the dogmas of papal primacy and papal infallibility. It was only at Vatican II (1962–65) that the church in its *ad intra* and *ad extra* relations was given a comprehensive treatment in the sixteen conciliar documents, the former aspect mainly, though not exclusively, in *Lumen Gentium*, and the latter chiefly, though not only, in the Pastoral Constitution on the Church in the Modern World (*Gaudium et Spes*). In the post–Vatican II era there has been such a veritable avalanche or tsunami of publications on the church that it would be a blatant lie, even for ecclesiologists, to claim to have acquired a passing familiarity with them all.

Third, "world Christianity" is a buzzword used in recent histories of Christianity to convey the idea that despite the fact that, at least since the fifteenth century, Christian missions were carried out from and by the West to the rest, Christianity, which originated in the Middle East, never was, never has been, and never will be a Western religion. Since its very beginning and throughout its history, Christianity has been, to use a neologism, polycentric, and massively so. As a result of the first Christian missionary efforts directed not only toward the West, in the Roman Empire—as is often recounted in the dominant narrative of Western church history textbooks—but also toward the East, in the Persian, Indian, and Chinese empires—a tale that is largely ignored—the church flourished in many different parts of the ancient world, for instance, in the five patriarchates, each with its own ecclesiastical, doctrinal, liturgical, and spiritual traditions. Today, despite the hegemony of Western countries and Western churches, whose missions rode the waves of Western colonialism, indigenous churches, especially non-Catholic, have always found subtle but effective ways to subvert their dominance and constructed their own inculturated forms of being church. This truth runs the risk of being ignored or even denied, especially by Roman Catholics, who tend to locate the center of their church in Rome, and, more specifically, in the Roman Curia, from which all decisions regarding church life, big and small, emanate to the whole world. Since there is an intimate correlation, albeit not identity, between the historical shapes of the church and the ecclesiologies that reflect and at times canonize them, it follows that given the resurgence of the reality of world Christianity, aided and abetted by powerful currents of globalization, "doing ecclesiology" today should take into account the new faces of world Christianity.

Fourth, in addition to globalization, worldwide migration is posing enormous challenges in economic, socio-political, and cultural arenas for countries of origination, transit, and destination. It has also changed the faces of religious, including Christian, communities, especially in the United States. If ecclesiology—like liberation theology—is something to be engaged in, to use Gustavo Gutiérrez's phrase, only at sundown, that is, only after having lived in solidarity and struggled with migrants, a contemporary theology of the church, not least in the United States, can only be a theology of "the church of migrants and a migrant church." Finally, it is to be noted that there is a strong historical correlation between migration and the emergence of world Christianity, since, as will be shown below, Christianity's expansion and establishment as indigenous churches throughout the world was brought about mainly not by the apostles and their supposed successors but by the migrants themselves.

Taking all these four elements together—ecclesiology, doing ecclesiology, world Christianity, and migration—I will seek to propose three basic theses. First, ecclesiology today must start "from below," that is, from the concrete economic, socio-political, cultural, and religious realities facing the church, affecting its identity (what it is theologically) and its mission (its manifold ministries). Hence, I will first give a bird's-eye view of world Christianity and migration as the two most pressing challenges to contemporary Christianity, and, consequently, to contemporary ecclesiology. Second, I will show that migration is not simply an adventitious event, something that has accidentally happened to the church; rather, migration, or more precisely, migratory movements, I argue, constitute church as church, that is, as an ecclesial community of migrants and as a migrant community. In other words, migration is taken as a theological category shaping ecclesiology. Third, I conclude by outlining the contour of this migrant ecclesiology in world Christianity.

WORLD CHRISTIANITY AND MIGRATION AS *LOCI THEOLOGICI*

World Christianity

In his introduction to a book on Christianities in Asia and Oceania,[3] M. Thomas Thangaraj notes that the expression "world Christianity" was first used by Francis John McConnell in his book *Human Needs and World Christianity*, published in 1929.[4] The term was used again by Henry Van Dusen in his Jarrell Lectures at Emory University in 1945, later published as a book under the title *World Christianity: Yesterday, Today, Tomorrow*.[5] Thangaraj

---

3. T. Thangaraj, "An Overview: Asian and Oceanic Christianity in an Age of World Christianity," in Heup Young Kim, Fumitaka Matsuoka, and Anri Morimoto, eds., *Asian and Oceanic Christianities in Conversation: Exploring Theological Identities at Home and in Diaspora* (Amsterdam: Rodopi, 2011), 11–12.

4. Francis J. McConnell, *Human Needs and World Christianity* (New York: Friendship Press, 1929).

5. H. P. Van Dusen, *World Christianity: Yesterday, Today, Tomorrow* (Nashville: Abingdon, 1947).

also mentions the two works, published in 1938 and 1949 respectively, by the eminent twentieth-century church historian Kenneth Scott Latourette, who did not use the expression "world Christianity" but its equivalents, namely, "World Christian Fellowship" and "World Christian Community."[6] The term was more recently used in ecumenical circles, notably by Ans J. van der Bent.[7]

The common concern of all these authors when speaking of "world Christianity" was to promote Christian missions and ecumenical unity. Their focus on these two issues was amply justified by their historical circumstances. In spite of the urgent call for missions at the World Missionary Conference in Edinburgh in 1910 (with its celebrated slogan "the evangelization of the world in this generation"), Christian missions by Western missionaries, both Catholic and Protestant, were severely hampered by the two World Wars. In many countries of the so-called Third World, indigenous churches began dissolving their institutional ties and dependence on their "mother churches" in Europe and the United States, and assuming their own responsibilities in the form of the three selfs, that is, self-supporting, self-governing, and self-propagating (e.g., the Protestant Three-Self Patriotic Movement and the Catholic Patriotic Association in China).

At the same time, concern for Christian missions was going hand in hand with that for the unity of the churches—ecumenical unity—and rightly so, since the success of missions depends on the unity of all the disciples of Jesus, as the World Missionary Conference at Edinburgh made clear. One of the results of the Edinburgh conference was the establishment of the International Missionary Council to unite all the Protestant missionary efforts in Asia, Africa, Latin America, Europe, and North America. In this context it was possible to speak of world Christianity, that is, a Christianity united within itself for the purpose of common witness to the gospel throughout the inhabited earth (*oikumene*) of the "six continents."

As important as Christian missions and ecumenical unity are, they are not what is meant by "world Christianity" in the current usage of the term. Rather, the expression refers to the historical, sociological, cultural, and theological *diversity* and *multiplicity* of Christianity, from its very beginning, throughout its two-thousand-year-long history, and arguably more so in the future. The legitimate concern for the unity of the church, especially after the emergence of heresies and schisms and, for the Catholic Church, during the centuries-long concentration of ecclesiastical power in the papacy, has masked this far-reaching ecclesial diversity and multiplicity in favor of an imagined and often

6. K. S. Latourette, *Toward a World Christian Fellowship* (New York: Association Press, 1938); and K. S. Latourette, *The Emergence of a World Christian Community* (New Haven: Yale University Press, 1949).

7. A. J. van der Bent, *God So Loved the World: The Immaturity of World Christianity* (Madras, India: Christian Literature Society, 1977; Maryknoll, NY: Orbis Books, 1979).

enforced uniformity. There is not, nor has there ever been, *one* Christianity; rather there exist Christiani*ties* (in the plural), all over the world and all the time. Christianity has always been, in contemporary parlance, "inculturated" or "contextualized" in all milieus, the former term preferred by Catholics and the latter by Protestants.[8]

The implications of world Christianity for ecclesiology are several and fundamental. Thangaraj has drawn out three corollaries from this conception of world Christianity. First, it recognizes all local forms of Christianity as forms of the Christian faith, however limited and partial they might be. Second, it relativizes all local expressions of Christianity, ruling out the use of any of them as the benchmark of Christianity. Third, it enables the revitalization of Christianity through the interaction among the diverse local Christianities.[9] In other words, in world Christianity, no one form of inculturated Christianity is privileged and normative for another, be it that of Rome (the "First Rome"), or Constantinople (the "Second Rome"), or Moscow (the "Third Rome"), or Canterbury, or Geneva. Each of the local incarnations of Christianity embodies, in its own unique and irreplaceable way, Christianity wholly but not perfectly, and all of them make up world Christianity. Christianity does not exist except as world Christianity, and world Christianity is not something ontologically prior to its local realizations, floating above history like a Platonic form, but rather is constituted into existence by each of its spatial and temporal realizations.

Thus, the most defining feature of the church is collegiality at all levels of church life, including parish, diocese, episcopal conference, the Roman Curia, and the papacy. How this collegiality is put into practice and what canonical structures are devised to promote it will determine the vitality of Christianity in the near future.

"The Age of Migration"

According to one statistical report, in 2013, 232 million people—3.2 percent of the world's population—lived outside their countries of origin. It is predicted that the migration rate will continue to increase over time. A 2012 Gallup survey determined that nearly 640 million adults would want to migrate if they had the opportunity to do so.[10] The recent wars in Iraq,

---

8. The recent literature on inculturation and contextualization is immense, particularly by African and Asian authors. For a helpful historical overview, see Robert A. Hunt, *The Gospel among the Nations: A Documentary History of Inculturation* (Maryknoll, NY: Orbis Books, 2010).

9. See T. Thangaraj, "An Overview: Asian and Oceanic Christianity in an Age of World Christianity," in Kim, Matsuoka, and Morimoto, eds., *Asian and Oceanic Christianities*, 15–17.

10. See Boundless, "Dimensionalizing Immigration: Numbers of Immigrants around the World," Boundless Economics, Boundless, July 21, 2015. https://www.boundless.com. There are legions of websites dedicated to the study of migration.

Afghanistan, and lately, in Syria, as well as the uprisings in various countries in the Middle East during the Arab Spring, have dramatically increased the number of migrants and refugees and highlighted their tragedy and sufferings. According to a recent report released by the United Nations Refugees Committee, a record 65.3 million people were displaced as of the end of 2015, compared to 59.5 million just 12 months earlier. Measured against the current world population of 7.6 billion, these numbers mean that one in every 113 people globally is now either an asylum seeker, an internally displaced person, or a refugee. Whereas at the end of 2005, an average of six persons were displaced per minute, today the number is 24 per minute. The three countries that account for more than half of the world refugees are Syria (4.9 million), Afghanistan (2.7 million), and Somalia (1.1 million). About half of the world's refugees are children.[11] Beyond and behind these cold numbers lie human faces struck by tragedies of immense proportions, with loss of land and home, family separation, physical sufferings, rape and sexual violence, psychological damage, lack of opportunities for education, uncertain future, and death itself. Global population movements—whether internal versus international/intercontinental, forced versus free, settler versus labor, temporary versus permanent, illegal/undocumented versus legal, or planned versus flight/refugee—currently constitute a global phenomenon of such immense proportions that our age has been dubbed the "The Age of Migration."[12]

While there have been observable and repeated patterns in past migrations, migration scholars such as the sociologist Saskia Sassen have singled out three very recent emerging flows that constitute what she calls "an epochal change." The first is the sharp increase in the migration of unaccompanied minors from Central America—especially from Honduras, Salvador, and Guatemala. The second is the surge of Rohingya refugees, a Muslim minority

---

11. See UN Refugee Agency, UNHCR's annual Global Trends report, http//www.unhcr. org.

12. This is the title of the best one-volume study of international migration; see Stephen Castles, Hein De Haas, and Mark J. Miller, *The Age of Migration: International Population Movements in the Modern World*, 5th ed. (New York: Guilford Press, 2014). On migration, the historical, sociological, anthropological, and political studies, in addition to specialized journals and websites, are numberless. The following general works are worth consulting: Paul Collier, *Exodus: How Migration Is Changing Our World* (Oxford: Oxford University Press, 2013); Alejandro Portes and Josh DeWind, *Rethinking Migration: New Theoretical and Empirical Perspectives* (New York: Berghahn Books, 2007); Caroline B. Brettell and James F. Hollifield, eds., *Migration Theory: Talking Across Disciplines* (New York: Routledge, 2008); David G. Gutiérrez and Pierette Hondagneu-Sotelo, eds., *Nation and Migration Past and Future* (Baltimore: Johns Hopkins University Press, 2009); Thomas Faist, Margit Fauser, and Eveline Reisenauer, *Transnational Migration* (Malden, MA: Polity, 2013); Joseph H. Carens, *The Ethics of Immigration* (Oxford: Oxford University Press, 2013); Karen O'Reilly, *International Migration and Social Theory* (New York: Palgrave Macmillan, 2012); and Ato Quayson and Girish Daswani, eds., *A Companion to Diaspora and Transnationalism* (Oxford: Wiley Blackwell, 2013).

who are being expelled from Myanmar (Burma). The third is the migration of war refugees toward Europe, chiefly from Syria, Iraq, Afghanistan, and several European countries, notably Eritrea and Somalia. The causes of these three recent flows of migration are often attributed to gang violence and religious persecution, but there are underlying factors such as international development policies resulting in ecological disasters, mining, land grabs, and plantation agriculture.[13]

Responses to Migration in World Christianity

In response to the migration crisis political organizations such as the United Nations and the European Union have set up agencies to study the problem of migration from various perspectives as well as to provide emergency relief. Religious authorities, especially Pope Francis, have awakened our sense of solidarity with these victims and urged churches and religious communities to welcome them into their midst. On the other hand, anti-immigration rhetoric and policies, especially against Muslims, have been on the rise in recent times, even in countries that have traditionally been hospitable to migrants such as Britain and the United States.

In my judgment, the polycentricity of world Christianity and the Age of Migration constitute the two most burning and intractable issues for contemporary Christianity, and hence, contemporary ecclesiology. There is no doubt that global migration brings with it innumerable and enormous challenges to countries of origination, transit, and destination. In addition, because migration exacerbates the diversity and multiplicity of world Christianity, it also poses no less complex and hitherto unimaginable problems to the church, especially in terms of ministry to these newcomers. To be concrete, how can an American parish make these strangers into its full-fledged members, with equal rights and responsibilities, in terms of inclusive hospitality, pastoral outreach, multilingual liturgy, culturally appropriate sacramental celebrations, religious education, popular devotions, and ethnic celebrations, in such a way that the parish embodies world Christianity?

World Christianity and migration do not only pose challenges but also present the church with undreamt-of opportunities to rejuvenate itself, to be enriched by new and diverse ways of being church, and to realize more fully its catholicity. To make all this possible, what is needed is brought into existence by migrants and that holds that the church is essentially an institutional migrant.

In what follows I will first show that historically, outside migration there is no American Catholic Church, and second, outside migration there is no

---

13. See Saskia Sassen, "Three Emergent Migrations: An Epochal Change," *SUR* (*International Journal of Human* Rights) 13, no. 23 (2016): 23–29.

Christianity at all. To put it in two Latin adages, first, *extra migrationem nulla ecclesia Americana*, and second, *extra migrationem nulla ecclesia.*

THE CHURCH OF MIGRANTS AND
THE MIGRANT CHURCH

Extra migrationem nulla ecclesia americana

This first thesis, that is, the American Catholic Church would not have existed at all without migration and migrants, is so obvious that it hardly needs elaboration; it is a fact that no self-respecting historian of the American Catholic Church would fail to point out. There had been, of course, Catholics in America prior to the establishment of the thirteen English colonies, namely, Mexicans, especially in California, Texas, and New Mexico, thanks to the Spanish missions, and Native Americans, especially in Michigan and Louisiana, thanks to the French missions. It must be admitted, however, that the American Catholic Church as such came into existence only with the arrival of English Catholics to Maryland in 1634. These migrants were eventually joined by waves and waves of Catholic migrants, especially in the nineteenth century, mainly from Ireland, Germany, French Canada, Italy, Poland, and other Eastern European countries. Immigration dramatically swelled the number of American Catholics, from a mere 195,000 in 1820 to over three million in 1860, and made them the largest denomination in the United States.

In spite of widespread anti-Catholic prejudice and discrimination, Catholic migrants went on assimilating the American culture, building churches in spite of their meager financial resources (the so-called brick-and-mortar Catholicism), engaging in education and health care (their schools and hospitals were the envy of the world), founding devotional societies, and forging a new type of Catholicism marked by cultural pluralism and lay involvement, while remaining faithful to their ethnic origins through the system of national churches.

The flow of Catholic immigrants to the United States slowed down after the Immigrant Act of 1924, which imposed national quotas that discriminated against immigration from traditionally Catholic countries. Because of its racist implications this Immigrant Act was abolished in 1965 by the Immigration and Nationality Act (Hart-Celler Act), which replaces national origins as the criterion for admission with professional skills and relationship with citizens and U.S. residents. This act opened the doors for migrants from Asia, Africa, the Middle East, and Southern and Eastern Europe.

By happenstance, in the 1970s, war and political events in these places brought to the United States a large number of immigrants from China,

Korea, the Philippines, Vietnam, and Central America, a substantial percentage of whom were Catholics. Furthermore, the population of American Catholics was drastically increased thanks to the coming of Mexican immigrants, both documented and undocumented. According to the statistics provided by the Center of Applied Research for the Apostolate (CARA), the number of foreign-born adult Catholics was 4.7 million in 1975; in 2014, the number ballooned to 21.5 million. Furthermore, Catholic migrant families provide a large number of priestly and religious (especially female) vocations, without whom quite a few dioceses and religious orders would have suffered greatly. Significantly, these new Catholic immigrants bring with them a new type of Catholicism, one that is quite different from that of the Irish and German migrants.[14]

Sadly, just as migrants often try to forget their past and erase memories of suffering and pain as they strive to survive in their new countries, the American Catholic Church runs the risk of forgetting its roots in migration and needs to have the black, brown, and yellow faces to remind it that without migrants it would not have existed at all and that its future depends on how the new migrants are welcomed into its midst, not as problems to be solved but as full-fledged members of the Body of Christ.

Extra migrationem nulla ecclesia

The second thesis, namely, apart from migration there is no church as a catholic (small "c") and global reality, is much harder to prove. One major obstacle to understanding the role of migration in the expansion of Christianity is the ahistorical conceptualization of apostolicity. There is the charming legend about the origin of the Apostles' Creed according to which the twelve apostles contributed to its composition, each formulating an article of its twelve articles, before dispersing throughout the world on their evangelizing mission. As a result, the expansion of Christianity is attributed chiefly to the work of the twelve apostles, and apostolic succession becomes the dogmatic cornerstone of the true church. Historically, however, apart from Paul, who was not one of the Twelve, the New Testament provides next to no information about the work of the Twelve except about the early missions of Peter and Philip.

It is here that Christian migrations provide the missing and much-needed information to understand the development of Christianity into a world religion. To understand that without migration the church as such would not have existed and that therefore the church is essentially a migrant, let's make a thought experiment. Suppose you want to write a general introduction to Christianity, or teach a course on church history, which events do you con-

---

14. Relevant statistics can be obtained by consulting the reports by the Center of Applied Research in the Apostolate (CARA) on its website.

sider pivotal and epoch making around which you organize your narrative: Ecumenical councils? The power struggles between emperors and popes? Papal elections and episcopal appointments? The division between the Greek church and the Latin church? The Protestant Reformation? The definition of the dogmas of papal primacy and infallibility? The reform of the Roman Curia? While not denying that these events and others might have an impact on the life of the church, none of them made Christianity into a universal and global body of believers, a world religion. Rather, I suggest, it is migration that achieved this. What if we make migration the linchpin of the history of Christianity and ecclesiology? Space allows me to offer only the barest outline of the eight migrations or migratory movements that stamp Christianity as a permanent institutional migrant, each of them producing a distinct face of the church.[15]

1. The first Christian migration, one that radically transformed Christianity from a Jewish sect into a worldwide migrant institution, occurred with the Jewish diaspora after the destruction of the Second Temple in A.D. 70.[16] The Jewish diaspora played an important role in the spread of Christianity in the first centuries of the Christian era. It is repeatedly reported in Acts that Paul, whenever he went, preached first to the Jews, most often in their synagogues, and that even though his mission to the Jews was a failure as a whole, the first important converts and leaders of the early church (e.g., Titus, Timothy, Apollo, Priscilla and Aquila, Barnabas, and many other men and women) came from diaspora Judaism. The face of the church here is that of Jewish-Christian migrants.[17]

2. Following on the heels of this first migration was another, much more extensive, exodus of the Christian community out of Jerusalem and Palestine. The destruction of the temple and the subsequent suppression of the Jewish revolts of 115–117 and 132–135 caused migrations not only of Jews but

---

15. A comprehensive history of Christianity from the perspective of migration and migrants still needs to be written.

16. Helpful works on the diaspora during the Greco-Roman time include Menahem Stern, "The Jewish Diaspora," in Shemuel Safrai and Menahem Stern, eds., *The Jewish People in the First Century: Historical Geography, Political History, Social, Cultural and Religious Life and Institutions* (Assen: Van Gorcum, 1974–76), 117–83; Emil Schürer, *The History of the Jewish People in the Age of Jesus Christ (175 B.C.–A.D. 135)*, trans. A. Burkill, rev. and ed. Geza Vermes and Fergus Miller (Edinburgh: Clark, 1973–87), 1–176; Tessa Rajak, *The Jewish Dialogue with Greece and Rome: Studies in Cultural and Social Interaction* (Leiden: Brill, 2001); and Erich S. Gruen, *Diaspora: Jews amidst Greeks and Romans* (Cambridge, MA: Harvard University Press, 2002).

17. The literature on early Jewish-Christians has recently grown by leaps and bounds, partly because of the rise of Jewish-Christian dialogue. From the historical point of view, the works of Daniel Boyarin and Amy-Jill Levine are of great relevance. Two further works deserve notice: Oskar Skarsaune and Reidar Hvalik, eds., *Jewish Believers in Jesus: The Early Centuries* (Peabody, MA: Hendrickson Publishers, 2007); and Judith M. Lieu, *Christian Identity in the Jewish and Graeco-Roman World* (Oxford: Oxford University Press, 2004).

also of Christians. The Christian community, numbering by that time in the thousands, emigrated en masse from Jerusalem and from Palestine as a whole, either by force or voluntarily, into different parts of the world.[18]

Five areas were the destinations of this second Christian migration where eventually Christians built a great number of vibrant and mission-minded communities. The first is Mesopotamia and the Roman province of Syria, with its three major cities, namely, Antioch, Damascus, and Edessa. The second is Greece and Asia Minor. The third is the western Mediterranean, including Italy, France, Spain, and North Africa. The fourth is Egypt, in particular Alexandria. The fifth is Asia, especially India. The face of the church here is that of the Mediterranean and Syrian migrants.[19]

3. The third migration, which had an enormous and permanent impact on the shape of Christianity, was occasioned by the Emperor Constantine's transfer of the capital of the Roman Empire from Rome to Byzantium and the subsequent establishment of the imperial court at Constantinople (the "New/Second Rome"). As a result, there were not only momentous geopolitical changes but also a shift of the Christian center of gravity. Gradually there emerged a new and different type of Christianity, commonly known as "Orthodox Christianity," both within the "Byzantine Commonwealth," which was part of the Holy Roman Empire, and outside the Byzantine/Roman sphere of influence, each church developing its own liturgy, theology, monasticism, spirituality, and organization. Migration, both forced and voluntary,

---

18. Histories of the early church are, of course, legion. However, studies on migration as a social phenomenon during the patristic era are scarce. The most useful single-volume histories of the early church include: Henry Chadwick, *The Early Church* (London: Penguin Books, 1967); Henry Chadwick, *The Church in Ancient Society: From Galilee to Gregory the Great* (Oxford: Oxford University Press, 2001); W. H. C. Frend, *The Rise of Christianity* (Philadelphia: Fortress, 1984); and Peter Brown, *The Rise of Western Christendom*, 2nd ed. (Oxford: Blackwell, 2003). Multivolume histories include: Kenneth Scott Latourette, *A History of the Expansion of Christianity*, rev. ed. (New York and London: Harper & Brothers, 1937–45); Hubert Jedin and John Dolan, eds., *History of the Church* (New York: Herder & Herder, 1965–81); Jean-Marie Mayeur, Charles et Luce Pietri, André Vauchez, Marc Venard, *Histoire du Christianisme des origines à nos jours* (Paris: Desclée, 1995). A helpful introduction to the various backgrounds of early Christianity is Everett Ferguson, *Backgrounds of Early Christianity* (Grand Rapids, MI: Eerdmans, 1987). One work that is highly useful for understanding Christianity as a world movement, with emphasis on the Christian expansion into Asia, is Dale Irvin and Scott W. Sunquist, *History of the World Christian Movement: Volume I: Earliest Christianity to 1453* (Maryknoll, NY: Orbis Books, 2001). For a history of Asian Christianity, see Samuel Hugh Moffett, *A History of Christianity in Asia: Volume I: Beginnings to 1500* (Maryknoll, NY: Orbis Books, 1998).

19. Whereas the story of the migration of Christians to the West is well known, that of Syrian missions to the East, particularly to India, is virtually ignored by older church history textbooks, partly on the assumption that the mission of St. Thomas to India is not historically reliable. For a comprehensive account of St. Thomas's mission to India and the St. Thomas Christians, see George Menachery, ed., *The Thomapedia* (Ollur, Kerala: St. Joseph's Press, 2000).

played a huge and determinative role in shaping the future of the Orthodox Church.

After the Islamic victory over the Byzantine Empire in the eighth century, like its non-Byzantine sister churches, the Byzantine church suffered grievously under Ottoman Muslim rule. The fateful year of 1453, when Constantinople, "God-protected city," was sacked by Mehmed II's Turkish army, spelled the end of the glorious history of the Great Church and the beginning of its long and still-ongoing "captivity." With the irreversible decline of "Second Rome," the Muscovite patriarchate arrogated the title of "Third Rome." In its turn, the Russian Orthodox Church has been deeply affected by migration. The Russian revolution of 1917 not only ended the Russian Empire but also fragmented the Russian church in the aftermath of the establishment of national Orthodox churches in Poland, Latvia, Estonia, and Finland. The face of the church here is that of Greek, Middle Eastern, and Slavic migrants.

4. The fourth major population movement in early Christianity was the migration of the Germanic tribes, which include the Vandals, the Goths, the Alemani, the Angles, the Saxons, the Burgundians, and the Lombards. The Vandals, the Goths (both the Ostrogoths and the Visigoths), and the Lombards invaded eastern and southern Europe, particularly Spain, whereas the Angles and the Saxons spread to the British Isles. Once converted to Christianity, these Germanic tribes established churches in their lands. The face of the church here is that of the migrating Germanic tribes.

5. Another mass migration, which radically altered the map of Christendom, coincided with the so-called discovery of the New World during the "Age of Discovery" under the royal patronage of Spain and Portugal. From the end of the fifteenth century, the two Iberian countries competed with each other in discovering and occupying new lands outside Europe. Once again, it was migration—the movement of massive numbers of religious missionaries and secular Europeans to Latin America and Asia—that built up a new form of Christianity that, though at first heavily marked by European Christian traditions, eventually developed distinctive ways of being Christian that reflect the cultures and religious traditions of their own indigenous peoples. The face of the church here is that of Spanish and Portuguese migrants and Latin Americans and Asians.

6. From about 1650 to the First World War (1914–18) migration played an increasingly vital role in the modernization and industrialization of the world economy.[20] Warfare, conquest, the emergence of empires and nation-states, and Europe's search for new wealth produced enormous migrations,

---

20. For an excellent account of world migrations, see Castles, De Haas, and Miller, eds., *Age of Migration*, 84–197. These pages survey migration before 1945, migration in Europe since 1945, migration in the Americas, migration in the Asia-Pacific region, and migration in Africa and the Middle East.

both voluntary and forced. By the nineteenth century other European powers joined the commercial and colonizing projects started by Portugal and Spain: France, Belgium, Germany, Great Britain, Italy, and Holland vied with one another in the "scramble for Africa," with most African countries, except Liberia and Ethiopia, falling under the domination of Europe. Almost all Asian countries, too, were colonized. Between 1800 and 1915 an estimated 50 to 60 million Europeans moved to overseas destinations, and by 1915, an estimated 15 percent of Europeans lived outside Europe. Again, it is the massive migrations of Europeans to Africa and Asia that, together with a large number of missionaries, especially Protestant, expanded Christianity in ways hitherto unimaginable and produced new forms of Christianity that eventually bear little resemblance to the European churches. In addition, the transatlantic slave trade from the sixteenth to the eighteenth century brought more than 12 million Africans—the largest forced migration in history—to the Americas and transformed the Christianity of this continent. The face of the church here is that of European colonialists, the peoples they conquered, especially Asians and Africans, and slaves.[21]

7. World War II, more than any other armed conflict, caused worldwide large-scale migrations. Since 1945 Europe experienced massive migrations, as the authors of *The Age of Migration* have noted: "The upsurge in migratory movements in the post-1945 period and particularly since the mid-1980s, indicates that large-scale immigration has become an intrinsic part of European societies."[22] Massive migrations were spawned by events such as decolonization, which was accompanied by the return of former colonists to their countries of origin and the migration of colonial subjects to colonizing countries. In Asia, while European countries were closing their doors to migrants, countries that were economically advanced or oil-rich but with small or declining demography (Brunei, Malaysia, Singapore, Japan, Saudi Arabia, and the Arab Emirates) import the work force from poorer Asian countries such as the Philippines, Indonesia, China, India, and Vietnam. The African continent was in full transformation. The wars of anticolonial liberation, the establishment of dictatorial regimes, the exploitation of mineral riches, the apartheid system in South Africa, and regional, interregional and tribal conflicts produced a steady stream of refugees and migrants. The face of the church now is that of Christian migrants in the diaspora.

8. Finally, in the Middle East the wars in Iraq, Afghanistan, Lebanon, and Syria caused massive migrations, as mentioned above. In particular, the Iraq War wrought havoc on the most ancient centers of Christianity, reduc-

---

21. On Asian migrants, see Sunil S. Amrith, *Migration and Diaspora in Modern Asia* (Cambridge: Cambridge University Press, 2011); and Judith M. Brown, *Global South Asians: Introducing the Modern Diaspora* (Cambridge: Cambridge University Press, 2006).

22. Castles, De Haas, and Miller, eds., *Age of Migration*, 123.

ing to rubbles Middle Eastern Christianity. In addition to wars, globalization and ease of international travel have made international, transnational, and transcontinental existence a daily fact of life. The contemporary face of the church is the global migrant institution and gives the "local church" a new meaning. For the first time, the Catholic Church is truly "catholic," that is, global, or "glocal." Christianity itself is now "World Christianity," a world religion that has always been but is becoming more than ever diverse, multiple, transnational, transcultural, and polycentric in all aspects of its life, due to the demographic shift of the Christian population from the Global North to the Global South, globalization, and the presence of migrants from everywhere to everywhere in all six continents.[23]

From this all-too-brief historical overview it is indisputable that without migration the church as such, and Christianity as a whole, could not be what it is today. Migration is not simply a historical factor that has wrought immense and indelible changes to the church. Rather, without it the church cannot fulfill its nature and mission. Again, to put it in a Latin adage, *extra migrationem nulla ecclesia*.

I hope I have so far established two theses: The first is historical: *extra ecclesiam nulla ecclesia americana*; the second, theological: *extra migrationem nulla ecclesia*. Migrantness, to coin a neologism, is a constitutive mark of the true church. Now, these two theses lead to a third: If the traditional maxim *Extra ecclesiam nulla salus* holds true, and if the new adage *Extra migrationem nulla ecclesia* also obtains, then from these two premises the conclusion would follow: *Extra migrationem nulla salus*. But this requires that we reconceive the church from the perspective of migration, which in turn demands that we do

---

23. See Peter C. Phan "World Christianity: Its Implications for History, Religious Studies, and Theology," *Horizons* 39, no. 2 (2012): 171–88, which contains a large bibliography pertinent to the theme of "World Christianity." See also Dale T. Irvin and Scott W. Sunquist, *History of the World Christian Movement: Volume I: Earliest Christianity to 1453* (Maryknoll, NY: Orbis Books, 2001); and Dale T. Irvin and Scott W. Sunquist, *History of the World Christian Movement: Volume II: Modern Christianity from 1453–1800* (Maryknoll, NY: Orbis Books, 2012); Douglas Jacobsen, *The World's Christians: Who They Are, Where They Are, and How They Got There* (Oxford: Wiley-Blackwell, 2011); Sebastian Kim and Kirsteen Kim, *Christianity as a World Religion* (London: Bloomsbury, 2008); Mark A. Noll, *The New Shape of World Christianity: How American Experience Reflects Global Faith* (Downers Grove, IL: IVP Academic, 2009); Noel Davies and Martin Conway, *World Christianity in the 20th Century* (London: SCM Press, 2008); Dyron B. Daughrity, *The Changing World of Christianity: The Global History of a Borderless Religion* (New York: Peter Lang, 2010); Charles Farhadian, ed., *Introducing World Christianity* (Oxford: Wiley-Blackwell, 2012); Justo L. González, *The Changing Shape of Church History* (Saint Louis: Chalice Press, 2002); Sheridan Gilley and Brian Stanley, eds., *The Cambridge History of Christianity: World Christianities c.1815–c.1914* (Cambridge: Cambridge University Press, 2006); and Hugh McLeod, ed., *The Cambridge History of Christianity: World Christianities c.1914–c.2000* (Cambridge: Cambridge University Press, 2006).

ecclesiology from this perspective as well. This brings us to the third part of my essay.

AN ECCLESIOLOGY OF MIGRATION

Early Christians, who believed that they were no longer "sojourners and strangers" but "fellow citizens" with Jews in God's household, paradoxically greeted one another as *paroikoi*, foreigners and migrants. Clearly, for them migration is an essential part of the Christian's permanent self-consciousness and theological—and not merely sociological—identity. No doubt this self-description has an eschatological and spiritual overtone insofar as Christians consider themselves to be the pilgrim people of God on the march toward the kingdom of God. At the same time, their social and political status as migrants and strangers, without a permanent residence and citizenship, as well as the persecutions they suffered, lent depth and poignancy to their theological reflections on their social condition.

An Early Ecclesiology of Migration

Among early Christian writings there is arguably no more eloquent description of Christians as migrants, and hence the church as a migrant, than the anonymous letter known as the *Letter to Diognetus*. Written in the second or third century by an unknown Christian to an equally unknown inquirer, it seeks to answer three questions concerning "what God they [Christians] believe in and how they worship him"; "the source of the loving affection that they have for each other"; and "why this new race or way of life has appeared on earth now and not earlier."[24] In the course of answering these three queries, the author contrasts, in a string of striking antitheses, the Christians with their contemporaries. Given the beauty of the text, a lengthy quotation may be permitted:

> For Christians cannot be distinguished from the rest of the human race by country or language or customs. They do not live in cities of their own; they do not use a peculiar form of speech; they do not follow an eccentric manner of life. This doctrine of theirs has not been discovered by the ingenuity or deep thought of inquisitive men, nor do they put forward a merely human teaching, as some people do. Yet, although they live in Greek and barbarian cities alike, as each man's lot has been cast, and follow the customs of the country in clothing and food and other matters of daily living, at the same time they give proof of the remarkable and admittedly extraordinary constitution of their own common-

---

24. For the English text of this letter, see C. Richardson, ed., *Early Christian Fathers* (Philadelphia: Westminster Press, 1957), 213–22.

wealth. They live in their own countries, but only as aliens [*paroikoi*]. They have a share in everything as citizens [*politai*], and endure everything as foreigners [*xenoi*]. Every foreign land is their fatherland, and yet for them every fatherland is a foreign land. They marry, like everyone else, and they beget children, but they do not cast out their offspring. They share their board with each other, but not their marriage bed. It is true that they are in the flesh, but they do not live according to the flesh. They busy themselves on earth, but their citizenship is in heaven. They obey the established laws, but in their own lives they go far beyond what the laws require. They love all men, but by all men are persecuted. They are unknown, and still they are condemned; they are put to death, and yet they are brought to life. They are poor, and yet they make many rich; they are completely destitute, and yet they enjoy complete abundance. They are dishonored, and in their very dishonor are glorified; they are defamed, and are vindicated. They are reviled, and yet they bless; when they are affronted, they still pay due respect. When they do good, they are punished as evildoers; undergoing punishment, they rejoice because they are brought to life. They are treated by the Jews as foreigners [*allophuloi*], and are hunted down by the Greeks; and all the time those who hate them find it impossible to justify their enmity. To put it simply: What the soul is in the body, that Christians are in the world. The soul is dispersed through all the members of the body, and Christians are scattered through all the cities of the world. The soul dwells in the body, but does not belong to the body, and Christians dwell in the world, but do not belong to the world. . . . The soul, which is immortal, is housed in a mortal dwelling; while Christians are settled among corruptible things, to wait for the incorruptibility that will be theirs in heaven.[25]

Needless to say, the portrait of the Christians as drawn in this celebrated letter should not be taken as a historically accurate description of the behavior of each and every early Christian. Surely, not all early Christians conducted themselves in the praiseworthy manner the letter claims. Rather than as factual description, the letter should be seen as presenting the ideal church and the corresponding normative behavior of Christians. On the other hand, it should not be dismissed out of hand as a piece of self-serving propaganda, either. Historical evidence tends to support many if not all of the letter's statements about early Christians. Whatever the historical validity of its claims about early Christianity and the value of its apologetics for the superiority of Christianity over pagan religions and Judaism, the letter's idealistic portrait

---

25. Richardson, ed., *Early Christian Fathers*, 217–18.

of the church can certainly be viewed as an exceptionally rich and profound theology of the church as a migrant. An extended commentary on this theology is not feasible here; suffice it to highlight its main points as significant contributions to a contemporary theology of the church as a migrant.

1. A Christian *qua* Christian does not possess a separate country, language, or customs. As Christians, therefore, migrants may adopt any of these things as their own, wherever they live. Moreover, though strangers, they must do their best to contribute to the welfare of their new homeland.

2. As best as they try to be inculturated into the new society and as much as "every foreign land is their fatherland," as Christians, migrants will and must remain to a certain extent strangers to their adopted country, of course not in language and customs, which they share with others, but in their religious worldview and moral behavior: "They live in their own countries, but only as aliens. They have a share in everything as citizens, but endure everything as foreigners." The theology of migration must therefore be not only transcultural, contextual, and crosscultural but also countercultural, by which the migrants can both incorporate and critique the surrounding cultures.

3. Because of their difference from the surrounding world, migrants, and especially Christian migrants, will inevitably experience discrimination and even persecution. They will be treated at times as "foreigners and enemies" by those to whom their beliefs and behaviors are incomprehensible and perhaps even an indirect reproach: "When they do good, they are punished as evildoers."

4. Even so, Christian migrants should not retaliate with violence against those who oppress them. Rather, "they are poor, and yet they make many rich . . . they are reviled, and yet they bless; when they affronted, they still pay due respect." Of course, this willingness to do good in spite of injustice is not a passive abdication of one's responsibilities for justice and fairness; rather, nonviolence and doing good are seen as the most effective ways to overcome hatred and injustice.

5. The motivation for such behavior of returning good for evil is hope, which is the virtue par excellence of migrants. This hope is not for material remuneration but for "the incorruptibility that will be theirs in heaven." Eschatology is then an intrinsic part of any theology of migration that sees it not only as a personal and societal curse—which it certainly is—but also as an urgent call for self-transcendence and for a collective action to overcome structural evils.

6. Finally, migration is a permanent feature of the church and not just a historical phenomenon of the early church or of any other period of church history. Like unity, catholicity, holiness, and apostolicity, "migrantness" is a note of the true church, because only a church that is conscious of being an institutional migrant and caring for all the migrants of the world can truly practice faith, hope, and love.

The Church as an Institutional Migrant

In describing the Christian migrant, early Christian writers had at their disposal the three biblical terms of *stranger* (or *alien*), *foreigner*, and *sojourner*. Though these terms are often used interchangeably in English translations of the Bible, they denote three distinct categories of people in biblical times. A *stranger* (Hebrew *zār*, Greek *xenos*, Latin *hospes*) is one who does not belong to the house or community or nation in which he or she lives and is often considered an enemy (Isa 1:7; Jer 5:19; 51:51; Ezek 7:21; 28:7, 10; Obad 11). A *foreigner* (Hebrew *nokri*, Greek *allotrios*, Latin *alienus*) is one of another race, and because non-Jews were regarded as idolatrous, the term also designates someone worshiping idols. Hence, Jews were forbidden to marry a foreigner (Deut 7:1–6). A *sojourner* (Hebrew *gēr*, Greek *paroikos*, Latin *peregrinus*) is someone whose permanent residence is in another nation, in contrast to the foreigner whose stay is only temporary. Sojourners were protected by the Law. Jews are commanded not to oppress them (Exod 22:21); they must even love them (Deut 10:19). Sojourners are grouped with orphans and widows as defenseless people whom God protects and whose oppressors God will judge severely (Jer 7:6; 22:7, 29; Zech 7:10; Mal 3:5). On the other hand, sojourners must observe some provisions of the Law, such as observance of the Sabbath and the Day of Atonement (Exod 20:10; Lev 16:29) and abstention from eating blood (Lev 17:10, 13), immorality (Lev 18:26), idolatry (Lev 20:2), and blasphemy (Lev 24:16).

The Good News of Jesus is that those who were strangers [*apēllotriōmenoi*] (Eph 2:12) from Israel, and so were "strangers and sojourners" [*xenoi kai paroikoi*] (Eph 2:19) have been made "fellow citizens [*sumpolitai*] with the saints and of the household of God [*oikeioi tou theou*]" (Eph 2:19). It is most interesting that early Christian writers, while convinced that Christians were no longer "strangers and sojourners" but "fellow citizens" with regard to Israel and constituting the household of God, considered themselves as *paroikoi*—sojourners, displaced people without a home and a nation, migrants—by far the early Christians' favorite term to describe themselves. This self-consciousness as foreigners, strangers, and sojourners is found in Clement of Rome's letter to the Christians in Corinth (ca. 96). It was sent from "the church of God which sojourns [*paroikousa*] in Rome" to "the church of God which sojourns [*paroikousei*] in Corinth." Polycarp, the bishop-martyr of Smyrna (d. 155), also addressed his letter to the Christians in Philippi: "To the church of God which resides as a stranger [*paroikousei*] at Philippi." Similarly, the *Martyrium Polycarpi* was sent "from the church of God which resides as a stranger [*paroikousa*] at Smyrna to the church of God residing as a stranger [*paroikousei*] at Philomelium and to all the communities of the holy and Catholic Church residing in any place [*paroikiais*]." While this self-awareness as sojourners and foreigners may be given an eschatological and spiritual interpretation, and thus a migrant ecclesiology is by necessity an eschatological ecclesiology, it was quite likely exacerbated by the fact that Christians in these areas—Rome, Corinth, and Asia Minor—were mostly migrants, without full civic rights, and were subject to discrimination and persecution.

Extra migrationem nulla salus

There is perhaps no moment when the migrantness of the church is more visible than in community worship, especially during the Eucharistic celebration. Daniel Groody has offered insightful reflections on the link between the Eucharist and migration, highlighting the connection between Jesus' actions and words at the Last Supper and the migrant's life: between "He Took the Bread" and the migrant's decision to migrate; between "He Broke the Bread" and the migrant's broken body; between "And Gave It to His Disciples" and the migrant's self-sacrifice for the good of others; between "Do This in Memory of Me" and the church's "option for the poor/migrant."[26] Thus, a migrant ecclesiology is quintessentially an Eucharistic ecclesiology.

Lastly, a migrant ecclesiology is also a christological ecclesiology. The theology of migration as proposed by the *Letter to Diognetus* is based, I suggest, on the theology of the migrant's life as *imitatio Christi*. After all, Jesus is the paradigmatic migrant who dwelt between the borders of two worlds. Through the Incarnation, ontologically, he stood between divinity and humanity and embraced both. Already as a child, he experienced migration to Egypt. As an adult, politically, he lived between colony and empire; culturally, between Roman and barbarian; linguistically, between Aramaic and Greek; religiously, between the Chosen People and the *goiim*. During his ministry, he was itinerant and homeless, having nowhere to lay his head, unlike foxes that have holes and birds that have nests (Luke 9:58). As a migrant, Jesus was a "marginal Jew," to use the title of John Meier's multivolume work on the historical Jesus. His migration carried him over all kinds of borders, both geographical and conventional: Palestine and the pagan territories, Jews and non-Jews, men and women, the young and the old, the rich and the poor, the Sadducees and the Pharisees, the powerful and the weak, the healthy and the sick, the clean and the unclean, the righteous and the sinners. Because his multiple border-crossings were a threat to those who occupied the economic, political, and religious centers of power, he was hung upon the cross, between heaven and earth, between the two cosmic borders, a migrant until the end.[27] That is why

---

26. See Daniel Groody, "Fruit of the Vine and Work of Human Hands: Immigration and the Eucharist," in *A Promised Land, a Perilous Journey: Theological Perspectives on Migration* (Notre Dame, IN: University of Notre Dame Press, 2009), 299–315.

27. On Jesus as a border crosser and migrant spirituality, see Peter C. Phan, *In Our Tongues: Perspectives from Asia on Mission and Inculturation* (Maryknoll, NY: Orbis Books, 2003), 13–50.

he could truly say that whoever welcomes a migrant/stranger, welcomes him: "I was a stranger [*xenos*] and you welcomed me."

We are now living in the "Age of Migration," and more than ever the church is called to be part of "world Christianity." Theology, as an ecclesial academic discipline, is challenged to interpret the signs of the time in the light of faith and faith in the light of the signs of the time. In this reinterpretation we are brought back to certain basic truths: outside migration there is no American Catholic Church; outside migration there is no church at all; and outside migration there is no salvation. Thus, we believe in the one, holy, catholic, apostolic, and migrant church.

11

The Holy Spirit as Foundation of Interreligious Dialogue

Toward an Asian Pneumatology

A biblical text that can be taken as a fruitful inspiration for these reflections on the foundation of interreligious dialogue is 1 Thess 5:19, in which the apostle Paul urges us not to "quench the Spirit." On the face of it, the exhortation, especially in its negative form (*to pneuma mē sbennute*), sounds rather straightforward and is often invoked by liberals to promote various initiatives for church reform over against conservatives who want to preserve the status quo.

Upon closer examination however the meaning of the injunction is far from clear.[1] To begin with, what is entailed by "quench" (*sbennuō*)? Which actions would count as "quenching" the Spirit—those that introduce new reforms in the church (*aggiornamento*) or those that bring the church back to the normative ancient practices (*ressourcement*) or both? Put positively, which actions would "light up" the Spirit or keep the Spirit's fire burning? The object of quenching is *to pneuma*, which is universally translated into English as "Spirit," with the capital "S." But may we use "spirit" with the lower case? If, however, we use "Spirit" with the capital "S," what does it stand for? Whose Spirit is it? Is it the Spirit of Christ? Does it refer to the Holy Spirit, named in the Christian tradition as the Third Person of the Trinity, or simply to God as spirit? If *to pneuma* connotes God or the Holy Spirit, how can God, who is infinite and all-powerful, be "quenched" or "extinguished" by finite humans? Does *to pneuma* refer instead to God's gifts or charisms, which we may refuse to recognize, or accept, or develop for our spiritual well-being and that of the church as a whole, and in that sense "quench" them? More pertinent to our

---

1. Most English translations of 1 Thess 5:19 use "quench" for *sbennuō* in the sense of "extinguish," "suppress," or "subdue." The New International Version renders this verse as "Do not put out the Spirit's fire," with allusion to Matt 3:11 (baptism with "the Holy Spirit and fire"), Luke 12:49 ("I came to bring fire to the earth"), and Acts 2:34 (tongues of fire). English translations of the Bible in this essay are taken from the New Revised Standard Version.

theme, in interreligious dialogue what must we do in order not to quench the Spirit, or, more positively, in order to light the fire of the Spirit and keep it burning brightly, for us Christians as well as for non-Christian partners in dialogue? Needless to say, determining the exact answers to all these questions will have large implications for the issues examined in this chapter.

As preliminaries to our reflections on the Holy Spirit as foundation of interreligious dialogue, a few words on the Pauline text may be helpful. According to Acts 17:1–9, Paul arrived in Thessalonica, the capital city of Macedonia, in A.D. 49 during his second missionary journey. His ministry there was carried out on three Sabbath days and was quite successful, especially among the God-fearing Greeks, including a great many "leading women." Some Jews, however, jealous of Paul's success, instigated a mob of ruffians to chase him out of the city, and Paul was forced to leave for Beroea. Worried about the faith of his new converts, Paul sent Timothy to inspect their situation, and after receiving Timothy's reassuring report, Paul wrote his first letter to the Thessalonians from Corinth sometime in 51–52. The Pauline authorship of 1 Thessalonians, in contrast to that of 2 Thessalonians, is generally not contested.

Toward the end of his letter, Paul gives the Thessalonians a series of exhortations, one of which is not to quench the Spirit. Here are the verses that seemingly form a thematic unity: "Do not quench the Spirit. Do not despise the words of prophets, but test everything; hold fast to what is good; abstain from every form of evil" (5:19–22). The first two injunctions are phrased negatively ("do not"), whereas the last three positively, though the fifth requires not doing something but avoiding doing it ("abstain"). With these exhortations in mind let's turn to our theme of interreligious dialogue and consider whether a theology of the Holy Spirit implicit in these injunctions, especially that of not to quench the Spirit with the capital "S," and perhaps even a theology of the spirit with the lower-case "s," can serve as a common foundation for interreligious dialogue. I begin with a brief survey of the various moves, especially among Western theologians, to find a fruitful foundation or starting point for interreligious dialogue. In the second part, I explore the possibility of a pneumatological or "spirit-based" approach to interreligious dialogue, drawing on the insights of the Federation of the Asian Bishops' Conferences (FABC) and some Asian theologians. I conclude by examining the practice of monastic interreligious dialogue as a paradigmatic case of this type of pneumatological approach.

IN SEARCH OF A COMMON FOUNDATION FOR INTERRELIGIOUS DIALOGUE

Recent theologies of religions can be categorized as different soteriologies on the basis of how they view the possibility of salvation outside Jesus and

Christianity, as Paul Knitter has done in his masterful survey *Introducing Theologies of Religions* by constructing a fourfold typology.[2] Alternatively, it is highly instructive to interpret these theologies of religions as attempts at establishing a theological basis for dialogue among the followers of different religions. To anticipate my historical mapping, my basic interpretation is that various theological realities have been harnessed to serve as a foundation for interreligious dialogue, and the quest for this basis has passed through seven stages: (1) from church (2) to Christ (3) to God (4) to the reign of God (5) to the Trinity (6) to the Holy Spirit, and finally (7) to the spirit/s (lower case, singular or plural).[3]

Two observations about this historical development are in order. First, these seven stages should not be taken as successive developments in which the previous theological reality is abandoned in favor of the next. Rather, the preceding reality is assumed and taken up into the following in a process of *Aufhebung*, that is, preserved but raised to a new context and thus given a wider meaning. Second, the theological move is from a particular and more historically specific reality to one with a wider and ultimately universal, albeit not less historically anchored, impact and significance. In other words, there have been a growing dissatisfaction with grounding interreligious dialogue in a particular truth peculiar to one religious tradition and a move toward finding a common starting point universally shared by all religious traditions. The theological itinerary has therefore been from the particular to the universal, with the latter currently proposed as a more fruitful starting point and basis for interreligious dialogue.

---

2. Paul Knitter, *Introducing Theologies of Religions* (Maryknoll, NY: Orbis Books, 2002). Refining the well-known categories of exclusivism, inclusivism, and pluralism, Knitter divides contemporary theologies of religions into four types or models, which he terms "replacement" ("Only One True Religion"), "fulfillment" ("The One Fulfills the Many"), "mutuality" ("Many True Religions Called to Dialogue"), and "acceptance" ("Many True Religions: So Be It"). A more recent review of Catholic theologies of religions is available in the massive volume *Catholic Engagement with World Religions: A Comprehensive Study*, ed. Karl J. Becker and Ilaria Morali (Maryknoll, NY: Orbis Books, 2010). A brief and lucid overview is available in David R. Brockman and Ruben Habito, eds., *The Gospel among Religions: Christian Ministry, Theology and Spirituality in a Multifaith World* (Maryknoll, NY: Orbis Books, 2010), 17–53.

3. I had developed this historical mapping before discovering that Gavin D'Costa proposes a similar (though not identical) sevenfold typology in his *Christianity and World Religions: Disputed Questions in the Theology of Religions* (Oxford: Wiley-Blackwell, 2009), 34–37. D'Costa's seven "isms" are trinity-centered, Christ-centered, Spirit-centered, church-centered, theo-centered, reality-centered, and ethics-centered. My account differs from D'Costa's in three significant respects: it is more historically based (rather than systematic); it focuses on the question of the foundation of interreligious dialogue (rather than the theology of religions); and it explores a more universal basis for interreligious dialogue (rather than identifying what D'Costa calls "non-negotiable" truths—for him, the first four—in interreligious dialogue. In addition, I do not share his thesis of "universal-access exclusivism."

1. Christianity's encounter with other faiths coincided with its very birth. Its beginnings were deeply marked by a hostile attitude toward Judaism and Greco-Roman and other "pagan" religions. The starting point for this interreligious encounter ("dialogue" would not be the right word for it) is the church, in and through which one comes to Christ and which is asserted to be the only ark of salvation. With respect to Judaism, the predominant tendency among New Testament writings, especially Matthew, John, and Hebrews, is to consider Israel to be "fulfilled" and superseded by the church, the True Israel and the New Covenant. Paul is an exception. Confessing to a "deep sorrow and unceasing anguish" over Israel's refusal to believe in Jesus and to join the church, Paul is nevertheless convinced of the "mystery" that Israel's infidelity is only partial and temporary until "the full number of the Gentiles has come in" and that "all Israel will be saved" (Rom 11:25–26). Paul categorically affirms that "the gifts and calling of God are irrevocable" (Rom 11:28).

With regard to Greco-Roman and "pagan" religions the attitude of the early Christian writers is uniformly condemnatory, seeing in them nothing but demonic superstition and depravity. In contrast, with respect to Greek philosophy, some Christian authors, for example, Clement of Alexandria, were more positive, viewing it as propaedeutic to Christianity. It would be wrong, however, to conclude that the early church as a whole was favorably disposed to Greek philosophy. Justin Martyr, whose doctrine of *logos spermatikos* and *sperma tou logou* is often taken to be evidence of his affirmative stance toward Greek philosophy and culture, is in reality far from appreciative since for him whatever true insights Greek philosophers have achieved about God were purloined from Hebrew scripture. For Justin as for all other church fathers (especially Augustine), only Christianity deserves to be called *religio*; it alone is the *vera religio*. Other religious traditions are at best "law" (*lex*) and "sects" (*secta*), and do not deserve to be called "*religio*." Non-Christians are called *pagani et infideles*, not believers. What they possess is not "faith" but only "belief."

This exclusive ecclesiocentrism is encapsulated in the celebrated phrase *extra ecclesiam nulla salus*. Though originally applied by Cyprian only to schismatics and heretics who in order to be saved must return to the church, which is the only ark of salvation, the exclusion of salvation is subsequently extended to pagans, Jews, and Muslims. No doubt the most peremptory and authoritative pronouncement on this doctrine is that of the general council of Florence in its decree for the Jacobites (1442). Citing *De fide ad Petrum* of Fulgentius of Ruspe (467–533), the council declares: "No one remaining outside the Catholic Church, not only pagans, but also Jews, heretics or schismatics, can become partakers of eternal life, but they will go to the eternal fire prepared for the devils and his angels, unless before the end of their life they are received into it."[4]

---

4. For the English translation, see J. Neuner and J. Dupuis, eds., *The Christian Faith in the Doctrinal Documents of the Catholic Church* (New York: Alba House, 1982), 279.

However, with the stubborn persistence of Judaism as a religious tradition, the threat of Islam as a political and military power, and the discovery of America and Asia with their huge populations of "barbarians" and "infidels," this absolute ecclesiocentrism based on a rigorist interpretation of especially Acts 4:12, 1 Tim 2:5 and Heb 11:6, died the death of a thousand qualifications. Theological principles of "God does not deny grace to anyone who does that which is within oneself"; "God has not bound his power to the sacraments"; and the inculpability of "invincible ignorance" were increasingly invoked to account for the possibility of salvation for the nonbaptized (the proverbial case of a child born in a forest or captured and raised in prison by the "Saracens").

2. Since 1949 the axiom *extra ecclesiam nulla salus* has officially been interpreted more broadly to make salvation possible for those who have not been in fact (*reapse*) incorporated in the church through baptism but only belong to it in "desire and longing" (*voto et desiderio*), even when such desire is merely "implicit."[5] This hermeneutical strategy reached its zenith at Vatican II, especially in *Lumen Gentium*, no. 16, *Ad Gentes*, nos. 3, 9, 11, and *Nostra Aetate*.[6] Thus, the church as a visible institution with all its means of grace and de facto membership in it no longer function as the exclusive and all-controlling vantage point for the religious encounter with other believers. Now "religion" as a generic and neutral descriptive term, equally applicable to Christianity as well as to other religions, gains theological respectability. The term and its plural form ("religions" and "world religions"), which are the Enlightenment's inventions, are adopted even by the official documents of the Roman magisterium, though it never tires of warning about the danger of indifferentism and "the dictatorship of relativism" lurking in the usage of "religion" as an umbrella term to denote supposedly equally valid religious ways.

As a result, a more frequent appeal is now made to the universal saving action of Christ as a basis for interreligious dialogue. There is a distinct theological advantage in this shift from church to Christ as the foundation for interreligious dialogue. As a particular social organization with a well-documented dark history, the church's claim to be the unique, universal, and necessary means of salvation carries little if any credibility, especially among the victims of its acts of persecution and violence, from Jews to pagans, Muslims, assortments of alleged heretics and schismatics, and the followers of other religions. By contrast, Christ, with his noble teachings and self-sacrificing life

---

5. See the August 8, 1949, letter of the Holy Office to the archbishop of Boston against the Jesuit Leonard Feeney, who held that salvation is possible only to Roman Catholics. See Neuner and Dupuis, eds., *Christian Faith*, 240–42.

6. The English translation of the documents of Vatican II is taken from Austin Flannery, gen. ed., *Vatican II: Constitutions, Decrees, Declarations* (Northport, NY: Costello Publishing, 1996).

and death, has been an object of admiration and imitation for not a few non-Christians and can thus credibly be presented as a universal savior. In addition, the church's claim that Christ is fully divine (as well as fully human) affords a more universal theological basis for interfaith encounter since divinity is by definition present and active in all places and at all times.

Presupposing Christ's ubiquitous and constant presence and activity in human history, Vatican II, speaking of non-Christian religions, affirms that "the Catholic Church rejects nothing of what is true and holy in these religions." Though recognizing the many differences between Christian teachings and practices and those of non-Christian religions, the council says that these "precepts and doctrines . . . often reflect a ray of that truth which enlightens all men and women." Consequently, the council urges Catholics to "acknowledge, preserve and encourage the spiritual and moral truths found among non-Christians, together with their social life and culture" (*Nostra Aetate*, no. 2).

Though the turn to Christology permits the acknowledgment of "elements of truth and grace" in non-Christian religions as "a secret presence of God" (*Ad Gentes*, no. 9), what has been called "the scandal of particularity," that is, the historical Incarnation of the Logos in Jesus of Nazareth, still casts a long shadow on interreligious dialogue. Indeed, it may be argued that the christological turn merely replaces one particularity (the church) with another (Jesus of Nazareth), albeit a more universal and credible one. The Christian claim about the uniqueness of Jesus as savior, which is tied with his historicity, is seen as a handicap in making Jesus a basis for dialogue. Aware of this difficulty, several theologians have sought to draw a distinction—albeit not separation, much less opposition—between the Logos *asarkos* and the incarnated Logos, between the Christ and Jesus, and argue that the Logos *asarkos* or the Christ is not exhaustively embodied in Jesus of Nazareth. Put differently, Jesus is wholly God (*totaliter Deus*) but not the whole God (*totus Deus*). Hence, it is in principle possible to hold that the Logos can manifest himself elsewhere, in other religions and other human beings, though not in the mode of hypostatic union.

3. But even the *theologoumenon* of the Logos *asarkos* or the Christ is judged by some theologians to represent a specifically Christian perspective and hence unsuitable to serve as a universal starting point for interreligious dialogue (except with Judaism and Islam). Another point of departure, more universal than Logos Christology, would be needed, namely, God himself. A theocentric approach would be preferable to both the ecclesiocentric and christocentric approaches. Of course, "God" is understood and named differently by various religious traditions. But these ways of conceptualizing and naming God should not be regarded as mutually exclusive theologies. Rather, they may be viewed as culturally and religiously conditioned modes of discourse about the Divine (or to use John Hick's term, "The Real"), each valid

in its own contexts and useful for different purposes, just as Joseph Jastrow's celebrated "illusion" can be seen as duck or rabbit, or light is interpreted as particle or wave, or maps of the same country are drawn by different cartographers for various uses. This theocentric model, it is argued, furnishes a truly universal foundation for interreligious dialogue, apart from any particular historical embodiment of the Divine.

4. Despite its theoretical advantages, the theocentric starting point for interreligious dialogue has been criticized on several grounds. First, it explicitly or implicitly smuggles a particular, often Christian, conception of the deity into the dialogue with other religions, and thus does not attend sufficiently to the theological particularities of each religion. Second, it does not address the fact that some religious traditions such as Buddhism and Jainism explicitly exclude considerations of the deity from their philosophies and practices. Third, it suffers from an exclusive focus on dialogue as a theological exchange carried out mostly among scholars, which, albeit legitimate and necessary, tends to neglect the other three aspects of interreligious dialogue, namely, common living, collaboration for peace and justice, and sharing of religious experiences. It is in the emphasis on common activities for justice, peace, and harmony that "kingdom of God" as a variation of theocentrism has been proposed as the basis for interreligious dialogue. This "regnocentric" or "basileiacentric" starting point is strongly favored by liberation theologians, especially in Asia, who combine the "preferential option for the poor" and interreligious dialogue as essential components of Christian mission.

5. The focus on the reign of God as the foundation of interreligious dialogue leads to the question of whether the Christian belief in Trinity, and more precisely, the economic Trinity, that is, the immanent Trinity present and active in history as Father/Creator, Son/Redeemer, and Spirit/Sanctifier, can itself be the foundation of interreligious dialogue. Attempts have been made to find not parallels, much less identities, between the Christian doctrine of the Trinity and the triadic if not trinitarian conceptions of reality espoused by other religions but to establish "homologies" among certain fundamental beliefs of various religions and to explore ways in which certain beliefs of one's religious tradition can be illuminated by those of others. In this way a basis for dialogue can be established which is both Christian and non-Christian.

6. Within this development of the trinitarian doctrine as foundation for interreligious dialogue, special attention has been paid to the role of the Spirit. Latin theology has often been accused of Christocentrism at the expense of the Holy Spirit. The balance has been redressed by recent events in church and theology that have brought the Spirit to the center of life and reflection. These events include the retrieval of the history of salvation (the kingdom of God) as the fundamental theological category, the focus on the economic rather than immanent Trinity, the discovery of hope (eschatology) as the basic character

of Christian existence, the worldwide explosion of the Pentecostal/charismatic movements and the gifts associated with the Holy Spirit, the vision of moral life as life in the Spirit and the consequent reshaping of moral and spiritual theology. This pneumatological turn supplies a new basis for interreligious dialogue that is of great appeal in dialogue with nontheistic as well as theistic religions, the so-called world religions, as well as primal and tribal religions.

7. Lastly, mention of primal and tribal religions and new religious movements (including independent or autonomous Christian churches) raises the question of whether spirits, that is, beings endowed with supernatural, though not necessarily divine, powers capable of good and for ill actions on behalf of humans, can also be a foundation for interreligious dialogue between Christianity on the one hand and Confucianism, Daoism, and a plethora of tribal, primitive, and popular religions. This question is of great importance, especially in light of what the missiologist Paul G. Hiebert refers to as the "excluded middle." Hiebert argues that Western theologians and missionaries have attended to the two opposed dimensions of reality, namely, the visible world of empirical things and the invisible world of the divine, but have neglected the in-between world, the "excluded middle" composed of "beings and forces that cannot be directly perceived but are thought to exist *on this earth.* These include spirits, ghosts, ancestors, demons, and earthly gods and goddesses who live in trees, rivers, hills and villages. These live not in some other world or time, but are inhabitants with humans and animals of this world and time."[7] This "excluded middle" can and should serve as a fertile starting point for interreligious dialogue, especially in Asia and Africa.

So far we have sketched a seven-stage movement in the quest for a foundation or at least a starting point for dialogue between Christianity and other religions. At least on the Christian side there has been, in my historical mapping, a move from the particular to the universal, or, better still, a sublation of the particular into the universal in which the previous foundation is expanded and rebuilt on a wider and more common basis. The next section will explore in detail the last two phases, which we have called "pneumatological" or "spirit-based," drawing on the insights of Asian Catholic theologies.

THE SPIRIT AS THE FOUNDATION OF INTERRELIGIOUS DIALOGUE

Perhaps the most convenient way to expound an Asian pneumatology, especially in connection with interreligious dialogue, is to provide a summary of

---

7. Paul G. Hiebert, "The Flaw of the Excluded Middle," in *Landmark Essays in Mission and World Christianity*, ed. Robert L. Gallagher and Paul Hertig (Maryknoll, NY: Orbis Books, 2009), 183.

and commentary on the document issued by the FABC's Office of Theological Concerns in 1997 entitled "The Spirit at Work in Asia Today."[8] The document is remarkable for its unusual length (about a hundred pages), comprehensiveness, and insightfulness. It intends to elaborate the implicit pneumatology of its previous documents dealing with interreligious dialogue, the local church, church and politics, and harmony. At the outset it states that pneumatology and Christology, far from opposing each other, are mutually complementary and illuminating: "The more we follow the leading of the Spirit, the deeper and closer will also be our understanding of the mystery of Jesus Christ."[9] *The Spirit at Work in Asia Today (SWAT)* is composed of six parts.[10] A few words on its key affirmations are in order.

The Spirit at Work in Various Religio-Cultural Traditions in Asia

Methodologically, it is highly significant that *SWAT* begins its treatment of the Holy Spirit with a lengthy exposition on the presence and activity of the Spirit in Asian cultures, religions, and socio-political realities (Parts I and II, comprising 43 pages, almost half of the total number of pages!), rather than with biblical and magisterial teachings, as is usually done in official church documents and Western theological texts. Implicit in this methodology is the conviction—still denied by the Roman magisterium and disputed by a number of theologians—that the Spirit is actively present in non-Christian religions and that these religions may be called "ways of salvation." In reflecting on the Spirit in Asian religious traditions, the authors of *SWAT* declare their intention to "discern the presence of the Spirit as expressed, believed, imaged and symbolized by believers themselves in these traditions."[11]

SWAT goes on to highlight what it terms "resonances" between the Spirit and various realities present in Asian religions. In Hinduism, it mentions *atman* (the self), *prana* (breath), *antarayamin* (inner controller/indweller), *ananda* (bliss/joy), *sakti* (power/energy, especially as female), and *agni* (fire). After pointing out a "deep resonance" between these Hindu concepts and the Christian concept of the Holy Spirit, *SWAT* asks: "Was the Spirit (apart from concepts congenial with the Spirit) present in the Indian Tradition? Yes.

---

8. For the text, see *For All the Peoples of Asia: Federation of Asian Bishops' Conferences. Documents from 1997 to 2001*, ed. Frans-Josef Eilers (Quezon City, Philippines: Claretian Publications, 2002), 237–327. Henceforth, *FAPA*.

9. *FAPA*, 238.

10. The six sections of *SWAT* are: (1) the Spirit at work in various religio-cultural traditions of Asia; (2) the Spirit at work in socio-political realities; (3) the Spirit at work in the biblical traditions; (4) the Spirit at work in the church; (5) toward an Asian theology of the Spirit; and (6) pastoral recommendations. I will not summarize the entire document but only highlight those aspects germane to my theme.

11. *FAPA*, 239.

If we are able to discern the signs of the Spirit we can read the history of Hinduism as a holy history, where the Spirit has led our brothers and sisters to the depths of the mystery of God and leads them towards Christ."[12]

Buddhism, with its stated nontheistic religious stance, presents a daunting challenge to elaborating pneumatology, and *SWAT* is well aware that "if one sets out to 'find God' in Buddhism, the result will be either frustrated disappointment or a distortion of tradition."[13] In spite of profound differences between Buddhism and Christianity, *SWAT* affirms that an encounter between them is possible and desirable, "beyond concepts, dogmas, symbols and rituals at the level of experience." It highlights the Buddhist experiences based on the Four Noble Truths, the Four Sublime States (i.e, *upeksa* [peace of mind], *karuna* [compassion], *mudita* [sympathetic joy], and above all, *maitri* [love]), and devotion (the ideal of the *bodhisattva*, especially the Amitabha Buddha and Avalokitesvara). Again, *SWAT* asks the pneumatological question: "As Christians come to share something of the vision and experience of the Buddha as lived out in the lives of the people with whom they share the Asian heritage, what can they perceive but the work of the Spirit which they too have experienced?"[14]

SWAT moves on to consider the two Chinese religious traditions, i.e., Confucianism and Daoism. Even though, unlike Buddhism, these traditions are not explicitly nontheistic, the transcendent being (e.g., Heaven or the Dao) does not play a significant role. Yet again *SWAT* concludes categorically: "In many ways, they [Confucianism and Daoism] reflect the workings of the Holy Spirit in the cosmos and particularly in humanity and its history. The Taoist virtues of docility, trust, humility, non-violence, detachment, equanimous love; and the Confucianist virtues of responsibility, honesty, loyalty and fidelity are but manifestations of the fruits of the one Spirit of God working in all sorts of different ways in different people in the world."[15]

The next object of discussion is what has been referred to under the umbrella category of "primal religions." *SWAT* sees them as characterized by two basic beliefs, i.e, in a supreme divine being (the Great Spirit) and in what has been called the "excluded middle" (the spirits). Primal religions (*SWAT* includes under this category Shamanism and Shintoism) are found primarily among indigenous peoples, also referred to as "tribals" or "aborigines," terms that often have a pejorative connotation of cultural backwardness. The document notes that the attitude fostered by primal religions toward the Great Spirit and spirits, of which some are benign and others evil, is both awe and fear. With regard to whether the Holy Spirit is active in primal religions,

---

12. Ibid., 241–42.
13. Ibid., 243.
14. Ibid., 248.
15. Ibid., 257.

SWAT frankly recognizes that until Vatican II these religious traditions have been condemned as idolatry and superstitions. However, since the council, a more positive appreciation of primal religions has been advocated, and the document notes that "much of the indigenous people's world view and ethos is compatible with the Christian faith," and that "traditional beliefs, rites, myths and symbols of indigenous peoples provide material for developing indigenous theologies and liturgical ceremonies."[16] Clearly, *SWAT* acknowledges the presence of the Holy Spirit in primal religions, albeit with some reservation, given their belief in evil spirits and practices to appease them.

No such qualm is to be found in *SWAT*'s discernment of the presence of the Spirit in Islam. The document opens its presentation of Islam with a categorical affirmation: "The Divine Spirit, who works unceasingly to renew the face of the universe, is also active in the religion of Islam to produce the Spirit's inimitable fruits in the lives of Muslims. . . . A study of the Qur'an, the Sacred Book of Islam, shows a constant effort to sow in the lives of believing Muslims those qualities that Christians recognize as the fruits of the Spirit."[17] The document singles out for admiration the Islamic teaching on love, compassion, and submission to God's will and the practices these virtues entail. The document is convinced that "by forming friendships with Muslims, by coming to know better their faith and practices, and by working together with them for good, it is God's Holy Spirit who is praised and worshiped."[18]

The Spirit at Work in Socio-Political Realities

Whereas it is a common practice to discern the presence of the Spirit in religions, it is rather unusual to do so with reference to socio-political events and movements. By so doing *SWAT* provides a basis for dialogue not only between Christianity and other religions but also between religions and nonreligious ideologies and movements (e.g., socialism and Communism), which are dominant in many Asian countries.

Acknowledging the extreme variety of Asian socio-political realities, *SWAT* mentions socio-political movements (e.g., the *Swaraj* and *ahimsa* movements in India, the anticolonialism struggle and the Communist ideology in China, Korea, and Vietnam, the *pancasila* ideology in Indonesia, and the "People's Power" in the Philippines), ecological movements, women's movements, workers' movements, political ideologies (e.g., atheistic Marxism, antitheistic capitalism, fundamentalism, communalism, national security ideology), and youth movements. *SWAT* urges Christians to discern the work of the Spirit in all these dizzyingly diverse realities as they combine biblical and church

---

16. Ibid., 261.
17. Ibid., 261–262.
18. Ibid., 266.

teachings on the Holy Spirit with the Asian religious, cultural, and socio-political heritage in the attempt to elaborate "an Asian pneumatology which might provide elements to discern the various spirits at work in Asia today."[19]

The Spirit at Work in the Biblical Tradition

SWAT presents a masterful summary of the teaching of the Bible on the Spirit and the Spirit's presence from creation to Jesus.[20] Of this summary four points deserve highlighting. First, the document strongly insists on the unity and inseparability between Word and Spirit throughout human history: "There is no Spirit without the Word and there is no Word without the Spirit."[21] Second, there is *mutual* dependence between Word and Spirit, one cannot operate without the other. One the one hand, the Spirit is presented as "the Spirit of Jesus" and as Jesus' gift; on the other, "the Spirit is at work in Christ."[22] Third, the Spirit operates with utter freedom; it blows where it wills. One place where *SWAT* discerns the activity of the Spirit is the sacred scriptures of non-Christian religions: "The Sacred Scriptures of the other religions are also reflections of the presence and activity of the Spirit in the non-Christian religious institutions."[23] Fourth, there is a need of discernment between the Spirit on one hand and evil spirits and false claims to have the Spirit on the other. This raises the question of criteria for discernment, and the document lists three: fruits of the Spirit, values of the kingdom of God, and the sense of faith of the church.

The Spirit at Work in the Church

Again, *SWAT* offers an insightful overview of the theology of the presence and activity of the Spirit in the church that can be termed "pneumatological ecclesiology." In particular, the document insists on the unity between the Spirit and the church, of which the Spirit is the soul as it were. It laments the danger of excessive institutionalization of the church's structures to the detriment of the charisms. It welcomes the rebirth of Spirit-centered spirituality in Protestant Pentecostalism, Catholic Charismatic Renewal, and other movements that celebrate the gifts of the Spirit (e.g., glossolalia, healing, prophecy, etc.) for the building up of the Body of Christ.

More pertinent to our theme, *SWAT* links the work of the Spirit in the church to interreligious dialogue. Paradoxically, the Spirit's presence *in* the

---

19. Ibid., 281.

20. *SWAT* lists ten activities of the Spirit as described by the Bible: The Spirit draws people to the Truth, begets people into the kingdom of God, teaches, witnesses, accuses by rousing a sense of sin, liberates, effects growth, prays, leads, and renews (*FAPA*, 294–97).

21. Ibid., 298.

22. Ibid., 288.

23. Ibid.

church enables the recognition of the Spirit's presence *outside* the church. It is the presence of the Spirit in the church that impels Christians toward dialogue with other religions and enables them to see in the "deeper meanings and intentions of people of other faiths . . . the voice of the Spirit bearing witness to the marvelous variety of God's self-revelation to man."[24]

Toward an Asian Pneumatology

Having discerned the presence of the Spirit in Asian cultures and religions, Asian socio-political movements, in the Bible, and in the church, *SWAT* essays an "Asian pneumatology." Of course, what is presented is but a sketch and not a systematic and comprehensive treatise. It is helpful to highlight its most salient features.

First, as has been seen above, methodologically an Asian pneumatology starts "from below," that is, from reflections on Asian cultures, religions, and socio-political movements. In this way, it, as *SWAT* rightly claims, "offers a broader theological framework in which we are able to relate the Spirit with the mystery of God's reign, and consequently understand and interpret our Asian experiences in a pluri-cultural and multi-religious context."[25] The document notes that "in the field of interreligious dialogue there is a shift from a theocentric view to a spirit-centered dialogue which stresses that the Spirit works in all peoples."[26] Thus, as I have shown above, "Spirit" represents the last two stages of the theological journey in quest of a universal foundation for interreligious dialogue.

Second, the Spirit is viewed primarily as mystery, that is, as that which cannot be fully and exhaustively expressed in anything finite and yet is present and active in all finite things: "Whatever has been manifest and expressed has been viewed as the mirror of the unmanifest, the unexpressed; the revealed as a fragment of the unrevealed."[27]

Third, of the myriad ways the Spirit is active in the world, an Asian pneumatology emphasizes three, i.e., ecological unity (binding humans with the cosmos), movement (crossing over all types of boundaries and divisions), and freedom (liberation from attachment and egoism and struggle for social justice and peace).

Fourth, since Asia is characterized by deep pluralism in all aspects of life, "the approach to the Spirit as the author of plurality strikes a highly responsive chord in Asian hearts."[28] Consequently, an Asian pneumatology will intentionally and explicitly cultivate what the FABC terms "receptive plural-

---

24. Ibid., 307.
25. Ibid., 318.
26. Ibid., 274.
27. Ibid., 318.
28. Ibid., 321.

ism," that is, the many and diverse ways in which Asian people respond to the Spirit: "We value pluralism as a great gift of the Spirit. . . . The many ways of responding to the prompting of the Holy Spirit must be continually in conversation with one another."[29]

Finally, such pneumatology carries profound implications for being church in Asia. In particular, it requires of Christians struggling in effective solidarity with the powerless, according primacy to charisms over institutions, and becoming a participative community of equals.

While concurring fully with *SWAT* on Asian pneumatology, I propose the following reflections to show that an Asian pneumatology—the theology of the Spirit (with a capital S) and spirit (with a lower-case s)—can serve as the most appropriate and fruitful foundation for interreligious dialogue. First, the Spirit—understood as the Third Person of the Trinity—is the *first* transcendent reality that humans experience, both chronologically and theologically. In any religious experience, it is the Spirit who is the first known and loved. From the Christian perspective, the proper *ordo* of both Christian living and Christian theology (and hence of dialogue between Christians and the followers of other religions) is: "*from* or *by the power of* the Spirit *in* the Son *to* the Father." In other words, the proper and necessary structure of Christian life, and also religious experience in general, is *from* the Spirit *in* the Son *to* the Father, and not *from* the Father *to* the Son *to* the Spirit (this is the order of the intratrinitarian eternal processions, not that of the economic Trinity), much less in the Father *and* the Son *and* the Spirit (the "and" obscures the specific relationships of the three divine persons). In brief, from the Christian perspective, the Spirit is the starting point and foundation of our encounter with the transcendent Being and with one another that leads us to the Son who leads to the Father.

Second, while a separation, let alone opposition, between Christ and the Spirit would postulate two distinct divine economies in the world and would therefore be theologically unacceptable, it is possible and necessary to distinguish between the activities of the Logos and those of the Spirit as well as between their modes and venues of operation. There is a *mutual* dependence and conditioning between the Logos and the Spirit. As pointed out by *SWAT*, the Spirit cannot function without the Logos (as often insisted upon in Western theology), but it must be no less strongly emphasized that the Logos cannot function without the Spirit. (In the same vein, it must be said that the Father cannot function without the Logos and the Spirit, and vice versa). This mutual dependence among the three divine persons in being and action is the corollary of the trinitarian structure of the Christian God. This truth is unfortunately often obscured in Western articulations

---

29. Ibid.

of the trinitarian processions from the Father to the Son to the Spirit—in descending and linear fashion—in spite of assertions of the divine *perichoresis*. This results in the total dependence of the Spirit not only on the Father but also the Son (hence, the oft-repeated formulas: "the Spirit of the Son," "the Spirit of Jesus," and the "Spirit of the Father"), and the implicit denial of the dependence of the Son (and the Father) on the Spirit (thus, there are no such formulas as "the Father of the Spirit," "the Son of the Spirit," and "Jesus of the Spirit"). In this way, the trinitarian/triadic structure of the Christian God is jeopardized. To put it in classical terminology, we should hold not only *Filioque*—the procession of the Spirit from the Father and/through the Son—but also *Spirituque*—the generation of the Son from the Father and/through the Spirit.

Third, mutual dependence among the trinitarian persons does not negate but rather requires a certain "autonomy" in being and action of each divine person, inasmuch as they have irreducibly *different* manners of being and action. Otherwise the divine persons cannot be distinguished among themselves. These differences entail that each person, and more relevant to our theme, the Spirit, can and does function "autonomously" from the Son in history, in different places and different times, where the Jesus of history could not reach due to his historical limitations. Only with this "autonomous" action of the Spirit, albeit not opposed to that of the Son, can we fully recognize the work of the Spirit outside of Jesus and Christianity, without the need to reduce the non-Christian religions to being simply "preparation" for Christianity (*praeparatio evangelica*) or to being "fulfilled" or "superseded" by it, thereby denying their integrity and otherness.

Fourth, in the dialogue with Asian religions, it is helpful to recall that "Spirit" has been conceptualized in diverse, at times diametrically opposed, ways. It has been interpreted in theistic, monotheistic, polytheistic, monistic, nondualistic, dualistic, humanistic, and even atheistic terms. This is not the place nor is it possible to go over all these philosophical and theological possibilities. The point is simply that better than any other Christian category, "Spirit" and "spirit" serve as a most acceptable starting point and foundation for interreligious dialogue in places with religious diversity as vast as in Asia. *SWAT* puts it concisely: "The 'Spirit' could be understood as the human or the divine Spirit. In nontheistic religions, such as Buddhism, Jainism or Taoism, it stands for the 'given' human potentiality to speak, seek and find total human liberation. But in the biblical, and some other theistic, traditions, this potentiality tends to be regarded as the divine Spirit operating immanently in the human person. In either case the diversity of tongues which defines the activity of the Spirit argues for religious pluralism."[30]

---

30. Ibid., 274.

To illustrate how a pneumatological approach is the most fruitful for interreligious dialogue I will conclude with brief reflections on how monastic interreligious dialogue has flourished precisely on the basis of such pneumatology.

MONASTIC INTERRELIGIOUS DIALOGUE AND THE SPIRIT

Given Asia's rich and diverse religious heritage, it is to be expected that modern interreligious dialogue finds its fertile soil in Asia, particularly in India. At first, the dialogue was with theistic religions, especially Hinduism. However, it has been no less vigorous with nontheistic religious traditions, in particular, Buddhism. This dialogue is carried out on four levels, i.e., common life, socio-political collaboration, academic exchange, and sharing of religious experiences. Furthermore. interreligious dialogue between Christianity, and more specifically, Roman Catholicism, and other religions flourished among monastic communities, both male and female.[31] For my thesis that pneumatology serves as the most comprehensive foundation for interreligious dialogue, two features of this interreligious dialogue stand out as highly significant. First, it has prospered as a sharing of religious experiences among monastics. Second, it has done so despite radical differences in the conception of the Ultimate or God.

In this context it may be asked: Is it fortuitous that historically, interreligious dialogue has been fostered primarily by monastics, both Christian and non-Christian, or is there an intrinsic connection, and not just accidental circumstances, between monastic life understood as life lived in the Spirit—in both Christian and non-Christian forms—and engaging in interreligious dialogue? In other words, are there deep resonances between monastic spirituality and the spirituality of interreligious dialogue? In answer to this question, Fabrice Blée's insightful reflections on what he calls the "desert of religious otherness" (*le désert de l'altérité religieuse*) prove very helpful. What is most important in interreligious dialogue, according to Blée, is the ability to make room within one's religious *self* for the religious *other* (to use Raimon Panikkar's expression, "intrareligious dialogue"). This empty space within one's religious self is a "desert"—a symbolic place of struggle and encounter with God/the Spirit. As Blée puts it concisely:

---

31. A comprehensive history and analysis of interreligious dialogue among monastic communities is given in Fabrice Blée, *Le désert de l'altérité: Une expérience spirituelle du dialogue interreligieux* (Montreal: Médiaspaul, 2004). The English translation was published by Liturgical Press in 2011.

Today, the desert is neither a geographical place nor a structure. The monk in dialogue intends to withdraw to the heart of religious otherness. Relationship with other believers needs more than ever this rich space of trials, temptations and union with the divine, a desert which, without a particular form and without distancing the monk from human activities, is ultimately the axis of the kingdom of God, where every communication becomes communion.[32]

The monks and nuns, non-Christian as well as Christian, are by vocation dedicated to making this place within themselves for the religious other, though of course they are not the only ones to do this. Once they have carved out this place of hospitality for the religious other (in *intrareligious* dialogue) they are naturally disposed and equipped to carry out *interreligious* dialogue.

The agent that enables the monk to perform this double task can be called God in theistic traditions, or Spirit (with the capital S), or just spirit (with the lower-case s) in nontheistic traditions, insofar as it is a force making humans perfectly human or more than human (liberated from *samsara* or from suffering) yet immanent within the human person itself. What matters is not how this experience is expressed verbally but what goes preverbally and postverbally. What precedes and follows theological exchanges in monastic interreligious dialogue is contemplation and prayer—not only in the same place (as during the celebrated Assisi prayer gatherings for peace in 1986 and 2002) but also *together*. This interreligious prayer is made possible by the presence of the Spirit/spirit who unites the pray-ers (the non-Christian and Christian praying monks) to the Pray-er (the Spirit) and to one another (spirits).

It is a happy coincidence that *SWAT* ends its exposition of an Asian pneumatology with the quotation from 1 Thessalonians: "The Church in Asia also needs to develop its faculty of discerning the Spirit at work in Asia today, within the church in the various charismatic and popular movements that have arisen, and in the Asian spiritualities, Asian aspirations for liberation and full human dignity. 'Do not stifle the Spirit or despise the gift of prophecy with contempt, test everything and hold on to what is good' (1 Thess. 5:19–21)."

---

32. Blée, *Le désert de l'altérité*, 22 (my translation).

12

Asian Catholicism and Confucianism

An Intercultural and Interreligious Dialogue

This chapter explores the encounter between two systems of thought and ways of life whose fortunes in East Asia have been intertwined for over four centuries and whose future prospects seem to be indissolubly wedded to each other. This task is made vastly complicated by the fact that there is a deep uncertainty about the identity of one of these two partners in dialogue. While there is a broad agreement as to what is meant by "Catholicism," there are sharp differences of opinion regarding "Confucianism." It has been seriously and extensively debated, for example, whether Confucianism is a religion at all or whether it is merely a philosophical anthropology or an ethical system or a socio-political theory, and even whether "Confucianism" itself is, historically speaking, a Western invention.

The subtitle of the chapter, "An Intercultural and Interreligious Dialogue," indicates my own position in these debates. I believe that Confucianism is to be regarded as a philosophical anthropology, an ethical system, a socio-political theory, and a religious way of life, all at once. These distinct categories, while useful in academic discourse, are not adequate representations of what is commonly referred to as Asian religions in general and Confucianism in particular. To encompass all these aspects of Confucianism, I will use culture and religion as the two broad perspectives for my exposition of the encounter between Confucianism and Catholic Christianity.

I begin with a bird's-eye view of the basic teachings of Confucius and the main developments of Confucianism. Next I give an account of the encounter between Confucianism and Roman Catholicism in East Asia, mainly in China, from the sixteenth century to the present. I end with reflections on some of the most important issues confronting an intercultural and interreligious dialogue between Confucianism and Roman Catholicism.

It is to be noted that my essay has a narrowly circumscribed focus, that is, the dialogue between Confucianism and Roman Catholicism. More precisely, it will consider only some and not all the issues that are crucial for that dialogue. It does not deal with the encounter between Confucianism and Christianity in general nor with the relationship between the Roman Catholic Church and other Christian churches in China on the one hand and the Chinese political system and the Chinese government on the other. It is of course impossible to wall off my reflections on the encounter between Roman Catholicism and Confucianism from these other larger issues, and I will occasionally refer to them. I hope that my reflections will make a contribution, however small, to the understanding of the future of Christianity, and in particular of the Roman Catholic Church, in East Asia.

KONGZI, THE *RU* TRADITION, AND CONFUCIANISM

Kongzi, Kong Fuzi, Confucius

"Confucius" is the Latinization by sixteenth-century Jesuit missionaries in China, most probably by Matteo Ricci, of the honorable title Kong Fuzi (literally, Master Kong). This Chinese expression itself was popularized if not invented by the Jesuits to designate a man proclaimed as China's greatest teacher of wisdom whose given name is Kong Qiu and courtesy name is Kong Zhongni and who was known to the Chinese as Kongzi— but not as Kong Fuzi, though the honorific *Fuzi* (master) was used by his disciples to address him or refer to him.[1] Born into a family of minor aristocracy in the small feudal state of Lu, near modern Qufu (Shandong Province), Confucius (551–479 BCE) lived in an age of great social and political upheaval known as the Spring and Autumn Period (772–481 BCE) of the Eastern Zhou dynasty (771–256 BCE). Of Confucius's life little is known with certainty, except that like others of his time, Confucius regarded public service as the proper goal of a gentleman (*junzi*). It is reported that at about the age of thirty-five, he visited the neighboring state of Qi but received no offer of employment from Duke Jing of Qi. He then returned to Lu and at the age of fifty took up a minor office of police commissioner. Disappointed with his failure to influence the duke of Lu, Confucius left Lu again and traveled for some thirteen years with a small band of disciples to visit various states. In around 484 Confucius returned to

---

1. Michael Nylan notes that the expression Kong Fuzi apparently first appeared on inscribed spirit tablets dedicated to the Sage during the Yuan period, but it was the Jesuit missionaries of the late sixteenth century who popularized the term in their attempt to elevate Confucius to the status equivalent to that of the fathers of the early church. See her *The Five "Confucian" Classics* (New Haven: Yale University Press, 2001), 363–64. Lionel Jensen however believes that the expression Kung Fuzi was invented by the Jesuits themselves. See his *Manufacturing Confucianism: Chinese Traditions and Universal Civilization* (Durham, NC: Duke University Press, 1997), 83–86.

Lu, where he was made a low-ranking counselor. He died some five years later in 479 at the age of seventy-three.

In the *Lunyu* (lit. "ordered sayings"), popularly known in English as the *Analects*, a collection of 497 verses purportedly containing Confucius's conversations with his disciples and compiled by the latter about a hundred years after his death, Confucius is alleged to have summarized his life as follows: "At fifteen, I set my mind upon learning; at thirty, I took my place in society; at forty, I became free of doubts; at fifty, I understood Heaven's Mandate; at sixty, my ear was attuned; and at seventy, I could follow my heart's desires without overstepping the bounds of propriety."[2] This barest autobiographical outline, though reflecting a historical core, is symbolic of the various stages of intellectual and spiritual progress of the "Confucian Way." This way comprises three pairs of stages. The first pair (learning and taking one's place in society) focuses on study and ritual practice. The second pair (freedom from doubt and understanding Heaven's Mandate) emphasizes the necessity of fully internalizing the new way of life and compliance with the will of Heaven. The third pair (being attuned and following one's heart's desires without overstepping the bounds of propriety) describes the state of complete harmonization between one's internal dispositions and the dictates of the moral order. These six stages contain all the essential elements of the so-called Confucian Way— personal self-cultivation through education for its own sake, socio-political engagement, and moral and spiritual transformation through compliance with a transcendent order of values. It is a way that can be practiced by anyone and does not necessarily correspond with any period of one's age.

Just as "Confucius" is the Latinization of the honorable title of Kong Fuzi, so the term "Confucianism" is also a Jesuit invention for the system of thought purported to be originally taught by the Chinese master. As Paul Rule has noted, until Nicholas Trigault published Matteo Ricci's journals in 1615, no European had ever discussed Confucius and the thought system associated with him, Confucianism. However, "Confucianism," if understood to mean some philosophical system or religious organization founded *ex nihilo* by Confucius, in the way Buddhism is founded by Siddhārtha Gautama and Christianity by Jesus of Nazareth, then it is a misnomer. In fact, Confucius explicitly disclaimed any intention to establish new

---

2. All the translations of the *Lunyu* are taken from *Confucius Analects, With Selections from Traditional Commentaries*, trans. Edward Slingerland (Indianapolis/Cambridge: Hackett, 2003). The text cited is indicated by the numbers of book and verse. Here, 2.4. Other recent important studies of *The Analects* include E. Bruce Brooks and A. Taeko Brooks, *The Original Analects: Sayings of Confucius and His Successors* (New York: Columbia University Press, 1990); and Bryan W. Van Norden, ed., *Confucius and the Analects: New Essays* (Oxford: Oxford University Press, 2002).

teachings or practices.[3] Rather, living in a state of political instability and moral decay of the Spring and Autumn Period of the Eastern Zhou dynasty, Confucius believed that the only way to reestablish harmony and prosperity in society was to return to the "Way of the Ancients," especially as was embodied by the legendary sage kings—the Jade, Shun, Yao, Yellow, and Yu emperors—and later by the founders of the Zhou dynasty—King Wen, King Wu, and the Duke of Zhou.

The Ru Tradition

Prior to Confucius then there had been an intellectual tradition to which he made appeal as a normative fount of wisdom and as a way of life and which is often referred to as *ru*.[4] That Confucius referred to this tradition, urging his disciple Zixia to be "a gentleman *ru*" (*junzi ru*) rather than "a petty *ru*" (*xiaoren ru*) is reported in the *Analects* (6.13). However, what is meant by *ru*, both etymologically and historically, is extremely obscure and has by no means been settled despite extensive scholarly studies. Etymologically, *ru* is said to be derived from the character *xu*, which itself is composed of two parts, meaning "cloud" and "above sky"; it is also associated with other homophonous characters meaning "wet," "soft," and "weak." These etymologies suggest that *ru* were people versed not in the military arts but in ritual, music, and dance.[5] Historically, according to Zhang Binglin (1869–1936), *ru* refers to three different kinds of people in the government office of the Zhou dynasty: first, to intellectuals or gentlemen equipped with skills and expertise in one or more areas of social life (*shu shi*); second, to professionals versed in the six arts of ritual, music, archery, charioteering, history, and mathematics; and third, to people who assisted the ruler to follow the way of yin-yang and to educate the people on this way.[6]

---

3. *Analects* 7.16: "The Master said: 'I transmit rather than innovate. I trust in and love the ancient ways. I might thus humbly compare myself to Old Peng.'"

4. Until the twentieth century, *ru*, M. Nylan points out, always referred to people, that is, people committed to the study and propagation of the classics (in this sense they are classicists), and never to a set of ideas in contrast to those of Buddhism and Daoism. See *The Five "Confucian" Classics*, 2.

5. On the early Confucians primarily as ritual masters, see Robert Eno, *The Confucian Creator of Heaven: Philosophy and the Defense of Ritual Mastery* (Albany: State University of New York Press, 1990).

6. Robert Campany notes that Zhang Binglin's reference to the "way of yin-yang" with regard to early Confucianism is inaccurate since the yin-yang theory has nothing to do with early Confucianism; it did not arise until around 250 BCE. Furthermore, according to Kang Youwei (1858–1927) and Hu Shi (1891–1962), *ru* refers not to the government officials of the Zhou dynasty but to those of the Shang dynasty (1600?–1100? BCE). Thanks to their knowledge of religious rituals these professionals were later employed as priests by the succeeding Zhou dynasty (Western Zhou, 1100?–771 BCE, and Eastern Zhou, 770–256 BCE).

By the time of the Warring States period (479–221 BCE) Confucius, as Han Feizi, a well-known critic of Confucius's ideas and practices, points out, was recognized as the preeminent master in the *ru* tradition. From here it was but a small step to identify *ru* with the teaching of Confucius, and the members of the *ru* tradition with his disciples. A complex of expressions associated with *ru* such as *rujia* (*ru* family), *rujiao* (*ru* teaching), *ruxue* (*ru* learning), and *ruzhe* (the *ru*) are used to designate what is now referred to as Confucianism and the adherents of the Confucian Way. Not that Confucianism is identical with *ru*. As has been mentioned, Confucius claims to be only a transmitter and not an inventor of tradition. Nevertheless, there is no gainsaying the fact that in transmitting the Way of the Ancients, Confucius has transformed it or at least is regarded to have done so by later writers, so that *ru* no longer refers merely to masters of dance, music, and ritual but to a specific tradition of thought and learning associated with Confucius and a community of scholars committed to studying and transmitting it.

Long before Confucius, there existed therefore a tradition of learning, which he claims to have transmitted. This intellectual tradition was initiated by the Zhou dynasty, especially the Duke of Zhou, who wanted to institute an official system of education (*guan xue*) to train specialists for civil service. This educational system was weakened during the Spring and Autumn period by the rise of semi-independent states and was replaced by private learning and education (*si xue*). Confucius is one of the earliest teachers to initiate this educational system and is said to have had three thousand students of whom seventy-two were intimate disciples. This community of Confucius's disciples eventually came to be known as the *rujia*, that is, a family or fellowship of the followers of the Confucian Way, devoted to the study and restoration of the Way of the ancient sage kings.

The Way of the sage kings is believed to be embodied in certain ancient writings or records. It was Confucius's lifelong ambition to collect, edit, preserve, and transmit them to later generations.[7] The earliest mention of the so-called Confucian classics is found in the *Book of Zhuangzi*, a Daoist work

---

7. With regard to Confucius's role in establishing these ancient records, later known as the "Confucian Classics," there are three opinions. A majority of Confucian scholars hold that there had been no "classics" proper before Confucius and that it is Confucius who established what is known as the classics. For other scholars, especially those of the Old Text School, the classics originated in the early years of the Zhou dynasty, and Confucius's role is essentially limited to arranging them as textbooks for his students. Another group of scholars, while crediting Confucius with a significant role in the formation of the classics by collecting, editing, arranging, and transmitting the ancient records, prefers not to make a generic judgment on Confucius's authorship of these classics as a whole but, using the historical and literary method, attempts to determine which parts of these classics were made by Confucius and his disciples and which parts came from later periods. See Xinzhong Yao, *An Introduction to Confucianism* (Cambridge: Cambridge University Press, 2000), 52–54.

compiled during the Warring States period. This work lists "Six Classics" (*liu-jing*): the *Classic of Poetry* or *Odes* (*shijing*), the *Classic of Documents* or *History* (*shujing* or *shangshu*), the *Records of Ritual* (composed of three texts: *Ceremonials* [*Yili*], *Rites Records* [*Liji*], and *Zhou Rites* [*Zhouli*]), the *Classic of Changes* (*yijing*), the *Spring and Autumn Annals* (*chunqiu*), and the *Classic of Music* (*yuejing*).[8] The last book is no longer extant (or has never existed); probably it was burned by order of the First Emperor of the Qin dynasty in 213 BCE, so that today reference is made to the "Five Classics" (*Wujing*).[9] These Five Classics, which deal with politics, legend, history, poetry, ritual, philosophy, and religion, were regarded as the foundational sources of Confucianism and were made the subject for civil service examinations.

In addition to the Five Classics, during the Song dynasty, Zhu Xi (1130–1200) singled out the *Analects*, two chapters of the *Record of Ritual*, namely, the *Great Learning* (*Daxue*) and the *Doctrine of the Mean* (*Zhongyong*), and the *Book of Mengzi* (Mencius) to form the "Four Masters" (*Sizi*), later designated as the "Four Books" (*Sishu*), which were also made the subject of civil service examinations by the Yuan dynasty (1260–1370) in 1313.

Confucianism

Partly because Confucianism was made into the state orthodoxy in 136 BCE by Emperor Wu (r. 140–87 BCE) of the Han dynasty (206 BCE–220 CE), with the worship of Confucius as the state cult, and Confucius himself awarded the title "Great Perfect, Most Holy Culture-Spreading First Teacher," and partly thanks to the Jesuit portraiture of the *xianru* (first *ru*) or *guru* (ancient *ru*), which they identified with the original teaching of Confucius, as the only orthodox teaching in China, Confucianism is often equated, in both Western and Eastern imagination, with "Chineseness" or Chinese culture. However, such identification is historically inaccurate because Confucius was only one of the great thinkers of his time and Confucianism was part of the "Hundred Families/Schools" (*baijia*) that flourished between 551 and 233 BCE. Sima Tan (170–110 BCE), a court historian of the Western Han dynasty, mentions six schools of philosophy vying for popular acceptance and imperial patronage during his time: Confucianism, Daoism (Laozi and Zhuangzi), Mohism

---

8. For a study of the classics, see the very helpful work of Nylan, *The Five "Confucian" Classics*, already cited.

9. The "Five Classics" were later expanded to the "Seven Classics" (added were the *Analects* and the *Classic of Filial Piety*). During the Tang dynasty (618–906 BCE) "Nine Classics" were inscribed on stone tablets (the *Classic of Changes*, the *Classic of Documents*, the *Classic of Poetry*, the three commentaries on the *Spring and Autumn Annals*, the *Zhou Ritual* (*zhouli*), the *Book of Etiquette and Ritual* (*yili*), and the *Records of Ritual*. Later, three more books were added to make "Twelve Classics": the *Classic of Filial Piety* (*xiaojing*) and the *Analects*. Finally, in the Song dynasty (960–1279), the *Book of Mengzi* (*Mencius*) was added to make the "Thirteen Classics."

(Mozi), the School of Law or Legalism (Han Feizi and Lizi), the School of Names (Hui Shi), and the School of Yin and Yang and the Five Phases (Agents or Elements). All these schools of thought, with sharply different views on fundamental philosophical issues and at times engaging in acrimonious polemics against each other, have contributed to the formation of what constitutes Chinese culture or "Chineseness."

Words ending in *ism* tend to essentialize the realities they refer to, masking their historical permutations and multiplicity of forms. Like other cultural, philosophical, and religious traditions, Confucianism is by no means homogeneous but has undergone continuous developments since its beginning in the sixth century BCE to our time and contains within itself self-contradictory positions. Of course, Confucian basic teachings are rooted in the Five Classics and the Four Books, but already in the years immediately following the Master's death, there were among his self-proclaimed disciples, e.g., Mengzi and Xunzi, profoundly different opinions regarding basic issues such as human nature and the process of self-cultivation.[10]

Even during the Western Han dynasty (206 BCE–8 CE, when thanks to the efforts of Jia Yi (200–168 BCE) and Dong Zhongshu (179–106 BCE) Confucianism became the state-sponsored orthodoxy, there was a debate between the "Old Text" and "New Text" Schools, so called because the texts of the former are written in the pre-Han (archaic) script, whereas those of the latter in the script current during the Han dynasty. The Old Text School arose as a reaction against the New Text School. The New Text School was championed by Dong Zhongshu and therefore accepted as orthodox, whereas the Old Text School was advocated by Liu Xin (?-23 CE) who was later accused of forging its texts. The New Text School tends to present Confucius not only as a sage but also as the "Uncrowned King," a divine being, and the "savior" of the world, whereas the Old Text School regards him simply as a transmitter of ancient wisdom. In addition, Han Confucianism became eclectic since it had to incor-

---

10. For interpretations of Confucianism and Chinese religious thought in general, besides classics such as Arthur Waley, *Three Ways of Thought in Ancient China* (London: G. Allen & Unwin, 1939); Benjamin I. Schwartz, *The World of Thought in Ancient China* (Cambridge, MA: Harvard University Press, 1985); and A. C. Graham, *Disputers of Tao: Philosophical Argument in Ancient China* (Chicago: Open Court, 1989), a very accessible history of the development of Confucianism is John H. Berthrong, *Transformations of the Confucian Way* (Boulder, CO: Westview Press, 1998). For an original exposition of Confucianism in dialogue with Western philosophy, see the three volumes by David L. Hall and Roger T. Ames, published by State University of New York Press, *Thinking Through Confucius* (1987); *Anticipating China: Thinking Through the Narratives of Chinese and Western Culture* (1995); and *Thinking from the Han: Self, Truth, and Transcendence in Chinese and Western Culture* (1998). On the history of Chinese philosophy in general, see Wing-Tsit Chan, ed., *A Source Book in Chinese Philosophy* (Princeton, NJ: Princeton University Press, 1969); Fung Yu-lan, *A History of Chinese Philosophy*, vols. 1–2, trans. Dek Bodde (Princeton, NJ: Princeton University Press, 1952); and Thomé Fang, *Chinese Philosophy: Its Spirit and Its Development* (Taipei: Linking Publishing, 1981).

porate elements of Daoism and the School of Law and even apocryphal writings (*chenwei*) in order to be acceptable to all the citizens.

Differences in various Confucian traditions are more pronounced in the turbulent period following the collapse of the Eastern Han dynasty (25–220 CE) known as the Six Dynasties period (222–589 CE) when the other two traditions, i.e., Buddhism and Daoism, reemerged to form with Confucianism the "Three Teachings/Religions" (*sanjiao*). In their struggle against their competitors, Confucian scholars, notably Wang Bi (226–249), developed a new form of hybrid Confucianism known as "The Study of Mystery" or "Mysterious Learning" (*xuanxue*), also referred to as Neo-Daoism. This form of learning, while remaining deeply rooted in the Confucian classics, interprets them, especially the *Classic of Change*, in Daoist language and categories. Mysterious Learning is the first serious and influential attempt to synthesize Confucianism and Daoism in order to resolve the debate about the relationship between moral codes/social institutions (*mingjiao*), which Confucianism favors, and the inborn tendencies of human nature (*ziran*), which Daoism promotes. The result is a new form of Confucianism enriched by the mystical elements of Daoism.

Another Confucian tradition emerged during the Song dynasty (960–1279), referred to in the West as Neo-Confucianism, which moves away from exegetical studies of the Confucian classics typical of the Han Learning to speculations on psychological and metaphysical issues of body-mind (*shenxin*) and nature-destiny (*xingming*). Major contributors to this new strand of Confucianism are the Five Masters of the Song Learning (*Song xue*): Zhou Dunyi (1017–1073), Shao Yong (1011–1077), Zhang Zai (1020–1077), and the two Cheng brothers, Cheng Hao (1032–1085) and Cheng Yi (1033–1107). However, the greatest master of the new school is Zhu Xi (1130–1200). As mentioned above, it was Zhu Xi who anthologized the "Four Books" which eventually became equal to the "Five Classics." In reinterpreting the Confucian tradition as a way of self-transformation, Zhu Xi follows the Cheng brothers' view of the dual concepts of "principle" (*li*) and "matter" (*qi*) as constitutive of the cosmos. Hence, the "Neo-Confucian" tradition is often called the "Study of Principle" (*li xue*) or the Rationalist School, or the Cheng-Zhu School. For Zhu Xi, to achieve self-transformation one must understand the *li* through the study of the classics (by "investigating things" [*gewu*]) and the practice of rituals. Zhu Xi's "School of Principle," which fuses scholarship with practice, and his commentaries on the classics became the required subject-matter and norm for the civil service examinations from the Yuan dynasty (1260–1368) until the end of the Qing dynasty.

However, Zhu Xi's interpretation of Confucianism did not go unchallenged. His contemporary Lu Jiuyuan (1139–1193) argues that the Supreme Ultimate that underlies and permeates all things is not *li* but *xin* (heart/mind).

All human beings are endowed by Heaven with the heart/mind, and therefore all have the innate ability to know intuitively what is good, to learn how to be good, and to do what is virtuous. This "Study of the Inner Mind" or "Learning of the Heart/Mind" (*xin xue*) School was developed and systematized under the Ming dynasty (1368–1644) by Wang Yangming (1472–1529). Wang eschews complex textual exegesis to accumulate knowledge of external things as a way of self-transformation. Instead, he advocates knowing the "original substance" (*benti*) within and acting on one's innate affections as the means to achieve sagehood.[11]

Under the Manchu/Qing dynasty (1644–1911), as part of anti-Qing sentiment, a movement called "Han Studies" (*Hanxue*) emerged which proposes evidence-based research (*kaozheng*) and a return to the ancient classics beyond the distortions of Buddhist-inspired "Song Studies" (*Songxue*) embodied in the "School of Principle" and the "Study of the Inner Mind." Underlying "Han Studies" is the conviction that behind all the divergent and politically inspired "Confucianisms" there is a common and pure source residing in the authentic teaching of Kongzi in which knowledge and action are united. Consequently, there was in this period a renewed interest in Confucius as a prophetic figure and religious founder.

Finally, as the Qing dynasty was facing collapse and as the empire was repeatedly humiliated with unequal treaties by the Western powers with their superior economic, technological, and military machinery, burning questions were raised regarding the social relevance of Confucianism for the new China—China with "science and democracy"— confronted with the urgent need of modernization. While the Qing dynasty assiduously promoted the Cheng-Zhu School to bolster its own regime, Confucian scholars such as Kang Youwei (1858–1927) revived the debate between the Old Text School and the New Text School. Kang favored the latter with its apotheosis of Confucius and proposed to make Confucianism the state religion (*guojiao*) as a means to strengthen China, making *kongjiao* (Confucian teaching/religion or better: "Confucianity") the Chinese equivalent of Christianity of the West. These scholars' political reform, which includes constitutional monarchy, lasted only a hundred days in 1898, thwarted as they were by the Empress Dowager Cixi (1835–1908). After the fall of the Qing dynasty (1911), there arose a powerful anti-Confucianism movement, crystallized in the May Fourth Movement (1919), led by radical liberals such as Chen Duxiu (1879–1942), Yi Baisha (1886–1921), Li Dazhao (1889–1927), and Hu Shi (1891–1962), laying all the ills of China at the feet of Confucius and Confucianism.

As a reaction against this extreme anti-Confucianism, a new movement led

---

11. Because this school was developed by Lu Jiuyuan and Wang Yangming, it is also known as the School of Lu-Wang. It is also referred to as the Idealistic School in opposition to Cheng-Zhu's rationalism.

by Confucian scholars known as "Modern New Confucian Learning" (*xiandai xin ruxue*) came into existence. This movement may be divided into three periods. The first, before the founding of the People's Republic of China (1949), was led by two groups of prominent scholars: those favoring the Cheng-Zhu School ("New Learning of Principle" [*xin songsue* or *xin lixue*]) and those following the Lu-Wang School ("New Learning of the Heart/Mind" [*xin xinxue*]). Among the first group, the most distinguished scholar is Fung Yu-lan (1895–1990), and among the second, Xiong Shili (1885–1968). The second period, which took place mainly outside of mainland China, particularly in Hong Kong, Taiwan, and the United States, was led by scholars such as Tang Yunyi, Mou Zongsan, Xu Fuguan, and Fang Dongmei (Thomé H. Fang). In 1858 they published "A Declaration of Chinese Culture to the Scholars of the World," in which they maintain that Confucianism is not against democracy, science, and technology and that a modernized China cannot do without Confucian humanistic values. The third stage of Modern New Confucian Learning is being carried out by these scholars' students and disciples such as Cheng Chung-ying, Tu Wei-ming, Liu Shuxian, and Yu Yingshi, who present Confucianism as a holistic tradition and culture, including metaphysics, ethics, politics, religion, and spirituality, with positive implications for modernization, as demonstrated in such countries as Japan, Korea, Taiwan, Hong Kong, and Singapore.[12]

Meanwhile, in mainland China, the Chinese Communist Party, founded in 1921, criticized Confucianism as feudalistic and backward. Maoist ideology replaced Confucian ideology. Later, Confucianism suffered a terrible blow during the Cultural Revolution (1966–1976), with its iconoclastic policies against the "Four Olds": old customs, old habits, old culture, and old thinking, emblems for what was considered Confucianism. After the deaths of Zhou Enlai and Mao Zedong (both in 1976) and the arrest of the Gang of Four, research and publications on Confucianism became acceptable again. The government restored the Kong family mansion, cemetery, and Confucian temple in Qufu and opened it to the public. In the 1980s several international conferences on Confucius were held in Qufu. The China Confucius Foundation was established in 1984, and the Shandong Publishing Commission Office has published the *Guide to Confucian Culture*, a set of books on Confucius and Confucianism.

The main purpose of this exceedingly sketchy overview of Confucianism and its various schools and developments throughout its more than two-

---

12. Tu Wei-ming's most significant works include *Centrality and Commonality: An Essay on Confucian Religiousness* (Albany: State University of New York Press, 1976/1986); *Selfhood as Creative Transformation* (Albany: State University of New York Press, 1985); *China in Transformation* (Cambridge, MA: Harvard University Press, 1994); and *Confucian Spirituality*, ed. with Mary Evelyn Tucker, vols. 1 and 2 (New York: Crossroad, 2003). Also, on Confucianism as a religious way of life, see Rodney Taylor, *The Religious Dimension of Confucianism* (Albany: State University of New York Press, 1990).

and-a-half-millennia history is to alert readers to the extreme complexity of a dialogue between Roman Catholicism and Confucianism. The preliminary question to such dialogue remains: With which Confucianism must the Catholic Church enter into dialogue? While a dialogue between Roman Catholicism and Confucianism can certainly dwell at the general level of the core philosophical, ethical, and religious concepts of both traditions, still it is necessary to be clear about how these concepts are understood, especially in different strands of Confucianism. Furthermore, from a practical point of view, such a dialogue cannot be carried out at the institutional or official levels since Confucianism, in contrast to Buddhism, Daoism, and other East Asian religions, does not have an authoritative teaching office (analogous to the Roman Catholic magisterium), a priesthood, and a governing authority. In fact, in China, Confucianism is not considered as a religion recognized by the government.[13] The question is not only with *which* Confucianism but also with *whom* among Confucians should the dialogue be carried out. Before broaching these themes a survey of the encounter between Roman Catholicism and Confucianism will provide some useful insights into how a dialogue between the two traditions should proceed in the future.

CONFUCIANISM AND ROMAN CATHOLICISM: A HISTORICAL ENCOUNTER

"The Luminous Religion from Daqin": Christianity's First Encounter with Chinese Religion

East Syrian Christianity in Persia, misleadingly referred to as the Nestorian Church, came to Xi'an, the ancient imperial capital in northwest China's Shaanxi Province, in 635 and was warmly welcomed by the Tang emperor Taizong (reigned 627–649).[14] On the stele erected in Xi'an in 781 and discovered in 1623/25, Christianity is called *Jingjiao* (the Luminous Religion or Religion of Light) of *Daqin* (Syria). The carved text of 1,756 Chinese characters, composed by the priest Jing-jing (his Syriac name is Adam), is a unique record of the encounter between the Christian faith and Chinese religions in the eighth century.

The stele contains a lengthy exposition of the Christian faith in prose and

---

13. The religions officially recognized by the Chinese government include Buddhism, Daoism, Roman Catholicism, Protestantism, and Islam.

14. The best one-volume, up-to-date history of Christianity in China is Jean-Pierre Charbonnier, *Christians in China*, trans. M. N. L. Couve de Murville (San Francisco: Ignatius Press, 2007). For a brief historical outline of Christianity in Asia, see Peter C. Phan, *The Blackwell Companion to Catholicism*, ed. James J. Buckley, Frederick Christian Bauerschmidt, and Trent Pomplun (Oxford: Blackwell, 2007), 203–20.

a shorter summary in verse. The first exposition, the more important of the two, refers to the Trinity, the creation of the world, the original fall of humanity, Satan's rule, the Incarnation, salvation, the Bible, baptism, evangelization, ministry, Christian morality, fasting, the liturgy of the hours, and the Eucharist. In expounding the essentials of the Christian faith Jing-jing makes ample use of Buddhist, Daoist, and Confucian expressions. He describes God as "unchanging in perfect repose," a formula used by the *Daodejing* to describe the *Dao* (Way). God is said to have produced "the four cardinal points" (a basic concept of Chinese geomancy) and "the two principles of nature," i.e., the yin and yang of Daoist and Confucian cosmology. He speaks of some people mistakenly identifying "nonexistence" (the Daoist "nameless nothingness") with "existence." He refers to Christianity as the ever-true and unchanging "Dao" itself. Jesus is said to have established his "new teaching of nonassertion," the key Daoist notion of *wu wei* (nonaction).

Jing-jing also adopts Confucian expressions. The messiah is said to teach "how to rule both families and kingdoms"—a Confucian phrase in the book of *Great Learning*. Buddhist concepts and images are also pressed into service. Jesus is said to have "hung up the bright sun" (i.e., crucifixion), taken an oar in "the vessel of mercy" (the bodhisattva or the Kuan-yin), and "ascended to the Palace of Light." In addition to this stele, there are numerous other Chinese written sources on Christianity of the T'ang period, often referred to as the "Dunhuang Documents," found in the library of the Dunhuang grottoes, which also contain a serious effort at interpreting the Christian faith in terms of Chinese religions.

The Catholic Church's First Entry into China

Unfortunately, East Syrian Christianity disappeared with the fall of the Tang dynasty in 907, its members scattered among the nomadic tribes in the north and northwest of China. Christianity did not come back to China until the Mongolian/Yuan dynasty (1279–1368), this time under the aegis of the Catholic Church. The mission to Rome in 1287 by Rabban Sauma (ca. 1225–1294), an Ulghur born in Beijing and a monk of the East Syrian Church, in the name of the Mongolian il-khan Arghun, revealed to the Roman church the existence of Christians in Mongolia and China. The first Catholic missionary to enter China proper, sent by Pope Nicholas IV, was the Franciscan friar Giovanni da Montecorvino, who reached Khanbalik (Beijing) in 1294, shortly after the death of Kublai Khan. The missionary built a church there and reported in 1305 that there were 6,000 converts. In 1307, Pope Clement V appointed him archbishop of Khanbalik and primate of Cathay (North China) and the entire Far East. When Giovanni da Montecorvino died in 1328, it was estimated that there were more than 10,000

Catholics. In 1338, at the request of the last Mongol emperor, Toghan Timur, Pope Benedict XII sent a group of missionaries, among whom was Giovanni da Marignolli. When the Yuan dynasty collapsed in 1368, the Catholic Church, which then numbered 30,000 and had enjoyed imperial support, disappeared with it. Compared with East Syrian Christianity, Roman Catholicism under the Yuan dynasty cannot be said to have made a serious effort at communicating the Christian faith in terms, both cultural and religious, understandable to the Chinese. To the Chinese, the Catholic Church could not but appear as a foreign religion, politically protected by an occupying foreign power and financially supported by a foreign religious institution.

Catholic Presence under the Ming Dynasty: A Sustained Dialogue with Confucianism

Almost 185 years later, the Catholic Church attempted once more to enter China, which under the Ming dynasty (1368–1644) had become isolationist, nationalist, and rigidly Confucian. Francis Xavier (1506–52) left Japan for mission in China in 1551 but died the following year on the small island of Sancian, within sight of the China coast, near Guangzhou.

Under the *padroado* (patronage) of Portugal, Francis Xavier's missionary dream was fulfilled by a small band of Jesuits, particularly Alessandro Valignano (1538–1606), Matteo Ricci (1552–1610), and Michele Ruggieri (1543–1607). From Macau, a small Portuguese colonial enclave (with a diocese established in 1576), Ricci and Ruggieri entered mainland China in 1583.

Following Valignano's accommodationist method, the two missionaries, Ricci in particular, learned the language, studied the Chinese classics, discarded the Buddhist monk's attire, presented themselves as members of the *ru*, dressed in Confucian scholars' garb, and tried to convert the Chinese through science (especially mathematics, astronomy, and map making). Ricci's goals were to reach Beijing and to convert the emperor, and through him, the Chinese people. Though he failed in his latter goal, he was allowed in 1600 by Emperor Wanli to reside in Beijing. In the last ten years of his life, Ricci, known in Chinese as Li Matou, was much more successful in his mission than in his previous seventeen years. Among his converts were the so-called Three Pillars of the Chinese Church: Paul Hsu (Xu Guangshi), Leon Li (Li Zhizao), and Michael Yang (Yang Tingyun), though the last was not taught by Ricci.

Other Jesuits who worked in Beijing until the fall of the Ming dynasty (1644) and beyond include Nicholas Longobardi (1559–1654), Adam Schall (1592–1666), and Ferdinand Verbiest (1623–88), the latter two directing the prestigious Bureau of Astronomy. At the end of the Ming dynasty there were 150,000 Chinese Catholics.

Roman Catholicism and Confucianism in
Conflict under the Manchu (Qing) Dynasty

At the beginning of the Qing dynasty, the prospects of Catholic missions were promising. Thanks to his accurate prediction of the solar eclipse on September 1, 1644, Schall was appointed by the second Manchu emperor Shunzi director not only of the Bureau of the Calendar but also of the Institute of Mathematics. The emperor also gave the Jesuits a piece of land, a church, a residence in the capital, and an annual subsidy. Verbiest, who succeeded Schall and served for twenty years, was much decorated by the third Manchu emperor, Kangxi (reigned 1662–1723).

Unfortunately, soon internal struggles among missionaries threatened to unravel Catholic missions in China. Until 1631, the Jesuits had enjoyed a monopoly in China mission. After 1630, however, other religious orders arrived, in particular, Dominicans (1631), Franciscans (1633), Augustinians (1680), and members of the Société des Missions Étrangères de Paris (1683). These newcomers brought with them not only conflicts between the two rival patronage systems—the Spanish and the Portuguese—but also the nascent colonizing ambitions of France and rivalries among religious orders. More tragically, they adopted different attitudes toward Chinese cultural and religious practices, in particular the sacrifice offered to Confucius and the veneration of ancestors. In Ricci's footsteps, most Jesuits (with the notable exception of Niccolò Longobardi, Ricci's successor), who worked mainly with the elite, tolerated these customs as nonsuperstitious acts of a political and civil nature, whereas the newly arrived missionaries, who labored among the uneducated masses, condemned them as idolatry.

These contrasting positions brought about what is known as the Chinese Rites Controversy, which began in 1633 and did not end until 1939. Popes Clement XI (in 1715) and Benedict XIV (in 1742) proscribed the Chinese rites. These condemnations proved disastrous for Catholic missions in China. In retaliation, the emperor Kangxi banished missionaries from China in 1722 unless they followed Ricci's policy, and his decision was confirmed by his successor Yongzheng. In the next 160 years sporadic persecutions broke out, Christians were ordered to apostatize, churches were seized, and native priests forced to secularize. Nevertheless, the Chinese Catholic Church survived. In 1800, there were reported to be 200,000 Catholics in all of China.

Catholic Missions in the Nineteenth Century

At the beginning of the nineteenth century, Catholic missions in China were complicated by the arrival of Protestants, mostly British, who devoted much of their energies to education and medical welfare. With the new missionaries, other colonial powers appeared on the scene. The Opium Wars of 1839–

42 and 1856–60, which humiliated China, concluded with favorable treaties for Britain, France, Russia, and the United States. These unequal treaties, besides forcing China to concede economic advantages to Western powers, stipulated the legal right for missionaries to preach and to erect churches in Chinese territories. Even the Chinese Christians were protected by the treaties as a special class, immune from Chinese laws. Catholic missions, in particular, were protected by France. Catholics were often segregated in isolated communities and were often regarded as foreign colonies, completely dependent on missionaries. In 1841, a Catholic mission prefecture was established in Hong Kong when the island was ceded as a British colony in that same year. From 1860 on, Catholic and Protestant missionaries flocked in great numbers to China, which soon became the world's largest mission field.

Eclipse of the Catholic Church under the Communist Regime in the Twentieth Century

By the middle of the nineteenth century, Christianity had been compromised by the Taiping Rebellion (1851–64), led by Christian-inspired Hong Xiuquan, against the Qing dynasty. At the beginning of the twentieth century, anti-foreign sentiments were rumbling and exploded in the 1900 Boxer Uprising (1898–1900). Identified in the Chinese eyes with Western imperialism, Christianity suffered heavily. With the overthrow of the Qing dynasty (1911), in which Christians played a role, and with the establishment of the Republic of China (1912–1949), led by the Christian Zhongshan (Sun Yat-Sen), Christianity enjoyed what may be called its Golden Age (1900–1920). The number of Chinese Christians was estimated at 366,000 in 1920. Now the foreign religion was welcomed as an antidote to Chinese traditionalism. Its victory was, however, short lived. In 1920, it was denounced by a group of college students as an anachronistic obstacle to China's modernization, and Christian missions were accused of being a tool of Western imperialism. Again, anti-Christian movements broke out in 1924 and lasted until 1927, this time supported by political parties, both Nationalist and Communist. Thousands of missionaries had to leave, mission schools and hospitals had to be closed, and physical properties damaged. In 1926, six Chinese bishops were consecrated.

With the victory of the Communists over Jiang Jiashi's (Chiang Kai-shek) *Kuomingtang* in 1949, Christian, and in particular Roman Catholic, missions ended. The Three-Self Patriotic Movement Committee was founded in 1954, which all churches were required to join. In 1957, the Chinese Catholic Patriotic Association was established. As a result, there are two Catholic groups in China: the government-approved Patriotic Catholic Association and the so-called Underground Church, loyal to Rome. In 1958, the first consecration of Catholic bishops without the approval of Rome took place. Since the 1980s there have been encouraging signs that the Vatican and Beijing have been working toward a rapprochement. Seminaries were allowed to open in Shanghai and Beijing in 1982 and 1983 respectively. In 2000, Pope John Paul II canonized 120 martyrs of China. Recently, two bishops were ordained with papal approval, following the appointment of a Vatican-approved bishop for Beijing. However, relations between the Vatican and the Chinese government remain volatile and unpredictable, since the latter is still holding firm to the power to name bishops, and there has recently been the appointment of several bishops without Vatican approval. Statistics of Chinese Christians are notoriously unreliable. Recent surveys put the number of Christians in Mainland China at 40 million, with 12 million Catholics, the rest being Protestants, especially Pentecostals.

Catholic and/or Confucian?

From this survey of the presence of the Catholic Church in China it is clear that the encounter between Christianity and Confucianism, which was initiated by the East Syrian Church in the seventh through ninth centuries, was taken up and expanded after the seventeenth century, principally by Jesuit missionaries with their accommodationist policies. The history of such accommodation—or to use the contemporary neologism of "inculturation"—is replete with triumphs and defeats, lights and shadows, humble acceptance and acrimonious rejection.[15] Though I have focused on China above, the same history of the encounter between Catholicism and Confucianism played out in countries within the Sinic sphere of influence, namely, Japan, Korea, Taiwan, and Vietnam, not to mention overseas Chinese communities.

A thumbnail sketch of this complex history of the Catholic-Confucian encounter may be drawn on two canvases: first, Catholic *and* Confucian, and, second, Catholic *or* Confucian. Of course, reality is much more complicated than these two stark options suggest. No Catholic would be totally for or totally against being a Confucian and vice versa. Both Catholicism and Confucianism contain beliefs and values that either side can appropriate, just as they also profess what one side considers as errors and unacceptable practices. The two alternatives, however, can serve as a useful heuristic device with which to view past approaches to the question of a possible dialogue between Catholicism and Confucianism.

---

15. For a discussion of the encounter between Catholicism and Confucianism, see John D. Young, *Confucianism and Christianity: The First Encounter* (Hong Kong: Hong Kong University Press, 1983); Julia Ching, *Confucianism & Christianity: A Comparative Study* (Tokyo: Kodansha International, 1977); Stephen Uhalley Jr. and Xiaoxin Wu, eds., *Christianity and China: Burdened Past Hopeful Future* (Armonk, NY: M. E. Sharpe, 2001); Peter K. H. Lee, *Confucian-Christian Encounters in Historical and Contemporary Perspectives* (Lewiston, NY: Edwin Mellen, 1991); and Liam Matthew Brockey, *Journey to the East: The Jesuit Mission to China 1579–1724* (Cambridge, MA: Harvard University Press, 2007).

On one side, then, there is the approach as practiced by the Jesuits, especially by Matteo Ricci and his followers. Alessandro Valignano (1539–1606), who was in charge of the Jesuit missions in East Asia with the title of visitor general, wanted Jesuit missionaries in China and Japan to "accommodate" Christianity to the local cultures, and as part of this policy he mandated a proficient knowledge of the native languages and personal adaptation to the local mores and customs. Matteo Ricci (1552–1610) arrived in Macao in 1582 and joined Michele Ruggieri (1543–1607) in the study of the Chinese language and of the Five Classics and the Four Books and in the translation of these works into Latin. A year later, both Ricci and Ruggieri were allowed to enter China and to reside at Zhaoqing in the Guangdong Province. From there Ricci gradually moved north, through Shaozhou, Nanchang, Nanjing, and finally Beijing and established Jesuit houses in these four cities. It was during this northward journey that Ricci made a fateful decision to discard the Buddhist monks' outward appearances and dress in the *ru* garb, presenting himself and other Jesuits as the *ru*, *xiru* (Western scholars), or *daoren* (men of the Way).

Of course, it was not simply a matter of sartorial style. Rather it was a missionary strategy, one that has vast and lasting implications for the Catholic–Confucian dialogue. Since Buddhism has many parallels with Catholicism, especially in monastic practices, Ricci, with the encouragement of Wang Pan, the magistrate at Zhaoqing, at first adopted the Buddhist monk's indigent clothing to make himself a Chinese to the Chinese. Subsequently, however, he realized that Buddhist monks were held in low regard by the Chinese populace and that in order to gain a hearing from the Chinese, he had to present himself as a bona fide member of the *ru* and establish missionary contacts with these Confucian scholars who were part of the Ming imperial bureaucracy, with the hope that through them he could convert the emperor. It is in this intellectual environment that Ricci composed his most celebrated work, *Tianzhu Shiyi* (the True Meaning of the Lord of Heaven), completed in 1596 and published in 1603. This work is presented as a dialogue between the "Chinese Scholar" and the "Western Scholar"—in fact, a dialogue between Confucianism and Catholicism on the basis of human reason alone.

Ricci is convinced that Confucianism as represented in the Five Classics—what he terms the "original" or "first" *ru*—is profoundly consonant with the Christian faith, with its belief in the one God designated as *Shangdi* (Lord on High) or *Tian* (Heaven), in contrast to Song Confucianism (now called "Neo-Confucianism"), which became, through the hands of Zhu Xi, atheistic with its speculations on *li* and *qi* and distorted by Buddhist ideas. Consequently, Ricci vigorously attacks Buddhism and Daoism as superstitious sects and extols the original *ru* as the only embodiment of authentic Chinese culture and religion. Ricci was practicing the method of *bu ru yi fo* [supplement *ru*, excise Buddhism], to use the expression of one of his most celebrated converts, the scholar-doctor Paul Xu Guangxi.[16] In this context, Confucius is elevated to the status of a Christian/Jesuit saint (Ricci's honorific title for him is *santo*), and the *ru*, whom Ricci calls *la legge de' letterati* (order of the literati), becomes the equivalent of the Society of Jesus. Such "manufacturing" of Confucius and the *ru* reaches its peak in the influential and massive work edited by Philippe Couplet and his fellow Jesuits, *Confucius Sinarum Philosophus sive Scientia Sinensis* (1687).

At the other end of the spectrum of missionary method stands the attitude of most mendicant friars, Dominicans and Franciscans, who came to evangelize Southeast China (especially the Fujin Province) in the 1630s, and the members of Missions Étrangères de Paris, sent by the Holy Congregation for the Propagation of Faith in the 1650s independent of the Portuguese *padroado*. These new arrivals worked mainly with the lower and poorer classes (whom of course the Jesuits did not neglect to evangelize, contrary to popular opinion). They were not versed in the Confucian classics nor were they interested in establishing a common cultural and religious ground between the Christian faith and Chinese culture. Consequently, they were much more inclined to highlight the opposition between the "pagan" way of life of the Chinese and the new Christian life which conversion imposes.

The differences between the Jesuits and the other missionaries with regard to Confucianism came to a head in the so-called Chinese Rites Controversy, which lasted three hundred years and brought into collision two fundamentally diverse attitudes to Confucian practices. The issues at hand were the cult of Confucius and the veneration of ancestors, both sacred obligations, the former for the *ru*, the latter for all Chinese. Most Jesuits tend to regard the rituals connected with these two cults as acts of filial piety and of "civil and political" significance, not religious worship, and hence permissible. The mendicant friars and the members of Missions Étrangères de Paris (most notoriously Bishop Charles Maigrot) saw them as superstition and proposed banning them. On the basis of conflicting reports from the missionaries, Rome issued confusing policies, at times prohibiting and at other times tolerating. In 1742, a total and absolute prohibition of these practices was issued by Pope Benedict XIV in his decree *Ex quo singulari*. It was not until 1939 that Rome lifted the ban on the traditional rites in honor of Confucius and the ancestors on the ground that they are only of "civil and political" import. In sum, then, a Chinese can be both Catholic *and* Confucian. One need not abandon one's Confucian heritage to be a Christian. The all-deciding question is of course: What is meant by "Confucian heritage"?

---

16. Another version of the motto reads: *qinru paifo* (draw close to *ru*/Confucianism, repudiate Buddhism).

A ROMAN CATHOLIC-CONFUCIAN DIALOGUE: CHALLENGES AND PROSPECTS

As I hope to have made it clear, there are many schools and strands of Confucianism, and there have been conflicting ways among Catholics in dealing with Confucianism. This double diversity must be kept in mind as we explore the encounter between Catholicism and Confucianism. In the remaining part of my essay I would like to highlight the new context in which Confucianism exists today, the challenges presented by this context to the encounter between Confucianism and Catholicism, and, finally, the prospects of a successful dialogue between these two religious traditions in East Asia.

A New Socio-Political Context

There is no need to belabor the point that the context in which Catholicism encountered Confucianism in East Asia, from the sixteenth to the twentieth centuries, has changed drastically. In China, Japan, Korea, and Vietnam, Confucianism has lost its preeminent position as an official religious and cultural tradition. Confucianism as a state-sponsored orthodoxy and the cult of Confucius—*kongjiao*—as a national religion (*guojiao*) have been dethroned. In their place, other ideologies are reigning supreme, Communism in China and Vietnam, and capitalism in most other East Asian countries. Thirty years ago, Julia Ching, writing on the encounter between Confucianism and Christianity, already noted this radical change in context which required new modes and venues of such encounter:

> At that time [before the collapse of the Qing dynasty], there was yet an identifiable Confucian world, where certain well-known moral values attributed to Confucian teachings were enshrined in the social order, and respected by legal institutions, in the countries of the Far East. Today, the situation has changed drastically.[17]

The drastic change Ching refers to is the dictatorial domination of Marxist socialism. Today, even that situation has also changed drastically. As far as economics is concerned, Communism, while still a one-party political system in China, North Korea, and Vietnam, is giving in to the forces of the free market economy. Capitalism, at least under the Communist Party's control, is being experimented with and seems to be on the ascendance in China and Vietnam. With it, and with globalization, consumerism and materialism are rampant in all East Asian countries, especially among the youth.

In the meantime, questions are being raised as to the cultural, moral, and

---

17. Ching, *Confucianism & Christianity*, 28.

religious values that should guide the life of the people and the nations where Confucianism was at one time the normative ideal. Of course, the fact that Confucianism is no longer the state-supported orthodoxy does not mean that its ideas and values have not been operative in the lives of individuals since the collapse of the Qing dynasty in China and the advent of modernity in East Asia. Nor does it mean that there has been a total moral and religious vacuum in East Asian countries. There are other religions such as Buddhism, Daoism, Islam, and even Christianity, not to mention popular religions, that continue to flourish, sometimes underground.

It has been mentioned that Confucianism has been enjoying a renaissance, albeit modest, in mainland China, and that it is in vigor in other countries such as Taiwan, Hong Kong, Singapore, the Republic of Korea, and overseas East Asian communities. It has even been suggested that Confucianism, with its emphasis on community, hard work, egalitarianism, education, and harmony, is the engine driving the economic miracle in the so-called Four Asian Tigers. Be that as it may, it is clear that the radically changed socio-political context of East Asian countries presents new challenges for the encounter between Catholicism and Confucianism.

New Challenges for Catholic-Confucian Encounter

At first glance, Catholicism and Confucianism seem to be on two different planes, having little to do with each other. The former is based on divine revelation, centered on God, and directed toward eternal salvation in union with the triune God, whereas the latter makes no claim to divine origination, is centered on humanity, and aims at this-worldly perfection of sagehood. Given these fundamental differences, it was not surprising that many Christians, especially Protestant missionaries to China in the nineteenth century, have tended to regard a common understanding between the two traditions impossible or, if they attempt a dialogue at all, end up by arguing for the superiority of Christianity on the grounds that Christianity has access to truths that are in principle unknowable to human reason, whether corrupted or not.

It is to the credit of Matteo Ricci that in his *Tianzhu Shiyi* he bases the dialogue between the "Western Scholar" and the "Chinese Scholar" on what human reason—what he calls the *lumen naturale*—can discover as true and can be known with certainty by both Christians and Confucians. Hence, he rightly does not discuss the death and resurrection of Jesus in this book. Nevertheless, even Ricci feels the need to dedicate a major portion of his book to the questions of the existence of the one God, divine creation, the immortality of the soul, and other philosophical questions.

Today, in the current context of Marxist socialism and capitalism, the primary and urgent issue seems to be the meaning of being human, and it is here—philosophical anthropology—that Catholicism and Confucianism can undertake a first and most fruitful dialogue before broaching the question of God. On the one hand, anthropology has been the preferred starting point of modern and contemporary theology, even among Catholics. On the other hand, Confucianism is essentially about becoming and being a perfect human being (*junzi*). Here is not the place to expound the essentials of Confucian anthropology. As Julia Ching explains, there are ample opportunities for mutual enrichment between Confucianism and Catholicism in doctrines such as the essential openness of the human to the Transcendent, the basic moral character of human nature, the ideal of sagehood (*sheng*), self-cultivation in virtue unto death if necessary, conscience and natural law based on human nature, the heart/mind (*xin*) as the locus of the encounter between Heaven and humans, the universal virtue of *ren*, the five human relationships, and the sense of community.[18]

This deepening of a common, albeit not identical, understanding of what it means to be human in the Catholic and Confucian traditions, enriching and correcting each other, is all the more urgent in societies such as are found in some East Asian countries where the question of God is not and cannot be explicitly raised, or where religious pluralism is such that a common understanding of the divine is not possible.

From the Catholic perspective, another area where a dialogue between Catholicism and Confucianism will be fruitful is ritual, liturgy, and worship. Admittedly, the cult of Confucius and the veneration of ancestors are no longer controversial, at least on the theological level. There are, however, aspects of Catholic worship and liturgy that will benefit greatly from an incorporation of the Confucian understanding of ritual (*li*). Whereas Catholic liturgy emphasizes strongly the transcendent dimension of worship as an act of cult directed toward God by the community, it often leaves undeveloped the personal, social, and political implications of worship. It is in this latter aspect that Catholic ritual can be enriched by the Confucian understanding and practice of ritual (*li*). Confucian *li* is variously translated as ritual, rites, ceremonies, moral codes or the rules of propriety. As James Legge explains, "They [the rules of *li*] are practiced by means of offerings, acts of strength, words, and postures of courtesy, in eating and drinking, in the observances of capping, marriage, mourning, sacrificing, archery, chariot-driving, audiences, and friendly missions."[19] The practice of *li* inevitably involves a social and political dimension insofar as it places the practitioner in his or her fivefold relationship, namely, those obtaining between ruler-subject, husband-wife, parent-child, sibling-sibling, and friend-friend.

With regard to rituals proper, there are two celebrations in which Catholic

---

18. See ibid., 68–105.

19. *The Li Ki or the Collection of Treatises on the Rules of Propriety or Ceremonial Usages*, trans. James Legge (Oxford: Clarendon Press, 1885), 388.

liturgy needs to be integrated with Confucian rituals, that is, weddings and funerals. There is no doubt that these two moments of the life cycle more than any others are deeply marked by Confucian ideas and practices and are most important for East Asians in the Confucian sphere of influence. Unfortunately, East Asian Catholics most often celebrate them in two distinct and parallel ceremonies, one at home (which is very elaborate) and the other in church, according to the Roman ritual (which is required). As a consequence, the "official" liturgical celebration of weddings and funerals is regarded as a canonical requirement but bereft of real significance, whereas the "private" ceremony in the family is invested with greater solemnity and existential meaning. In light of this dichotomy, the Confucian–Catholic dialogue must make ritual and worship one of the most urgent items for consideration. The goal for such dialogue is a harmonious integration of the two rituals, especially for weddings and funerals, in such a way that they can enrich each other.

Prospects

In concluding his comprehensive introduction to Confucianism, Xinzhong Yao discusses its modern relevance. Yao enumerates three values by which Confucianism can be of great significance to contemporary society: an ethic of responsibility, a comprehensive understanding of education, and a humanistic understanding of life.[20]

First, in terms of responsibility, Confucianism places a paramount emphasis on the person's responsibility to self, family, nation, and world. In this respect, says Yao, "Confucianism can make a contribution to a new moral sense, a new ecological view and a new code for the global village."[21] Second, in terms of education, Confucian intellectualism is essentially a tradition based on learning and education. However, learning and education in the Confucian tradition, Yao points out, does not aim at mere accumulation of information and technical skills, though these are not neglected. Rather it aims at self-cultivation: "Confucian education is designed to penetrate the inner world of a learner, based on the conviction that cultivation of the virtues is more important than adjustment of external behavior."[22] Its goal is to form a "gentleman" (*junzi*), that is, a moral aristocrat, an exemplar of ritually correct behavior, ethical courage, and noble sentiment, a person of *ren*, with "sageliness within" and "kingliness without." Third, in terms of humanism, Confucianism represents an essentially anthropocentric faith. Thus, Yao reminds us, "Confucianism does not lack a transcendental dimension, nor does it want

---

20. See Yao, *An Introduction to Confucianism*, 279–86.
21. Ibid., 279.
22. Ibid., 281–82.

in metaphysical depth. The belief in Heaven and the Heavenly endowed mission underlies Confucian philosophy, politics, and religion."[23]

It is in these three areas that an encounter between Catholicism and Confucianism has very bright prospects. If these prospects are effectively realized, then both Catholicism and Confucianism will be relevant not only in East Asia but for all the world. Julia Ching puts it best when she describes how Confucianism can be dead or alive:

> And so, is Confucianism relevant? If we mean by the word sterile textual studies, a society of hierarchical human relationships excluding reciprocity, the permanent dominance of parents over children, of men over women, a social order interested only in the past and not in the future, then Confucianism is not relevant, and may as well be dead.

> But if we also mean by it a dynamic discovery of the worth of the human person, of his possibilities of moral greatness and even sagehood, of his fundamental relationship to others in a human society based on ethical values, of a metaphysics of the self open to the transcendent, then Confucianism is very relevant, and will always be relevant.[24]

Ironically, if one substitutes "Confucianism" with "Roman Catholicism," most of the negative characteristics and positive assets apply as well. Consequently, it is in the interest of both religious traditions to engage in a mutual critique and reciprocal learning so as to preserve and enhance their futures in the world.

---

23. Ibid., 285.
24. Ching, *Confucianism & Christianity*, 63.

Part III

PRACTICE

13

Christian Social Spirituality

A Global and Asian Perspective

The focus of this chapter is the social dimension of Christian spirituality in a global perspective. Two aspects of Christian spirituality will be explored, namely, its sociality and its globality. The former is an intrinsic element of Christian anthropology and ethics, the latter a new perspective imposed by the complex phenomenon known as globalization and the seemingly opposite need of Christian spirituality to be deeply rooted in local cultures.[1] I begin with a brief description of some urgent socio-political and economic challenges that globalization presents to Christian spirituality today. Next, an outline of Christian social spirituality, especially from the Roman Catholic tradition, will be presented. Finally, I make this Christian social spirituality more concrete by locating it in the situation of Asia and the social teachings of the Asian bishops and theologians.

CHRISTIAN SPIRITUALITY
IN THE GLOBALIZED WORLD

A balanced Christian spirituality—as the Irish theologian Donal Dorr has convincingly argued on the basis of the prophet Micah's triple injunction to act justly, to love tenderly, and walk humbly with God (Mic 6:8)—must be personal (religious conversion to God), interpersonal (moral conversion to face-to-face relationships with other people), and public (political conversion to the "poor").[2] These three conversions are not parallel, much less alternative, paths to God. Rather, they are inextricably intertwined with each other such that one without the other two would fail to achieve its goal. Furthermore, Christian spirituality in all its three dimensions must be lived out in the

---

1. The term "glocalization" was coined by the eminent theorist of globalization Roland Robertson to express this double movement, i.e., globalization and localization. See his *Globalization: Social Theory and Global Cultures* (London and Thousand Oaks, CA: Sage, 1992).

2. See Donal Dorr, *Spirituality and Justice* (Maryknoll, NY: Orbis Books, 1984), 8–18.

current socio-political, economic, and cultural context that today is encapsulated in the word "globalization."

Globalization

There is already a vast literature on globalization in its economic, political, and cultural aspects.[3] While some historians still question whether globalization with the implied dissolution of the system of nation-states is occurring or will ever occur, most agree that vast changes in societies and the world economy have been taking place, at least since the sixteenth century, as the result of dramatically increased international trade and cultural exchange, and that globalization is a useful shorthand for this phenomenon. Arjun Appadurai identifies five areas where this global connectivity has occurred: "ethnoscapes" (movements of people, including tourists, business travelers, legal and illegal immigrants, and refugees); "finanscapes" (global flows of money and capital, thanks to currency markets, stock exchanges, and commodity markets); "ideoscapes" (the global spread of ideas and ideologies); "mediascapes" (global instant communication through the mass media, especially the Internet); and "technoscapes" (the spread of technologies around the globe).[4]

As with any movement of this scope, there are both supporters and opponents. Pro-globalists highlight the benefits of globalization and cite hard statistics to support their contentions: since the 1950s, the percentage of people in developing countries living below U.S. $1 per day (adjusted for inflation and purchasing power) has been reduced to half; life expectancy has almost doubled, and child mortality has decreased in the developing countries since World War II; democracy has increased dramatically throughout the world since 1900; worldwide, per-capita food supplies have grown since the 1960s; global literacy has improved significantly since 1950, especially among women; and the availability of life necessities such as electricity, cars, radios, telephones, televisions, and clean water has increased. In sum, globalization with its capitalist economy, free trade, global political institutions, and cultural exchange is said to bring about a more efficient allocation of resources, lower prices, better employment, higher output, and democracy.[5]

---

3. For a helpful study of globalization from the Catholic perspective, see *Globalization and Catholic Social Thought: Present Crisis, Future Hope*, ed. John A. Coleman and William F. Ryan (Maryknoll, NY: Orbis Books, 2005); and the entire volume 2, no. 1 of *Journal of Catholic Social Thought* (Winter, 2005): 1–276. For very helpful reflections on globalization and bibliography, see the Globalization website at Emory University, Atlanta, Georgia: http://www.sociology.emory.edu/globalization.

4. See Arjun Appadurai, "Disjuncture and Difference in the Global Economy," *Public Culture* 2, no. 2 (1990): 1–24.

5. John Coleman briefly lists the good effects of globalization: "The positive effects of globalization include increased consciousness of being one world. Information is also more

Antiglobalists, on the other hand, reject this rosy depiction of globalization, which they claim is more accurately characterized as "corporate globalism." They are made up of a variety of groups and movements with diverse, even opposing, ideologies: left-wing parties, right-wing state nationalists, religious fundamentalists, national liberation movements, environmentalists, peasant unionists, antiracism organizations, progressive church groups, and so on. Despite their different agendas, antiglobalists argue that globalization has not taken the interests of poorer nations and the welfare of workers into account. Rather, unrestricted free trade benefits the so-called "core" states—those of the First World, with higher-skill, capital-intensive production and with military superiority—rather than the so-called "semi-periphery" and "periphery" countries, that is, long-independent states outside the West and poor, recently independent colonies (especially in Africa, Latin America, and Asia) respectively, which focus on low-skill, labor-intensive production and extraction of raw materials and have weak military power. In their view, globalization promotes a corporatist agenda at the expense of the poor, imposes credit-based economies with an unsustainable growth of debt as a result, and is an instrument of neoimperialism and neocolonialism.[6]

Any fair assessment of globalization must, of course, recognize both its benefits and its deleterious effects, the former no doubt exaggerated by proglobalists and the latter by antiglobalists. It is not the competence of Christians qua Christians to render a judgment on globalization as a process of internationalizing trade, capital, labor forces, and technology. But it must be admitted that such an economic, political, and cultural process is by no means morally neutral. On the contrary, it is driven by certain assumptions about the meaning of human life and activities, especially economic ones, that have profound ethical and spiritual implications for the church's mission fostering peace, justice, and the integrity of creation.

Challenges of Globalization to Christian Social Spirituality

To live the social dimension of Christian spirituality responsibly in our globalized world, Christians must have an adequate grasp of the destructive effects, intended and otherwise, of globalization. Without pretension to completeness, the following can be noted.[7]

---

democratically available, and human rights language now permeates a wider global consciousness." See *Globalization and Catholic Social Thought*, 13.

6. John Coleman lists four negative effects of globalization: insensitivity to human suffering, inattention to ecological sustainability, polarization between and within cultures, and the erosion of the abilities of states to provide for societal needs. See *Globalization and Catholic Social Thought*, 13–14.

7. See Donal Dorr, *The Social Justice Agenda: Justice, Ecology, Power and the Church* (Maryknoll, NY: Orbis Books, 1991), 7–41.

First, *the ever-expanding gap between the rich and the poor.* Even though virtually all countries may stand to benefit from globalization, as pro-globalists claim, so far the strongest gains, and this is admitted even by pro-globalists, have been made by the "core" countries and, to a lesser extent, by only some of the "semi-peripheral" and "peripheral" ones. Consequently, the gap *between* the rich and the poor countries and between the wealthy and the destitute *within* each country is becoming ever wider. While the inevitable fact that there are rich and poor people does not constitute social injustice, that there is dehumanizing poverty alongside extravagant wealth and that this wealth and the luxurious lifestyle it provides to a small group of humanity are obtained at the expense of impoverished men, women, and children—who constitute the majority of the world population—is a morally scandalous exploitation.

Second, *international debt.* As a result of the economic policies of the wealthy nations and their banks, especially the International Money Fund, many countries, particularly in Africa and Latin America, are saddled with crushing debts, with the unpaid interest added to the original loans. Loans were made to fund misguided "development" programs that benefit more the donor countries of the First World and the corrupt dictators of the receiving countries than the poor people themselves whom the loans were designed to help. Ironically, it is the poor who most often have to shoulder the burden of the debt repayment.

Third, *ecological destruction.* Through globalization, the First World, which has had severe pollution problems, is exporting them to poorer countries. Unscrupulous multinational companies have dumped toxic industrial waste and even radioactive materials in the Third World, where laws against pollution are nonexistent or less stringent. Furthermore, the large-scale cutting down of the tropical rain forests and the rapid erosion of land due to overgrazing are producing the "greenhouse effect," which raises the Earth's temperature and causes massive floods and hurricanes. These ecological disasters harm not only humans but also the Earth's flora and fauna.

Fourth, *chronic unemployment.* Globalization exports Western methods of mass production, automation, and computerization. While these technological advances have reduced the drudgery of heavy manual labor, they have also produced what has been called "structural unemployment," that is, large-scale chronic and inevitable unemployment inherent in the use of high technology and in the economic system itself. Furthermore, corporations are not loath to moving their factories or outsourcing jobs to countries where production costs are lowest, thus causing unemployment in former places of manufacturing.

Fifth, *increase in immigrants and refugees.* The scarcity of jobs and food shortages, in addition to war and racial/ethnic and religious persecutions, have caused massive immigration in many countries of the Third World. These refugees, political and economic, suffer immense physical and emotional damage, even when settled in countries that are willing to accept them.

Sixth, and perhaps most important, globalization exports *the Western model of economic development*, that is, production of material goods as cheaply and efficiently as possible and selling them for maximum financial profit. Such a purely economic analysis does not take into account the costs in ecological destruction, structural unemployment, and human misery. Furthermore, the highly consumerist lifestyle of the First World is not sustainable with the Earth's resources were it to be reproduced in the Third World. Consequently, an alternative model of development must be devised, to be adopted by both the First World and the Third World, one that rejects the ideology of limitless "growth" and omnivorous consumption, cares for human and ecological resources, and promotes other human values in addition to economic ones.

Other Social Challenges

The six challenges mentioned above, which are directly tied with globalization, are, of course, not the only ones that concern Christians today. Other social issues, listed here without detailed comment, continue to confront Christian social spirituality; they include racism, sexism, political oppression, human rights violations, abortion, the arms race, and lately, stateless terrorism. The question is raised as to what Christians can and should do as part of their social spirituality to remove or at least reduce the negative effects of these challenges on both individuals and society.

CONTOURS OF CONTEMPORARY CHRISTIAN SOCIAL SPIRITUALITY

Christian Spirituality

Spirituality as a way of living has three connotations. In its broadest sense, (1) spirituality refers to the human capacity for self-transcendence in acts of knowledge and love of realities other than oneself. More narrowly, (2) it refers to the religious dimension of life by which one is in touch with a more-than-human, transcendent reality, however interpreted and named (e.g., the Empty, the Holy, the Ultimate, or God). More strictly still, (3) it indicates a particular way of living one's relationship with this transcendent reality, through specific beliefs, rituals, prayers, moral behaviors, and community participation (e.g., Hindu, Buddhist, Jewish, Christian, Muslim, etc.). It is important to note that there is no generic spirituality untethered from a historical and particular tradition and community. Even when one attempts to construct one's own spirituality, one can do so only by drawing on various elements of preexisting spiritual traditions.

Needless to say, Christian spirituality embodies all these three connotations, i.e., human self-transcendence toward the Ultimate Other carried out within a particular religious tradition. More precisely, it is a particular way of relating to the Holy and Ultimate Being revealed as "Abba/Father" by Jesus of Nazareth in his ministry, death, and resurrection, a relationship mediated by Jesus himself and actualized by the power of the Holy Spirit, who has been poured out upon the community of Jesus' followers called church. In other words, Christian spirituality is theocentric (relationship with God), Christic (mediated by and modeled after Christ), pneumatological (empowered by the Spirit), and ecclesial (realized in and through the church).

Christian Social Spirituality

As pointed out above, Christian spirituality is at once and inextricably personal, interpersonal, and political. Here, our focus is only on the political dimension, and the question is what a Christian as individual and the church as community of believers can and should do to meet the challenges of globalization to promote peace, justice, and the integrity of creation. Within Roman Catholicism, this question has been the subject of extensive reflection in recent decades, especially by liberation theologians of various stripes and by popes, especially John Paul II. From these sources a rough sketch of Christian social spirituality may be drawn. It would include at least the following elements.[8]

---

8. The following works are to be noted: Gustavo Gutiérrez, *We Drink from Our Own Wells: The Spiritual Journey of a People* (Maryknoll, NY: Orbis Books, 1983); Pedro Casaldáliga and José-María Vigil, *Liberating Spirituality: A Spirituality of Liberation*, trans. Paul Burns and Francis McDonagh (Quezon City, Philippines: Claretian Publications, 1996), with a very helpful bibliography; Jon Sobrino, *Spirituality of Liberation: Toward Political Holiness*, trans. Robert R. Barr (Maryknoll, NY: Orbis Books, 1988); Antonio González, *The Gospel of Faith and Justice*, trans. Joseph Owens (Maryknoll, NY: Orbis Books, 2005). Obviously, Catholic social spirituality is rooted in Catholic social thought. For studies of Catholic social thought, see *One Hundred Years of Catholic Social Thought*, ed. John Coleman (Maryknoll, NY: Orbis Books, 1991); Charles E. Curran, *Catholic Social Teaching 1891–Present: A Historical, Theological, and Ethical Analysis* (Washington, DC: Georgetown University Press, 2002); Judith Merkle, *From the Heart of the Church: The Catholic Social Tradition* (Collegeville, MN: Liturgical Press, 2004); Thomas Massaro, *Living Justice: Catholic Social Teaching in Action* (Lanham, MD: Sheed & Ward, 2000); and *Modern Catholic Social Teaching: Commentaries & Interpretations*, ed. Kenneth Himes (Washington, DC: Georgetown University Press, 2005). Of Catholic social thought, John Coleman says that it is made up of eight basic principles: human dignity (based on the fact that humans are made in God's image and are called to be co-creators of society and culture); the human person as a social, dependent, and interdependent being; the common good (the sum total of institutional arrangements that guarantee and promote human flourishing); subsidiarity (higher forms of governance must not coopt or dissipate the proper roles of local units); solidarity (moral obligations to come to the aid and support of others); the preferential option for the poor (rooted in God's and Jesus' preferential identification with the poor); justice (commutative, distributive, and social); and integral humanism (authentic or integral human development). See *Globalization and Catholic Social Thought*, 15–18.

Unconditional and Total Commitment to the Reign of God

At the heart of Christian social spirituality lies a total commitment to the service of the kingdom of God or the kingdom of heaven that Jesus proclaimed and inaugurated. The kingdom of heaven, that is, God's rule in and through Jesus, is, however, no mere transcendent and spiritual reality in the postmortem, empyreal realm. God's gracious sharing of God's triune life with us brings about not only forgiveness of sins and reconciliation with God but also truth, justice, peace, and the integrity of creation. Furthermore, this gift of socio-political, economic, and ecological well-being is at the same time a task; it is, to play on German words, both *Gabe* (gift) and *Aufgabe* (task). It demands that we dedicate ourselves to making, by means of collective action, God's gifts into a universal historical reality, especially for those who have been deprived of them by oppressive, unjust, and exploitative systems.

This single-minded and total commitment to the reign of God is *the* essential and distinctive feature of Christian social spirituality in general and of liberation spirituality in particular. It informs the way Christian social spirituality understands the ministry of the historical Jesus, the Trinity, and the Incarnation.

Understanding Jesus of History, Trinity, Incarnation Anew

It is well known that liberation theologians are interested in discovering the "true Jesus" of history. However, their concern is not to retrieve the *ipsissima verba et gesta Jesu* (Jesus' very words and deeds), as is done in various "quests for the historical Jesus," most recently, in the Jesus Seminar, by nature an uncertain and inconclusive enterprise. Rather, it is to discover the *ipsissima intentio Jesu* (Jesus' very "cause"), that to which he dedicated his entire ministry and on account of which he was killed, his all-consuming passion and exclusive obsession. Contemporary biblical scholarship has shown beyond dispute that Jesus' cause is nothing other than the kingdom of God—the kingdom of truth, justice, peace, love, forgiveness, reconciliation, grace, and ecological harmony—that he proclaimed and brought to all, particularly to those the Bible calls the "poor."[9]

The task of social spirituality is not to demythologize Jesus from the dogmatic incrustations of the "Christ of faith" but, in Jon Sobrino's pregnant

---

9. For a study of the theme of the kingdom of God in Jesus' preaching in the context of the quest for the historical Jesus, see James D. G. Dunn, *Jesus Remembered* (Grand Rapids, MI: Eerdmans, 2003), 383–541. Dunn's conclusion is pertinent: "In short, the evidence we have points to one and only one clear conclusion: that Jesus was remembered as preaching about the kingdom of God and that this was central to his message and mission" (387). Contemporary biblical scholars whose works are important for the rediscovery of the historical Jesus include, besides those of the "Jesus Seminar," Raymond Brown, Bruce A. Chilton, Martin Hengel, Gerd Theissen, Larry Hurtado, John Meier, N. T. Wright, Luke Timothy Johnson, among many others.

expression, to "de-manipulate" Jesus from the vested interests of the rich and the powerful, to rescue him from contamination by idolatry and from the injustices committed throughout history in his very name, and to restore the centrality of the reign of God to his life and ministry. It will then be clear that the goal of Jesus' ministry is neither to preach about himself nor to found a religious organization but to proclaim God, and not just any God, such as the inaccessible Unmoved Mover dwelling in the empyreal realm, but the God of the reign and the reign of God in history.

Christian social spirituality also professes faith in the triune God, but it sees the problem of faith today to consist not so much in atheism as in idolatry. The real issue for Christian social spirituality is not whether God *exists* but whether the God one worships is the *true* God, a masked idol or the God who reveals himself as the Father of Jesus and the Sender of the Spirit and whose reign is one of truth and justice and peace, especially for the poor and the marginalized. This triune God, constituted by the three divine persons in absolute equality, perfect communion, and mutual love, is Christianity's social agenda in a nutshell. Like the all-embracing Trinity in Andrej Rublev's famous icon, Christians welcome all, especially those deprived of human dignity, to the table of life, peace, justice, and love.

Because social spirituality by its very nature is rooted in history, it puts a premium on the doctrine of the Incarnation. However, while affirming Jesus' real humanity over against monophysitism and docetism, social spirituality does not understand the Incarnation to refer simply to the once-upon-a-time physical conception and birth of the Word of God from Mary. Rather it takes this divine enfleshment to mean that in Jesus God has truly become history and therefore can be encountered only within history; that God has "emptied" Godself and therefore can be encountered only in those who have been "emptied" of their humanity; that God has assumed a particular culture, i.e., the Jewish one and therefore can be encountered only in the particularities of each culture; and that God has become a Jew in colonized Palestine and therefore can be encountered only within the struggle for the political freedom, human rights, and economic well-being of victims of new forms of colonialism.

Honesty about and Fidelity to Reality

One fundamental implication of a full-throated acceptance of the Jesus of history, of the God of the reign, and of the Incarnation for Christian social spirituality is what Jon Sobrino calls "honesty about the real" and "fidelity to the real."[10] By the former, Sobrino means an objective and adequate knowledge of the socio-political and economic condition of the majority of people and to recognize it for what it is; namely, human life today is being assaulted by sys-

---

10. See Sobrino, *Spirituality of Liberation*, 14–19.

tematic impoverishment and institutionalized violence. Without this honesty to the real, any attempt to live a Christian social spirituality is a castle built on sand. By the latter, Sobrino means the willingness to accept the risks of life and limb for being honest about reality and for trying to transform this negative reality into one of truth, justice, and peace.

Because of the need to be honest about and faithful to reality, Christian social spirituality insists on the use of the methodology of Pierre Cardijn's Young Christian Workers movement, i.e., "see-judge-act."[11] It is imperative to "see" reality clearly and accurately, and not be blinded by personal bias or collective ideology. In terms of social spirituality, it is necessary to see poverty with the eyes of the poor and to understand injustice and oppression from the perspective of the victims. Consequently, it is a vital part of contemporary Christian social spirituality to fully grasp, by means of a thorough social analysis, the nature of globalization as an economic, socio-political, and cultural process and its deleterious impact on the poor.

Following and Imitating the Jesus of the Reign of God

Christian spirituality, whatever its form or orientation, is in essence a following (*sequela*) or imitation (*imitatio*) or discipleship of Jesus. But the crucial question is: which Jesus? As mentioned above, Christian social spirituality focuses on the Jesus of the reign of God. Pedro Casaldáliga, bishop of São Felix, Brazil, and José-Maria Vigil, a Spanish-born and naturalized Nicaraguan theologian, have drawn a detailed portrait of this Jesus that includes the following features: Jesus who reveals the true God; who is deeply human; who is devoted to the cause of the poor; who proclaims the God of the reign; who is poor among the poor; who subverts the established order; who inaugurates and realizes the reign of God; who denounces the forces opposed to such reign; who is free and promotes freedom in others; who brings abundant life; who is compassionate; who welcomes people of different faiths; who defends the full dignity of women; who does not avoid conflicts for the sake of God's reign; who is persecuted and martyred; and who is the way, the truth, and the life of God's reign.[12] Christian social spirituality aims at appropriating the teachings and deeds of such a Jesus in one's life.

---

11. Clodovis Boff develops this "see-judge-act" into a full-fledged theological method of socio-analytical, hermeneutical, and practical mediations in his *Theology and Praxis: Epistemological Foundations*, trans. Robert Barr (Maryknoll, NY: Orbis Books, 1987). See Peter C. Phan, "A Common Journey, Different Paths, the Same Destination: Method in Liberation Theologies," in Peter C. Phan, *Christianity with an Asian Face* (Maryknoll, NY: Orbis Books, 2003), 26–46.

12. See Casaldáliga and Vigil, *Liberating Spirituality*, 96–99.

Option for the Poor

Following the Jesus of the reign of God requires what liberation theologians term the "option for the poor." Such an option, which is not exclusive but preferential, is not inspired by the Marxist notion of class struggle but is rooted in the action of the triune God who throughout history has always taken the side of the oppressed and the poor and empowered them to reclaim their freedom. As Casaldáliga and Vigil assert, "the option for the poor becomes a 'mark' of the true church, of discipleship of Jesus, of Christian spirituality."[13]

An essential element of social spirituality, this option for the poor is no mere theological posturing but rather entails attitudinal changes and concrete actions: removing oneself from the privileged and dominant classes, real sharing of day-to-day life with the poor, taking up the cause of the poor and the oppressed in active solidarity that respects them as agents of their own liberation.[14]

Persecution and Martyrdom

In a world where power and wealth are often acquired through violence and exploitation, this fundamental option will sooner or later bring Christians engaged in social spirituality into a deadly conflict with the rich and the powerful whose political domination is challenged and economic interests are threatened by such an option. It is not that social spirituality seeks class conflicts; rather these *inevitably* arise as a result of Christians doing in their time what Jesus did in his—assisting those who are oppressed and impoverished to gain liberation from the powers that exploited and dominated them. Indeed, Jesus repeatedly warned his followers that they would suffer persecution and even death at the hands of their family members, political leaders, and religious authorities, as he himself did. His predictions were amply borne out throughout history, and recently, in many parts of the world where Christians—lay as well as clerical—have been maimed and murdered.

Martyrdom has become once again the mark of Christian discipleship and authentic social spirituality. Sobrino has persuasively argued that persecution is not only a historical inevitability for a church that wants to remain faithful to Jesus' mission to and for the poor but also "an a priori theological necessity"[15] insofar as it is rooted in the persecution that Jesus suffered because of his service to the reign of God. Hence, it is necessary for a Christian social spirituality to develop a "spirituality of persecution," not as something peripheral and secondary but as its central element, by which "the possibility and reality of

---

13. Ibid., 140.

14. Implicit in the option for the poor is the philosophical assumption in social spirituality that action (*praxis*) and not philosophical reflection (*theoria*) provides the integral and holistic approach to reality and to God. See González, *The Gospel of Faith and Justice*, 2–5.

15. Sobrino, *Spirituality of Liberation*, 90.

persecution in some form and in some degree be taken seriously as an essential ingredient of the Christian life."[16] In this readiness to accept persecution as a historical inevitability and a theological necessity, the three "theologal" virtues of faith, hope, and love acquire a new maturity and depth. It is in persecution that faith encounters the silence of God the Father, as Jesus did on the cross; hope meets its ultimate test and passes it, as Jesus entrusted his life to his Father at the moment of his death; and love finds its supreme fulfillment, since there is no greater love than laying down one's life for one's friends.

Sobrino goes on to show that persecution and martyrdom enrich Christian life with five new spirits: a spirit of *fortitude* with which one bears the burdens of witnessing to the gospel; the spirit of *impoverishment* by which one patiently accepts the fact that one must lose one's life in order to find it; the spirit of *creativity* with which one devises new ways to live and reflect on the Christian life; the spirit of *solidarity* by which one grows in the awareness that one is not saved alone but always with others; and the spirit of *joy* because one knows that martyrdom makes one more like Jesus and the church more faithful.[17]

Contemplation in Liberation

As air for birds and water for fish, prayer is the absolute sine qua non for any spirituality, Christian or otherwise. But within social spirituality, prayer acquires a new dimension. If in the past prayer was done for the most part in the church, the monastery, the desert, or the private study, today there is a consensus in social spirituality that while these locales still retain their importance, prayer must be done in liberative action and vice versa. In the past it was felt necessary to withdraw from the world in order to contemplate and commune with God, Today, the world is seen as the proper arena for contemplation and prayer, and action in favor of justice and peace; and the integrity of creation is an intrinsic part of and even a form of prayer and contemplation.

This contemplation in liberation and liberation in contemplation, which is another key hallmark of contemporary social spirituality, reconfigure both where we meet God today and what kind of God we meet. As to the locale of the divine–human encounter, there is no longer a separation between the sacred and the profane, between the temple and the marketplace, between church and world, between salvation and liberation. Indeed, the place from which God is contemplated and in which God is encountered is no other than the everyday life with its evolving history and its diverse and even conflictive kinds of economic systems, political regimes, social structures, cultural traditions, and religious beliefs and practices. Furthermore, because the vantage point from which contemplation and prayer are done is the underside of history, the God contemplated and prayed to is no other than the Father

---

16. Ibid., 92.
17. See ibid., 96–102.

of Jesus, the God of the reign of truth and life, justice and peace, grace and freedom.

This unity between contemplation and liberative action is not an excuse to neglect setting aside a certain amount of time every day (e.g., at least half an hour) for prayer on the specious ground that "everything is prayer." Casaldáliga and Vigil issue a useful warning against the temptation of activism without a serious dedication to prayer and contemplation: "It is true that all Christian action genuinely carried out in faith, 'in a state of prayer,' is in some sense a living of prayer, but it is not comparable to prayer itself. Charity is charity, service is service, and prayer is prayer."[18]

Political Holiness

One widely used expression to characterize the new Christian social spirituality with its emphasis on contemplation in liberation is "political holiness." Admittedly, such holiness is traditional in the sense that it is nourished by the liturgy and the sacraments, strengthened by prayer and contemplation, and seasoned by the practice of virtue and asceticism. However, political holiness is a helpful shorthand to highlight the new features of Christian social spirituality in the global context and to give primacy to certain virtues that have been neglected and downplayed in traditional spirituality. To summarize what has been said so far of Christian social spirituality, political spirituality, like that of Jesus himself, is oriented to the kingdom of God, lived out not away from but within history and the world, animated by the preferential option for the poor and a willing acceptance of persecution and even martyrdom, and actualized within the unity of contemplation and liberation.

As a consequence, political holiness fosters a set of virtues and practices that were either neglected or even derogated by traditional spirituality. For example, whereas traditional spirituality uniformly regards anger as a vice to be controlled, political spirituality sees it as a necessary and beneficial emotional reaction to systemic and organized injustice and oppression. This anger is the opposite of indifference and lack of courage. Rather than a vice to be avoided, this moral indignation is a force impelling compassion for victims and action to help them regain their humanity. As Casaldáliga and Vigil note, "it affects us, shakes us and moves us, imperatively. We feel questioned by it, in the depths of our being. We see it bringing an inescapable challenge: we know we cannot compromise with, tolerate, live with or agree to injustice, because to do so would be to betray what is innermost and deepest in ourselves."[19]

Political holiness also prizes certain virtues often ignored in the past. For example, whereas obedience, humility, meekness, chastity, mortification, renunciation, and what Nietzsche derides as unmanly Christianity are

---

18. Casaldáliga and Vigil, *Liberating Spirituality*, 122.
19. Ibid., 23.

often extolled in traditional spirituality and asceticism (not always untainted by sadism or masochism), political holiness, while not denigrating these virtues, promotes a greater appreciation for more "active" and "social" virtues and practices directed toward the building of a just and peaceful world. There is a greater awareness of the "structural evils" and "social sins," in addition to personal sins. Hence, conversion is not only a turning away from evil actions and an immoral way of life, a transformation of the heart, but also a commitment to the struggle for the cause of Jesus, that is, to the removal of unjust and oppressive structures and the establishment of a peaceful and just society. Of course, social spirituality recognizes the necessity of both conversions, transformation of the heart and structural change, since they are mutually conditioned. A conversion of the heart without a commitment to social transformation runs the risk of individualism and escapism; on the other hand, efforts at social change without a conversion of the heart are doomed to failure and prone to despair, especially when success is not immediate.

In this context, another virtue is given primacy, namely, hope, which, of the three theologal virtues, is the most neglected. Yet, in social spirituality, hope, especially hope in the resurrection, is the primary virtue: "Political holiness is a holiness of active hope, which is able to overcome the defeatism of the poor in the face of the status quo, the established powers, the regrouping of capitalism and imperialism, in the face of the wave of neoliberalism, the thrust of capitalism against labor, North against South. It is a holiness capable of enduring the hours of darkness for the poor, upholding the asceticism of hope against all hope."[20] Of course, such hope must be backed up by vigorous and effective action in favor of social justice; otherwise, Karl Marx's dismissal of religion in general, and of Christianity, in particular, as the opium of the people would prove uncomfortably close to the truth.

Back to Globalization: A Spirituality for Our Time

It is by now clear that in an age such as ours a social spirituality as outlined above is more urgent than ever. When the gap between the rich and the poor is ever expanding; when the burdens of the debts that the Third World owes to the First World are being borne by the poor; when the ecology is being destroyed for economic development; when unemployment is chronic and built into the economic system; when more and more immigrants and refugees have to leave their home for survival; and when the Western consumerist model of economic development is being imposed on other parts of the world, and all of this in the name of globalization, then Christians have to ask: is there a way of being human, Christian, and church that leads to a more just, equitable, peaceful, and harmonious society?

---

20. Ibid., 180.

From the Christian point of view, one way is to make the heart and soul of Jesus' life and ministry, namely, the kingdom of God, the central focus of one's life. In so doing, one must see-judge-act. Reality—and here, globalization—must be seen, that is, carefully investigated in all its dimensions, both positive and negative, and this investigation must be carried out from the perspective of the victims, and not only of the beneficiaries, of globalization. Next, a judgment must be rendered on this reality, in the light of the reign of God. The reign of God, and nothing else, serves as the all-encompassing and decisive criterion. Finally, one must act, individually and collectively, to remove unjust and oppressive structures and establish a society and a church that approximate as closely as possible the utopia of the reign of God. In this action, one follows Jesus as his disciple, in solidarity with the poor and the marginalized, accepting persecution and death as the inevitable price of one's service to God's reign, and hoping and trusting in the resurrection of Jesus, which is the first fruits and the guarantee of our own resurrection, especially of those who are most impoverished, oppressed, exploited among us.

SOCIAL SPIRITUALITY: AN ASIAN PERSPECTIVE

One of the remarkable developments in contemporary theology is the rapid spread of liberation theology and, with it, Christian social spirituality throughout the globe. It seems as if where globalization reaches, there liberation theology and social spirituality arrive too, as an antidote to the deleterious effects of globalization on its victims because of their class, gender, and race.[21] The previous pages have shown how social spirituality developed in Latin America.[22] In Africa, too, social spirituality has received sustained attention.[23] While a study of social spirituality in the global perspective must

---

21. For a helpful overview of liberation theology in its global development, see Christopher Rowland, ed., *The Cambridge Companion to Liberation Theology* (Cambridge: Cambridge University Press, 1999).

22. In addition to the works by Gustavo Gutiérrez, Pedro Casaldáliga, José-María Vigil, and Jon Sobrino already cited above, those on spirituality by Leonardo Boff, Clodovis Boff, Juan Luis Segundo, José Comblin, Ignacio Ellacuría, Segundo Galilea, Carlos Mesters, João Batista Libânio, Oscar Romero, Pablo Richard, Ivone Gebara, María Clara Bingemer, and a host of younger theologians deserve a close reading. To note that liberation theology has spread throughout the globe is not to deny that in recent times it has suffered an eclipse, due in part to the opposition of Cardinal Josef Ratzinger (Pope Benedict XVI), Prefect of the Congregation for the Doctrine of the Faith. However, as Christopher Rowland has rightly noted, "We are dealing with a movement whose high point as the topic of discussion may now have passed, but whose influence, in a multitude of ways, direct and indirect, is as strong as ever" (*The Cambridge Companion to Liberation Theology*, 248).

23. See, for example, Patrick A. Kalilombe, "Spirituality in the African Perspective," in Rosino Gibellini, ed., *Paths of African Theology* (Maryknoll, NY: Orbis Books, 1994), 115–35;

take into account its development on all the continents, in the remaining pages, because of space limitations, focus will be given to the Asian context.[24]

Asia's Spiritual Quest

It is no exaggeration to say that Asia, understood here to include East Asia (the Far East), West Asia (the Middle East), South Asia, and North Asia (Central Asia), embodies a longstanding and dynamic spiritual quest. After all, it is the cradle of all of the world's major religions (e.g., Hinduism, Buddhism, Judaism, Christianity, and Islam), many other spiritual traditions (e.g., Daoism, Confucianism, Zoroastrianism, Jainism, Sikhism, and Shintoism), innumerable tribal and indigenous religions, and an untold number of new religious movements and sects. Despite its bewildering diversity and multiplicity, the Asian spiritual quest is characterized by certain common cultural and religious values, which Pope John Paul II describes succinctly:

> The people of Asia take pride in their religious and cultural values, such as love of silence and contemplation, simplicity, harmony, detachment, non-violence, the spirit of hard work, discipline, frugal living, the thirst for learning and philosophical inquiry. They hold dear the values of respect for life, compassion for all beings, closeness to nature, filial piety towards parents, elders and ancestors, and a highly developed sense of community. . . . Asian people are known for their spirit of religious tolerance and peaceful coexistence. . . . Asia has often demonstrated a remarkable capacity for accommodation and a natural openness to the mutual enrichment of peoples in the midst of a plurality of religions

---

and Diane B. Stinton, *Jesus of Africa: Voices of Contemporary African Christology* (Maryknoll, NY: Orbis Books, 2004). Works by other theologians such as Mercy Oduyoye, Bénézet Bujo, Jean-Marc Ela, J. N. K. Mugambi, John S. Pobee, Kwame Bediako, John S. Mbiti, Charles Nyamiti, Peter K. Sarpong, Justin S. Ukpong, François Kabasélé Lumbala, and Magesa Laurenti deserve serious study.

24. My chief resources here will be the teachings of the Federation of Asian Bishops' Conferences (FABC) and the Special Assembly of the Synod of Bishops for Asia, which met in Rome on April 19–May 14, 1998 (the Asian Synod for short). The FABC was founded in 1970, on the occasion of Pope Paul VI's visit to Manila, Philippines. Its statutes, approved by the Holy See *ad experimentum* in 1972, were amended several times and were also approved again each time by the Holy See. For the documents of the FABC and its various institutes, see Gaudencio Rosales and C. G. Arévalo, eds., *For All the Peoples of Asia: Federation of Asian Bishops' Conferences: Documents from 1970 to 1991*, vol. 1 (New York/Quezon City: Orbis Books/ Claretian Publications, 1992); Franz-Josef Eilers, ed., *For All the Peoples of Asia: Federation of Asian Bishops' Conferences: Documents from 1992 to1996*, vol. 2 (Quezon City: Claretian Publications, 1997), and Franz-Josef Eilers, ed., *For All the Peoples of Asia: Federation of Asian Bishops' Conferences: Documents from 1997 to 2002*, vol. 3 (Quezon City: Claretian Publications, 2002). For a history of the FABC, see Edmund Chia, *Thirty Years of FABC: History, Foundation, Context and Theology* (Hong Kong: FABC Papers, 2003).

and cultures. . . . Many people, especially the young, experience a deep thirst for spiritual values, as the rise of new religious movements clearly demonstrates.[25]

As a consequence, Christian social spirituality must be developed in dialogue with Asia's deep religiousness. Second, Asia is also steeped in extreme and dehumanizing poverty. This poverty is not an accidental phenomenon but the result of systemic exploitation perpetrated by colonialism in the past and globalization today.[26] The church in Asia, as Sri Lankan theologian Aloysius Pieris has repeatedly insisted, must be baptized in the Jordan of Asian multi-religiousness and in the Calvary of Asian poverty.[27] A third characteristic of Asian Christianity is its numerical minority (some 3 percent of the Asian population), and this suggests a focus on mission and evangelization as the primary task of the church. A Christian social spirituality must address these three concerns.

Spirituality in Dialogue with Asian Religions

Because Asia is the birthplace of most if not all religions, and because Christians form but a tiny minority of the Asian population, Asian Christians, more than their fellow believers in any other part of the world, cannot live their Spirit-empowered lives apart from non-Christian religions.[28] At first, most missionaries, both Catholic and Protestant, were pessimistic about

---

25. Pope John Paul II's apostolic exhortation *Ecclesia in Asia*, §6. English translation in Peter C. Phan, ed., *The Asian Synod: Texts and Commentaries* (Maryknoll, NY: Orbis Books, 2002), 286–340.

26. Of globalization, the Asian bishops say: "While the process of economic globalization has brought certain positive effects, we are aware that it 'has also worked to the detriment of the poor, tending to push poorer countries to the margin of economic and political relations. Many Asian nations are unable to hold their own in a global market economy' (*Ecclesia in Asia*, 39). The phenomena of marginalization and exclusion are its direct consequences. It has produced greater inequalities among people. It has enabled only a small portion of the population to improve their standards of living, leaving many to remain in poverty. Another consequence is excessive urbanization, causing the emergence of huge urban conglomerations and the resultant migration, crime and exploitation of the weaker sections" (*For All the Peoples of Asia*, vol. 3, 6).

27. See Aloysius Pieris, *An Asian Theology of Liberation* (Maryknoll, NY: Orbis Books, 1988); *Love Meets Wisdom: A Christian Experience of Buddhism* (Maryknoll, NY: Orbis Books, 1988); *Fire and Water: Basic Issues in Asian Buddhism and Christianity* (Maryknoll, NY: Orbis Books, 1996); *God's Reign for God's Poor: A Return to the Jesus Formula: A Critical Evaluation of Contemporary Reformulations of the Mission Manifestation in Roman Catholic Theology in Recent Jesuit Documents* (Kelaniya: Tulana Research Centre, 1999); *Mysticism of Service: A Short Treatise on Spirituality with a Pauline-Ignatian Focus on the Prayer-Life of Christian Activists* (Kelaniya: Tulana Research Centre, 2000).

28. On interreligious dialogue in Asia, see Peter C. Phan, *Being Religious Interreligiously: Asian Perspectives on Interfaith Dialogue* (Maryknoll, NY: Orbis Books, 2005).

the spiritual values of these religious ways of life. But the goodness of non-Christians (some of them are holier than Christians!), with whom very often Christians share their daily lives intimately as family members, give the lie to the church's pre–Vatican II teaching that heathens are condemned to hell, that Christianity is the only acceptable way to God, and that non-Christian religions are infested with superstition and depravity. Clearly, non-Christians are good and holy not in spite of but *because* of the beliefs and practices of their religions. From the Christian perspective, these elements of truth and grace must be regarded as fruits of the Spirit, who is the gift of God and the risen Christ, but who is active outside of, albeit not independently from, the visible spheres of action of Jesus and the church, in ways known to God alone.

But if this is true, then the Asian Christian spiritual quest must be carried out in sincere and humble dialogue with other religions to learn from, among other things, their sacred scriptures, doctrinal teachings, moral and spiritual practices, prayers and devotions, and monastic and mystical traditions. It is to the credit of the Society of Jesus that many of its members were the first missionaries in Asia to develop a Christian spirituality in dialogue with Asian cultures and religions. Jesuits such as Francis Xavier and Alessandro Valignano in Japan, Matteo Ricci in China, Roberto de Nobili in India, and Alexandre de Rhodes in Vietnam, notwithstanding whatever deficiencies of their accommodationist policies from the perspective of today's contextual theology, were visionary pioneers who paved the way, often at great personal costs, to a Christian spirituality enriched by other religious traditions and in turn enriching them through interfaith dialogue.

In more recent times, bold and even controversial efforts have been made to incorporate monastic and spiritual practices of non-Christian religions into Christian spirituality. In India, French priest Jules Monchanin (who took the name of Prama Arabi Ananda), French Benedictine Henri Le Saux (also known as Abhishiktananda), English Benedictine Dom Bede Griffiths, Belgian Cistercian monk Francis Mahieu, and Indian Jesuit Ignatius Hirudayam, to cite only the better-known ones, have been active in incorporating into their Christian experience of God as Trinity the Hindu advaitic quest for God as *sat* (being), *cit* (truth), and bliss (*ananda*). Moreover, through their Ashram Movement, they have assimilated into Christian worship and monasticism the Hindu sacred scriptures, religious symbols, ascetic practices, meditation techniques, religious songs and dance, sacred art, clothing, and postures.

In Japan, the resource for spiritual enrichment has been mainly Zen Buddhism. Not surprisingly, the first efforts at dialogue with Zen were made by the Quakers. Among Catholics, Jesuits Hugo M. Enomiya-Lassalle, Kakichi Kadowaki, and William Johnston and Dominican priest Oshida have been instrumental in enriching Christian spirituality with Zen meditation practices. Dialogue with Buddhism, especially in its Theravada branch, has been carried out extensively in Thailand and Sri Lanka. Dialogue with Islam is active in certain parts of India and in Indonesia. In countries heavily influenced by Confucianism, such as China, Taiwan, Vietnam, and Korea, Christian spirituality has recently incorporated the rituals of the cult of ancestors after it had been severely condemned by the church for several centuries.

From a practical point of view, interfaith dialogue as a part of the Asian Christian spiritual quest is a genuine opening of persons of different faiths to one another with a view to share and be enriched by another faith; moreover, it serves a multiplicity of functions. It helps overcome fear of the other, removes misunderstandings of and prejudices against other religions, promotes collaboration with others in areas of life beyond religion, and enhances the understanding and practice of one's own faith.

The Pontifical Council for Interreligious Dialogue of the Roman Catholic Church and the Federation of Asian Bishops' Conferences have suggested four modes in which interfaith dialogue can be carried out. First, the dialogue of *life* consists in sharing daily life together, which fosters mutual understanding, neighborly assistance, and cordial friendship among adherents of different religions. Second, the dialogue of *collaborative action* brings believers of different faiths to work together to promote justice, human rights, peace, human development, and ecological well-being. Third, the dialogue of *theological reflection* enables a deeper understanding of and enrichment by the beliefs and practices of religions other than one's own. Lastly, the dialogue of *spiritual experience*, which is the deepest and most transformative, brings people together to *pray*, each in the way of his or her tradition, and later, possibly, to pray *together*, in a common way.

Spirituality as Discipleship to Jesus: Service to the Reign of God

As with Latin American spirituality, Asian Christian spirituality takes discipleship and imitation of Jesus as its central focus.[29] The question then arises as to which Jesus would appeal to Asian cultural and religious sensibilities. There are, of course, many and diverse Asian Christologies, and the participants at the Asian Synod suggested several images of Jesus. Among them were "Jesus Christ as the Teacher of Wisdom, the Healer, the Liberator, the Spiritual Guide, the Enlightened One, the Compassionate Friend of the Poor, the Good Samaritan, the Good Shepherd, the Obedient One."[30] Running through these diverse Christologies and linking them together is the view that at the heart of Jesus' ministry stands the kingdom of God of which he,

---

29. For a clear and comprehensive presentation of Asian liberation theologies, see Michael Amaladoss, *Life in Freedom: Liberation Theologies from Asia* (Maryknoll, NY: Orbis Books, 1997).

30. *Ecclesia in Asia*, §20.

the Eschatological Prophet, is the personal embodiment. It was in the service of this reign of justice, peace, forgiveness, reconciliation, and love that he was crucified. Christian spirituality insofar as it is an imitation of Christ must therefore take the form of service to God's reign.[31]

But what form of service to God's reign is most appropriate to the spiritual quest in Asia? The answer is determined by the socio-political and economic contexts of the continent. While some countries such as Japan, South Korea, Singapore, Taiwan, and Hong Kong have a well-developed economy, they form but a small portion of the Asian population. By contrast, several Asian countries are among the poorest nations on earth, and the majority of Asians are oppressed people who for centuries have been kept economically, culturally, and politically on the margins of society. Of special concern are women's oppression within a patriarchal and androcentric culture, abortion of female fetuses, marginalization of outcasts and tribal or indigenous people, the exploitation of migrant and child labor, and sex tourism. Though Western colonialism has ended, its deleterious legacy is now being extended by neocolonialism through economic globalization. Politically, Asia is a complex array of ideologies ranging from democracy to military dictatorship and communism.

In this economic and socio-political context, Asian spirituality as *imitatio Christi* must take the form of the preferential option for the poor, which is a distinctive hallmark of Latin American spirituality and which has been appropriated by the Asian churches. Spirituality as service to the kingdom of God occupies a central place in Asian theologies of liberation, such as the theologies of Choan-Seng Song, Tissa Balasuriya, Aloysius Pieris, Michael Amaladoss, Samuel Rayan, Felix Wilfred, R. S. Sugirtharajah, Carlos H. Abesamis, Aruna Gnanadason; *minjung* theology (Korea); homeland theology (Taiwan); the theology of struggle (the Philippines); *Dalit* theology (India); Asian feminist theology (Virginia Fabella, Chung Hyun Kyung, Mary John Mananzan, Kwok Pui-lan, Elizabeth Tapia). This kind of spirituality allows Asians to overcome the pronounced individualism of their religions and ethics and to view the spiritual quest as necessarily including the quest for social justice. It requires Asian Christians to make the "preferential option for the poor," join with those who are oppressed in their struggle for human rights and freedom, and to name and fight against the forces that enslave their fellow Asians (e.g., communism, neocapitalism, sex tourism, human labor trafficking, ecological destruction, etc.). Finally, spirituality as service to the reign of God directs Asian eyes away from the golden age located in the mythic past and turns them toward the *eschaton*, which is the risen Christ himself, who will "come again" to judge the living and the dead and to bring the reign of God to ultimate fulfillment.

---

31. For a challenging study of Asian Christology, see George M. Soares-Prabhu, *The Dharma of Jesus*, ed. Francis Xavier D'Sa (Maryknoll, NY: Orbis Books, 2003).

Spirituality as an Ecclesial Quest: Realizing the Church's Mission

The third dimension of Christian spirituality is its ecclesiality. By this is meant that spirituality is not a private and solitary pursuit for the salvation of one's soul or the mystical union of the "one with the One." Rather, it is a communal quest carried out in the bosom of the church, together with other members of the body of Christ, by means of the church's resources such as the Bible and the sacraments. Thus, Asian Christian spirituality is fundamentally biblical, sacramental, and liturgical.

Furthermore, because it is ecclesial, Asian spirituality is also missionary, since the church, as Vatican II has affirmed, is missionary by nature.[32] But what is meant by mission in Asia is different from what has been understood in pre–Vatican II theology of missions (*missio ad gentes*), which was predicated upon two basic concepts, i.e., salvation of souls and planting the church. Mission as saving souls is inspired primarily by Matt 18:19–20. Jesus' command to go and make disciples of all nations, baptize them in the name of the Father and the Son and the Holy Spirit, and teach them to observe all that he has commanded is taken to mean proclaiming, through words and deeds, the Good News of God's salvation to the heathens and converting them to the Christian religion. Salvation is exclusively that of the soul, for which conversion and baptism are absolute requirements. Missions are made urgent by the doctrine of original sin, according to which all humans are born as enemies of God, and by the belief that very few indeed will be saved. All non-Christian religions are condemned as idolatry and superstition or at least as powerless human attempts at self-salvation. On the other hand, mission as church planting (*plantatio ecclesiae*) is inspired by Luke 14:23. In this parable the master orders his servants to go out to the roads and country lanes and bring everybody to the banquet so that his house may be full. Conversion and baptism are the first steps toward the final goal of mission, i.e., establishing the church, with all its institutional and sacramental structures. This model is operative mostly in mainline churches, especially the Roman Catholic Church.

By contrast, it is customary today to distinguish between "mission" and "missions." By *mission* is meant God the Father's own "mission" or activities in history through Jesus and in the power of the Holy Spirit (*missio Dei*). This mission actualizes in time and space the eternal relations among the divine persons in the Trinity itself. It is the mission of the church only insofar as the church is empowered to participate in it. *Missions* refers to the various forms and activities by which the church carries out God's mission at a particular place and time. Today there is a keen awareness that missions are not restricted

---

32. For a magisterial history of Christian missions in Asia, see Samuel Hugh Moffett, *A History of Christianity in Asia, Vol. I: Beginnings to 1500* (Maryknoll, NY: Orbis Books, 1992); and *A History of Christianity in Asia, Vol. II: 1500–1900* (Maryknoll, NY: Orbis Books, 2005).

to certain individuals, i.e., missionaries, but are incumbent on *all* Christians. "Missions" here are understood as serving God's kingdom of truth, love, and justice. This model is rooted in Luke 4:18–19, which speaks of Jesus' mission of preaching the Good News to the poor, releasing the captives, giving sight to the blind, setting the oppressed free, and proclaiming the favorable year of the Lord. Salvation is understood not in spiritualistic and individualistic terms (as salvation of souls) nor in ecclesiastical terms (as planting the church) but as comprising, as we have seen above, the social, political, economic, and cosmic dimensions of human existence.

Furthermore, while not denying the necessity of witness, proclamation, baptism, and church planting, this model of mission focuses on finding the most effective way to carry out God's mission amid cultural diversity, religious pluralism, and massive poverty. This modality is dialogue, based on the mystery of God's incarnation. The modes of dialogue, as has been mentioned above, are four: common life, action, theological exchange, and religious experience. Furthermore, this dialogue is carried out in three areas, as the Federation of Asian Bishops' Conferences has repeatedly emphasized, namely, liberation, inculturation, and interreligious dialogue.

So far we have shown how interfaith dialogue and liberation are constitutive dimensions of Asian Christian spirituality. But inculturation is no less essential for Asian Christian spirituality.[33] By it is meant the double movement of bringing the gospel into a particular culture and using the categories of a particular culture to express and live the gospel, a process by which the local culture and the gospel are enriched and transformed. The Asian bishops have stressed that the primary agent of the inculturation of the Christian faith in Asia is the Holy Spirit, and that the persons responsible for this process are not experts but the local church. Inculturation must be carried out in all aspects of church life, including theology, liturgy, preaching, catechesis, and styles of spirituality. The intrinsic connection between inculturation and spirituality is evident in the fact that the test of true inculturation is "whether people become more committed to their Christian faith because they perceive it more clearly with the eyes of their own culture."[34]

Because of this missionary character of Asian spirituality, in addition to the well-known spiritualities of various schools and religious orders imported from the West (e.g., Benedictine, Franciscan, Dominican, Carmelite, Jesuit, etc.), there has been an interesting development in the Asian churches, namely, the founding of Asian missionary societies with their own distinctive spiritualities that reflect Asian cultures and religious traditions. These missionary

---

33. On inculturation in Asia, see Peter C. Phan, *In Our Own Tongues: Perspectives from Asia on Mission and Inculturation* (Maryknoll, NY: Orbis Books, 2003); and James H. Kroger, ed., *Inculturation in Asia: Directions, Initiatives, and Options* (Hong Kong: FABC Papers, 2005).

34. *Ecclesia in Asia*, §22.

societies of apostolic life focus on mission to non-Christians (*ad gentes*), in foreign countries (*ad exteros*), and for life (*ad vitam*). Notable among these are the Mission Society of the Philippines, the Missionary Society of St. Thomas the Apostle (India), the Catholic Foreign Mission Society of Korea, the Missionary Society of Heralds of Good News (India), the Missionary Society of Thailand, and the Lorenzo Ruiz Mission Society (the Philippines).[35]

A final characteristic of this missionary spirituality is its emphasis on the laity since, given the vast not-yet-evangelized Asian territories and the insufficient number of clergy and religious, the laity, both women and men, especially catechists, are assuming an increasing role in church missions. This lay character of Asian spirituality also gives a preponderant place to popular devotions (in addition to liturgy and sacraments), especially devotion to Mary and the saints.

Mission as well as spirituality is contemplative action and active contemplation. Mission is convincing only if it is steeped in spirituality. In Pope John Paul II's words, "In Asia, home to great religions where individuals and entire peoples are thirsting for the divine, the church is called to be a praying church, deeply spiritual even as she engages in immediate human and social concerns. All Christians need a true missionary spirituality of prayer and contemplation."[36] Such a spirituality is nothing more than life lived under the power of the Spirit (interreligious dialogue), in imitation of Christ (liberation), and for the sake of the church's mission (inculturation). Such spirituality by nature is also social spirituality.

---

35. On Asian mission societies, see James H. Kroeger, "The Asian Churches' Awakening to Mission," in Phan, ed., *The Asian Synod*, 189–211.

36. *Ecclesia in Asia*, §23.

14

Local Spiritualities, Popular Religions, and Christian Higher Education in Asia

The general theme of this chapter is the relationship between popular religions and local spiritualities and their promotion in everyday higher education in Asia.[1] As such, "local spiritualities" is of course wider than "popular religions," and "everydayness" may be understood as the arena where popular religions are practiced. What is meant by "local spiritualities" and "popular religions" will be elucidated in the course of the chapter. For the moment, their overlapping relationship may be expressed by saying that all popular religions are local spiritualities but not all local spiritualities are popular religions. Given the distinction, albeit not opposition, between these two realities, their place in Christian higher education is consequently different, and hence the way Christian universities and colleges in Asia deal with them must also be different from, albeit intimately related to, each other.

I will begin with a discussion of local spiritualities and their relation to Christian spirituality in terms of inculturation. Next I examine the nature of popular religions and the obligation of the church to enter into a dialogue with them. I conclude with reflections on how Christian colleges and universities in Asia can promote among themselves a fruitful conversation about and the practice of local spiritualities and popular religions.

To state my basic thesis in a nutshell, the task facing Christian higher education in Asia with regard to local spiritualities is how to express the Christian faith in terms of local cultures, a project generally referred to in Roman Catholic circles as "inculturation" and among Protestants as "contextualization." With regard to popular religions, on the other hand, the challenge for Christian higher education in Asia is to enter into a respectful dialogue with them, an enterprise that may lead to mutual ritual participation, or to use a neologism, "inter-riting." These two tasks—inculturation and interreligious dialogue—have been objects of extensive, at times heated, debates in mainline

---

1. Ideas in this chapter repeat and expand on topics treated in earlier chapters.

Christian churches. In fact, the World Council of Churches and the Roman Catholic Church, especially in the fifty years after the Second Vatican Council (1962–65), have issued countless documents stressing the need for and various approaches to inculturation and interfaith dialogue.

I hasten to add that according to the Federation of Asian Bishops' Conferences (FABC), these two tasks are intimately connected with a third, namely, liberation, so much so that one cannot be fulfilled without the other two. Furthermore, according to the FABC, these three activities should be carried out in the form of dialogue, and this triple dialogue constitutes the mode of Christian mission in Asia. Here I will focus principally on inculturation and interreligious dialogue, and will refer to liberation by way of conclusion.

A final preliminary remark is in order. It is well known that in Asia Christian missions, both Catholic and Protestant, have devoted a great part of their resources, personnel as well as money, to promoting education at all levels, and that Christian institutions of higher learning count among the best in Asia. However, the fact that they belong to different Christian denominations and do not share the same theological outlook and approaches, especially with regard to the two realities under consideration, poses difficult challenges to my presentation. On the one hand, for some groups, for example Roman Catholics, I may be preaching to the choir, and some of the points I will be making regarding inculturation and interreligious dialogue may sound like old news. On the other hand, for others, particularly those steeped in the Evangelical and Pentecostal traditions, what is common practice among Roman Catholics and other denominations may appear novel and perhaps even unorthodox. In this chapter I hope to be able to persuade the latter group of the necessity of both inculturation and interreligious dialogue and to show the former that in spite of the abundant literature on these two activities, there is still a lot left to be said, and therefore I hope to offer some new insights on them, especially in the context of higher education in Asia.

CHRISTIAN SPIRITUALITY, A LOCAL SPIRITUALITY TO BE LOCALIZED WITH OTHER LOCAL SPIRITUALITIES

To begin with, a few words about spirituality in general and Christian spirituality in particular are in order.[2] In its broadest sense, spirituality refers first of all to the human capacity for self-transcendence actualized in acts of knowledge of and love for realities other than oneself. Second, and more narrowly, spirituality refers to the religious dimension of life by which one is in

---

2. For a more comprehensive treatment of Christian spirituality in our globalized world, see Chapter 13.

touch with the more-than-human, transcendent reality, however interpreted and named (e.g., Emptiness, the Holy, the Ultimate, the Real, the Absolute, Heaven, or God). Third, and more strictly still, spirituality indicates a particular way of living one's relationship with this transcendent reality, through specific beliefs, rituals, prayers, moral behaviors, and community participation (e.g., Hindu, Buddhist, Jewish, Christian, Muslim, etc.).[3] Needless to say, Asian spirituality embodies all these three connotations. It is (1) human self-transcendence (2) toward the Ultimate Other (3) within a particular religious tradition.

Because spirituality is lived in a specific religious tradition or, as is common in Asia, a mixture of traditions, there is, of course, no generic spirituality, untethered from a historical and particular tradition and community. Even when one attempts to construct one's own spirituality and elects to be "spiritual" but not "religious," to use a common contemporary slogan, one can only do so by drawing on various elements of preexisting spiritual traditions. In other words, an institutional dimension is essential to any spiritual quest.[4] A spirituality that is like a Platonic form, floating above space and time, valid always and everywhere, does not and cannot exist. Here, then, is the first principle regarding spirituality: All spiritualities are necessarily and intrinsically local and localized, not only in the spatial sense but also in all the ways in which a reality is particularized in terms of time, economics, politics, culture, and religion. In a sense, to speak of spirituality as "local" is a redundancy.

This is also true of Christian spirituality, which is a particular way of relating to God as Abba/Father, mediated by Jesus of Nazareth in his ministry, death, and resurrection, and made possible by the power of the Holy Spirit, who has been poured out on the community called the church. Spirituality is essentially life in the Spirit. It is, however, not antithetical to the body and matter. According to Paul, "spirit" (*pneuma*) and "spiritual" (*pneumatikos*)—from which "spirituality" is derived—are the opposites of "flesh" (*sarx*), "fleshly" (*sarkikos*), and "soul" (*psyche*) and "soul-ly" (*psychikos*), but not of "body" (*soma*), "bodily" (*somatikos*), and "matter" (*hyle*). The Pauline opposition is not between two ontological orders: the incorporeal and the immaterial on the one hand and the corporeal and the material on the other. Such metaphysical dualism did not attach to the use of *spiritualitas* until the twelfth century. Rather, the opposition is between two ways of life, one that is led by

---

3. For a survey of these different spiritualities, see the series of monographs published by Paulist Press entitled Classics of Western Spirituality. Beyond Western spirituality, see the series World Spirituality published by Alban Books, Ltd., and World Spirituality published by Crossroad Publishing.

4. For a study of Christian spirituality in a global perspective, see James Wiseman, *Spirituality and Mysticism: A Global View* (Maryknoll, NY: Orbis Books, 2006).

and in accord with the Spirit ("spiritual") and therefore leading to life, and the other opposed to the Spirit ("fleshly") and bringing about death. Christian spirituality then is essentially *life empowered by the Spirit of Christ*, by which men and women are made sons and daughters of God by adoption and brothers and sisters of Christ into whose image they must be fashioned. Such a life is adorned with the Spirit's gift of virtues (1 Cor 13:13; Col 1:9; Rom 8:21; Gal 5:13; 2 Cor 3:17), fruits (Gal 5:23–24), and charisms of different kinds to build up the Christian community (1 Cor 12:4–11, 28–30; Rom 12:6–8; Eph 4:11–13).[5] In short, Christian spirituality as relationship with God is *pneumatological* (empowered by the Spirit), *christological* (mediated through and modeled after Christ), and *ecclesial* (realized in the church). Hence, Asian Christian spirituality realizes these three dimensions necessarily in the context of Asian societies, cultures, and religions.

Consequently, an essential part of the church's mission is to incarnate the Christian faith into the local context. Besides interreligious dialogue and liberation, as will be discussed below, Asian Christian churches must also take on the task of inculturation, namely, making Christianity not only *in* and *for* Asia but also *of* Asia. In the recent past, this task was not always considered an essential part of Christian mission. Western pieties and devotions were imported into Asia, especially in the Roman Catholic Church. Hymns, prayers, songs, liturgical books, sacramental rituals, sacred vestments, plastic arts and architecture, monastic institutions, canon law, and the various spiritualities of religious orders, both male and female, and so forth, are imposed on the local churches. At best, these foreign spiritual elements and traditions were adapted to the local conditions; they are, as it were, fully-grown trees transplanted into another soil and climate and thus undergoing only superficial changes.

In contrast, inculturation (or contextualization or indigenization) is understood as a creative encounter between a particular, already inculturated form of Christianity (there is no culture-free, pure form of Christianity!) and a particular local culture from which another form of Christianity, a *tertium quid*, will emerge, one that preserves some continuity with past Christianities elsewhere but is not identical with them. It is like a seed planted in a new soil out of which a different tree, though of the same species, will grow. No one form of Christianity should and may be taken as normative for all others. So it is with Asian spirituality. It is, of course, Christian spirituality but in Asian

---

5. For a comprehensive history of Christian spirituality, see the following three volumes: Bernard McGinn, John Meyendorff, and Jean Leclerq, eds., *Christian Spirituality: Origins to the Twelfth Century* (New York: Crossroad, 1988); Jill Raitt, ed., *Christian Spirituality: High Middle Ages and Reformation* (New York: Crossroad, 1988); and Louis Dupré and Don E. Saliers, eds., *Christian Spirituality: Post-Reformation and Modern* (New York: Crossroad, 1991).

"style," transformed by the cultural and religious values of each ethnic group and country in Asia.[6] We may call these cultural and religious values and practices as embodied and lived in a particular country "local spiritualities."

Having stated these general principles of inculturation, I would like to expand briefly on Christian spirituality *as itself a local spirituality* to be localized again and again as it enters new cultures and encounters other local spiritualities. This statement does not seem to require lengthy and elaborate proof. Indeed, it can be succinctly justified on two theological principles. The first is the Incarnation. Just as the Word of God was made flesh not in a generic human form but in a particular Jew, namely, Jesus, who lived in a specific place and during a particular time, with all the specificities and the limitations this embodiment entails, so the Christian faith, and by implication, the Christian way of life must also be incarnated into a particular place and time.

However, as illuminating as the incarnation metaphor is, it is misleading with regard to the inculturation of Christian faith and Christian spirituality. It may wrongly suggest that like the Logos, Christian faith and Christian spirituality are nonspatial and nontemporal realities descending pure and culture-free from heaven as it were into a particular culture. Christian faith and spirituality are nothing of the sort, of course. As historical realities, they were first expressed in biblical cultures—Hebrew and Greek—and then in those of the Roman Empire, both East and West; of the Anglo-Saxon and Teutonic worlds; of Spain, Portugal, Italy, Holland, Britain, France, Germany, Denmark, and the United States, just to mention some of the countries from which missionaries came to evangelize Asia. It is the Christianities and Christian spiritualities (note the plural form!) of these countries, very different among themselves, that were imported to Asia, and not the allegedly pure and culture-free gospel. Inculturation, then, is not the encounter between the contextually free, culturally universal, and permanently valid Christian spirituality on the one hand and the locally situated, culturally limited, and temporarily valid spiritualities on the other. Rather, inculturation is an encounter, at times harmonious, at other times contentious, between an essentially local Christian spirituality and other equally local spiritualities. Christian spirituality, no less than other spiritualities, are affected by limitedness, partiality, bias, incompleteness, and errors.

The second theological principle is what Andrew F. Walls call "the translation principle."[7] By translation is meant not only the verbal rendering of a

---

6. See Peter C. Phan, *In Our Own Tongues: Perspectives from Asia on Mission and Inculturation* (Maryknoll, NY: Orbis Books, 2004); and Peter C. Phan, ed., *The Asian Synod: Texts and Commentaries* (Maryknoll, NY: Orbis Books, 2002).

7. Andrew Walls, *The Missionary Movement in Christian History: Studies in the Transmission of Faith* (Maryknoll, NY: Orbis Books, 1996), 26.

text, for example, the Bible, from its original language into another language, either by formal equivalence (word-for-word translation) or by dynamic or functional equivalence (sense-for-sense translation), but also, and primarily, the whole process of crosscultural transmission of certain elements of one culture (the original culture) into another culture (the receptor or target culture). Missiologists such as Andrew Walls and Lamin Sanneh among many others have pointed out that it is through what Walls terms "the infinite translatability of the Christian faith"[8] that Christianity survived the vicissitudes of history and became a world or global religion.[9]

As applied to Christianity, this crosscultural process of transmission is, Walls notes, governed by two apparently opposing principles. First, the "indigenizing principle," by which Christianity becomes part of the local culture and thanks to which the newly Christian converts can feel at home in their new religion, engaging in familiar spiritual practices, though now endowed with new meanings. Second, the "pilgrim principle," by which the local culture and, with it, the new Christian converts are brought out of their particularities and transformed into something new, more universal, and that is the Christian way of life.[10] In sum, Christian spirituality is essentially one local spirituality among many, to be localized again and again with other local spiritualities with which it comes into contact.

By "Asian local spiritualities" are meant those cultural and religious values and practices by which people of a country or ethnic group in Asia actualize self-transcendence in acts of knowledge of and love for realities other than themselves, especially the Transcendent. These local spiritualities may be but are not necessarily connected with a particular religion such as Hinduism, Buddhism, Islam, Jainism, Sikhism, Shintoism, Confucianism, and Daoism, to name only the major religious traditions of Asia. They are part of what is called "primal religion," or what Aloysius calls "cosmic religion," in distinction from the so-called world religions or, in Pieris's term, "metacosmic religion."[11]

The relation between popular spirituality ("cosmic religion") and historical religions ("metacosmic religions") is well explained by Pieris:

> These two species of religions (cosmic and metacosmic) relate to each other as natural complements. In fact, a metacosmic religion (whether agapeic or gnostic) cannot be firmly rooted (that is, inculturated) in

---

8. Ibid., 22.

9. See also Andrew Walls, *The Cross-Cultural Process in Christian History* (Maryknoll, NY: Orbis Books, 2002); and Lamin Sanneh, *Translating the Message: The Missionary Impact on Culture* (Maryknoll, NY: Orbis Books, 1989).

10. See Walls, *Missionary Movement in Christian History*, 7–9.

11. See Aloysius Pieris, *An Asian Theology of Liberation* (Maryknoll, NY: Orbis Books, 1988), 54.

tribal societies except within the context of their cosmic religion; conversely, a cosmic religion is an open-ended spirituality that awaits a transcendental orientation from a metacosmic religion. It is therefore not a question of one replacing the other, but one completing the other in such a way as to form a bidimensional soteriology that maintains a healthy tension between the cosmic *now* and the metacosmic *beyond*.[12]

What then is Asian popular spirituality without which Christian spirituality cannot firmly be rooted in the Asian soil and by which it is completed so as "to form a bidimensional soteriology"? In answer to this question, we may cite Pope John Paul II's statement in his apostolic exhortation *Ecclesia in Asia*:

> The people of Asia take pride in their religious and cultural values, such as love of silence and contemplation, simplicity, harmony, detachment, non-violence, the spirit of hard work, discipline, frugal living, the thirst for learning and philosophical enquiry. They hold dear the value of respect for life, compassion for all beings, closeness to nature, filial piety towards parents, elders and ancestors, and a highly developed sense of community. In particular they hold the family to be a vital source of strength, a closely knit community with a powerful sense of solidarity. Asian peoples are known for their spirit of religious tolerance and peaceful co-existence. Without denying the existence of bitter tensions and violent conflicts, it can still be said that Asia has often demonstrated a remarkable capacity for accommodation and a natural openness to the mutual enrichment of peoples in the midst of a plurality of religions and cultures.[13]

To avoid triumphalism and orientalism, it is important to read John Paul II's statement not as a taxonomy of the so-called Asian culture, much less a historical portrait of each and every Asian person. Rather, it enumerates a set of moral and spiritual *ideals* and *values* to which Asian people characteristically aspire and which they practice in varying degrees in their daily lives. Indeed, as Christian spirituality is inculturated in a particular locale, it is, by virtue of the indigenizing principle, incorporated into the local spiritualities; and at the same time, local spiritualities, by virtue of the pilgrim principle, are brought out of their particular localities and made part of Christian spirituality.

As an example of this mutual enrichment between Christian spirituality and local spiritualities, let's take the fourth commandment of the Jewish-Christian decalogue, "Thou shall honor your father and your mother," and see whether it has been indigenized into what Pope John Paul II refers to as

---

12. Ibid.
13. Pope John Paul II, *Ecclesia in Asia* (Vatican City: Libreria Editrice Vaticana, 1999), no. 6.

one element of Asian local spiritualities, namely, "filial piety towards parents, elders and ancestors." A passing familiarity with the history of Catholic missions in China and the three-centuries-long so-called Chinese Rites Controversy can testify to how a lack of understanding and repeated condemnations of this practice has had a disastrous impact on Christian missions not only in China but also in countries within the sphere of Sinic influence such as Korea, Japan, and Vietnam. This failure at inculturation has also deprived Christian spirituality of the riches of local spiritualities. For instance, note how "your father and your mother" is now expanded by John Paul II to include "parents, elders and ancestors." Furthermore, imagine how the elaborate rituals of ancestor worship in Asia can offer immense resources for enriching the rather jejune connotation of "honor" in the commandment "Thou shall honor your father and your mother."

On the other hand, by not being integrated into Christian spirituality, ancestor veneration has lost a precious opportunity to be universalized and become a religious practice that is meaningful for all Christians. Instead, it still remains a regional, albeit quaint and exotic, practice in Western eyes. How Asian universities and colleges can promote this twofold process of indigenizing Christian spirituality and universalizing local spiritualities will be discussed in the last part of my presentation.

CHRISTIAN SPIRITUALITY AND POPULAR RELIGIONS

In his statement on Asia, Pope John Paul II refers not only to the continent's plurality of cultures but also plurality of religions, and consequently calls for not only inculturation but also interreligious dialogue.[14] With regard to interreligious dialogue, because Asia is the birthplace of most if not all religions, and because Christians form but a tiny minority of the Asian population, Asian Christians, more than their fellow believers in any other part of the globe, cannot live their Spirit-empowered lives apart from non-Christian religions.

As is well known, however, the history of Christianity in Asia was not always marked by respect for and dialogue with other religions. At first, most missionaries, both Catholic and Protestant, and especially Evangelical and Pentecostal, with very few exceptions, were dismissive of the spiritual values of these religious ways of life and often condemned them as fruits of religious superstition and moral depravity. But the goodness of non-Christians (some of them are holier than Christians!), with whom many Christians share their daily life intimately as family members, gives the lie to the church's age-old teaching that non-Christians are heathens destined for

---

14. On inculturation, see *Ecclesia in Asia*, nos. 21–22. On interreligious dialogue, see ibid., no. 31.

hell, that non-Christian religions are the work of the devil, that Christianity is the only true and exclusive way to God, and that there is no salvation outside the church (*extra ecclesiam nulla salus*). Furthermore, it is increasingly recognized that non-Christians are good and holy, not in spite of but *because* of the beliefs and practices enjoined on them by their religions. From the Christian perspective, these elements of truth and grace must be regarded as fruits of the Spirit, who is the gift of God and the risen Christ, but who is active outside of, albeit not independently from, Jesus and the church, in ways known to God.

In its ground-breaking Declaration on the Relation of the Church to Non-Christian Religions, known by its Latin title *Nostra Aetate*, Vatican II, while affirming the necessity of Christian mission, declares: "The Catholic Church rejects nothing of what is true and holy in these religions. It has a high regard for the manner of life and conduct, the precepts and doctrines which, although differing in many ways from its own teaching, nevertheless often reflect a ray of truth which enlightens all men and women" (no. 2). It goes on to assert: "The church, therefore, urges its sons and daughters to enter with prudence and charity into discussion and collaborate with members of other religions. Let Christians, while witnessing to their own faith and way of life, acknowledge, preserve and encourage the spiritual and moral truths found among non-Christians, together with their social life and culture" (no. 2).[15]

Arguably Vatican II's mandate to undertake dialogue with non-Christian religions has been carried out with greater vigor in the Catholic Church in Asia than anywhere else in the last fifty years. No area of church life has been left out of consideration, including theology, ethics, worship, and spirituality. It is, however, in spirituality that dialogue has proved most fertile and transformative. The FABC has recommended that dialogue take place in four interdependent forms: *common living* as friendly and helpful neighbors; *common action* for the sake of peace, justice, and ecological integrity; *theological exchange* to remove misunderstandings and to enrich one another intellectually; and shared *religious experience* in which people of different faiths pray and worship together.[16] Of the four, the last—sharing religious experience—presupposes and strengthens a common spirituality. To be able to build an interreligious spirituality requires a sincere and humble dialogue with other religions in an effort to learn from, among other things, their sacred scriptures, doctrinal teachings, moral and spiritual practices, prayers and devotions, and monastic and mystical traditions to enrich one's spiritual life.

---

15. *The Basic Sixteen Documents Vatican I*, ed. Austin Flannery (Northport, NY: Costello, 2007), 570–71.

16. See Peter C. Phan, *Being Religious Interreligiously: Asian Perspectives on Interfaith Dialogue* (Maryknoll, NY: Orbis Books, 2005); Kwok Pui-lan, "Interfaith Encounter," in *The Blackwell Companion to Christian Spirituality*, ed. Arthur Holder (Malden, MA: Blackwell, 2005), 532–49.

It is to the credit of the Society of Jesus that many of its members were the first missionaries in Asia to develop a Christian spirituality in dialogue with Asian cultures and religions. Jesuits such as Francis Xavier (1506–1552) and Alessandro Valignano (1539–1606) in Japan, Matteo Ricci (1552–1610) in China, Roberto de Nobili (1577–1656) in India, and Alexandre de Rhodes (1591–1660) in Vietnam, notwithstanding whatever deficiencies of their accommodationist policies, were visionary pioneers who paved the way, often at great personal costs, to a Christian spirituality enriched by other religious traditions and in turn enriching them through interfaith dialogue.[17]

In more recent times, bold and even controversial efforts have been made to incorporate monastic and spiritual practices of non-Christian religions into Christian spirituality. In India, French priest Jules Monchanin (also known as Swami Paramarubyananda, 1895–1957), French Benedictine Henri Le Saux (1910–1973, also known as Swami Abhishiktananda), English Benedictine Dom Bede Griffiths (1906–1993), Belgian Cistercian monk Francis Mahieu (1912–2002), and Indian Jesuit Ignatius Hirudayam, to name only the better-known ones, have been active in incorporating into their Christian experience of God as Trinity the Hindu advaitic quest for God as *sat* (being), *cit* (truth), and bliss (*ananda*). Moreover, through their Ashram Movement, they have assimilated into Christian worship and monasticism the Hindu sacred scriptures, religious symbols, ascetic practices, meditation techniques, religious songs and dance, sacred art, clothing, and postures.[18]

In Japan, the resource for spiritual enrichment has been mainly Zen Buddhism. Not surprisingly, the first efforts at dialogue with Zen were made by the Quakers. Among Catholics, the Jesuits Hugo M. Enomiya-Lassalle (1898–1990), Kakichi Kadowaki (1926–2017) and William Johnston (1925–2010), the Carmelite priest Agostino Ichiro Okomura (1923–2014), and the Dominican priest Vincenzo Shigeto Oshida (1922–2003) have been instrumental in enriching Christian spirituality with Zen meditation practices. Dialogue with Buddhism, especially in its Theravada branch, has been carried out extensively in Thailand and Sri Lanka. Dialogue with Islam is active in certain parts of India and in Indonesia. In countries heavily influenced by Confucianism such as China, Taiwan, Vietnam, and Korea, Christian spirituality has recently incorporated the rituals of the cult of ancestors after it had been severely condemned by the church for several centuries.

Important as interreligious dialogue is for the Asian churches, the focus of my reflections is not on this activity as such but on the encounter between

---

17. See Peter C. Phan, *Mission and Catechesis: Alexandre de Rhodes & Inculturation in Seventeenth-Century Vietnam* (Maryknoll, NY: Orbis Books, 1998).

18. See Francis X. Clooney, *Hindu Wisdom for All God's Children* (Maryknoll, NY: Orbis Books, 1998).

Christianity and popular religion(s), to be more precise, the encounter between popular religion in Christianity and popular religion in Asian religions. Needless to say, this subject is extremely complex, not least because of the highly contested meaning, nature, and function of the so-called popular religion, also known by other terms such as "folk religion" and "common religion."[19] Each of these three appellations has strengths and weaknesses as the expression for what is understood by popular religion. By "popular" is not meant "fashionable" (or in young Americans' parlance, "cool" and "awesome") but "of the people," "people" generally understood as the poor, majority class. In this sense, popular religion is contrasted with "official religion," "elite religion," and "esoteric religion." Like these three types of religion, popular religion has an institutional organization, a social formation, and an intellectual component, though in a different configuration.

As mentioned above, popular religion exists in both Christianity and Asian religions in various combinations of its three features of institutional organization, social formation, and intellectual component. All Asian religions have popular or folk religion as one of their major building blocks, especially Hinduism, Buddhism, Islam, Daoism, and Shinto. Indeed, more than Christianity, these religions cannot be appreciated without their popular religions.

In general, popular religion has eight distinctive elements.[20] First, its image of God or gods is that of a deity at once gracious and stern and constantly involved in the life of believers, dispensing reward for good deeds and punishment for bad ones. Second, the deity is approached not directly but through a series of mediators who intercede for believers (in Christianity: Jesus, Mary, the saints, and local patrons). Third, it is kept vibrant by social activities such as periodic celebrations and feastings, processions, eating, dancing, and singing. Fourth, it comprises a plethora of devotional activities such as prayer, novenas, vow-making, pilgrimages, and personal cult to a favorite mediator. Fifth, it has a strong material culture, including sacred objects such as statues, images, rosaries, relics, medals, sanctuaries, shrines, holy water, candles, and incense. Sixth, it is sustained by associations, societies, and clubs, each with an appropriate supernatural patron. Seventh, it has a distinctive cosmology, characterized by a view of the world as an interconnected and controlled place in which divine favors can be obtained and earthly life is intimately connected

---

19. Studies on popular religion are legion. For our purposes I strongly recommend Robert Schreiter's lucid and insightful chapter 6 ("Popular Religion and Official Religion") of his book *Constructing Local Theologies* (Maryknoll, NY: Orbis Books, 1985, 2015), 139–64. On the Catholic Church's position on popular religion, see Peter C. Phan, ed., *Directory on Popular Piety and the Liturgy: Principles and Guidelines. A Commentary* (Collegeville, MN: Liturgical Press, 2005).

20. See Schreiter, *Constructing Local Theologies*, 146–49.

with life after death. Eighth and lastly, popular religion has an extensive albeit ambiguous relationship to official religion. On the one hand, its flourishing depends on the approval of the custodians of official religion and on its being incorporated into it. On the other hand, its practitioners tend to neglect the teachings and practices of official religion.

There are different approaches and interpretations of popular religion.[21] On the negative side, there are two: the elitist and the Marxist evaluations, the former regarding popular religion as a corruption of the official and orthodox religion into false beliefs and superstitious practices, and the latter viewing it as the false consciousness imposed by the ruling class on the proletariat.

On the positive side, there are five approaches. First, the baseline approach views popular religion as the first and basic complex of religious elements of a particular location and culture that are later taken up and incorporated into a more universal world religion such Hinduism, Buddhism, Judaism, Christianity, and Islam. Second, the romanticist approach views popular religion as the genuine religion of the people, which is corrupted and brought under control by the institutional religion and its clergy. Third, the remnant approach sees popular religion as elements of religious beliefs and practices of the primal religion that continue to exist, though under different forms and meanings, as constituents of world religions. Fourth, the subaltern approach views popular religion as the symbolic creation of the oppressed class to resist and subvert the domination of the ruling class and its official religion. Fifth and lastly, the social-psychological approach views popular religion as collective responses to the social and psychological needs of displaced people, for example, rural people moving into the cities, to find security, identity, and community.

It is important to note that all of these seven approaches have strengths and weaknesses proving helpful insights into the origin, nature, and functions of popular religion. Given the complex and multidimensional reality of popular religion within both Christianity and Asian religions, it is obvious that the interreligious encounter between Christianity and Asian religions is not between a popular-religion-free Christianity and popular-religion-laden Asian religions. Rather, it is a two-way, interacting, and mutually influencing dialogue between the above-mentioned eight elements of the popular religion of Christianities and the equivalent elements of the popular religions of Asian religions. It is an extremely complex and challenging encounter, fraught with dangers such as various forms of so-called syncretism, but one without which Christianity cannot be planted in the indigenous soil and become a local spirituality of everydayness. How to foster this type of local Christian spirituality, especially in Asian Christian universities and colleges, is the topic of the final part of my presentation.

---

21. See ibid., 149–59.

LOCAL SPIRITUALITIES AND POPULAR RELIGIONS IN ASIA'S CHRISTIAN HIGHER EDUCATION

With a deep awareness that Christian institutions of higher learning differ, at times markedly, in their theological orientations, I will endeavor to offer some general reflections on the theme of this meeting, namely, promoting conversation on local spiritualities in Christian higher education in Asia.

The first and obvious thing to note is that Christian institutes of higher learning in Asia, more than anywhere else, lend themselves to the kind of inculturation of the Christian faith into local spiritualities and interreligious dialogue with popular religions we have been speaking about thanks to the ethnic, cultural, and religious composition of their student bodies, staff, and faculty. Except in the Philippines, as a rule they come from diverse cultural backgrounds, and most of them are non-Christians. While our institutions should as part of their mission promote Christian ideas and values in their educational programs and disciplinary curricula, I take it that none of them is engaged in or permits or tolerates evangelization under the form of proselytism, that is, efforts to convert non-Christian students, staff, and faculty to the Christian faith through pressure and blandishments. No institution will, therefore, measure the success of their objectives and goals by the number of baptisms produced. Furthermore, most of the institutions, I presume, have chapels or churches on campus where Bible studies, religious services, devotional practices, and sacramental celebrations are held daily or weekly, attendance at which is presumably not compulsory. In addition, like most colleges and universities in the United States, their institutions may have chaplaincies to serve the spiritual needs of the university.

The question of where conversation about the interaction between Christianity on the one hand and local spiritualities and popular religions on the other can and should occur on campus regularly and intentionally may be answered by examining the three venues mentioned above, namely, chaplaincy, church services, and educational programs and disciplinary curricula. First, where possible, it is highly desirable that chaplaincy staff come from diverse cultural and religious backgrounds. For example, at Georgetown University where I work, the chaplaincy office is headed by a Jesuit priest, but there are full-time Protestant, Jewish, Muslim, and Hindu chaplains. By their presence and activities these chaplains embody and promote religious diversity and tolerance, interreligious collaboration, and interfaith worship. Studies of sacred texts (especially the Tanak, the Bible, the Qur'an, and the Hindu classics) and religious services are conducted regularly and are open to people of diverse faiths. One of my students this semester is a Jewish woman, but she sings in the choir at Sunday Mass, and she told me that she has attended Mass and listened to Catholic homilies more than any Catholic she knows. Chaplaincy, needless to say, also assists students through counseling when they have or are liable to go through psychological and spiritual crises, for example, after the sudden and tragic death of a classmate, or ecological and national catastrophes. Solemn and public Mass is celebrated for all students, faculty, and staff at the beginning of the academic year to invoke God's blessings on the university and during the Commencement exercises at the end of the school year. These are fertile moments not for producing conversion to the Christian faith but for promoting interreligious understanding and harmony. To fulfill this goal and to spark fruitful conversation on local spirituality and popular religion on campus, the selection of chaplains is of paramount importance, since not every ordained minister is well equipped for these tasks.

The second venue that offers plenty of opportunities for extended conversation about local spiritualities and popular religions is the campus church or chapel, in the sense of both the physical building and liturgical celebrations and divine worship carried out therein. Every Christian university and college should have a sacred building, preferably at the center or at least at a prominent location on the campus. For instance, at Georgetown University, there is a splendid chapel in the proverbial university quadrangle, an artistic jewel and a vibrant symbol of all the ideals, values, and religious faiths that animate the university. This chapel, with appropriate decorations, hosts major religious feasts of all the faiths represented on campus. Nearby is a small meditation center to which members of any faith of the university can retreat for quiet reflection and prayer, and where Hindu yoga, Buddhist meditation, and Christian contemplation are practiced.

While chaplaincy and church activities offer rich opportunities for the practice of inculturation and interreligious dialogue, educational programs and disciplinary curricula are what distinguish Christian colleges and universities as centers of higher learning. I take it that the main goals and objectives of Asian Christian colleges and universities are not the establishment of professional programs, especially in law, politics, business, medicine, and science—a constant temptation in trying to compete with prestigious secular universities and to respond to the immediate and urgent needs of their countries. On the contrary, at the heart of their educational philosophy, I submit, must be the integral formation of the entire person, and this cannot be achieved without the students' serious and scholarly engagement with the humanities, irrespective of their majors and career choices. This is called liberal arts education, an essential part of which is the study of religion and religious traditions. Of course, practical concerns will dictate the number of courses and credits for religious/theological studies in the core curriculum, and to be honest, intense pressure is often brought by faculty in other disciplines to reduce them to a minimum on the grounds that religious/theological studies are not practical (read: do not make money) or that they are merely religious propaganda or indoctrination (read: that is how religion has been taught to these faculty).

To dispel this misapprehension, religious/theological issues must be shown to lie at the center of human existence, not in the sense that without religion an ethically good life is impossible (indeed, it is possible!) but in the sense that no matter what one thinks about religion, whether as a good thing or a bad thing, it must be recognized that there is no important area of human life—business, law, medicine, politics, and science—in which religion does not matter and therefore must be seriously studied. Consequently, a university education without a scholarly study of religion/theology, including local spiritualities and popular religions, is essentially defective, and a Christian university that does not make religious/theological studies the center of its educational philosophy and programs fails in its mission. As a result, adequate financial resources must be used to secure for departments of religious/theological studies the best and brightest faculty, with the highest academic qualifications and excellent teaching experience, and to set up programs of studies with rigorous standards, so that both faculty and programs of religious/theological studies will command the respect and admiration of the entire university. For this to happen, there must be religious/theological studies faculty members capable of participating in university-wide conversation on any topic of significance, be it in business, law, politics, medicine, and science.

So far I have argued for the absolute necessity of religious/theological studies in Christian colleges and universities in Asia, and I would be very pleased if I have been preaching to the choir. In the remaining time I will broach the narrower issue of how to promote on campus conversation on local spiritualities and popular religion in everyday living. Beside chaplaincy, church activities, and academic programs and curricula, there is the highly controversial issue of shared ritual participation or "inter-riting."

For monotheistic religions with well-defined doctrines and sharply drawn boundaries such as Judaism, Christianity, and Islam, it would seem that shared ritual participation, wherein members of different religious traditions pray, worship, and celebrate sacred rituals together, is to be rejected since, so it is argued, it inevitably leads to religious relativism and syncretism.

On the other hand, especially in Asia, religions are not seen as impermeable and mutually exclusive institutions, with officially defined dogmas, clearly marked and hermetically sealed boundaries, and for-members-only rituals. Rather, religions are widely viewed as diverse but complementary ways to the Divine and to achieve full human flourishing, and may be adopted in various ways, depending on a particular need at a particular stage of one's life. Whichever religion is deemed to best satisfy this need is adopted without scruples about doctrinal orthodoxy, membership requirements, or ritual purity. For instance, there is in China the *san jiao* (three religions) tradition, in which a mandarin is a Confucian when performing his government function, a Daoist when he is at home enjoying harmony with nature, and a Buddhist when he dies. It is also said, perhaps with some exaggeration but not without a grain of truth, that a Japanese is born a Shinto, marries as a Christian, and dies as a Buddhist. In India, inter-riting is a pervasive fact of life, especially among Hindus but also among Muslims. The same thing may be said of most other Asian countries. Perhaps the most interesting case of inter-riting is a religion founded in Vietnam in the 1940s known as Cao Dai, which originated as an intentional combination of Buddhism, Daoism, Confucianism, and Christianity.

Moreover, this inter-riting is inevitable when Christianity enters into dialogue with local spiritualities and popular religion. Indeed, as I have pointed out above, there is no non-cultural Christianity; it is itself a historical product born out of the encounter between the already-inculturated Christian faith and local spiritualities and popular religions. This concomitant process of inculturation (the indigenizing principle) and transformation (the pilgrim principle) is ever ongoing. Indeed, it is this form of hybrid Christianity that is lived in the everydayness of life and that is most meaningful to ordinary Christians. It is primarily a "way of life" and not a "view of life." How can Christian colleges and universities in Asia contribute to the success of this process?

I would like to suggest two main ways in which this contribution can be made. First, in terms of practice. Ritual sharing, as Maryanne Moyart suggests, can be done on two fronts, namely, as a community response to external events ("outer-facing") and as an act of hospitality to members of religions other than one's own to promote interreligious dialogue ("inner-facing").[22] Inter-riting should be strongly encouraged to create a common religious "We" among diverse religious communities to galvanize concerted efforts to meet serious challenges facing the community such as natural disasters, acts of war and terrorism, and political and economic emergency situations. Inter-riting on those occasions serves to express sadness and mourning for the dead and solidarity with the survivors of the victims, to organize relief efforts, and to solidify religious collaboration. Such ritual participation can and should also be organized for major cultural feasts such as New Year's Day, National Independence Day, the Day for the Dead, World Day of Prayer for Peace, and so on.

While "outer-facing" ritual sharing is widely practiced today and is no longer controversial, "inner-facing" ritual participation for the sake of interreligious dialogue is highly contested and often meets with vigorous opposition,

---

22. Maryanne Moyart and Joris Geldhof, eds., *Ritual Participation and Interreligious Dialogue: Boundaries, Transgressions and Innovations* (London: Bloomsbury, 2015), 1–3.

especially on the part of religious authorities.[23] On the opposition side, the main argument is that to be possible and authentic, ritual sharing presupposes common core beliefs; where such shared faith is absent, inter-riting would lead to religious syncretism or indifferentism. In response, supporters of inter-riting point out that ritual performances do more than express belief; they "engage the entire person (not just the mind); they impact on all the senses (vision, hearing, smell, taste, and touch); they evoke powerful emotions (or soothe emotions that are too overwhelming); they stimulate religious experiences, stir the imagination, and attune the body to the divine."[24] Because of the evocative and transformative effects of rituals on the entire person, especially on the body, rituals can and often do alter the community's beliefs. Thus, we have to hold both principles, traditionally expressed in the Latin adages, *lex credendi, lex orandi* (what we believe determines how we pray) and *lex orandi, lex credenda* (how we pray determines what we believe).

It is here that Christian colleges and universities can, I suggest, make their second contribution to the conversation about local spiritualities and popular religions, one that is proper to their nature and mission as institutes of higher learning. I mentioned above that one of the main objections of opponents of ritual sharing is the danger of syncretism. It must be acknowledged that until recently Christian literature on syncretism has for the most part taken a negative stance toward it. It is feared that in this process Christianity will dilute and even lose its orthodoxy and identity. It is to be noted in passing that the syncretistic movement is a two-way street: not only does Christianity borrow elements of other religions to form new types of Christianity but also other cultures borrow elements of Christianity to form new religious movements, such as the already mentioned Cao Dai in Vietnam, the Iglesia Filipina Independiente (the Aglipayan Church) in the Philippines, numerous new religious movements in Japan and Korea, hundreds of marginal churches in China, and thousands of Independent churches in Africa and Latin America.

It must be admitted that to date syncretism remains a highly controversial and deeply contested phenomenon, and unfortunately there is still much that requires careful study.[25] It is here that Christian institutions of higher

---

23. For a helpful discussion of the pro-and-con reasons regarding inter-riting, see ibid., 3–10.

24. Ibid., 7.

25. For a lucid exposition of syncretism as a theological problem, see Schreiter, *Constructing Local Theologies*, 165–81. Other useful studies on religious syncretism include: Gailyn Van Rheenen, ed., *Contextualization and Syncretism: Navigating Cultural Currents* (Pasadena, CA: William Carey Library, 2006); Eric Maroney, *Religious Syncretism* (London: SCM Press, 2006); Anita Maria Leopold and Jeppe Sinding Jensen, eds., *Syncretism in Religion: A Reader* (New York: Routledge, 2004); Charles Stewart and Rosalind Shaw, eds., *Syncretism/Anti-Syncretism: The Politics of Religious Synthesis* (London and New York: Routledge, 1994); Jerald D. Gort,

learning can and should make a much-needed contribution. Since rarely does a single college or university have the financial and academic resources to carry out this study by itself, the association should pull together common resources to investigate the phenomenon of syncretism in Asia. This study can focus on three areas: first, where Christianity and Asian religions have come to form a new religion or religious movement, with Asian religions providing the basic framework; second, where Christianity provides the basic framework for the syncretistic movement but is radically reinterpreted and substantially reshaped, often without dialogue with and control by church authorities; and third, where selected elements of Christianity are borrowed and incorporated into another religious system. In this study, special attention should be given to the phenomenon called "double religious belonging," which, as I pointed out above, is a common practice in Asia. In this study, Christian theologians may be helped by existing research on how non-Christian religions in Asia, especially Buddhism, have accomplished this syncretistic movement as they spread out of their countries of origin without losing their fundamental identity and structure.

To conclude. I have been speaking of inculturation and interreligious dialogue as ways of promoting conversation about local spiritualities and popular religions in Asian Christian institutes of higher learning. These two tasks, however, must be linked with a third, that is, liberation, without which Christian spirituality, and by implication, Christian colleges and universities in Asia, would remain an elitist enterprise. Christian spirituality is essentially *imitatio Christi* in the service of the reign of God. It was in the service of this reign of justice, peace, forgiveness, and reconciliation that Jesus lived and died.

While some Asian countries such as Japan, South Korea, Singapore, Taiwan, and Hong Kong have a well-developed economy, they are but a minority. By contrast, several Asian countries are among the poorest nations on earth, and the majority of Asians are poor and oppressed people who for centuries have been kept economically, culturally, and politically on the margins of society by a variety of forces. Of special concern are women's oppression within a patriarchal and androcentric culture, abortion of female fetuses, marginalization of the outcasts and the tribal or indigenous people, exploitation of migrant and child labor, sex tourism and human trafficking, violation of human rights, and ecological destruction.

In this economic and socio-political context, Asian spirituality as *imitatio Christi* must take the form of the preferential option for the poor, which is a distinctive hallmark of Latin American spirituality and has been appropri-

---

Hendrik M. Vroom, Rein Ferhout, and Anton Wessels, eds., *Dialogue and Syncretism: An Interdisciplinary Approach* (Grand Rapids, MI: Eerdmans, 1989); and William H. Harrison, *In Praise of Mixed Religion: The Syncretism Solution in a Multifaith World* (Montreal: McGill-Queen's University Press, 2014).

ated by Asian churches. Spirituality as service to the kingdom of God occupies a central place in Asian theologies of liberation, such as *minjung* theology, homeland theology, the theology of struggle, *Dalit* theology, feminist theology, and ecological theology.[26] This kind of spirituality allows Asians to overcome the pronounced individualism of their native religions and ethics and to view the spiritual quest as necessarily comprising the quest for social justice. It requires Asian Christians to join with those who are oppressed, Christians and non-Christians, in their struggle for liberation and for full human flourishing. Finally, spirituality as service to the reign of God directs Asian eyes away from the golden age located in the mythic past and turns them toward the *eschaton*, which is the risen Christ himself, who will come again in glory to judge the living and the dead and to bring the reign of God to ultimate fulfillment.

---

26. See, for example, Kim Yong Bock, *Minjung Theology: People as the Subjects of History* (Singapore: Christian Conference of Asia, 1981); V. Devasahayam, ed., *Frontiers of Dalit Theology* (Madras: Indian Society for Promoting Christian Knowledge, 1997); Chung Hyun Kyung, *Struggle to Be the Sun Again: Introducing Asian Women's Theology* (Maryknoll, NY: Orbis Books, 1990); Kwok Pui-lan, *Introducing Asian Feminist Theology* (Cleveland: Pilgrim Press, 2000); Aruna Gnanadason, *Listen to the Women! Listen to the Earth!* (Geneva: World Council of Churches, 2005).

15

"Always Remember Where You Came From"

An Ethic of Migrant Memory

The voice, rich and resonant, tinged with part nostalgia, part pride, rumbled from an old black man, deep furrows in his brow but radiant with hope and strength. February being Black History Month in the United States, he was asked what advice he would like to give to his fellow black Americans. Eyes strained at the camera, the right index finger raised for emphasis, he intoned: "Always remember where you came from." The message was delivered, solemnly and persuasively. In this kind of broadcast, however, television trades only in sound bites, and so the old man was not afforded the time to elaborate on his pithy counsel. But it was not difficult to conjure up, behind those words "where you came from," years of unspeakable sufferings and humiliations and violence when black slaves, like cattle, were bought and sold, forced to serve their white masters as their gods, and lynched when they rebelled.

"ALWAYS REMEMBER WHERE YOU CAME FROM"

With a black man in the White House, though himself not a descendant of slaves, it is easy, especially for those blacks who have made it, armed with degrees from elite white universities, to forget this long and painful chapter of their history. The old black man's timely admonition to his fellow black nationals to remember where they came from was all the more poignant in light of recent shootings and killings of unarmed black men by white police officers, who were not even indicted, stories that went viral on global social media.

As I was ruminating on the theme of this chapter, namely, migration and ethics, it dawned on me that the old black man's admonition to remember one's roots was compelling not only for black Americans but also for millions of migrants and refugees who have come to the United States, especially after the passage in 1965 of the Hart-Celler Act, a by-product of the civil rights movement and part of President Lyndon Johnson's Great Society program. The primary aim of this act was to abolish the racially based quota system imposed by the 1921 National Origins Formula, and to favor the immigration of people from central, northern, and Western Europe, especially from countries such as Italy, Greece, and Portugal. The law replaced the racial quotas with preference categories based on family relationships and job skills that were in demand to boost the American economy. However, after 1970, following an initial influx of migrants from those European countries, immigrants started pouring in from unexpected countries such as Korea, China, India, the Philippines, Vietnam, and Pakistan, as well as countries of Africa and Central America, and then, most recently, from the Middle East. Compared with their predecessors, the great majority of these new migrants, whose racial and ethnic origins had been judged by nativists to be unassimilatable into the American melting pot, did not come voluntarily in search of a better economic future but to flee from war and violence.

For the descendants of predominantly white migrants from Europe in the nineteenth and early-twentieth centuries, their ancestors' experiences of leaving their countries and their loved ones, often never to be seen again, in search of a better life in the United States, painful as they were, are now but distant and dim memories, ensconced in long-forgotten family lore or buried in dusty national archives, retrievable perhaps through curiosity-driven programs such as Ancestry.com. In contrast, for recent migrants from Asia, Africa, Latin America, and the Middle East, victims of war and torture, memories of their pains and sufferings are agonizingly fresh, blood-oozing wounds and mutilations branded on their bodies, rape and piracy on the high seas, hunger and thirst in the jungle and the desert, despair and anguish carved into the deep folds of their psyche haunting them on sleepless nights or jerking them awake with screams of terror.

To these migrants and refugees, what does the old black man's eloquent injunction "Always remember where you came from" mean? Perhaps, for black Americans who are urged to forget the horrors of slavery to bring about a color-blind society, and for descendants of white immigrants who are not aware of their roots because of the passage of time or because they are now part of the dominant social group, remembering one's past is an urgent ethical imperative lest forgetfulness of where they came from blunts their sense of solidarity with the new immigrants. But for new arrivals after the 1970s, most of whom are refugees escaping from war and violence, does the old man's advice to remember where they came from not wiggle the knife deeper into their physical and psychological wounds? While it is debatable whether such remembering produces a beneficial or a harmful effect on the migrants' psychological well-being, it may be asked whether it constitutes a *moral* duty for them, and if so, why.

Most treatises on the ethics of immigration have emphasized, and rightly so, the duty of the host country and the local church to welcome the strangers and the migrants into their communities. A quick survey of recent works on the ethics of migration shows that the virtue of hospitality has received the lion's share of scholarly attention, which is unsurprising, given the sacred duty of hospitality in ancient societies and in biblical history. Kristin E. Heyer writes eloquently on "inhospitality to immigrants" as a social sin and "civic kinship and subversive hospitality" as the hallmark of Christian immigration ethics.[1] The Jesuit ethicist William O'Neill draws on biblical texts to offer rich reflections on Christian hospitality and solidarity with the stranger.[2] As can be seen from the title of O'Neill's essay, hospitality toward migrants is often paired with solidarity with them. These twin attitudes are examined in one of the most comprehensive texts on the theology of migration.[3] In one of the earliest texts on the theology of migration in Asia, hospitality is also twinned with solidarity.[4] A recently published book that deals with migration and mission also has a chapter on hospitality to migrants.[5]

Politically, the practice of hospitality has taken, especially in the United States, France, and the United Kingdom, the form of a sanctuary movement that works to provide asylum to refugees who have a reasonable proof of being likely to be subjected to persecution in their own countries on account of one of five protected grounds: race, religion, nationality, political opinion, and social group. Susanna Snyder has written one of the most insightful studies of migration, asylum seeking, and the role of the church.[6] In the same vein, a large number of studies have been produced on the various rights of migrants and their families. This is the most common approach in migration studies,

---

1. See Kristin E. Heyer, *Kinship across Borders: A Christian Ethic of Immigration* (Washington, DC: Georgetown University Press, 2002), esp. chapters 2 and 5.

2. See William O'Neill, "Christian Hospitality and Solidarity with the Stranger," in Donald Kerwin and Jill Marie Gerschutz, eds., *And You Welcomed Me: Migration and Catholic Social Teaching* (Lanham, MD: Rowman & Littlefield, 2009), 149–55.

3. See Daniel G. Groody and Giacchino Campese, eds., *A Promised Land, A Perilous Journey: Theological Perspectives on Migration* (Notre Dame, IN: University of Notre Dame, 2008). The essays that discuss hospitality and solidarity at some length include Donald Senior, "'Beloved Aliens and Exiles': New Testament Perspectives on Migration," 20–34 and Peter C. Phan, "Migration in the Patristic Era: History and Theology," 35–61.

4. See Anthony Rogers, "Globalizing Solidarity through Faith Encounters in Asia," in Fabio Baggio and Agnes M. Brazal, eds., *Faith on the Move: Toward a Theology of Migration in Asia* (Quezon City, Philippines: Ateneo de Manila University Press, 2008), 203–18.

5. See Timothy A. Lenchak, "Israel's Ancestors as *Gerim*: A Lesson of Biblical Hospitality," in vanThanh Nguyen and John M. Prior, eds., *God's People on the Move: Biblical and Global Perspectives on Migration and Mission* (Eugene, OR: Pickwick, 2014), 18–28.

6. See Susanna Snyder, *Asylum-Seeking, Migration and Church* (Burlington, VT: Ashgate, 2012).

and it is adopted not only by Christian scholars but also by secular theorists of migration and political, national, and international organizations.

Presupposing all these reflections on hospitality and related virtues toward the stranger, this chapter takes a somewhat different tack by focusing not on the ethical responsibilities of the citizens and the churches of the host countries but on those of the *migrants* themselves. Of course migrants, and refugees in particular, live in extremely precarious circumstances and need a welcoming home to recover their human dignity and ample assistance to secure their well-being. But they are not, and must not be treated as, objects of charity. They are primarily agents charged with moral responsibilities. Among the latter, I would argue, is the duty of *remembering*. In what follows I first explain *why* migrants should remember "where they came from," to cite the old man's solemn injunction. Next, I discuss *what* they as migrants should remember of their pasts. Lastly, I examine *how* migrants should remember their past for the sake of the host country, the receiving church, and the migrants themselves.

"WHERE YOU CAME FROM": *WHY* SHOULD MIGRANTS REMEMBER?

At first sight it seems counterintuitive that migrants ought to remember "where they came from." For most migrants, especially those who voluntarily leave their own countries in search of better economic opportunities for themselves and their families, and those who have done well in their adopted countries, "home" is at worst a place plagued by poverty and backwardness, at best a destination for occasional, nostalgic visits, but not a place to remember with pleasure, much less their final resting place. The primary concern of these voluntary migrants is to blend into the so-called melting-pot as quickly and as effectively as possible so as to guarantee acceptance into the new society and professional success. To urge them to remember where they came from sounds like a tasteless joke. This is true particularly of their children, the one-and-a-half and second generations, who most often know next to nothing of their parents' country of origin, its history, language, and culture. If ever the migrants' descendants embark on a journey of discovery of their family roots, it would often take the form of academic research; or if they happen to travel to their ancestors' homeland, the trip is more an imaginative reconstruction of what their migrant parents would have gone through than an actual journey down memory lane.

By contrast, people who are forced to flee their native countries for physical safety, most of whom do not possess the necessary skills to succeed economically and socially in the new countries, tend to remember their homelands and their former lives there with fondness and longing. Unfortunately, however, because of the extremely painful circumstances that force them to emigrate, often with as much of their material possessions as they literally can carry, and because their flights to safety and freedom are invariably filled with anguish and tragedies, refugees are psychologically conditioned to suppress their memories of their escape. If they remember their former lives at all, their memory is tinged with sadness and nostalgia, and when doing so, their memory is distorted by exaggerating the quality of their standard of living in the old country in contrast to the lowly one they now have.

Because of real or perceived heavy losses, not rarely including the deaths of family members and friends, refugees often succumb to feelings of bitterness and hatred toward the people whom they deem responsible for their losses and current condition. They do not adapt easily to the culture of the host country, remaining permanent foreigners living in a foreign land. They endlessly plot— mostly in grandiose rhetoric—a revolution against or an overthrow of the— illegitimate in their eyes—government that has caused their exile and robbed them of their freedom, and dream of an eventual return to the old country and of being buried there. This has happened to many of my fellow Vietnamese refugees—including my parents—who fled to the United States after the Communist takeover of South Vietnam in 1975. To these refugees, the injunction to remember where they came from—especially if by this expression is meant the inhuman circumstances forcing their migration—is tantamount to asking them to descend to hell once again. Thus, to voluntary migrants, this mandate sounds like a tasteless joke; to forced migrants and refugees, a cruel one.

Why, then, ought migrants to remember where they came from, and indeed, what are the things they must keep in their memory that are subsumed under the expression "where they came from"? We will return to the second question below. As for the first question, the most direct and peremptory answer is that this is a *divine command*. Again and again, Yahweh enjoins the Israelites to remember where they came from: "You shall not wrong or oppress a resident alien, *for you were aliens in the land of Egypt*" (Exod 22:21). Again: "You shall not oppress a resident alien; you know the heart of an alien, *for you were aliens in the land of Egypt*" (Exod 23:9). Again: "When an alien resides with you in your land, you shall not oppress the alien. The alien who resides with you shall be to you as the citizen among you; you shall love the alien as yourself, *for you were alien in the land of Egypt*" (Lev 19:33–34).[7] The italicized words occur like a refrain throughout the Hebrew scriptures and serve as the ethical foundation for Israel's various duties to the strangers and aliens among them.

It is true that these words are addressed not to migrants as such but to *former* migrants who have settled in the new land and are now citizens. But

---

7. English translations of the Bible are taken from the New Revised Standard Version.

arguably the command, "Remember where you came from," applies to both since most often migrants, both voluntary and forced, eventually become citizens. If anything, the obligation is even more stringent for erstwhile migrants, as they are more tempted to forget their past now that they enjoy all the privileges accruing to them as successful citizens. Furthermore, the Israelites-now-citizens may be psychologically inclined to erase their experiences as aliens and slaves in Egypt because they were painful, experiences that Yahweh does not fail to recall to their memory: "I have observed the misery of my people in Egypt. I have heard their cry on account of their taskmasters. Indeed, I know their sufferings" (Exod 3:7).

Indeed, it is this memory of past sufferings associated with migration that grounds ethical behavior toward migrants. Yahweh reminds the Israelites that they have a connatural empathy with migrants because "you know the heart of an alien." But how can one know the depths of "the heart of an alien" if one does not nurture in one's own heart the memory of oneself as a migrant? It takes one to know one, as the saying goes. Without this memory of oneself as migrant, how can one identify oneself with other migrants and fulfill the Lord's command: "You shall love the alien as yourself"? "Yourself" here is a migrant/alien, not a citizen, or a generic human being. It is oneself as *migrant* that is the measure of one's love toward other migrants, even if legally one is now no longer a migrant. Perhaps the divine command may be paraphrased as "You shall love the migrant in the measure in which you love yourself *as a migrant.*" In other words, being migrant is a *permanent* identity and not a phase of life that can eventually be shed as one acquires a better social status. And it can become permanent—an "indelible character"—to use an expression of Catholic sacramental theology—imprinted in the "heart" only if one always and constantly remembers where one came from.

There are thus at least two fundamental reasons why migrants ought to remember where they came from. First, *theological*: to proclaim the great works of God (the *magnalia Dei*) and to rejoice and give thanks to God for the deeds God has done for all migrants—to quote Mary's words in her *Magnificat*: "My soul magnifies the Lord and my spirit rejoices in God my Savior . . . for the Mighty One has done great things for me" (Luke 1:4–47, 49). Of these mighty deeds Yahweh himself reminds the Israelites before making a covenant with them: "You have seen what I did to the Egyptians, and how I bore you on eagles' wings and brought you to myself" (Exod 19:4). The God of the Hebrews, the God of Abraham, Isaac, and Jacob, is a God who loves and accompanies the migrants with mighty deeds: God is a migrant God (*Deus Migrator*).[8] To remember having been a migrant, then, is an act of *imitatio Dei*,

---

8. For a rearticulation of Christian beliefs in terms of migration, see Peter C. Phan, "*Deus Migrator*—God the Migrant: Migration of Theology and Theology of Migration," *Theological Studies* 77, no. 4 (2016): 845–68.

and to act justly and lovingly toward migrants is nothing less than an act of liturgical worship, glorifying, praising, and thanking God for God's mighty deeds, carrying on God's wings the ancient "aliens in Egypt" and migrants of all times and in all places.

Second, *ethical*: to do for migrants what God has done for them. There is an intrinsic and indissoluble connection between the theological and the ethical reasons. Note the conjunction "for" in the words that follow the command to love the migrants: "*for* you were aliens in the land of Egypt." The reason why we must not wrong and oppress migrants is *because* we were, or, more precisely, *are* migrants. The underlying ethical reasoning seems to be as follows: First, being a migrant enables one to know "the heart of a migrant"; second, knowledge of the migrant's heart is cultivated by remembering one's own personal experience of being a migrant; and third, remembering one's past as a migrant provides the ethical grounding for one's just and loving treatment of migrants. Remembering "where one came from" is therefore a moral imperative in the ethics of migration.

"WHERE YOU CAME FROM": *WHAT* MUST MIGRANTS REMEMBER?

Granted the moral imperative for migrants to remember where they came from, what exactly does "where they came from" stand for? How much of it should be remembered, or forgotten? Is migration memory always selective? If so, what is the principle of selection? It is common knowledge that we remember clearly things that bring us joy and pleasure; today, thanks to ubiquitous digital cameras we can record them and email photos to friends so that they too can share in these happy moments simultaneously, in real time. It is also a well-known fact that we easily remember life-changing events, be they happy such as marriage and the birth of our children, or painful and tragic such as divorce and the death of our loved ones, even though in the latter case we may try, albeit rarely with success, to erase them from our memory because they bring renewed pains and sufferings when remembered. Be that as it may, memories, remembered as well as suppressed, are the stuff that makes us who we are—our ever-shifting identity—just as imagination, which lives on hope, is the construction site of our final destiny.

Migrants, like everyone else, remember and forget things that are pleasurable as well as things that are painful, and, like everyone else, they tend to suppress the latter, especially those surrounding their flights from their countries. Thus, "where they came from" is not an objective collection of fixed facts and events of their past but a highly selective medley of memories, some embellished, others diminished, some real, others imagined, that make up the psychological and spiritual blocks with which migrants rebuild their lives in the new country. Notwithstanding this amalgamative and partial character of their memories, there are certain realities of where they came from that migrants ought, and indeed should be encouraged and empowered, to preserve and promote in order to maintain their self-identity and bring their own contributions to the common good of their host country.

The first thing of "where they came from" that migrants must remember is, of course, their culture and all the things that go under this broad umbrella term. While it is important for migrants to learn the local language and to familiarize themselves with the history and cultural traditions of the host society in order to be able to fulfill the duties of citizenship responsibly, it is their right as well as their duty to preserve and promote their own language, cultural traditions, and values, and to transmit them to their children. Happily, today, at least in the United States, this cultural right is by and large respected, in the educational system as well as in the society at large, as the melting-pot paradigm of cultural assimilation has been abandoned in favor of multiculturalism. In general, there is a deep and genuine appreciation for and promotion of cultural diversity, especially in countries with a large presence of migrants. There are, of course, pockets of political resistance and cultural chauvinism, but efforts at imposing a national language and a homogeneous culture are doomed to failure. The reason for this is that migrants' constant connection with their countries of origin is greatly facilitated by the omnipresent reality of globalization, the widespread use of social media, the rampant accessibility of the Internet, and the ease of international travel. Geographically, "where they came from" can be brought close to migrants with a click of the mouse; culturally, ethnic foods, music, entertainment media, fashion, and newspapers and magazines are available around the corner.

Sadly, however, migrants, and especially their children, are sometimes embarrassed by their cultural customs and practices. In the new country these may appear as quaint, old-fashioned, and even superstitious, subject to misunderstanding and ridicule by their new, modern neighbors; and in a misguided effort at shedding their ethnic background, migrants are tempted to jettison their age-old and rich cultural heritage. Furthermore, migrants may be prevented from celebrating their native customs and feasts by their work schedules and calendar differences (for example, the lunar New Year's Day celebrations). In view of this very real danger of forgetting where they came from, it is all the more imperative for migrants to find ways to remember and celebrate their cultural traditions in the new country.

Another part of "where they came from" is the migrants' religious heritage. Unlike earlier immigrants from Europe, migrants to the United States since the 1960s bring with them their own, non-Christian religious traditions—typically, Hinduism, Buddhism, Sikhism, and Confucianism from Asia and

Islam from Africa and the Middle East—and are not willing to renounce their faiths and convert to Christianity, and in the process are turning America into the most religiously diverse country on earth, to quote the title of Diana Eck's popular book.[9] Migrants to European countries such as Britain, France, and Germany bring with them Islam, and their religious practice is consistently more vibrant than that of Christians of mainline churches. Of course, for migrants remaining faithful to their non-Christian religions in the new country is challenging. They are under heavy pressure to convert to Christianity, not only from proselytizing Christians but also from life in the pervasive albeit nominal Christian society with its Christian calendar and festivals (for example, Christmas and Easter) and interfaith marriages.

Fortunately, with the proliferation of non-Christian places of worship and religious organizations, non-Christian migrants in the West (though, unfortunately, less so for Christian migrants in non-Christian countries) can continue to practice and propagate their religions. This growing and increasingly vocal presence of non-Christian migrants in the heartlands of Western Christianity constitutes a formidable challenge to hitherto dominant Christianity. It is here that migrants can make an important contribution to the religious life of their adopted countries, but only on condition that they do not forget their own non-Christian religious faiths. The coexistence of many diverse, at times conflictive, religious traditions makes interreligious dialogue both a real possibility and an urgent need, with enormous benefits to not only the migrants and their new fellow religious believers in the host countries but also to the religious communities in their home countries, where religiously inspired wars and violence have often caused their migration in the first place.

A third element of the migrants' past that must be remembered is their own brand of Christianity. Again, as they participate in the life of Western Christian churches, migrants are unavoidably shaped by their worship styles, spiritual practices, and organizational structures, which are often governed by result-oriented efficiency, streamlined bureaucracy, financial solvency, and legal protection. These concerns are, of course, legitimate and even necessary to assure a smooth functioning of church activities in a complex society. However, the dark side of all this is that Christian "communities" tend to operate like corporations and not like the "family of God."[10] It is here that Christian

---

9. See Diana Eck, *A New Religious America: How a "Christian Country" Has Now Become the Most Religiously Diverse Nation on Earth* (San Francisco: HarperSan Francisco, 2001). See also Robert Wuthnow, *America and the Challenges of Religious Diversity* (Princeton, NJ: Princeton University Press, 2005).

10. The image of "family/household of God" is used in the New Testament to refer to the church (see, for instance, 1 Tim 3:15). Though this image can be misused to justify patriarchalism and androcentrism, as has often been done in the Christian tradition, it can also convey intimacy and mutuality.

migrants from the so-called Third World can bring to the Western churches their experiences of local churches as neighborhood communities or *comuni-dades de base*, where lay leadership, popular devotions, shared prayer, group solidarity, and personal friendship play a large role in church life. It is a fact, albeit not yet widely acknowledged, that the presence of Catholic migrants has "rescued" many dioceses in the West, especially in the United States, with their numerous priestly and religious vocations, and revitalized parishes with their regular church attendance and generous financial contributions. It is also a fact, similarly not yet widely recognized, that migrants have transformed the membership, organization, and spiritual life of Christian churches in Asia such as those of Japan, Taiwan, Hong Kong, and South Korea.

Finally, for migrants, part of "where they came from" that must be remembered and even publicly honored includes their individual and unique experiences of migration. Of course, these experiences are extremely diverse: migration experiences of voluntary migrants are very different from those of refugees. Voluntary migrants do not normally incur economic loss and physical pain; still they may suffer cultural shock, discrimination, separation from their families, and loneliness. Forced migrants and refugees, by contrast, in addition to the above-mentioned pains, are always subjected to traumatic and life-shattering sufferings. More than other migrants, they are psychologically conditioned to erase from their memory their migration experiences. Though this erasure may sometimes be necessary for their psychological well-being, total forgetfulness will not only be detrimental to their spiritual development but also will deprive them from making one of the most precious contributions to the ethics of migration. Without this memory it is impossible to form "the heart of an alien," which is the deepest source and motivation for ethical behavior toward migrants, as Yahweh's command makes it clear: "You shall not oppress a resident alien; *you know the heart of an alien*, for you were aliens in the land of Egypt" (Exod 23:9; italics added). Consequently, these memories of migration should be recorded, preserved in museums and archives, and celebrated in literature, art, and liturgical celebrations.

If an effective ethics of migration is to be developed, it must not only be based on the abstract principles of human rights and justice but also bathed in the blood and tears, the hunger and thirst, the griefs and pains, the tortures and, yes, the deaths of so many migrants on their way to freedom. Perhaps this is "the where they came from" that runs the greatest risk of being erased and forgotten not only by the migrants but also by the now-citizens whose migrant roots have dried up and withered and whose memories of their ancestors' migration have been lost forever in the mists of the past. If we want an ethics of migration that will propel both citizens and migrants to act justly and lovingly toward strangers and aliens in our midst, we must practice the old black man's injunction: "Always remember where you came from."

"WHERE YOU CAME FROM":
HOW MUST MIGRANTS REMEMBER?

Just as there are many "whys" and many "whats" to remember, there are also different ways to remember. *How* must migrants remember where they came from, especially the pains and sufferings inflicted upon them by their political enemies who caused their exile? In recent literature on the spirituality of peacemaking and reconciliation, there is an emphasis not on to "forgive and forget" past acts of injustice and violence but on opening up the space for the victim's journey toward God, his or her enemies, and the self. This spirituality goes beyond the strategies and methodologies of conflict resolution and applies to reconciliation between both individuals and among groups and nations. Individual reconciliation occurs when two persons, the offender and the victim, are brought together to a new place, the former recognizing his or her guilt, and the latter having his or her dignity restored and forgiving the oppressor. The same dynamic applies, analogously, between groups and nations. In this spirituality of reconciliation and peacebuilding an important role is given to memory and remembering, and I would like to make use of some of the insights, especially those developed by Miroslav Volf, to answer the question of how migrants should remember where they came from. In his *Exclusion and Embrace*, Volf deals with the challenges of reconciliation in contexts of persisting enmity in which the dividing line between victims and perpetrators is thin and in which today's victims can become tomorrow's perpetrators.[11] "Embrace," a spiritual attitude toward the oppressor, is marked by two key stances: acting with generosity toward the perpetrator of injustice and maintaining flexible identities with porous boundaries. "Embrace," which is made possible by God's grace, does not negate the necessity of justice. Rather, it includes justice as a dimension of grace extended toward wrongdoers. Nor is "embrace" opposed to boundary maintenance. On the contrary, it assumes the necessity of establishing and maintaining the self's boundaries but enables these boundaries to remain porous so that the self, while not being obliterated, can journey with others in reconciliation and mutual enrichment.

As a model of "embrace" Volf cites the father's attitude toward his son in the so-called parable of the Prodigal Son in which the father forgives his son and accepts his new identity as "the-father-of-the-prodigal-son." For Volf, however, the supreme exemplar of "embrace" is Christ's action in his death as an "inclusive substitute" for the ungodly. On the cross, Christ forgives and opens his arms to embrace sinners, thus creating a space for them in God. For Volf, "embrace" is ultimately rooted in God's unconditional love and in God's trinitarian nature in which there is the mutual indwelling of the three divine

---

11. Miroslav Volf, *Exclusion and Embrace: A Theological Exploration of Identity, Otherness, and Reconciliation* (Nashville, TN: Abingdon Press, 1996).

persons whose identity boundaries are therefore reciprocally porous. Further-more, Volf points out that total "embrace" will be achieved only eschatologi-cally, at the "Last Judgment," which he interprets as the final reconciliation between God and humanity, in which judgment is not eliminated but is an indispensable element of reconciliation.

One of the central concerns of *Exclusion and Embrace*, which is of great relevance to our question of how migrants should remember where they came from, is truth telling in the context of enmity and conflict, especially truth telling about the past, a theme that Volf explores in much greater depth in his later work *The End of Memory: Remembering Rightly in a Violent World*.[12] There is an intended paradox between the title and the subtitle of the book. Volf wants to put an end to one kind of memory and suggests the practice of another, and the operative word is *"rightly."* The question is not *whether* to remember but *how*. One does, of course, forget things but not things that leave an indelible mark upon one's body or psyche or soul. One cannot not remem-ber them, but *how* must they be remembered?

The book was sparked by an event in the author's life in 1984 when as a conscript in the army of the then-Communist Yugoslavia, he was considered a security threat simply because he was a son of a pastor, had studied theology abroad, and had an American wife. He was spied on by his comrades and was subjected to interrogations, though not physical torture, especially by a cap-tain, a certain G. The question that kept haunting Volf after he was freed was how he should remember this abuse, especially Captain G. himself, not with hatred and a desire for vengeance but out of fidelity to Jesus and his God who command us to forgive and love our enemies. The topic of the book then is *"the memory of wrongdoing suffered by a person who desires neither to hate nor to disregard but to love the wrongdoer."*[13] Note that the required task is not simply to forgive the victimizer but to love him or her. The problem then becomes: Once remembering of the injury is rooted in the decision to forgive and love the injurer, how to remember the wrongdoing *rightly?* For Volf, remember-ing the wrongdoing rightly involves remembering it and its implications with regard to three realities: the injured, the community out of which the injury arose and to which it may be applied, and the perpetrator himself or herself.

Volf structures his argument along three basic questions that make up the three parts of his book: what is involved in remembering past wrongs; how should we remember; and how long should we remember. With regard to the first question, Volf reminds us that memory of wrongs suffered is a Janus-faced organ: as a "shield," it can help form our identity, bring about healing, produce justice by acknowledging the reality of wrongs, link us with other

---

12. Miroslav Volf, *The End of Memory: Remembering Rightly in a Violent World* (Grand Rapids, MI: Eerdmans, 2006).

13. Ibid., 9.

victims, and protect victims from further violence. Sadly, as a "sword," it can also wound, breed indifference, reinforce false self-perceptions, and re-injure.

This leads to the question of *how* we as *Christians* should remember. Volf suggests a triple remembering: "remember truthfully," "remember so as to be healed," and "remember so as to learn."[14] In this way, Volf argues, we remember not simply as individuals but also as members of a community that can teach us to remember rightly, that is, "remembering that is truthful and just, that heals individuals without injuring others, that allows the past to motivate a just struggle for justice and the grace-filled work of reconciliation."[15]

But *how long* should we remember? With the help of Freud, Nietzsche, and Kierkegaard, Volf argues for the possibility of a healthy forgetting or non-remembering. He goes further in asserting that "memories of suffered wrongs will not come to the minds of the citizens of the world to come, for in it they will perfectly enjoy God and one another in God."[16] Note the important point Volf is making: In heaven, "we will not forget so as to be able to rejoice; we will rejoice and *therefore* let those memories slip out of our minds."[17] Thus, the "end" of memory of which the book speaks is both its *termination* (since we should not remember forever) and its *goal* or *telos*, that is, "the formation of the communion of love between all people, including victims and perpetrators."[18] To conclude, I will expand Volf's threefold remembering to find an answer to the question of how migrants should remember where they came from.

Remembering Truthfully

As alluded to above, migrants tend to remember their past tendentiously, either exaggerating their pains and sufferings, or erasing the most traumatic ones of them, or embellishing their former lives in the old country. However, in order for them to regain their human dignity, migrants must remember where they came from truthfully. This truthful remembering, which corresponds to Volf's "Remember truthfully," has three aspects: first, establishing the facts of abuses against oneself; second, disclosing the structures of lying and the patterns of violence of the oppressive regime; and third, making public the history of abuses through reports and honoring the memories of the victims.[19] This knowing the truth is absolutely essential for achieving real

---

14. See Miroslav Volf, "Memory of Reconciliation—Reconciliation of Memory," *Proceedings of the Fifty-Ninth Annual Convention*. The Catholic Theological Society of America 59 (2004), 1.

15. Ibid., 128.

16. Ibid., 177.

17. Ibid., 214.

18. Ibid., 232.

19. This truth-finding about human-rights violations was one of the three tasks assigned to the Truth and Reconciliation Commission in South Africa, the other two being determining

reconciliation since, as Robert Schreiter has convincingly shown, systematic violence is built upon "a narrative of the lie" intended to destroy and replace the truths that provide the victims with a sense of self-identity and security.[20] This truth seeking is not only necessary for the possibility of closure for the survivors and the relatives of the victims but also establishes a pattern of truthfulness on which a new moral order can be built.

Remembering Justly

Knowing the truth, however, does not necessarily lead to the migrant's reconciliation with those who inflict pain and suffering on them. Indeed, it may lead to revenge, hatred, and retribution. To achieve reconciliation, knowing the truth must be followed by doing justice. Without justice, reconciliation is immoral. But what kind of justice? Certainly, not simply punitive justice whereby the wrongdoers are apprehended, tried, convicted, and punished. Punitive justice must also be corrective, providing the wrongdoers with an opportunity for moral conversion; otherwise, punitive justice is not very different from revenge.

There are, however, three other levels of justice, as Schreiter has pointed out, that need to be attended to. First, restitutional or restorative justice, which seeks to make amends by providing reparation or restitution for the victims. In this sense, migrants, and specially refugees, have the right to recover what they have lost. Even though reparation can only ease and not erase the damages and the pains inflicted on the victims (the dead cannot be brought back to life, health cannot be restored, and the lost years cannot be recovered!), nevertheless it is a necessary and important symbol for the recovery of the dignity of the victims. Second, there is structural justice by which inequalities in the society are removed. Third, there is legal justice by which a just and equitable legal system is established and the rule of law maintained.[21] In these two levels of justice, migrants can play an important role by making use of all the means at their disposal in their new countries, including political organizations and economic pressure.

Remembering Forgivingly

The third and, by common agreement, the hardest part of reconciliation, is forgiveness. This "remembering forgivingly" corresponds to Volf's "Remem-

---

reparations for the victims of gross human-rights violations and granting amnesty to perpetrators of human-rights abuses who have made a full and frank disclosure of their misdeeds.

20. See Robert Schreiter, *Reconciliation: Mission and Ministry in a Changing Social Order* (Maryknoll, NY: Orbis Books, 1992), 34–36.

21. See Robert Schreiter, *The Ministry of Reconciliation: Spirituality & Strategies* (Maryknoll, NY: Orbis Books, 1998), 122–23.

ber so as to be healed." One reason why forgiveness is hard is that at first sight it appears to require forgetting the violent deeds suffered, as the common adage "forgive and forget" seems to indicate. But, of course, most victims of physical torture and political repression find it impossible to forget their wounds as these are indelibly burnt into their flesh and their psyche, and consequently feel that forgiveness is beyond their power. To forgive seems to imply betraying the past, especially the dead. Here it is useful to note that rather than "forgive and forget," we should "remember and forgive."[22] Or, as Schreiter puts it, "*in forgiving, we do not forget; we remember in a different way.*"[23] It is possible to remember *in a different way* because in forgiving the balance of power has shifted from the oppressor to the victim: it is the victim, and the victim alone, who has the power to forgive. In forgiving, the victim breaks loose of the oppressor's hold, becomes free of the power of the past, and is able to live by a story other than that of fear and suffering.

There is another reason why forgiveness is hard. Normally, a condition for forgiveness is the offender's acknowledgment of guilt, repentance, and asking forgiveness from the victims. But it is a rare oppressor who sincerely does these things, not even when confronted with his or her evil deeds. More often than not, wrongdoers shamelessly deny any responsibility or flee to another country and there enjoy a comfortable life off their ill-gotten wealth, while their victims are left with a greater sense of injustice. It is here that human forgiveness takes on the characteristics of divine forgiveness. According to the Christian faith, God forgives humans not because of but *prior* to their repentance, out of God's gratuitous love and mercy. It is God's forgiveness that leads the sinner to repentance and not vice versa. Repentance is not the condition but the *fruit* of God's forgiveness. In imitation of God's gratuitous mercy and love, and by God's grace and power, the victims forgive their torturers and oppressors *prior* to and not as a consequence of their repentance and asking for forgiveness, with the hope that this forgiveness will lead them to repentance and change. Like God's forgiveness, the victim's forgiveness has a gift-like and miraculous quality. Ultimately, it is this gratuitous forgiveness—beyond truth and justice—that makes real reconciliation between abusers and victims possible. Only then the legal and social processes of amnesty and pardon can be put into action.[24]

---

22. See Donald W. Shriver, *An Ethic for Enemies: Forgiveness in Politics* (New York: Oxford University Press, 1995), 6–9.

23. Schreiter, *Ministry of Reconciliation*, 66.

24. On amnesty and pardon in the process of reconciliation, see Schreiter, *Ministry of Reconciliation*, 124–26; R. Scott Appleby, *The Ambivalence of the Sacred: Religion, Violence, and Restitution* (Lanham, MD: Rowman & Littlefield, 2000), 167–204; and William Bole, Drew Christiansen, and Robert Hennemeyer, *Forgiveness in International Politics: An Alternative Road to Peace* (Washington, DC: United States Conference of Catholic Bishops, 2004).

Remembering Constructively

The ultimate goal of truth finding, restoring justice, and forgiveness is to build a society in which all citizens can live in freedom, equality, and harmony, and in which, at the minimum, abuses of human rights will not occur again. This task of social reconstruction corresponds to Volf's "Remember so as to learn." Such praxis for change requires establishing structural justice through various social reforms and legal justice through the reform of law and the judiciary. Moreover, there is the need of a democratic system of government in which all citizens can exercise their civil rights and duties. There is a need as well of an economic system in which all have an equal opportunity at earning a living wage and in which the basic needs of the poor and the weak are provided for. Last but not least, the cultural and religious dimensions of human life must also be nurtured and developed through education, the mass media, and other means, so that the whole person, and not only certain dimensions of it, can achieve full flourishing. Perhaps the contribution of migrants to this fourth aspect of remembering is often indirect but no less effective, by means of individual and collective activities to promote justice, peace, education, social services, and economic development during their diaspora. Their role, of course, is vastly expanded if they, or their descendants, can one day return to their old countries to take part in the reconstruction of their homeland.

"Always remember where you came from!" The old black man's words continue to reverberate down the corridors of the history of migrations—old and new. Unless migrants understand *why* they must remember their past, *what* of this past they must remember, and *how* they should remember it, they will fail to meet the challenges and forfeit the unique opportunities the *Deus Migrator* has given them.

16

Pope Francis's *Laudato Si'* and Ecological Theology

Call to Action for the Catholic Church in Asia

Though this chapter was written several months prior to the November 8, 2016, American presidential election, its opportuneness and urgency, sadly, are dramatically increased by the elevation of Donald Trump as president of the United States of America. Widely denounced for his xenophobic, racist, bigoted, and narcissistic attitude, his shameless boasting about his ability to grab female genitalia at will, and his total lack of political experience, Trump is also castigated for his denial of global warming. Unencumbered by scientific data, he blithely dismisses global warming as a hoax perpetrated by the Chinese government to harm American economic interests. During his campaign Trump repeatedly promised to cancel U.S. participation in the Paris climate agreement that had been negotiated in late 2015 by nearly two hundred countries to reduce greenhouse gas emissions in an effort to reverse the ecological damage, a promise he has since carried out.

In the last presidential election American Catholics made up 23 percent of the electorate. Fifty-two percent of Catholic voters, 60 percent of white Catholic voters, and 56 percent of Catholics who go to church regularly reportedly cast their votes for Trump, a fact that the hierarchy of the American Catholic Church must not conveniently erase from their conscience when issuing solemn declarations about moral norms and Christian behavior. Apparently, Pope Francis's vigorous appeal to save the environment fell on deaf ears as a majority of American Catholics entered the voting booths. There might have been many reasons for Catholics, especially white working-class Catholic males, to choose Trump over Hillary Clinton, but perhaps the most important one was the hope for the appointment of conservative judges to the Supreme Court to overturn abortion-legalizing *Roe v. Wade*. For them, anti-abortion concerns trumped (no pun intended!) urgent care for the environment. Ironically, with the destruction of Earth there is no possibility of a healthy life, and even survival, for the babies that may have been saved by an anti-abortion decision of the Supreme Court!

Pope Francis's *Laudato Si': On Care for Our Common Home* (*LS*) is the first encyclical devoted exclusively to the issue of ecology. In its opening paragraphs (nos. 3–6) Francis recalls the teaching of his predecessors John XXIII, Paul VI, and Benedict XVI on the moral obligation to safeguard the environment. However, all of their statements on ecology are *obiter dicta*, and none of the earlier documents of Catholic social teaching offers a sustained treatment of the subject.[1] In a sense *LS* encapsulates the twin foci of Francis's pontificate, which are implied in his choice of "Francis" as his name. Three days after his election to the papacy on March 13, 2013, he explained the reason for his choice: "Francis was a man of poverty, who loved and protected creation." Protection of the environment and love for the poor are the two basic themes of the encyclical, and they are strictly intertwined since, as the pope insists, it is the poor who suffer the most from ecological destruction: "The deterioration of the environment and of society affects the most vulnerable people on the planet" (no. 21). The encyclical is an urgent clarion call to the whole world to heed the cry of the poor and the cry of the devastated Sister Earth that, in Francis's arresting description, "is beginning to look more and more like an immense pile of filth" (no. 21).

It is still too early to tell, but all the signs seem to indicate that *LS* is fated to meet with the same fierce opposition as Pope Paul VI's *Humanae Vitae*, which condemns "artificial contraception." The difference is that this time opposition comes from the opposite side of the ideological spectrum, that is, conservatives, especially in the United States, who believe that global warming is a scientific hoax perpetrated by anticapitalistic ultraleftists to destroy profitable fossil-fuel industries and to curb the globalization of the Western technocratic paradigm of production and consumption.[2]

Of course, deniers of climate change in opulent countries of the First World can easily avoid its deleterious effects on their health and environment by having multinational corporations export ecologically polluting industries to Third-World or Majority-World countries, where they can operate cheaply and unencumbered by the legal constraints that are imposed in their own developed countries. In the process, they damage the environment, as *LS* notes, "leaving behind great human and environmental liabilities, such as

---

1. Pope Francis, *Laudato Si': On Care for Our Common Home*, with Commentary by Sean McDonagh (Maryknoll, NY: Orbis Books, 2016, henceforth *LS*). Of special note is John Paul II's World Day of Peace Message *Peace with God the Creator, Peace with All Creation* (January, 1, 1990).

2. Prominent among opponents of the encyclical are the leading figures of the U.S. Republican Party, such as veteran climate change deniers James Inhofe and Rick Santorum, and the leaders of fossil-fuel industries such as Arch Coal.

unemployment, abandoned towns, the depletion of natural reserves, deforestation, the impoverishment of agriculture and local stock breeding, open pits, riven hills, polluted rivers and a handful of social works that are no longer sustainable" (no. 51).

The intent of this chapter is not to summarize and evaluate the encyclical as a whole, which is unnecessary, as there are already a good number of studies, both popular and scholarly, that offer a summary and a critical analysis of it.[3] Rather my task is to read *LS* with Asian eyes, from the Asian perspective, and this I will do by raising three questions. First, which ideas of the encyclical would hold the greatest interest and thus have the greatest relevance for Asians? Second, are there any aspects of the teaching of the encyclical that would be enriched by incorporating the teachings of the Asian Catholic Church and insights from the philosophical and religious traditions of Asia? And third, which most urgent remaining ecological issues still need to be addressed?

LAUDATO SI': AN ENCYCLICAL FOR ASIA?

In a broad sense the question of whether the encyclical is directed to the people of Asia, irrespective of religious faith, should be responded affirmatively since Pope Francis addresses not only Catholics and other Christians but also the whole of humanity since "the environmental challenge we are undergoing, and its human roots, concern and affect us all" and since "all of us can cooperate as instruments of God for the care of creation, each according to his or her own culture, experience, involvements and talents" (no. 15). But there is a special sense in which the people of Asia will find *LS* to be of particular relevance in light of both its teachings on environmental protection and the ecological situation of their continent.

It is interesting to note that there is in Asia no leading politician or prominent business leader who would deny the reality of climate change and ecological destruction. All it takes for them to dispel any thought of climate change as a scientific and political hoax is to step outside their office into the street in any Asian metropolis; they would be choked by smoke-filled air, assaulted by

---

3. See, for example, Donal Dorr, *Option for the Poor & for the Earth: From Leo XIII to Pope Francis* (Maryknoll, NY: Orbis Books, 2016); John Fleming & John Ozolins, *Laudato Si': A Critique* (Redland Bay, QLD: Conner Court Publications, 2016); Elizabeth-Anne Stewart, *Preaching and Teaching Laudato Si': On Care for Our Common Home* (Amazon Digital Services, 2016); Kevin Irwin, *A Commentary on Laudato Si': Examining the Background, Contributions, Implementation, and Future of Pope Francis's Encyclical* (Mahwah, NJ: Paulist Press, 2016); Nellie McLaughlin, *Life's Delicate Balance: Our Common Home and Laudato Si'* (Dublin: Veritas Publications, 2016); Anthony Kelly, *Laudato Si'* (Adelaide, SA: ATF Press, 2016).

the acrid smell, contaminated by disease-bearing water, and overwhelmed by scorching heat. In calling for environmental protection in Asia Francis is thus preaching to the choir, but the scientific information he provides on global warming (chapter 1) is no less useful, his discussion of the "human roots of the ecological crisis" (chapter 3) no less enlightening, his message about "integral ecology" (chapter 4) no less apposite, and his call for "ecological conversion" and "ecological education and spirituality" (chapter 6) no less urgent, given the fact that in all the areas in which human life is adversely affected by ecological degradation Asia (along with Africa) is the most vulnerable continent.

Unfortunately, because of their lack of scientific education, many Asians—like most people in the Majority World—are not intellectually equipped to understand *why* climate change and its attendant ecological catastrophes occur. They tend to view natural disasters—floods, typhoons, hurricanes, drought, torrential and prolonged rains, ice storms, heat waves, and other weather-related excessive phenomena—as unavoidable natural cycles, or worse, to accept apocalyptic interpretations of them as God's punishments for human sins. Thus, they are unable to see, as Pope Francis puts it, "the human roots of the ecological crisis" and that "a certain way of understanding human life and activity has gone awry, to the serious detriment of the world around us" (no. 101). As a consequence, they fail to acknowledge their own responsibility for ecological destruction and for taking up the task of protecting the environment.

By presenting a scientifically accurate and yet highly accessible explanation of how climate change results from human activities (chapter 1) *LS* makes a great contribution—normally not expected of a religious document—to the diffusion of the much-needed understanding of the *causal connection* between the release of greenhouse gases (carbon dioxide, methane, nitrogen oxides, and others) into the atmosphere, the depletion of the ozone layer, global warming, the melting of the polar ice, the rise of the sea level on the one hand and human activities such as the burning of fossil fuel (coal, petroleum, and gas), deforestation, the dumping of industrial and nuclear waste and chemical products, and the increasing use of fertilizers, insecticides, fungicides, herbicides and agrotoxins on the other.

Unless this causal connection between global warming and human activities is clearly understood and acknowledged, communal efforts "to resolve the tragic effects of environmental degradation on the lives of the world's poorest" (no. 13) in "a new and universal solidarity" (no. 14) would be impossible. For Catholics, especially those who do not possess the requisite scientific knowledge—in fact, a majority of Asian Catholics—to verify for themselves the fact of global warming, especially over against the denial of it by powerful interest groups, the affirmation by the highest teaching authority of the church that "our common home is falling into serious disrepair" (no. 61) serves as a rich and helpful source of information and an incentive for concerted action to promote an "*integral ecology*" (no. 137).

Thanks to Pope Francis's clarion call "to hear *both the cry of the earth and the cry of the poor*" (no. 49), we are now encouraged to pay attention to the catastrophic impact of global warming and climate change on the Asian poor, especially in three areas. First, loss of safe habitable land. It was recently reported that 35 million people who live in the delta area of Bangladesh would be displaced and lose their livelihood if the global sea levels rise by one meter (3.3 feet).

Second, lack of access to fresh water and the pollution of water. While 97.5 percent of Earth's water is found in its oceans, only 3 percent is fresh water. During the twentieth century, due to the threefold increase of the human population, industrialization, and irrigation of agriculture, water consumption jumped sevenfold; and it is predicted that by 2025, two-thirds of the world's population will experience water shortages. Sixty percent of the world's population live in Asia, yet only 36 percent of the world's fresh water is available to them, and water scarcity drives up its price for the poor. (It was reported in 2002 that in Pakistan water costs 1.1 percent of the people's daily wages, whereas in the United States, it costs as little as 0.006 percent.)

Furthermore, as Pope Francis points out, "the quality of water available to the poor" is toxic: "Every day, unsafe water results in many deaths and the spread of water-related diseases, including those caused by microorganisms and chemical substances. Dysentery and cholera, linked to inadequate hygiene and water supplies, are a significant cause of suffering and of infant mortality. Underground water sources in many places are threatened by the pollution produced in certain mining, farming, and industrial activities, especially in countries lacking adequate regulation or controls. It is not only a question of industrial waste. Detergents and chemical products, commonly used in many places of the world, continue to pour into our rivers, lakes and seas" (no. 29). Sadly, to those living or visiting Asia the pope's description of water pollution is all too familiar.

Water scarcity has caused violent conflicts not only in the Middle East over the Tigris and Euphrates rivers, and Africa over the Nile, but it is also the source of potential conflicts in Asia: between Pakistan and India (the Indus River), between India and Bangladesh (the Ganges and the Brahmaputra rivers), among Thailand, Myanmar, and China (the Salween River), and among Thailand, Cambodia, Laos, and Vietnam (the Mekong River). The melting of the glaciers on the Himalayas, which is caused by global warming, will affect the waters of the Ganges, Brahmaputra, Irrawaddy, Mekong, Salween, Yangtze, and Yellow rivers. It has been said that in international economy and politics water promises to be to the twenty-first century what oil was in the twentieth century. Finally, the pope goes on to note, "the control of water by large multinational businesses may become a major source of conflict in this century" (no. 31). Transnational water has become a highly profitable commodity, and private companies have attempted to capture the "water market." Needless to say, privatizing water for profit further deprives the Asian poor of their right to safe water.

Third, the loss of biodiversity. According to many scientists, in our time the Earth is experiencing the sixth greatest extinction of life since life began 3.8 billion years ago. In 2015, the extinction of species was taking place one thousand times faster than at the end of the Ice Age, and this unprecedented loss of biodiversity is compounded by global warming. *LS* points out that "each year sees the disappearance of thousands of plant and animal species which we will never know, which our children will never see, because they have been lost forever. The great majority become extinct for reasons related to human activities" (no. 33). In Asia, much of the biodiversity found in tropical countries is disappearing at an alarming rate. For example, orangutans, which live only in Indonesia and Malaysia, are facing extinction by illegal logging and the clearance of their habitat for palm oil plantations. Golden-headed langurs and black-crested gibbons are disappearing in northeastern Vietnam.

Loss of biodiversity occurs not only on land but also in the waters. *LS* notes: "Oceans not only contain the bulk of our planet's water supply, but also most of the immense variety of living creatures, many of them still unknown to us and threatened for various reasons. What is more, marine life in rivers, lakes, seas and oceans, which feeds a great part of the world's population, is affected by uncontrolled fishing, leading to a drastic depletion of certain species" (no. 40). *LS* points out that "carbon dioxide increases the acidification of the ocean and compromises the marine food chain" (no. 24). In Asia, in a single year, the Yellow River can dump into the South China Sea 751 tons of heavy metals along with 21,000 tons of oil. In addition to acidification, climate change also contributes to the deoxygenation of sea water. Recent ocean models project that there will be a decline between 1 and 7 percent in the global ocean oxygen in this century, which has a negative impact on fish and other marine organisms.

Loss of biodiversity in the oceans is also caused by fishing with giant deep-sea-bottom trawlers, which is heavily subsidized by governments and which strips the oceans bare. A study by the International Union for the Conservation of Nature in 2012 found that 12 percent of all the marine species in the tropical eastern Pacific Ocean were threatened with extinction. In addition, mining for copper, manganese, nickel, cobalt, and rare metals on the floor of the Pacific Ocean at 2.5 miles beneath the surface will also do irreparable damage to marine life. Two marine ecosystems are especially at risk: the coral reefs and the mangrove forests. *LS* notes: "Many of the world's coral reefs are already barren or in a state of constant decline" (no. 41). Coral reefs, which are comparable to the great forests on dry land, provide shelter, livelihood, and security for nearly half a billion people across the globe. Like coral reefs, mangrove forests provide food and shelter for fish. Tragically, in the last forty years, millions of acres of mangrove areas have been destroyed. In Asia, Thailand has lost 27 percent of its mangrove forests; Malaysia 20 percent; the Philippines 45 percent; and Indonesia 40 percent.

From these brief considerations of the disastrous impact of global warming on Asia, and especially the Asian poor, in three areas, namely, loss of habitable land, access to healthy water, and biodiversity, it is clear that *LS*, though not specifically written for Asia, is highly relevant for the continent. As the encyclical argues, not only has the "environmental, economic, and social ecology" been degraded (nos. 139–42), but also the "cultural ecology" (nos. 143–46) and the "ecology of daily life" (nos. 147–55) have been seriously harmed. These three ecologies constitute what *LS* terms "integral ecology," which must be preserved by means of a worldwide and concerted effort (chapter 4). As *LS* points out somberly, ecological destruction has led to a decline in the quality of human life and the breakdown of society: "The social dimensions of global change include the effects of technological innovations on employment, social exclusion, an inequitable distribution and consumption of energy and other services, social breakdown, increased violence and a rise in new forms of social aggression, drug trafficking, growing drug use by young people, and the loss of identity" (no. 46). Furthermore, ecological degradation has also led to "global inequality" between the rich countries of the Global North and the developing and poor countries of the Global South (nos. 48–52). A quick survey of the Asian contemporary social and economic scene will confirm Pope Francis's succinct litany of the challenges Asia is facing as the result of ecological degradation.

"THE GREAT SAGES OF THE PAST"

In calling for the restoration of integral ecology Pope Francis appeals not only to the Judeo-Christian biblical tradition with its emphasis on the universe as God's creation (nos. 76–83), universal communion (nos. 89–92), and the common destination of goods (nos. 93–95), but also to the wisdom of Saint Francis of Assisi as expressed in his celebrated *Canticle of the Creatures* (no. 87), whose opening line serves as the title of the encyclical. Furthermore, introducing a theological novelty, he cites the teaching of the Ecumenical Patriarch Bartholomew (nos. 7–9) and twenty-one episcopal conferences, including those of the Philippines (no. 41), Japan (no. 85), and the Federation of Asian Bishops' Conferences (no. 116).

It is noteworthy that the Federation of Asian Bishops' Conferences (FABC) is probably the first official church body to be deeply concerned about ecology.[4] Already in 1988, at the Eleventh Bishops' Institute for Inter-religious Affairs in Sukabumi, Indonesia, it was stated that "the ecological question or the harmony and balance of the natural environment in relation to the life of man is a fundamental one. The destiny of humankind is inextricably bound up with the way they cultivate the earth and share its resources. Harmony and peace call for respect for the earth. She is the mother of whose dust we are made and to whose womb we shall return. The usurpation of the fruit of the earth by some and the deprivation of others of the same results in the rupture of harmony among peoples."[5]

Among the institute's many pastoral recommendations, there is one regarding the environment:

> Respect for nature and compassion for all living things are ingrained in the Asian religions and cultural traditions. Today in Asia owing to many factors, the natural environment with which man should be in harmony is being wantonly destroyed through deforestation, industrial pollution, depositing of nuclear wastes, etc. Christian life and witness should manifest greater sensitivity to nature and to all sentiments. Hence we recommend that Christians join forces and cooperate with all movements of followers of other religions and secular groups engaged in maintaining balance and harmony in our ecosystem, and protecting nature and its riches from destruction.[6]

Concern for the environment recurred as a constant refrain in the FABC's Plenary Assemblies and in the various documents of its offices in the ensuing years. At the Sixth FABC Plenary Assembly, in 1965, on "Christian Discipleship in Asia Today," it is stated in the Final Statement: "Ecology is once again brought to our pastoral attention. And urgently so, since we see in the

---

4. For a collection of the FABC's and its various offices' documents, see Gaudencio Rosales and C. G. Arévalo, eds., *For All the Peoples of Asia: Federation of Asian Bishops' Conferences. Documents from 1970 to 1991*, vol. 1 (Maryknoll, NY: Orbis Books, 1991); Franz-Josef Eilers, ed., *For All the Peoples of Asia: Federation of Asian Bishops' Conferences. Documents from 1992 to 1996*, vol. 2 (Quezon City, Philippines: Claretian Publications, 1997); Franz-Josef Eilers, ed., *For All the Peoples of Asia: Federation of Asian Bishops' Conferences. Documents from 1997 to 2001*, vol. 3 (Quezon City, Philippines: Claretian Publications, 2002); Franz-Josef Eilers, ed., *For All the Peoples of Asia: Federation of Asian Bishops' Conferences. Documents from 2002 to 2006*, vol. 4 (Quezon City, Philippines: Claretian Publications, 2007); and Vimal Tirimanna, ed., *For All the Peoples of Asia: Federation of Asian Bishops' Conferences. Documents from 2007 to 2012*, vol. 5, (Quezon City, Philippines: Claretian Publications, 2013). These volumes will be cited as *FAPA*, followed by their respective years of publication.

5. *FAPA* (1992), 320.

6. Ibid., 323.

countries of Asia the continuing and unabated destruction of our environment. . . . Life, especially in a third world setting, is sacrificed at the altar
of short term economic gains. The Lord, the Giver of Life, calls our discipleship in Asia into a question on the time bomb issue of ecology. Choosing
life requires our discipleship to discern and act with other faiths and groups
against the forces of ecological destruction."[7]

Note that the FABC's approach to ecology is framed in terms of "harmony"
and "wholeness," which are said to be characteristic ideals of Asian peoples:
"When we look into our traditional cultures and heritages, we note that they
are inspired by a vision of unity. The universe is perceived as an organic whole
with the web of relations knitting together each and every part of it. The nature
and the human are not viewed as antagonistic to each other, but as chords in a
universal symphony."[8] It is out of this sense of universal harmony and wholeness that concern for ecology is born and nourished. Indeed, there is a fourfold
harmony to be achieved: with God, with oneself, with others, and with nature.
A disturbance in any one of these four relations brings about disharmony in
the other three; conversely, harmony in any one of them strengthens harmony
in the other three. Thus, harmonious ecology is rooted in harmonious relation
with God, with oneself, and with others. By the same token, there cannot be
harmony with God, with oneself, and with others without harmonious ecology. Indeed, the idea of harmony is so central to Asian thought and life that
the Theological Advisory Commission (now Office of Theological Concerns)
has produced a seventy-page document entitled *Asian Christian Perspectives on
Harmony*, in which ecological degradation figures among the most destructive
forces causing disharmony in Asia.[9]

Ecology is also discussed at the FABC's Seventh Plenary Assembly, in
2000, with the theme "A Renewed Church in Asia: A Mission of Love and
Service."[10] The Tenth Plenary Assembly, in 2012, with the theme "A New
Evangelization" notes how the ecological issue was brought to worldwide
attention by the monumental disaster in Japan caused by a tsunami on March
11, 2011: "Our Assembly has likewise noted the unabated abuse of creation
due to selfish and shortsighted economic gains. Human causes contribute significantly to global warming and climate change, the impact of which affects
the poor and the deprived more disastrously. The ecological concern, the care
for the integrity of creation, including intergenerational justice and compassion, is fundamental to a spirituality of communion."[11]

As important as these FABC documents are, they are not cited by *LS*.

---

7. *FAPA* (1997), 11.
8. *FAPA* (1992), 319.
9. See *FAPA* (1997), 237–38. The entire document is found on pp. 229–98.
10. See *FAPA* (2002), 7.
11. *FAPA* (2014), 45.

Instead, the encyclical quotes three other lesser-known texts. The first is a brief statement of the Colloquium on Faith and Science held in Tagaytay, the Philippines, by the FABC Office of Education and Student Chaplaincies in 1993 entitled *Love for Creation, An Asian Response to the Ecological Crisis.*[12] The statement provides a helpful analysis of the ecological problem in its scientific, cultural, political, theological, and pastoral dimensions. The second document is the pastoral letter on ecology of the Conference of Catholic Bishops of the Philippines, whose title, *What Is Happening to Our Beautiful Land?*, is echoed in the title of *LS*'s first chapter, "What Is Happening to Our Common Home?" The letter begins with a graphic list of the ecological damage that has been done to the forests, seas, and land of the Philippines and ends with a recommendation of activities that can and must be undertaken by individuals, churches, and the government "to respect and defend life." The third document is a rather lengthy letter of the Catholic Bishops of Japan titled *Reverence for Life: A Message for the Twenty-First Century from the Catholic Bishops of Japan* (January 1, 2001).[13] Chapter 3, titled "Life and Death," discusses eight issues, one of which is the environment. It recalls Rachel Carson's prophetic voice warning the world in 1962 about the "silent spring" and ends with the following beautiful words, which *LS* quotes (no. 85): "God cares even for the flowers of the field, dressing each with beauty and loving it. To sense each creature singing the hymn of its existence is to live joyfully in God's love and hope."

So far we have examined only the teachings on ecology of the Catholic Church in Asia. However, the "Great Sages of the Past," to whom *LS* refers (no. 47) and from whom we can acquire "true wisdom, as the fruit of self-examination and generous encounter between persons" (no. 47), include also the spiritual masters of Asian religions. *LS* explicitly calls for a dialogue and collaboration among religions for the defense of the Earth, a call repeatedly made by the FABC: "The majority of people living on our planet profess to be believers. This should spur religions to dialogue among themselves for the sake of protecting nature, defending the poor, and building networks of respect and fraternity" (no. 201).

Among the many causes of the ecological crisis, Pope Francis highlights what he calls "the globalization of the technocratic paradigm," which "exalts the concept of a subject who, using logical and rational procedures, progressively approaches and gains control over an external object" (no. 106). In this case, the "external object" is the material world, which technocracy tries to dominate by means of "a technique of possession, mastery and

---

12. The text is available at http://www.usanews.com.
13. The Japanese bishops issued a revised and enlarged edition of this document on January 1, 2017. The ecological problems are discussed in chapter 3, section 3, entitled "Threats to Life," which cites Pope Francis's *LS*.

transformation" (no. 106). At the basis of this technocratic paradigm is the conception of the material world and everything existing therein as valuable only to the extent that they can be made to serve human needs and wants and not as valuable in themselves, by their independent existence and autonomous value. This conception is called "excessive anthropocentrism" (no. 116). In order to counter the technocratic paradigm and excessive anthropocentrism the pope develops philosophical and theological arguments derived from Christian sources (chapter 20). Starting from the Christian belief in God's creation of nature or the universe, Francis affirms the existence of a "universal communion": "All of us are linked by unseen bonds and together form a kind of universal family, a sublime communion which fills us with a sacred, affectionate and humble respect" (no. 89). The pope goes on to emphasize that "universal communion" includes the material universe: "Everything is related, and we human beings are united as brothers and sisters on a wonderful pilgrimage, woven together by the love God has for each of his creatures and which also unites us in fond affection with brother sun, sister moon, brother river and mother earth" (no. 92).

Here I would like to extend Francis's reflections on universal communion by invoking the Buddhist and Daoist perspectives. Admittedly, Pope Francis's belief in a personal God and in God's creative act is fundamentally different from the nontheistic and noncreationist stance of Buddhism and Daoism. Yet, in spite of this difference, these two Asian religious traditions offer insights into reality that strengthen the pope's position. In brief, the technocratic paradigm can be countered by the Buddhist notion of "interdependent/dependent co-arising/origination" (Sanskrit: *pratītyasamutpāda*), and excessive anthropocentrism by the Daoist view of universal harmony.

By "interdependent/dependent arising/origination" is meant that all things (*dharma*) do not exist as independent and permanent realities or "selves," but are constantly changing or "co-arising" (*samutpāda*) dependently (*pratītya*) on other things, which are also co-arising dependently on the things that co-arise dependently on them. The doctrine of interdependent origination is expressed in the following terse formula: "When this is, that is; This arising, that arises; When this is not, that is not; This ceasing, that ceases."[14] As a result of interdependent origination there is nothing that is permanent (*anicca*), nothing that is substantial (*anattā*), The Buddha's primary interest is practical: he wants to trace suffering (*dukkha*) back to a chain of twelve causes (the twelve *nidāna*), the last of which is lack of knowledge (*avidyā*), and to show that by abolishing these twelve causal links a person can break the cycle of rebirth

---

14. For a helpful explanation of "interdependent origination" in Buddhist thought, see Richard Combrich, *What the Buddha Thought* (London: Equinox, 2009), 129–43; and Paul Williams with Anthony Tribe, *Buddhist Thought: A Complete Introduction to the Indian Tradition* (London: Routledge, 2000), 62–72.

(*saṃsāra*) and reach enlightenment (*nirvāna*), which alone is not subject to interdependent origination.

There is no need to go in detail here into the Buddha's teaching on the Four Noble Truths and the Eightfold Path toward enlightenment, which are undergirded by the ontological principle of interdependent origination. My purpose is simply to argue that the Buddhist concept of interdependent origination implicitly rejects the technocratic paradigm that views the world in terms of subject–object for the purpose of domination and exploitation. Interdependent origination—as the term implies—affirms universal and mutual conditioning among all things. No being can exist without an other: one person without all other persons; humanity without ecology; and, vice versa, ecology without humanity.

This interdependence of all things is dramatically expressed by the Vietnamese Buddhist monk Thich Nhat Hanh. In a short post titled "Clouds in Each Paper" he writes:

> If you are a poet, you will see clearly that there is a cloud floating in this sheet of paper. Without a cloud, there will be no rain; without rain, the trees cannot grow: and without trees, we cannot make paper. The cloud is essential for the paper to exist. If the cloud is not here, the sheet of paper cannot be here either. So we can say that the cloud and the paper inter-are.
>
> "Interbeing" is a word that is not in the dictionary yet, but if we combine the prefix "inter" with the verb "to be," we have a new verb, inter-be. Without a cloud, we cannot have paper, so we can say that the cloud and the sheet of paper inter-are.
>
> If we look into this sheet of paper even more deeply, we can see the sunshine in it. If the sunshine is not there, the forest cannot grow. In fact nothing can grow. Even we cannot grow without sunshine. And so, we know that the sunshine is also in this sheet of paper. The paper and the sunshine inter-are. And if we continue to look we can see the logger who cut the tree and brought it to the mill to be transformed into paper. And we see the wheat. We know that the logger cannot exist without his daily bread, and therefore the wheat that became his bread is also in this sheet of paper. And the logger's father and mother are in it too. When we look in this way we see that without all of these things, this sheet of paper cannot exist.[15]

Because of interdependent origination, humanity and ecology "inter-are." "Interbeing" is the only mode of existence possible, not only among humans

---

15. "Clouds in Each Paper," at http://www.awakin.org (March 25, 2000). See also Thich Nhat Hanh, *The Wisdom of Thich Nhat Hanh* (New York: One Spirit, 2000), 233–252.

themselves but also between humanity and ecology. The animals and the material world are not just "objects" for us humans as "subjects" to manipulate, dominate, and exploit. Their value and worth are not measured by their usefulness to humans; rather, they possess their autonomous value in themselves because they and we co-arise interdependently. Without them we cannot exist, and, vice versa, without us they cannot exist. They and we "inter-are."

The FABC Theological Advisory Commission in its document *Asian Christian Perspectives on Harmony,* already cited above, explains how in the Mahayana tradition the historical Buddha becomes identified with the goal he reached by destroying the twelve causes producing suffering, namely, *nirvāna,* the Ultimate "No-Self," or Absolute "Emptiness." It goes on to say: "The human task is to follow the example of the historical Buddha and to reach this ultimate state of emptiness, which is stillness, quietness and limitless rest, but the dynamic stillness which reaches out in compassion to all living beings still in the throes of suffering."[16] For arguments against excessive anthropocentrism we turn to the Daoist tradition of universal harmony. As mentioned earlier, the FABC regards harmony and wholeness as characteristic ideals of the Asian way of life. Daoism is both a philosophical school (*daojia*) and a religious practice (*daogiao*) that is distinguished from Confucianism and Buddhism (*fojiao*). The classics on which Daoism is founded are the *Daodejing,* also known as the *Laozi,* and the *Zhuangxi.* The defining concept of the Daoist religion is the Dao itself. Literally meaning the "way" or the "path," the Dao refers to the proper course of human conduct, especially as taught by the ancient sages. It soon came to be understood as the metaphysical basis of the natural order itself, primordial yet eternally present. In its primordial state, Dao is described as "nothingness," null and void. But the Dao also manifests itself and becomes present in the sensible world through *qi* (literally, breath, steam, vapor, or energy). *Qi,* both energy and matter, is the basic building block of all things in the universe, responsible for movement and energy, and is the vital substance of life. Daoist rituals and religious practices aim at preserving this *qi* by combatting the forces of aging, illness, and death. The goal, at once temporal and spatial, is to bring the various parts of the body back into unified harmony and thus to achieve immortality.

Again, it is not necessary to delve into all the intricate philosophical and cosmological speculations and alchemy of Daoism here. Suffice it to note for our present purposes that central to Daoism as a religious practice is the ethics of "noncontrivance" (*wu wei*). According to Zhuangxi, the Dao acts spontaneously in individuals, society, and nature. Similarly, humans must respect and submit to natural changes. In this way they and the world can become one.

---

16. *FAPA* (1997), 260.

By contrast, contrivance should be avoided because it is counterproductive and contrary to the spontaneity (*tzu-jan*) of the Dao. The ethic of noncontrivance means that humans must not act against nature; rather human action, like the Dao's, must be nonpurposive, nondeliberative, and yet continuously transforming, as natural as water flowing downward and fire rising upward.

Clearly, such an ethic of noncontrivance and spontaneity runs counter to the kind of anthropocentrism that makes humans the center or the summit of creation and technological domination of nature the goal of knowledge. Even though Daoist thought and practice are not based on the belief in God the Creator, they provide a powerful stimulus to "hear the cry of nature itself; everything is connected" (no. 117).

GOING FORWARD AND FURTHER

In his evaluation of *LS*, Donal Dorr says that the encyclical "is an exceptionally important document, which will surely rank with the Vatican II Pastoral Constitution on the Church in the Modern World (*Gaudium et Spes*)."[17] That is not a hyperbole, in light of both contents and methodology. In terms of methodology, the encyclical starts with a clear, accessible, and accurate presentation of the scientific data on the ecological crisis, without which theological elaborations would be no more than abstract speculation. As mentioned above, *LS* offers a very helpful introduction to the ecological crisis and provides people with inadequate scientific education the means to articulate the causal connections between human activities—individual and corporate—and global warming. Furthermore, the fact that Pope Francis quotes the teachings of episcopal conferences is a welcome departure from the earlier view that they do not constitute a proper teaching authority of the hierarchical magisterium.

In terms of contents, again, according to Dorr, "Francis's account of an integral ecology represents a major breakthrough in Catholic social teaching."[18] Dorr goes on to list eleven areas where such breakthroughs occur: a rich Bible-based theology of ecology; a comprehensive account of the major environmental issues; the affirmation of human activities as causing the ecological crisis; the strong linkage between "the cry of the earth" and " the cry of the poor"; the danger of the "technocratic paradigm"; the proposal of an alternative economy; the "ecological debt" of the rich countries; a recognition of the contributions of local cooperatives and indigenous communities; encouragement to adopt ecologically friendly practices; an emphasis on the need for

---

17. Dorr, *Option for the Poor & for the Earth*, 436.
18. Ibid.

enforcement measures at the national and international levels; and the need to pressure politicians to take radical enforcement measures.[19]

On the debit side, Dorr notes three areas where *LS* could be improved: the population issue, the theology of the "Cosmic Christ," and an evolution-based theology of creation in the form of the "New Story."[20] With regard to the Asian context, the first issue obtains pride of place. *LS* mentions the "reduction in the birth rate" and "certain policies of 'reproductive health'" (no. 50) and views them as ways in which rich countries try to avoid facing the consequences of their consumerist lifestyle on the environment by blaming it on the birth rate in the Majority World. The encyclical goes on to quote the *Compendium of the Social Doctrine of the Church* of the Pontifical Council for Justice and Peace: "While it is true that an unequal distribution of the population and of the available resources creates obstacles to development and a sustainable use of the environment, it must nonetheless be recognized that demographic growth is fully compatible with an integral and shared development" (no. 50).

In light of the demographic explosion in Asian countries such as India, China, the Philippines, Indonesia, and Vietnam, and especially in the poorest countries of Asia, such a treatment of the impact of the demographic explosion on the environment is little short of being cavalier. Perhaps *LS* is still hampered by the teaching of *Humane Vitae*, but the ecological crisis in 2016 is quite different than in 1968 and should have provided an occasion for a serious reexamination of Pope Paul VI's admittedly noninfallible teaching. At any rate, what Pope Francis said on January 19, 2014, on his way back to Rome from the Philippines to the effect that one need not reproduce like rabbits in order to be good Catholics is a good place to start an open and honest discussion of "responsible parenthood."

With the publication of *Laudato Si'* no one can accuse the leadership of the Catholic Church of turning a blind eye to an issue on which the survival not only of the human family but of the planet Earth itself depends. Pope Francis has sounded a clarion call for an "ecological conversion," a call addressed to the whole of humanity but also one that Asia will need to heed and respond to actively and promptly because being a continent of the poorest of the poor, it has to respond to the cry of the Earth to make a decent human life possible for its own people.

---

19. Ibid., 437–38.
20. Ibid., 439–43.

Index